The Islam
in
Islamic Terrorism

The Importance of Beliefs, Ideas, and Ideology

The Islam in Islamic Terrorism

The Importance of Beliefs, Ideas, and Ideology

Ibn Warraq

Copyright © Ibn Warraq, 2017

All rights reserved. No part of this book may be reproduced in any form or by any means, electronic or mechanical, without permission in writing from the publisher except by reviewers who may quote brief passages in their reviews.

Published by New English Review Press
a subsidiary of World Encounter Institute
PO Box 158397
Nashville, Tennessee 37215
&
27 Old Gloucester Street
London, England, WC1N 3AX

Cover Art and Design by Kendra Mallock

ISBN: 978-1-943003-08-2

First Edition

NEW ENGLISH REVIEW PRESS
newenglishreview.org

There was a time when scholars and other writers in communist eastern Europe relied on writers and publishers in the free West to speak the truth about their history, their culture, and their predicament. Today it is those who told the truth, not those who concealed or denied it, who are respected and welcomed in these countries. …

Historians in free countries have a moral and professional obligation not to shirk the difficult issues and subjects that some people would place under a sort of taboo; not to submit to voluntary censorship, but to deal with these matters fairly, honestly, without apologetics, without polemic, and, of course, competently. Those who enjoy freedom have a moral obligation to use that freedom for those who do not possess it. We live in a time when great efforts have been made, and continue to be made, to falsify the record of the past and to make history a tool of propaganda; when governments, religious movements, political parties, and sectional groups of every kind are busy rewriting history as they would wish it to have been, as they would like their followers to believe that it was. All this is very dangerous indeed, to ourselves and to others, however we may define otherness-dangerous to our common humanity. Because, make no mistake, those who are unwilling to confront the past will be unable to understand the present and unfit to face the future.

—Bernard Lewis, *Islam and the West*

To
Peter
A Civilizing Influence.

Contents

Preface and Acknowledgements   15

Introduction   17

1 - Root Cause Fallacy   24
    Islamic Terrorism: Not Caused by Poverty or Lack of Knowledge of Islam   24
        MA, RHF, and Education   25
        Ordinary Muslims   26
        Poverty and the Plight of Women   28
        Variations of the Socioeconomic Argument   29
        Land and Wealth: Mistaken Identifiers   31
    Nor by Israeli-Arab Conflict   34
        Rival Ideologies   37
        Antisemitism   38
    Nor by U.S. Foreign Policy   40
        Setting the Record Straight   44
        U.S. Aid   45
        The True Victims   47
    Nor by Western Imperialism   47
    Nor by the Crusades   49

2 - Explanations of Islamic Terrorism   53
    Human Agency, Free Will, and Responsibility   53
        Fundamental Differences   56
    Importance of Ideology as a Motivating Force   59
    Soviet Union and Communism   61
    The Ideology of Nazism   63
    Islam or the Ideology of the Islamic Terrorists   64

3 - Marx, Freud, and Darwin among the *Jihādists*   71
    Reductionist Views of Islamic Terrorism   71
    Importance of Religion in the Middle East   72

4 - Islamic Doctrines as Motivating Factors 76
    The Koran 77
    Shari'a Supremacism 79
    The *Sunna* and Muhammad 80
        The Sunna 80
        Muhammad 82
        Hadīth 83
    Shari'a 84
        Position of Women and Non-Muslims 85
    Beliefs: God and *Tawhīd* **86**
    Commanding Right and Forbidding Wrong 87
        Forbidding Wrong 89
        By Tongue 89
        Or Hand 90
        Or Heart 91
        Al-Ghazālī on Emigration 91
        Privacy versus Hidden Sin 92
        Categories of Wrongdoing 94
        Forbidding Wrong and Rebellion 94
    The Hereafter: Blood and Death, not Life, in Islam 96
        Contempt for Life 97

5 - *Jihād*: Definitions, Descriptions, and Discussions 101
    Definitions of *Jihād* 101
    Descriptions of *Jihād* 104
        Encyclopaedia of Islam, First Edition, 1913 104
        Encyclopaedia of Islam, Second Edition, 1960–1986 105
    Discussions: Modern Scholars on *Jihād* 107
        Majid Khadduri, *War and Peace in the Law of Islam*, 1955 107
        Fazlur Rahman, *Islam*, 1966 109
        Mustansir Mir, "*Jihād* in Islam," 1991 109
        Rudolph Peters, *Jihād in Classical and Modern Islam*, 1996 111
        David Cook, *Understanding Jihād*, 2005 113

6 - *Jihād*: Theory and Practice   114
    Jihād in the Koran   115
    Early Muslim Scholars on *Jihād*   117
    Hadīth on *Jihād*   120
    Six Canonical Collections 120
        Bukhārī   120
        More on *Jihād from the Canon* 123
    Some Legal Definitions: *Dar al-Islam, Dar al-Harb, Dar al-Sulh* 125

7 - The Goals of *Jihād*: Apocalypse and Conversion   128
    The *Mahdi*   129
    The Martyr   130
    The Rewards of Martyrdom   131
        In the Koran 131
        In the Hadīth 132
    The Law Schools on *Jihād* 134
    The Spiritual Nature of *Jihād*   136
    Greater Jihād and Lesser *Jihād*   138
    Non-Canonical Distinction   138
        Military Mysticism: Sufis Soldiers and Jihād   143
    Conclusion   146

8 - Muhammad's Campaigns and Early Conquests   147
    The Ideology of Islam   154

9 - The First Terrorists? Khārijites, Violence, and the Demand for the Purification of Islam of Its Unpious Accretions 158
    The Basic Doctrine of the Khārijites   161
    Later History of the Khārijites   165
    The Significance of the Khārijite Movement   167

10 - Sahl ibn Salāma, Barbahārī, and *Bid'a*: Religious Violence in Ninth- and Tenth-Century Baghdad   170
    "Fanatical Terrorism" and Barbahārī   174

11 - Religious Violence in Baghdad between 991 CE and 1092 CE 178
12 - Ibn Taymiyya   184
    Early Life and Education   185
    Clash with Authorities and Imprisonment   186
    Ibn Taymiyya's Character   187
    Call to *Jihād*   188
    Concern for Commanding Right and Forbidding Wrong   191
    Ibn Taymiyya's Anti-Mongol *Fatwas*   193
    Groups to Be Fought   195
    Innovations, Heresies, and Religious Minorities   197
    More Innovations 198
    Sufis and Shī'ites   200
    Jew, Christians, and *Ahl Dhimmi*   203
    The Great Regenerator of *Jihād*   205

13 - The Qādīzādeli Movement in Seventeenth-Century Istanbul 210
    Qādīzāde Mehmed   212
    Qādīzādeli Influence   215
    Influence of Ibn Taymiyya 216

14 - Ibn 'Abd Al-Wahhāb and Eighteenth-Century Renewal and Reform   217
    The Eighteenth Century   217
    Rudolph Peters on Fundamentalism and a Religious Riot in Eighteenth-Century Cairo 218
    The Birth of Wahhābism   223
    Najd and the Hanbalī Tradition   224
    Pre-Wahhābi Beliefs and Practices 225
    Muhammad Ibn al-Wahhāb (1703–1792) 226
    Influences and Some of His Doctrines   228
        Tawhīd   230
        Takfīr and Qitāl   234
        Jihād   235
        The Bedouin 237
        Ijtihād and Taqlīd   238
        Imāma   239

  Commanding Right and Forbidding Wrong   240
 Ibn al-Wahhāb: Other Writings   241
 Real Causes and Aims of Wahhābism   242
 Critiques of Wahhābism and the Ikhwān   243
 The Influence of Wahhabism   246

15 - Sayyid Abu 'l-'Alā' Mawdūdī   250
 Thirteenth and Fourteenth Century India Under Islamic Rulers 250
 Shaykh Ahmad Sirhindī and the Sixteenth Century   251
 Shāh Walī Allāh and the Eighteenth Century   252
 Sayyid Ahmad Brēlwī [1786-1831]   254
 Sayyid Abu'l-a'la Mawdūdī   259
  Mawdūdī's Beliefs   264
  Mawdūdī on Jihād   266
  Mawdūdī and Shari'a 267

16 - Brigadier S.K. Malik and *The Qur'anic Concept of War*   271

17 - Hasan al-Banna and the Muslim Brotherhood   278
 Brotherhood Ideology   279
 Violence Necessary   282
 The Brotherhood and the Totalitarian Core of Islam   284

18 - Grand Mufti Haj Amin al-Husaini and the Nazis   289
 Al-Husaini, Islam, and Violence   291
 A True Radical Muslim Hero   294
 Consolidating Efforts   295

19 - Sayyid Qutb   299
 Core Ideas   301
 The Solution: *Jihād*   304

20 - Muhammad 'Abd al-Salām Faraj and *The Neglected Duty*   308

21 - Abdullah Azzam and *Defense of the Muslim Lands*   314
 Scholar's Ink, Martyr's Blood   317

22 - Ayman al-Zawahiri and *Knights under the Prophet's Banner*   320

23 - Ayatollah Ruhollah Khomeini and the Iranian Revolution   324
    Historical and Political Background to Khomeini's Rise to Power: Nawab Safavi and the *Fidā'iyīn-i Islam*   324
    The Influence of the 1979 Iranian Revolution in the Islamic World   329
    Ruhollah Khomeini   329
    An Islamic Revolution   332
        Growing with Blood   335
    A Constitution of Islam   337
    The Islamic Republic of Iran   338
        A Disregard for Human Rights 339
        Khomeini's Victims   343
    State Terror   346

24 - Conclusion: "The Life of the Muslim *umma* is solely dependent on the ink of the scholars and the blood of the martyrs."   349

Selected Bibliography   357
    A. Reference   357
    B. Koran Translations and Concordance   357
    C. Primary sources: Islamic   358
        C.1. Life of Muhammad   358
        C2. Early Islamic Conquests   359
        C3. Koranic Commentators and other Classical Islamic scholars   359
        C4. Ibn Taymiyya   359
    D. *Hadith* 360
    E. Modern Radical Islam: Primary Sources   360
    F. Secondary Sources   362

Index   377

Preface and Acknowledgements

THE PRESENT WORK was originally 165,000 words. I have cut it down by a third, as I was advised by many friends that a shorter book is always better than a longer one. It seems the general, educated public no longer reads long books, and publishers are reluctant to take on weighty, daunting tomes. I should have liked to have included a much longer section on India. I shall perhaps post the long version on my website in a year or two.

All my Koranic citations are given in the following manner; for example, the citation "Q2. *al-Baqara*, the Cow, 256" refers to Sura 2, called *al-Baqara* in Arabic, which means the Cow, and the final figure "256" is number of the verse. However, when I have to a give a long list of suras from the Koran, my system becomes rather clumsy. For example, I give the following Koranic references in footnote 167 below: Q2:216; Q2:221; Q3:28; Q3:85; Q4:101; Q4:144; Q8:39; Q9:14, 17, 23, 28, 29, 36, 39, 41, 73, 111, 123; Q25:52. Imagine how lengthy and cumbersome that would be if here I were to insist on keeping the following schema: "Q2. *al-Baqara*, The Cow, 216"; and so on.

Originally, I had planned to thank everyone who has shown me any kindness over the last few years. But it all became rather complicated. First, the list became absurdly long, and while awaiting permission to publish their names, I kept remembering ever more people I had forgotten to mention. There is always the possibility I have missed someone. Second, I am not at all sure that I am doing the people I mention any favors, since, alas, Ibn Warraq remains "mad, bad, and dangerous to know." I should not like to embroil anyone not directly involved in the book's production in any controversy that may ensue on publication of a work critical of Islam. Therefore, I shall only name those who have helped me directly with the book, and whose permission I have received to do so.

It gives me great pleasure to single out my anonymous editor, who, with her professionalism and patience, did a remarkable job on the original, unwieldy manuscript, and made it presentable. I am beholden to Rebecca Bynum, who took on the onerous task of publishing my work though she was already busy with all her political commitments. Rebecca further meticulously edited the work, and got it ready to send to the printer in record time.

Finally, I should like to thank Nancy and Tom Klingenstein for their friendship, kindness, and support which made all my research possible.

It is no empty formality to insist that I alone am responsible for the opinions voiced in the present work.

Introduction

Consider the following claims:

1. Marc Sageman, a "government counterterrorism consultant," asserts that terrorism is not "the result of the beliefs and perceptions held by the terrorists."[1]

2. "The idea of the sacred Koran has existed for 1400 years, give or take, [but] we have seen Islamic terrorism only over the past 40 or so. Clearly, the Koran is not the issue."[2]

I BELIEVE THAT both of these views are wrong. To understand the behavior of Islamic terrorists, to make sense of their motives, we must take their beliefs seriously. The acts of ISIS or the Taliban or any other *jihādist* group are not random acts of violence by a mob of psychopathic, sexually frustrated, impoverished vandals, but carefully and strategically planned operations that are part of a long campaign by educated, affluent Muslims who wish to bring about the establishment of an Islamic state based on the Shariʻa—the Islamic Holy Law, derived from the Koran, that is the very word of God, and from the Sunna of the Prophet and the Traditions (*ahādīth*, pl. of *hadīth*), which are the sayings and doings of Muhammad and his companions.

Nor has Islamic terrorism emerged, *ex nihilo*, in the "past 40 or

---

[1] Marc Sageman, *Leaderless Jihād: Terror Networks in the Twenty-First Century* (Philadelphia: University of Pennsylvania Press, 2008), 22.
[2] Anonymous, letter to author, July 2014.

so" years. From its foundation in the seventh century, violent movements have arisen seeking to revive true Islam, which its members felt had been neglected in Muslim societies, who were not living up to the ideals of the earliest Muslims. Groups such as the seventh-century Azraqites sought to revive forgotten beliefs and rituals and to cleanse the body of Islam of the corrupt practices that had tarnished the pristine Muslim religion. Today, Deobandi extremists, for example, can only be understood against developments within Islam during the eighteenth and nineteenth centuries, in particular the philosophy of Shah Wali Allah, who died in 1762.

What of the religious violence in ninth- and early tenth-century Baghdad associated with such ideologues as Sahl ibn Salāma, and Barbahārī, and their rejection of innovations (bid'a); followed by more religious violence in Baghdad between 991 CE and 1092 CE? The violent Qādīzādeli Movement in seventeenth-century Istanbul may well have influenced the movement launched by Ibn 'Abd al-Wahhāb in Arabia in the eighteenth century, which in turn has influenced almost every modern terrorist movement. Wahhābi extremism spread as far as India and we are still feeling its effects, far beyond Arabia, to this day.

As Barbara Metcalf, professor emerita of history at the University of California, Davis, has noted, when faced with the decline of their culture, Muslims "drew on their own traditions for interpretations and patterns of action."[3] Extremists like the Deobandi in India are drawing upon their own tradition and their own history of Islamic activism that reaches back to the foundation of Islam. Similarly, all the other modern Islamist ideologues from Hasan al-Banna to Ayatollah Ruhollah Khomeini examined in this book, draw their inspiration from Islamic traditions, the canonical texts, Islamic history, and seminal Islamic thinkers such as Ibn Taymiyya (also studied in the present work) to justify their political actions and activism, which often end in violence.

Madeline C. Zilfi, who specializes in the Middle Eastern and Islamic history of the last centuries of the Ottoman Empire, writes of the Qādīzādeli Movement (see chapter 11), "The issues that shaped religious discourse in seventeenth-century Istanbul indeed echoed those that had arisen in earlier centuries."[4] But she also points out:

---

3 Barbara Metcalf, *Islamic Revival in British India: Deoband 1860–1900* (Princeton, NJ: Princeton University Press, 1982), 3.

4 Madeline C. Zilfi, "The Kadizadelis: Discordant Revivalism in Seventeenth-Century Istanbul," *Journal of Near Eastern Studies* 45, no. 4 (1986): 251–52.

It is my contention that the fate of the *ilmiye* [the Ottoman religious institution] between the sixteenth and late eighteenth centuries, while reflecting concerns similar to those of its secular counterparts, was uniquely shaped by ideological conflict within the body of Ottoman religious. In this regard, it is appropriate to focus on the "high" versus "folk religion" features of such conflict. This, like 'ulama'-state tensions, is endemic to Islamic history.[5]

Again, one cannot escape one's past; these concerns recur in surprisingly similar forms.

In her important 1988 work, *The Politics of Piety*, Zilfi writes of the fundamentalist preacher Kadizade: "His views, which he had made plain countless times before, trumpeted the fundamentalist ethic, the drive to rid Islam of beliefs and practices that had accumulated since the era of the Prophet and the original Islamic community at Medina."[6] Zilfi continues:

> The newly aroused tensions between innovation and fundamentalism in large part determined the character of religious politics in the seventeenth century. Constraints and austerity on the one hand and innovation and license on the other are a recurring point counterpoint in Islam. The appeal of the fundamentalist ethic bears on the relationship of the Islamic community to its own past, to the austerity and righteousness of the epoch of the Prophet Muhammad and the patriarchs.[7]

Thus the fundamentalists' acts must be referred back to Islam's past.

One can argue that the dialectic between innovation and fundamental, "orthodox" Islam is centuries old. As Zilfi contends:

> The reason Islamic fundamentalists receive such enthusiastic endorsement in the Islamic community lies in that community's attitude to its own romanticized past, perceived as a period of righteousness. Ever since the epoch of the Proph-

---

5 Madeline C. Zilfi, *The Politics of Piety: The Ottoman Ulema in the Postclassical Age (1600–1800)* (Minneapolis, MN: Bibliotheca Islamica, 1988), 14.
6 Ibid., 134.
7 Ibid.

et and his noble companions, there has been a gradual distancing, it was felt, from its ideals. Since all human activity is seen as a sacred matter, any change in behavior, manners or dress, is seen as an unacceptable innovation that represents a falling away from the norms established by the Prophet and his companions. As a tradition (hadith) reminds us, every innovation is heresy, every heresy is error, and every error leads to hell.[8]

As the reader will learn in the pages of this book, there is a seamless path from the acts of the Khārijites in the seventh century, passing, *en route*, the violent religious riots in ninth-, tenth-, and eleventh-century Baghdad, fifteenth- and seventeenth-century Istanbul, eighteenth-century Najd (Arabia), and the nineteenth-century Wahhābis of India known as the Hindustanee Fanatics, to the Taliban, al-Qaeda, and the modern *jihādists*.

Bernard Lewis, professor emeritus of Near Eastern studies at Princeton University, writing in 1993 with his customary elegance, also refers to Islam's past to underline its relevance today:

> No one, least of all the Islamic fundamentalists themselves, will dispute that their creed and political program are not compatible with liberal democracy. But Islamic fundamentalism is just one stream among many. In the fourteen centuries that have passed since the mission of the Prophet, there have been several such movements—fanatical, intolerant, aggressive, and violent. Led by charismatic religious figures from outside the establishment, they have usually begun by denouncing the perversion of the faith and the corruption of society by the false and evil Muslim rulers and leaders of their time. Sometimes these movements have been halted and suppressed by the ruling establishment. At other times they have gained power and used it to wage holy war, first at home, against those whom they saw as backsliders and apostates, and then abroad against the other enemies of the true faith. In time these regimes have been either ousted or, if they have survived, transformed—usually in a fairly short period—into something not noticeably better, and in some ways rather worse, than the old establishments that they had

---

8 Zilfi, "Kadizadelis: Discordant Revivalism," 253.

overthrown. Something of this kind is already visibly happening in the Islamic Republic of Iran.⁹

Thus, fundamentalist movements have been endemic in Islamic history, and modern *jihādists* are constantly drawing upon their Islamic tradition to legitimate, morally and culturally, their acts and programs.

One such movement was that of the Isma'ilis, who emerged from among the extremist Shi'a in the first half of the eighth century. The first of many assassinations for which the Isma'ilis were later renowned occurred on October 16, 1092. A powerful vizier in the Seljuq empire, Nizam al-Mulk, was the target. Our source, Rashid al-Din (ca.1247–1318), a Persian historian in Ilkhanate-ruled Iran (during the Mongolian period), writes that when Hasan-i Sabbah asked who would rid this state of the evil of Nizam al-Mulk, "a man called Bu Tahir Arrani laid the hand of acceptance on his breast, and, following the path of error by which he hoped to attain the bliss of the world-to-come…struck [Nizam al-Mulk] with a knife, and by that blow he suffered martyrdom."¹⁰

As Lewis writes in *The Assassins: A Radical Sect in Islam* (1967), "It was the first of a long series of such attacks which, in a calculated *war of terror* brought sudden death to sovereigns, princes, generals, governors, and even divines who had condemned Ismaili doctrines and authorized the suppression of those who professed them" (emphasis added).¹¹ For the Isma'ilis, the assassins were heroic warriors fighting the enemies of the imam (Muslim ruler), ready to give their lives killing oppressors, thereby manifesting their loyalty, faith, and selflessness. The assassins "earned immediate and eternal bliss."¹²

In sending out their assassins to kill the unrighteous, the Isma'ilis were able to draw upon an old, and perhaps minor, Islamic tradition which nonetheless found favor within dissident and extremist sects.

"The ancient ideal of tyrannicide," Lewis explains, "the religious obligation to rid the world of an unrighteous ruler,"

---

9 Bernard Lewis, "Islam and Liberal Democracy," *Atlantic* (February 1993), http://www.theatlantic.com/magazine/archive/1993/02/islam-and-liberal-democracy/308509/.
10 *Encyclopaedia of Islam*, vol. 3, "H–Iram," ed. B. Lewis et al., 2nd ed. (Leiden: Brill, 1971), s.v. "Hasan-i Sabbāh."
11 Bernard Lewis, *The Assassins: A Radical Sect in Islam* (London: Weidenfeld & Nicolson Ltd, 1967; New York: Basic Books, 2003), 47.
12 Ibid., 48.

certainly contributed to the practice of assassination, as adopted and applied by the Ismailis. But there was more to it than that. The killing by the Assassin of his victim was not only an act of piety; it also had a ritual, almost a sacramental quality. It is significant that in all their murders, in both Persia and Syria, the Assassins always used a dagger; never poison, never missiles, though there must have been occasions when these would have been easier and safer. The Assassin is almost always caught, and usually indeed makes no attempt to escape; there is even a suggestion that to survive a mission was shameful."[13]

Lewis, it must be remembered, calls the Assassins "the first terrorists."[14] He quotes an Isma'ili poet: "Brothers, when the time of triumph comes, with good fortune from both worlds as our companion, then one single warrior on foot a king may be stricken with terror, though he owns more than a hundred thousand horsemen."[15]

And for a campaign of terror to be sustained, two things were required: organization and ideology. "There had to be an organization capable both of launching the attack and surviving the inevitable counter-blow; there had to be a system of belief—which in that time and place could only be a religion—to inspire and sustain the attackers to the point of death," writes Lewis.[16] The Isma'ili religion, "with its memories of passion and martyrdom, its promise of divine and human fulfilment, was a cause that gave dignity and courage to those that embraced it, and inspired a devotion unsurpassed in human history."[17]

Hasan-i Sabbah has inspired many contemporary Islamic fundamentalists: he and his Assassins are regarded as "heroes of Islam," attracting more disciples than ever.[18]

* * *

The desire not to offend Muslims, the wish not to be considered

---

13 Ibid.,127.
14 Ibid.,129-30.
15 Ibid.,130.
16 Ibid.,131.
17 Ibid.,131.
18 Amir Taheri, *Holy Terror: The Inside Story of Islamic Terrorism* (London: Sphere Books, 1987), 34–35.

"Islamophobic," and the long American tradition of not wanting to question the religion of fellow citizens have made any criticism of Islam difficult. This strategy of turning a blind eye to the obvious Islamic component in Islamic terrorism has been taken to absurd and dangerous lengths.

The centrality of religion in the Islamic world is something that Western liberals fail to understand or take seriously. Since most liberal are, in this postmodern world, agnostic, atheists, or simply indifferent to religion, they have trouble understanding that Muslims really do take the Koran literally as the word of God, and really do believe that Muhammad, their Prophet, received God's message through angels or occasionally directly. As I write in chapter 4, in the section entitled "Koran":

> The Koran is considered a revelation from God, *ipsissima verba*, the very words of God. The Koran is understood, not in an allegorical, analogical, metaphorical, or Pickwickian sense, but in a literal sense to be the word of God, and to be obeyed literally. It is a practical manual. Muslims use the Koran as guide to conduct, both private and public. The Koran gives details of the moral and legal duties of believers; it is the basis of their religious dogma, beliefs, ritual, and one of the sources of their law.

To understand how the doctrines of Islam motivate and direct Islamic terrorism, one must take the history of Islamic terrorism back to the Muslim conquests during the first years of Islam. In their rationale, the conquests in the Sind (India), Iraq, and Iran in the early eighth century bear a close resemblance to the wars and agenda of modern *jihādists*; they all depend upon the religious duty of carrying out a *jihād* in the name of and for the cause of God, and to establish Islam. The other central doctrine of Islam with profound implications for Islamic activism—the doctrine or principle of Commanding Right and Forbidding Wrong—has seldom been discussed. *Jihād* can be seen as a special case of this principle in action.

CHAPTER 1
ROOT CAUSE FALLACY

IN THE WAKE of the terrorist attacks on September 11, 2001, many analysts, journalists, and pundits decided, without much thought, that the United States was targeted because of its foreign policy. Others opined, just as dogmatically, that we had to dig out the root causes, which were essentially socioeconomic, with poverty as the favorite explanation. Others followed with their own preferred explanations, which ranged from the Arab-Israeli conflict; lack of education of the *jihādists*, who, it is claimed, had absolutely no knowledge of Islam; sexual deprivation and frustration, to the Crusades and Britney Spears, that is Western decadence; and, rather fatuously, global warming (strange how global warming seems to goad only Muslims to acts of terrorism).

I argue below that neither poverty, nor the lack education of the terrorists, nor the Israel-Arab conflict, nor the foreign policy of the United States, nor Western imperialism, nor the Crusades provide an adequate explanation for Islamic terrorism.

Islamic Terrorism: Not Caused by Poverty or Lack of Knowledge of Islam

The most common explanation for Islamic terrorism is the lack of economic opportunities for the members of the various terrorists groups, in other words, poverty. The second most frequent claim is that all the terrorists are totally ignorant of the tenets of Islam and have no knowledge of, no education in, the contents of the Koran. The thought behind the latter claim is that the terrorists are not justified in invoking Islamic scripture—if they had any real knowledge of Islam they would not commit these acts of terror in its name.

We begin with a study conducted between 1977 and 1979 under the leadership of an Egyptian sociologist, Saad Eddin Ibrahim, of two militant Egyptian Islamic groups: Al-Takfir wa-l-Hijra (incorrectly translated as "Repentance and Holy Flight," or RHF) and Al-Fanniya al-'Askariya ("Technical Military Academy," or MA). I start with this study because Ibrahim is a serious Egyptian scholar keenly aware of the cultural nuances of an Islamic country not available to outsiders, which gives his conclusions more authenticity and weight, and because his study is the first of its kind, appearing long before Western scholars came on the scene in the wake of the 9/11 attacks in 2001. Furthermore, Ibrahim addresses both the question of poverty and the level of education of various members of the terrorist organizations in general, and the depth of their knowledge of Islam in particular.

In 1977, "demanding the release of RHF members being detained by the government," RHF kidnapped a former cabinet minister "and then carried out their threat to kill [him] when the release did not materialize. Crackdowns and shootouts resulted in scores of dead and wounded around the country."[1] Three years earlier MA had "attempted to stage a coup d'état." That plot "was foiled while in process but only after dozens had been killed and wounded."[2] Although the two leaders of both groups had been executed, many of their second-echelon leaders were still in prison. At first distrustful, the jailed militants ultimately decided that Ibrahim's team of researchers "seemed honest and credible enough [to allow the team] to spend approximately four hundred hours interviewing them over a two-year period," amounting to "more than ten hours per person for the thirty-three militants" interviewed.[3]

MA, RHF, and Education

I shall begin with a word about the similarities between the leaders of the militant Egyptian Islamic groups under discussion. MA began under the leadership of Salih Siriya, who turns out to be "a modern, educated man with a Ph.D. in science education":

---

[1] Saad Eddin Ibrahim, "Anatomy of Egypt's Militant Islamic Groups: Methodological Notes and Preliminary Findings," in *Egypt, Islam and Democracy: Critical Essays* (1996; Cairo: The American University in Cairo Press, 2002), 2. First published under the same title in *International Journal of Middle East Studies* 12, no. 4 (December 1980): 423–53.
[2] Ibid., 3.
[3] Ibid., 6.

A Palestinian by birth and in his mid-thirties, he had been a member of the Muslim Brotherhood branch in Jordan (known as the Islamic Liberation Party, Hizb al-Tahrir al-Islami). After the defeat of 1967 he intermittently joined various Palestinian organizations, tried to cooperate with various Arab regimes that claimed to be revolutionary (Libya and Iraq, for example), spent brief periods in jail, and finally settled in Egypt in 1971 and joined one of the specialized agencies of the Arab League in Cairo. It was from that vantage point that he began to attract the attention of some religious students. Underground cells, called usar (families) by the group, began to form in Cairo and Alexandria."[4]

Also in his thirties and educated in Cairo, with a B.S. in agricultural science, RHF founder Shukri Mustafa "had been arrested in 1965, tried, and jailed for a few years on charges of being a member of the Brotherhood."[5]

Both Siriya and Mustafa were seen by rank and file members of their groups as "extremely eloquent, knowledgeable about religion, well-versed in the Quran and Hadith, and highly understanding of national, regional, and international affairs. Both were perceived as virtuous, courageous, fearless of death, and even eager for martyrdom (*istishhad*)."[6] Mustafa in particular was considered by RHF members to be "an authority on matters of doctrinal theology, Islamic jurisprudence, worship, and Islamic social transaction."[7]

Ordinary Muslims

Now we come to the ordinary members themselves. As Ibrahim notes, "the class affiliation of most members of these militant Islamist groups is middle and lower-middle class,"[8] whose

> educational and occupational attainments...was decidedly higher than that of their parents. All but five...were university graduates or university students...enrolled in college at the time of their arrest. The rest were secondary school ed-

---

4 Ibid., 14.
5 Ibid., 14-15.
6 Ibid., 15.
7 Ibid., 16.
8 Ibid., 18.

ucated. Occupationally, only...47 percent...were classifiable, the rest being students. Most of these were professionals... employed by the government: five teachers, three engineers, two doctors, and two agronomists. Three were self-employed (a pharmacist, a doctor, and an accountant), and one worked as a conductor for a bus company. Among those who were students at the time of their arrest...six majored in engineering, four medicine, three in agricultural science, two in pharamacy, two in technical military science, and one in literature....[F]our of [these] majors require very high grades in Egypt's statewide examination of *thanawiya 'amma*:[9] medicine, engineering, technical military science, and pharmacy. These four majors accounted for fourteen out of the eighteen students....In other words, student members of the two militant Islamic groups were decidedly high in both motivation and achievement.[10]

Incidentally, 80 percent of the members had perfectly ordinary family backgrounds.

Fifteen years later, Ibrahim's findings were still considered valid, and enthusiastically endorsed by Egyptian economist Galal A. Amin, who called Ibrahim's work a "pioneer study."[11] Amin wrote, "It is striking how rare it is to find examples of religious fanatcism among either the higher or the very lowest social strata of the Egyptian population,"[12] and quoted Albert Hourani, a much respected Arab historian and intellectual who "reached similar conclusions in connection with the growth of the Muslim Brothers' movement in the late 1930s, pointing out that it was 'spreading in the urban population-among those in an intermediate position: craftsmen, small tradesmen, teachers and professional men

---

9 *Thanawiya 'amma* means "General Secondary" in Modern Standard Arabic. It refers to a series of standardized tests in Egypt that lead to the General Secondary Education Certificate for public secondary schools and serves as the entrance examination for Egyptian public universities. In the context of Egypt's education system, it refers to the general (as opposed to technical or vocational) secondary education track, the completion exams at the end of the track, and the diploma a student earns by passing the exams.
10 Ibrahim, "Anatomy of Egypt's Militant Islamic Groups," 18–19.
11 Galal A. Amin, *Egypt's Economic Predicament: A Study in the Interaction of External Pressure, Political Folly and Social Tension in Egypt, 1960–1990* (Leiden: E.J. Brill, 1995), 137.
12 Ibid., 136.

who stood outside the charmed circle of the dominant elite."'[13]

That same year the Palestinian journalist Khaled Amayreh observed in a *Jerusalem Post* article that the claim that "Islamic terrorism in Israel, as elsewhere, is the product of poverty, backwardness and ignorance" is "simply nonsense. Islamic fundamentalism (a more accurate term is Islamic revival) is not a product or by-product of poverty. Several studies have shown that a substantial majority of Islamists and their supporters come from the middle and upper socio-economic strata."[14]

Amayreh elaborated:

> In the Jordanian parliamentary elections of 1994, to cite just one example, the Muslim Brothers won by landslide margins in such middle-class Amman districts as Jabal Amman and Shmesani, as they did in the poorer neighborhoods. Likewise, in the West Bank and the rest of the occupied territories, the Islamist movement has attained much more popularity and acceptance in towns like Hebron, Nablus, and Ramallah than it has in rural areas and refugee camps, which have a lower standard of living.
>
> Moreover, successive student council elections in West Bank colleges and universities have consistently shown that city dwellers are more likely to vote for "Islamic blocs" than are villagers. The fact that city dwellers, who are generally more educated and better off economically, have consistently lent more support to Islamists refutes the widely held assumption that Islamist popularity thrives on economic misery.[15]

Poverty and the Plight of Women

Geraldine Brooks, a foreign correspondent for the *Wall Street Journal*, wrote about her experiences researching the plight of women in the Middle East in the late 1980s.[16] While in Egypt Brooks was assisted by Sahar, a well-educated, well-connected (her father worked for an American car company) Egyptian woman of twenty-five who wore thick

---

13 Ibid.,137, quoting Albert Hourani, *A History of the Arab Peoples* (London: Faber and Faber, 1991), 349.

14 Khaled Amayreh, "Reality Behind the Image," *Jerusalem Post*, February 24, 1995.

15 Ibid.

16 Geraldine Brooks, *Nine Parts of Desire: The Hidden World of Islamic Women* (1994; New York: Anchor Books, 1996).

make up, stiletto heels, elaborate hairdos, and elegant dresses. "Then one morning," Brooks remembers, "I opened the door and faced a stranger. The elaborate curls were gone. Wrapped away in a severe blue scarf. The make-up was scrubbed off and her shapely dress had been replaced by a dowdy sack. Sahar had adopted the uniform of a Muslim fundamentalist....I'd had assumed that the turn to Islam was the desperate choice of poor people searching for heavenly solace. But Sahar...belonged somewhere near the stratosphere of Egypt's meticulously tiered society."[17]

Asked about her decision, "Sahar mouthed the slogan of Islamic *Jihād* and the Muslim Brotherhood: 'Islam is the Answer.'" Imported ideologies of capitalism and socialism had failed, it was time to "follow the system set down so long ago in the Koran. If God had taken the trouble to reveal a complete code of laws, ethics and social organization, Sahar argued, why not follow that code?"[18]

As Brooks explains, "Islamic movements were on the ascendant in almost every university in the Middle East. And the faculties in which they were most heavily represented were the bastions of the most gifted....The students who were hearing the Islamic call included students with the most options...the elites of the next decade: the people who would shape their nations' futures."[19]

Variations of the Socioeconomic Argument

Brooks's conclusion puts into question a slightly more refined variation of the socioeconomic argument the idea that it is a lack of economic opportunities and means of bettering one's position in society that is responsible for young people turning to Islamic terrorism. Martin Kramer, director of the Moshe Dayan Center for Middle Eastern and African Studies at Tel Aviv University, for example, surmises that the Islamic world contains potential members of the elite who get excluded from political power for one reason or another. "So while they are educated and wealthy, they have a grievance," Kramer observes in a letter to Daniel Pipes, historian and the president of the Middle East Forum, and publisher of its *Middle East Quarterly*, "their ambition is blocked, they cannot translate their socio-economic assets into politcal clout. Islamism is particularly useful to these people, in part because of its careful manipulation, it is possible to recruit a following among

---

17 Ibid., 7-8.
18 Ibid., 8.
19 Ibid., 164.

the poor, who make valuable foot-soldiers."[20] Kramer goes on to cite the "Anatolian Tigers, businessmen who have a critical role in backing Turkey's militant Islamic party, as an example of this counter-elite in its purest form."[21]

Does Brooks's conclusion that even students who have the world at their feet, who have not been rejected and yet choose to follow the radical Islamic path, serve as a counterargument to Kramer's conjecture that it is those who have been rejected who comprise the majority of Islamists? Surely Kramer's argument cannot account for all educated recruits to the Islamists' cause.

In 2008, Marc Sageman, a government counterterrorism expert who had worked with Islamic fundamentalists during the Soviet-Afghan War, and had studied their development, wrote in *Leaderless Jihād: Terror Networks in the Twenty-First Century*: "In terms of socioeconomic background of the family of origin, the vast majority of the terrorists [in his sample of more than 500] came from the middle class."[22] The first wave of the old guards

> came from a higher socio-economic status, almost equally divided between upper class and middle class. An example of the upper class is of course Osama bin Laden himself, the very wealthy scion of a construction empire who grew up with royal princes of Saudi Arabia. A second is his deputy. Ayman al-Zawahiri, who comes from one of the most prominent families in Egypt, with a grandfather who held prestigious diplomatic and academic and uncle who was the founding Secretary General of the Arab League.[23]

The second wave was young people mainly from the middle class.

As Pipes pointed out in 2001,

> wealth does not inoculate against miltant Islam. Kuwaitis enjoy a Western-style income, and owe their very existence to the West, yet Islamists generally win the largest bloc of seats in parliament....The West Bank is more prosperous than

---

20 Martin Kramer, letter to Daniel Pipes, August 2, 2001, cited in Daniel Pipes, *Militant Islam Reaches America* (New York: W.W. Norton and Company, 2002), 57.
21 Ibid.
22 Sageman, *Leaderless Jihād*, 48.
23 Ibid., 49.

Gaza, yet militant Islamic groups usually enjoy more popularity in the former than the latter. Militant Islam flourishes in Western Europe and North America, where Muslims have an economic level higher than the national averages. And... [i]n the United States, the difference between Islamists and common Muslims is largely one between haves and have-nots. Muslims have the numbers; Islamists have the dollars.[24]

Pipes also makes clear that "a flourishing economy does not inoculate against radical Islam. Today's militant Islamic movements took off in the 1970s, precisely as oil-exporting states enjoyed extraordinary growth rates."[25]

Land and Wealth: Mistaken Identifiers

In general, observes David Wurmser of the American Enterprise Institute, Westerners attribute too many of the Arab world's problems "to specific material issues" such as land and wealth. This usually means a tendency "to belittle belief and strict adherence to principle as genuine and dismiss it as a cynical exploitation of the masses by politicians. As such, Western observers see material issues and leaders, not the spiritual state of the Arab world, as the heart of the problem."[26]

Islamists themselves seldom invoke poverty as their principal grievance. Here is an illuminating reply to this kind of explanation from the Ayatollah Khomeini in an August 24, 1979, speech given in Qom: "Economics is a matter for the donkey (*khar*). Our people made the revolution for Islam, not for the Persian melon (*kharboza*)."[27] Even more conclusive is Khomeini's lengthy riposte, uttered in late 1979, in which he spells out the *raison d'être* of the Iranian Revolution:

> This movement which from start to finish took about fifteen, sixteen years...in which much blood was given and young people were lost....[I]t is our belief that this was all for Islam.

---

24 Pipes, *Miltant Islam*, 58, quoting Khalid Duran, "How CAIR Put My Life in Peril," *Middle East Quarterly* 9, no. 1 (Winter 2002): 43.
25 Ibid., 58.
26 David Wurmser, "The Rise and Fall of the Arab World," *Strategic Review* 21, no. 3 (Summer 1993): 33–46; quoted in Daniel Pipes, "God and Mammon: Does Poverty Cause Militant Islam?" *National Interest*, no. 66 (Winter 2001/2002): 14–21.
27 Quoted in Saïd Amir Arjomand, *After Khomeini: Iran under His Successors* (Oxford and New York: Oxford University Press, 2009), 56.

I cannot, and no intelligent person can, imagine that it could be said that we gave our blood so that melons would be less expensive, that we gave up our young men so that houses would be less expensive....

...It is for Islam that a person can give up his life. Our saints also gave up their lives for Islam, not for economics....[T]hat a person would want an economic system and would sacrifice his life so that the economic situation would be improved! This is not sensible!"[28]

In the preface to his translation of a work by celebrated Iranian exegete and historian al-Tabarī' (839–923 CE), Israeli scholar of Islamic studies Yohanan Freidmann, echoing Khomeini, summarizes the goals of the early Muslims as explained directly to their Persian adversaries: "Unlike the pre-Islamic Arabs, the Muslims do not fight for worldy possessions or in order to improve their standard of living. Their only objective is to spread the new faith of Islam."[29]

Bringing the argument to February 2015, here is how ISIS recruit Aqsa Mahmood describes her background and motivations to journalist Beenish Ahmed in an interview: "The media at first used to [portray] the ones running away to join the *Jihād* as being unsuccessful, [and say that they] didn't have a future and [came] from broke [sic] down families etc. But that is far from the truth." Mahmood elaborates:

> Most sisters I have come across have been in university studying courses with many promising paths, with big, happy families and friends and everything in the Dunyah ["world"] to persuade one to stay behind and enjoy the luxury. If we had stayed behind, we could have been blessed with it all...a relaxing and comfortable life and lots of money....
>
> ...[W]e sacrificed all of that for the best in *al-ākhira* [the

---

28 Quoted in Suzanne Maloney, *Iran's Political Economy since the Revolution* (Cambridge: Cambridge University Press, 2015), 84. *Mavaz'-e Imam Khomeini*, ed. Mohammad Reza Akbari (Isfahan, Iran: Payam-i 'Itrat, 1999), 1:243–44.

29 *The Battle of a-Qadisiyya and the Conquest of Syria and Palestine*, trans. Yohanan Friedmann, vol. 12 of *The History of al-Tabarī* (Albany: State University of New York Press, 1991), xvi.

"Hereafter"]. [We] were not stupid young brainwashed females[;] we[']ve come here to [S]yria for ALLAH alone."[30]

It is true that some Islamists refer to economic circumstances, including the poverty of their fellow Muslims, when justifying their acts of terrorism, but they are thinking only of Islamic justice. Their priority is the establishment of an Islamic state where God-made laws replace man-made laws. If they were truly thinking first and foremost of ameliorating the economic situation of all Muslims, the Jemaah Islamiyah, a Southeast Asian militant extremist Islamist group linked to al-Qaeda, for example, would not have bombed the tourist districts of Kuta in Bali in October 2002, killing 202 people. The Islamic terrorists not only killed thirty-eight Indonesians, but also slowed the tourist trade on which so many locals depended; tourism accounts for five percent of Indonesia's Gross Domestic Product. In other words, Islamic terrorism was the cause, not the result, of poverty.

A similar conclusion can be drawn regarding the Luxor Massacre of fifty-eight tourists and four Egyptian nationals on November 17, 1997. This massacre, probably instigated by the Al-Gama'a al-Islamiyya, an Egyptian Sunni Islamist group designated as a terrorist organization by the United States, was also directly responsible for empty hotel rooms and unemployed tourist guides. A great many Egyptians depend upon the tourist industry for their livelihoods; 700,000 people work in travel agencies and hotels, and many times that number rely indirectly on tourism (as many as 1.5 million in 2014).[31] "We are facing the biggest crisis in the history of tourism in Egypt," Tourism Minister Mamdou el-Beltagi reported to the government daily *Al-Ahram*. "It would be naive to say that this grisly crime will not have a major negative impact."[32] There is some evidence to suggest that the Islamic terrorists responsible for the murders were deliberately targeting the Egyptian economy, hoping to provoke the government to take repressive measures, which

---

30 Beenish Ahmed, "How a Teenage Girl Goes from Listening to Coldplay and Reading Harry Potter to Joining ISIS," *Think Progress*, February 24, 2015, http://thinkprogress.org/world/2015/02/24/3626720/women-isis/.

31 Kevin Rushby, "Can Middle East Tourism Ever Recover?" Travel, *Guardian*, November 24, 2015, https://www.theguardian.com/travel/2015/nov/24/can-middle-east-tourism-ever-recover-terrorist-attacks-egypt-tunisia

32 Douglas Jehl, "Massacre Hobbles Tourism in Egypt," International Business, *New York Times*, December 25, 1997, http://www.nytimes.com/1997/12/25/business/international-business-massacre-hobbles-tourism-in-egypt.html

in turn would have strengthened support for antigovernment forces.[33] Islamic terrorist attacks have had a similarly devastating effect on the economies of Algeria, Tunisia, Libya, Aden, and Yemen.[34]

Nor by Israeli-Arab Conflict

The existence of Israel is not the cause of Islamic terrorism.

In Terrorism: How the West Can Win (an underrated book he edited and contributed to), Israel's prime minister Benjamin Netanyahu makes clear that Islamic terrorism is "not a sporadic phenomenon born of social misery and frustration."[35] We must avoid simplistic analyses of Islamic terrorism as "a result of certain 'root causes,' such as poverty, political oppression, denial of national aspirations, etc.," Netanyahu warns, for "terrorism is not an automatic result of anything. It is…an evil choice." He continues: "No resistance movement in Nazi-occupied Europe conducted or condoned terrorist attacks against German civilians, attacking military and government targets instead. But today's terrorists need the flimsiest pretexts to perpetrate their crimes, targeting the innocent with particular relish."[36] Thus,

> the root cause of terrorism lies not in grievances, but in a disposition toward unbridled violence. This can be traced to a world view which asserts that certain ideological and religious goals justify, indeed demand, the shedding of all moral inhibitions. In this context, the observation that the root cause of terrorism is terrorists is more than a tautology.[37]

And so we come to Israel and the Arabs. Writing in 1986, Netanyahu sets the record straight:

> It is argued that the absence of progress toward a peaceful settlement between Arabs and Israelis induces terrorism. The truth is exactly the reverse. Arab terrorism is the not the

---

33 Lawrence Wright, T*he Looming Tower: Al-Qaeda and the Road to 9/11* (New York: Vintage 2007), 256–57.

34 Rushby, "Can Middle East Tourism Recover?"

35 Benjamin Netanyahu, "Defining Terrorism," in *Terrorism: How the West Can Win*, ed. Benjamin Netanyahu (New York: Farrar, Starus, Giroux, 1986), 7.

36 Benjamin Netanyahu, "Terrorism: How the West Can Win," in Netanyahu, Terrorism, 203.

37 Ibid., 204.

result of breakdowns of peace negotiations; it is, more than any other factor, the cause of such breakdowns. (Arab leaders showing the slightest inclination toward peaceful coexistence risk immediate assassination by the terrorists.)[38]

What about American support for Israel? According to Netanyahu,

> The antagonism of Islamic and Arab radicalism to the West… is sometimes explained as deriving from American support for Israel. But the hostility to the West preceded the creation of Israel by centuries, and much of the terrorists' animus is directed against targets and issues that have nothing to do with Israel…. Middle Eastern radicals…hated Israel from its inception *because it is an organic part of the West.* That is, because Israel represents for them precisely the incarnation of those very traditions and values, formeost of which is democracy, which they hate and fear."[39] (emphasis in original)

As early as 1995, Netanyahu had warned: "It is impossible to understand just how inimical—and how deadly—to the United States and to Europe this rising tide of militant Islam is without taking a look at the roots of Arab-Islamic hatred of the West. The enmity toward the West goes back many centuries….And this would be the case even if Israel had never been born."[40] Or as Wagdi Ghuniem, a militant Islamic cleric from Egypt, put it: "[S]uppose the Jews said 'Palestine—you [Muslims] can take it.' Would it then be ok?…No! The problem is belief, it is not a problem of land."[41]

---

38 Ibid.

39 Benjamin Netanyahu, "Terrorism and the Islamic World," in Netanyahu, *Terrorism*, 62–63.

40 Benjamin Netanyahu, *Fighting Terrorism: How Democracies Can Defeat Domestic and International Terrorism* (New York: Farrar, Straus and Giroux, 1995), 82; quoted in Douglas Murray, *Neoconservatism: Why We Need It* (New York: Encounter Books, 2006), 118–19.

41 Wagdi Ghuniem, speech delivered at "Palestine: 50 Years of Occupation," a program sponsored by the Islamic Association for Palestine and held in the Walt Whitman Auditorium, Brooklyn College, Brooklyn, NY, May 24, 1998; quoted in Steven Emerson, "Islamic Militants on the Lecture Circuit in the United States," *Journal of Counterterrorism* (Summer 1998), available at http://www.steveemerson.com/4256/islamic-militants-on-the-lecture-circuit-in.

In September 2001 Christopher Hitchens, journalist and political analyst, wrote in *The Nation*: "Does anyone suppose that an Israeli withdrawal from Gaza would have forestalled the slaughter in Manhattan? It would take a moral cretin to suggest anything of the sort; the cadres of the new *jihād* make it very apparent that their quarrel is with Judaism and secularism on principle, not with (or not just with) Zionism."[42]

In 2012, Yoram Ettinger, Israel's consul general in Houston, Texas from 1985 to 1988 and minister for congressional affairs—with the rank of ambassador —at Israel's embassy in Washington, D.C. from 1989 to 1992, wrote:

> The most-frequently mentioned (supposed) cause of anti-U.S. Islamic terrorism is U.S. support of Israel and U.S. policy toward the Palestinians. Nevertheless, 9/11 was planned while former U.S. President Bill Clinton and then-Prime Minister Ehud Barak offered the Palestinians the entire store. The Oct. 12, 2000 murder of 17 sailors on the *USS Cole* happened when Israel and the U.S. offered unprecedented concessions to the Palestinians at Camp David. The Aug. 27, 1998 bombing of the U.S. embassies in Kenya and Tanzania (257 murdered and more than 4,000 injured) took place while Clinton was brutally pressuring then-Prime Minister Benjamin Netanyahu. The murders of 19 U.S. soldiers in Riyadh and the Khobar Towers, in 1995 and 1996, were carried out while then-interim Prime Minister Shimon Peres implemented unprecedented concessions for the Palestinians. The February 1993 World Trade Center bombing (six murdered and more than 1,000 injured) transpired while Israel conducted the pre-Oslo talks with the PLO. The Dec. 21, 1988 Pan Am-103 terrorist attack (270 murdered) took place a few months following the groundbreaking recognition of the PLO by the U.S. The 1983 murder of 300 Marines and 58 French soldiers in car bombings at the U.S. Embassy and Marines base, and at the French military headquarters in Beirut, all occurred while the U.S. military confronted Israeli tanks in Lebanon and the U.S. administration blasted Israel for its war against the PLO.[43]

---

42 Christopher Hitchens, "Against Rationalization," *Nation*, September 20, 2001, https://www.thenation.com/article/against-rationalization/.
43 Yoram Ettinger, "The Root Causes of Anti-US Islamic Terrorism," *Israel Hayom*,

The passing of time and further reflection has not altered this conclusion: Islamic terrorism far predates the existence of Israel.

Rival Ideologies

Islamic terrorists see the United States as preaching and practising a rival ideology: "Islamic rogue regimes view the U.S. as their key moral and strategic adversary. U.S.-style freedom of religion, expression, markets and association constitute a lethal threat to all Islamic regimes."[44] Osama bin Laden confirmed this insight in an interview about the September 11, 2001, World Trade Center atrocity: "The immense materialistic towers, which preach Freedom, and Human Rights, and Equality, were destroyed."[45] He did not call the towers a symbol of capitalism, but of "freedom, human rights and equality"—and it's these three fundamental Western principles that are the targets of the Islamic terrorists.

Barry Rubin, the late director of the Global Research in International Affairs Center at the Interdisciplinary Center, in Herzliya, Israel, also makes some valid observations regarding U.S. support for Israel and Islamic anti-Americanism in his masterly 2001 essay, "The Truth about U.S. Middle East Policy":

> It is strange that the height of anti-Americanism in the Middle East came at the height of U.S. proposals to support an independent Palestinian state with its capital in East Jerusalem....The attempt to reduce all of U.S. Middle East policy to the phrase "support for Israel"—and then misrepresent what that stance acutally entailed—was really an attempt to exploit xenophobia as a tool justifying radical groups and dictatorial regimes. The real complaint was that the United States helped Israel survive, then sought a diplomatic solution that would undermine both the case for Islamist revolution and the justification for the regimes' dictatorial rule.[46]

January 11, 2012, http://www.israelhayom.com/site/newsletter_opinion.php?id=1180.
44 Ibid.
45 Osama Bin Laden, interviewed by Tayser Allouni, Al Jazeera, October 21, 2001, in *Messages to the World: The Statements of Osama Bin Laden*, ed. Bruce Lawrence, trans. James Howarth (London: Verso, 2005), 112.
46 Barry Rubin, "The Truth about U.S. Middle East Policy," in *Anti-American Terrorism and the Middle East: A Documentary Reader—Understanding the Violence*, ed. Barry Rubin and Judith Colp Rubin (Oxford and New York: Oxford University Press, 2002), 94. Originally published under the same title in *Middle East Review of International*

Neither Ettinger nor Rubin, however, mention two other fundamental elements of Islamic terrorist ideology that, in themselves, are enough to explain this hostility to Israel and all those who come to her succour. First, virulent antisemitism is central to all Islamic doctrine. As Andrew Bostom points out in his definitive analysis and anthology, *The Legacy of Islamic Antisemitism* (2008), "The uncomfortable examination of Islamic doctrines and history is required to understand the enduring phenomenon of Muslim Jew hatred, which dates back to the origins of Islam."[47]

Antisemitism

Islamic antisemitism is not a modern creed derived from Nazism but is simply confirmed by it. Modern Islamic terrorists justify this hatred by copious references to the Koran, the biography of Muhammad, the *sunna* and *hadīth* —in other words all the scriptures and revered texts of Islam. Jews cannot be trusted, they are the permanent enemies of Muslims, and must be subjugated, made to pay a tax, or killed, and fought until the Day of Judgment. In the *hadīth*, according to *Sahīh al-Bukhārī*, "The Day of Judgment will not come about until Muslims fight the Jews (killing the Jews), when the Jew will hide behind stones and trees. The stones and trees will say O Muslims, O Abdulla, there is a Jew behind me, come and kill him. Only the Gharkad tree would not do that because it is one of the trees of the Jews."[48] (We shall return to this theme when examining the doctrines of the Islamic terrorists.)

The second Islamic principle concerning Jews and Israel is well-described by Jan Willem van der Hoeven, director of the International Christian Zionist Center in Jerusalem: "Once the forces of Islam conquer a land or territory, it is to remain under Islamic dominion forever, and it is a mortal affront to the supremacy of Islam when such territories would ever be lost to the dominion of Islam and revert to previous—infidel—ownership as was the case in Palestine. It was a Muslim controlled territory (under the Muslim Turks and later the Muslim Arabs) and reverted by the decree of the U.N. resolution back to its previous

---

Affairs 5, no. 4 (December 2001), http://www.rubincenter.org/meria/2001/12/brubin.pdf. This important article deserves to be better known, and should be reprinted as a pamphlet, and translated into as many languages as possible, particularly Arabic, Persian, and Urdu.

47 Andrew Bostom, *The Legacy of Islamic Antisemitism: From Sacred Texts to Solemn History* (Amherst, MA: Prometheus Books, 2008), 33.

48 Bukhārī, *Sahīh, The Authentic Hadīth: Book of Jihād and Campaigns*, trans. Muhammad Muhsin Khan, Hadīth 2925 (Riyadh, Saudi Arabia: Darussalam, 1997), 4:113.

owners: the Jews."⁴⁹

Article 11 of the August 18, 1988, Covenant of the Islamic Resistance Movement (the Hamas Covenant) makes clear the doctrinal issue by using *waqf*, a term, according to *The Dictionary of Islam*, that "in the language of the law signifies the appropriation or dedication of property to charitable uses and the service of God. An endowment. The object of such an endowment or appropriation must be of perpetual nature, and such property or land cannot be sold or transferred."⁵⁰ Here is an essential excerpt from Article 11 of the Hamas Covenant:

> The Islamic Resistance Movement believes that the land of Palestine is an Islamic *Waqf* consecrated for future Muslim generations until Judgment Day. It, or any part of it, should not be squandered: it, or any part of it, should not be given up. Neither a single Arab country nor all Arab countries, neither any king or president, nor all the kings and presidents, neither any organization nor all of them, be they Palestinian or Arab, possess the right to do that. Palestine is an Islamic *Waqf* land consecrated for Muslim generations until Judgment Day. This being so, who could claim to have the right to represent Muslim generations till Judgment Day?
>
> This is the law governing the land of Palestine in the Islamic Sharia (law) and the same goes for any land the Muslims have conquered by force, because during the times of (Islamic) conquests, the Muslims consecrated these lands to Muslim generations till the Day of Judgment.⁵¹

Many Islamists claim that large parts of Europe that were once conquered by Muslims still belong to them. Hasan al-Banna, founder of

---

49 Jan Willem van der Hoeven, "The Main Reason for the Present Middle East Conflict: Islam and Not "The Territories," EretzYisroel.Org, 2000–2001, http://www.eretzyisroel.org/~jkatz/mainreason.html.

50 Thomas Patrick Hughes, *Dictionary of Islam: Being a Cyclopaedia of the Doctrines, Rites, Ceremonies, and Customs, Together with the Technical and Theological Terms of the Muhammadan Religion* (London: W.H. Allen, 1885; Delhi: Rupa & Co, 1988), s.v. "*waqf*."

51 "Hamas Covenant 1988: The Covenant of the Islamic Resistance Movement," August 18, 1988, text available at Yale Law School, Lillian Goldman Law Library, The Avalon Project: Documents in Law, History, and Diplomacy, http://avalon.law.yale.edu/20th_century/hamas.asp.

Egypt's Muslim Brotherhood, argued that "Andalusia [the Muslim name for Spain], Sicily, the Balkans, south Italy, and the Roman sea islands were all Islamic lands that have to be restored to the homeland of Islam....[I]t is our right to restore the Islamic Empire its glory."[52] Of course, in a culture imbued with the ethics of shame and honor, the very existence of Israel and the loss of the land of Palestine is a doubly shameful reminder of Islamic humiliation.

More recently Bernard Lewis is reported to have said that "the only real solution to defeating radical Islam is to bring freedom to the Middle East. Either 'we free them or they destroy us,'" but as Daniel Pipes pointed out, "There are plenty of born-free Muslims in the West who are Islamists. Take, for example, the four 7/7 bombers in London. Freedom did nothing for them."[53]

Nor by U.S. Foreign Policy

United States foreign policy is another popular explanation for the virulent anti-Americanism of the Islamic terrorists that is offered as a general cause of all terrorist acts. However, as Barry Rubin very convincingly argues in his above-cited essay,[54] U.S. foreign policy regarding the Islamic world has been conciliatory and accommodating rather than confrontational and antagonistic. Rubin writes:

> During the 1940s and early 1950s, U.S. leaders wanted to play an anti-imperialist role in the Middle East. They tended to oppose continued British and French rule in the region and to voice support for reform movements. When Gamal Abdel Nasser took power in Egypt in 1952, American policymakers welcomed his coup....In 1956, in an unusual break in its close relationship to England and France, the United States opposed their plot to overthrow Nasser during the Suez crisis because it thought this action would antagonize the Arab world and increase Soviet influence.[55]

---

52 "Oh Youth," *The Complete Works of Imam Hasan al-Banna: 1906–1949*, 12, https://thequranblog.files.wordpress.com/2008/06/_9_-oh-youth.pdf, available at The Quran Blog—Enlighten Yourself, June 7, 2008, https://thequranblog.wordpress.com/2008/06/07/the-complete-works-of-imam-hasan-al-banna-10/.

53 Daniel Pipes, "We Free Them or They Destroy Us," Lion's Den: Daniel Pipes Blog, September 13, 2006, http://www.danielpipes.org/blog/2006/09/we-free-them-or-they-destroy-us.

54 Rubin, "Truth about Middle East Policy."

55 Ibid., 81-82.

Rubin goes on to argue that much of the instability of the region was caused by the Arab states themselves:

> America was dragged into crises when Muslim Iraq attacked Muslim Iran, when Arab Muslim Iraq seized Arab Muslim Kuwait, and when Arab Muslim but secularist Egypt threatened Arab Muslim Jordan and Saudi Arabia. Usama bin Ladin's anger was most provoked by the presence of U.S. troops in Saudi Arabia starting in 1990. Yet this action not only protected Saudi Arabia and freed Kuwait from an Iraqi threat but was sanctioned by the Arab League. The grievance most closely associated with bin Ladin's turn to an anti-American strategy and the September 11 attacks was clearly based on a U.S. action that was pro-Arab and pro-Muslim.[56]

With the help of Rubin's "The Truth about U.S. Middle East Policy," let us consider the many ways the United States has assisted both Muslims and Arabs.

Palestine. When chairman of the Palestine Liberation Organization (PLO) Yasir Arafat was besieged in Beirut by the Israeli army in 1982, the United States arranged for him safe passage out of Lebanon and adopted a conciliatory approach to the PLO, turning a blind eye to terrorism by some PLO member groups. This policy became unacceptable when the PLO refused to denounce and renounce violence in 1990. Between 1993 and 2000, the U.S. was in effect Palestine's patron, even forgiving Arafat's past acts of terrorism that killed American citizens, including U.S. diplomats. Arafat was subsequently invited to the White House on numerous occasions. The U.S. raised money for the Palestinian Authority (the interim self-government body established in 1994 following the Gaza-Jericho Agreement to govern the Gaza Strip and Areas A and B of the West Bank), which it refrained from criticizing in public.

Several U.S. presidents made symbolic gestures of solidarity with the Palestinian people and its leaders, as, for example, when President Bill Clinton spoke in Gaza to the Palestinian leaders in 1998. The U.S. oversaw negotiations that led to a peace agreement producing an independent Palestinian state with its capital in East Jerusalem in 2000. And when Arafat rejected U.S. peace efforts, refusing to implement agreed

---
56 Ibid., 83.

upon cease-fires, American leaders still did not criticize him or give up hope. Despite all efforts, patience, and diplomacy on the part of the U.S., Arabs and Muslims were jubilant when bin Ladin attacked the U.S. on September 11, claiming that Palestinians themselves had suffered because of American policies.

Iran. The Carter, Reagan, and Clinton administrations all made serious détente efforts with Iran. While it is true that America maintained some sanctions against Iran in order to discourage Iran's sponsoring of terrorism, development of weapons of mass destruction, and ongoing opposition to Arab-Israel peace efforts, American leaders constantly sought ways to end sanctions through diplomatic compromise, never interfering in Iran's internal affairs.

Afghanistan and Others. Covert aid from the United States saved Afghanistan from the Soviets in the 1980s, Kuwait and Saudi Arabia from Iraq (the First Gulf War: August 2, 1990–February 28, 1991), the Muslim peoples of Bosnia from Bosnian Serbs (1992–1995), and Kosovo from the Federal Republic of Yugoslavia, consisting of the Republics of Montenegro and Serbia (1998–1999). While the U.S. risked American lives to help Muslims for humanitarian reasons, bin Ladin and his apologists blamed the United States for Muslim suffering in Bosnia and Kosovo, as elsewhere. What mattered to bin Ladin was that Americans—infidels, in other words—deployed troops on Saudi-Muslim soil and attacked a Muslim nation, Iraq.

Successive U.S. presidential administrations took pains to cushion Muslim sensibilities, exonerating Islam from any responsibility for terrorist attacks by using euphemisms and stock phrases such as "A great world religion has been hijacked by a minority of criminals" and "Islam is a religion of peace" when addressing these attacks in public statements.

Pakistan and Turkey. Ignoring Pakistan's sponsorship of terrorism against India, the U.S. government backed the Pakistani government. It also backed Turkey against Greece over the Cyprus conflict, a crisis resulting from the invasion of the island by Turkey and the eventual illegal declaration of independence by the Turkish Cypriot assembly in 1983.

Somalia. Similarly, the U.S. intervened in Somalia to protect the Muslim people for humanitarian reasons, sending U.S. forces to protect Muslims suffering from anarchy, civil war, and brutal warlords, but because there were no American interests in play, humanitarian actions were portrayed by bin Ladin, journalists, Muslim intellectuals in the Middle East, and many others as American imperialism and aggression against Muslims.

Iraq. When President Saddam Hussein of Iraq began to seek Arab leadership in 1989 and repeatedly denounced the United States, U.S. policy makers responded cautiously, in order to avoid offending Arabs, and continued to provide Iraq with credits and other trade benefits, despite hard evidence that the money Iraq obtained was being used illegally to buy arms.

Nonetheless the U.S. supported continued sanctions against Iraq because Hussein refused to cooperate with United Nations inspectors. Since Baghdad's government reneged on its commitments to allow UN inspectors free access to military sites these sanctions were kept in place. Iraq's government deliberately allowed its own people to suffer, and using that suffering as propaganda maintained its aggressive stance toward its Arab and Muslim neighbors. Bin Ladin and his apologists portrayed American policy as a deliberate attempt to injure and kill Iraqi people.

The Persian Gulf. The U.S. kept its military forces out of the Persian Gulf to avoid offending the sensibilities of the Arab and Muslim peoples there. It entered only when requested,

> first to reflag Arab oil tankers and later to intervene against Iraq's invasion of Kuwait. Its forces never went where they were not invited and left whenever they were asked to do so by the local states. American forces also stayed away from Mecca and Medina to avoid offense to Islam. Once Kuwait was liberated, the United States…advocated the concept of the Damascus agreement, in which Egypt and Syria would have played a primary role in protecting the Gulf. It was the Gulf Arab states that rejected implementation of this idea. Nevertheless, bin Ladin, other Arabs, and Iran's government portrayed the U.S. presence as an imperialist plot to dominate the area and subjugate its people.

> The United States rescued Egypt at the end of the 1973 war by pressing Israel to stop advancing and by insisting on a cease-fire. The United States became Egypt's patron in 1980s, after the Camp David peace agreement, providing large-scale arms supplies and other military and financial assistance while asking little in return….[N]one of this help gave the United States any leverage over Egyptian policies, or even goodwill in the state-controlled Egyptian media and in the

statements of that country's leaders. Bin Ladin and his allies, however, portrayed Egypt as a puppet of the United States.[57]

Setting the Record Straight

It is important to record at least some of the ways that the United States has not reacted to events in the Middle East, despite deliberate provocation on the part of Middle Eastern regimes:[58]

- The United States has not attacked Iran despite the overwhelming evidence that Iran has sponsored terrorist attacks on Americans—attacks that have cost hundreds of American lives in Lebanon and Iraq. Following the Iranian revolution of 1979, the U.S. demanded economic sanctions to change specific policies. They were expanded in 1995 to include firms dealing with the Iranian government. In 1979 Iran was in violation of all international laws when it took American hostages at the U.S. Embassy in Tehran—strictly speaking an act of war—but President Carter sought diplomatic means to resolve the situation.
- Similarly, when Syria was shown to have participated in anti-American terrorism, the United States did not coerce or seek to subvert it. The U.S. tried to win over Syria during the First Gulf War, which was a consequence of the Iraqi invasion of Kuwait in 1990, and in the subsequent peace process. Even when Syria walked out, the U.S. did not apply pressure, but sought diplomatic ways to gain Syria's cooperation.
- Nor did the United States seek to destroy Arafat and the PLO even when they were known to have been responsible for anti-American terrorism and to have aligned with the USSR. The U.S. refrained from criticizing the PLO when they broke agreements and cease-fires promised in 2000 and 2001.
- The U.S. did not threaten or punish when Egypt purchased missiles from North Korea in the late 1980s and early 1990s, and refused to cooperate with the War on Terror in 2001.
- Nor did the United States retaliate when Jordan supported Iraq during the First Gulf War. Jordan continues to receive American aid—amounting to $1,211,821,880 in 2013 and in $772,939,966 in 2014.[59]

---

57 Ibid., 85–87.
58 Rubin, "Truth about Middle East Policy," 89–91.
59 Jordan 2014 figures, USAID, https://explorer.usaid.gov/country-detail.html#Jordan. USAID is the leading U.S. Government agency that "works to end extreme global poverty and enable resilient, democratic societies to realize their potential," Who We Are, https://www.usaid.gov/who-we-are.

- "When the U.S. companies' holdings were nationalized and oil prices were raised steeply, the United States did not try to overthrow regimes or force or threaten them to lower prices."[60]
- The U.S. "did not take advantage of the USSR's disappearance as a superpower to impose anything on anybody and certainly not to establish American domination in the region. Despite having won the Cold War, the United States did not seek to take revenge on regimes that had supported the losing side."[61]

U.S. Aid

It is important as well to point out that the U.S has spent billions of dollars in aid to the Middle East.

In 2013, Face the Facts USA, a project of George Washington University, reported that "[o]ver the last six decades, the U.S. has invested $299 billion in military and economic aid for Middle East and Central Asian countries currently in turmoil. Egypt tops a list of 10 nations, receiving $114 billion since the end of World War II. Iraq comes in second, getting nearly $60 billion from the U.S. (over and above war costs)."[62]

As Rubin points out, the United States bent over backwards to maintain good relations with Muslims and Arabs even after several thousand Americans were murdered in the terrorist attacks of 9/11: "U.S. leaders spent much of their time urging that there be no retaliation against Muslims or Arabs in the United States. American policy makers repeated at every opportunity that they did not see Islam as the enemy and tried everything possible to gain Arab and Muslim support or sympathy for the U.S. effort."[63]

Both the Bush and Obama administrations reiterated on every relevant occasion that "Islam is a religion of peace, and terrorism has nothing to do with the tenets of Islam." Consider these quotes from President George W. Bush on Islam and terrorism. "I believe that Islam is a great religion that preaches peace," Bush stated in 2007 on an Arabic speaking television station,[64] recalling language he used during remarks made to

---

60 Rubin, "Truth about Middle East Policy," 91.
61 Ibid.
62 "Billions in U.S. Aid Haven't Bought Peace in the Middle East," *World Post*, May 06, 2013, http://www.huffingtonpost.com/2013/05/06/us-aid-middle-east_n_3223151.html.
63 Rubin, "Truth about Middle East Policy," 88.
64 George W. Bush, quoted in Daniel Pipes, "Bush Returns to the 'Religion of Peace' Formulation," *Lion's Den: Daniel Pipes Blog*, October 4, 2007, http://www.danielpipes.

reassure Muslims and Americans not long after 9/11 at the Islamic Center of Washington, D.C.:

> These acts of violence against innocents violate the fundamental tenets of the Islamic faith. And it's important for my fellow Americans to understand that. The English translation is not as eloquent as the original Arabic, but let me quote from the Koran, itself: In the long run, evil in the extreme will be the end of those who do evil. For that they rejected the signs of Allah and held them up to ridicule.
>
> The face of terror is not the true faith of Islam. That's not what Islam is all about. Islam is peace. These terrorists don't represent peace. They represent evil and war.[65]

Although the United States has handled relations with the Middle East with political restraint and humanitarian generosity, the Middle East has neither recognized America's protection, nor acknowledged its responsibility for acts of terrorism against Americans—and for squandering billions in American aid. As Rubin sums it up: "[I]f the root cause of this…anti-Americanism" is "internal, it is dependent on those needs and forces rather than anything the United States actually does.... Those who have declared war on America are playing the dangerous game of exaggerating outside menaces to justify their incompetence at home and aggressiveness abroad. They deliberately misunderstand American policy and society, successfully soiling them also in the eyes of others."[66]

All the states of the Middle East, including Turkey and Iran, see themselves in modern history as passive victims of Western imperialist manipulation. This attitude and the attendant conspiracy theories with which the Middle East is awash are a means to avoid taking responsibility for its present lamentable state. Its anti-Western, anti-American rhetoric is a convenient way to cover up its own failures.

---

org/blog/2007/10/bush-returns-to-the-religion-of-peace.

65 The White House: President George W. Bush, "'Islam Is Peace' Says President: Remarks by the President at Islamic Center of Washington, D.C.," news release, September 17, 2001, https://georgewbush-whitehouse.archives.gov/news/releases/2001/09/20010917-11.html.

66 Rubin, "Truth about Middle East Policy," 106.

The True Victims

Historically, the image of the West slowly picking the Ottoman Empire to pieces during the eighteenth and nineteenth centuries and driving into World War I to hasten its demise in order to seize its lands is nonsense. As Efraim Karsh, professor and head of the Mediterranean Studies Programme, King's College, University of London, wrote,

> [T]he Ottoman Empire was not a hapless victim of European imperialism but an active participant in the great-power game; the destruction of this empire was predominantly self-inflicted; there was no Arab yearning for regional unity; the European powers did not break the Middle East's political unity but rather over-unified the region; Britain neither misled its Arab allies nor made simultaneous contradictory promises regarding post-war settlement in the Middle East; and the creation of the post-Ottoman regional order was no less of the making of the local actors than of the great powers.[67]

What, for example, has U.S. foreign policy to got to do with the armed conflict between Islamist groups (such as the Islamic Armed Movement and the more hard-line Armed Islamic Group) and security forces between 1991 and 2002 that left over 150,000 Algerians victims and more than 6,000 missing?[68] As I wrote ten years ago, many of the victims of Islamic fundamentalism are Muslim—Muslim men, women, and children, Muslim writers, intellectuals, and journalists.[69] The Algerian armed groups have everything essential in common with all other Islamic terrorist groups, a fact obscured by the reality that in this case the victims have been largely, though not entirely, fellow Muslims.

Nor by Western Imperialism

It is still claimed by many analysts and experts in the West, and even by Muslim intellectuals and Muslim states, that one of the reasons

---

67 Efraim Karsh, *The Tail Wags the Dog: International Politics and the Middle East* (New York: Bloomsbury, 2015), 9.

68 Dalia Ghanem-Yazbeck, "The Decline of Islamist Parties in Algeria," Sada: Middle East Analysis, Carnegie Endowment for International Peace, February 13, 2014, http://carnegieendowment.org/sada/?fa=54510.

69 Ibn Warraq, "Reason, Not Revelation," in *Virgins? What Virgins? And Other Essays* (Amherst, MA: Prometheus Books, 2010), 384. "Reason, Not Revelation" was a paper originally given at The Hague in 2006.

the United States was attacked is its imperialist past. But of course, the United States has never been an imperialist power in the Middle East. Indeed it played an anti-imperialist role, as for example, when President Eisenhower intervened during the Suez Crisis of 1956. Eisenhower dissuaded the European powers from launching a military operation against Egypt, when the latter seized and nationalized the Suez Canal in which Great Britain had heavy economic investments.

Fifteen of the nineteen Islamic terrorists involved in the September 11, 2001, attacks on America were Saudi nationals. But Saudi Arabia has never been colonized by any Western power. The coastal strip known as the Hijaz, which contains the holy sites of Islam, Mecca and Medina, was, in fact, a part of the Ottoman Empire. These holy sites were attacked and captured by the fundamentalist and violent Islamic group, the Wahhābis in 1803 and 1804, who destroyed various shrines such as the one built over the tomb of Fatima, the Prophet's daughter.

The Wahhābis also massacred thousands of Shias. Ibn 'Abd al-Wahhāb, the founder of Wahhābism, was not motivated by anticolonial animus—he was not even aware of any Western presence in the Islamic world. He was mainly concerned with saving Muslim souls and purifying Islam of its impious accretions.

The British left Egypt in 1956, but Islamic acts of terrorism began in 1970s and were directed at various Egyptian governments and leaders. The French departed Algeria in 1962, but since that date Islamic terrorists have targeted fellow Algerians, leaving, as noted above, more than 150,000 Algerians dead. More than fifty years later, the terrorism continues, with attacks perpetrated by such groups as al-Qaeda in the Islamic Maghreb, al-Murabitun, and Jund al-Khalifa on Algerian government interests in 2013, 2014, and 2015.

Putative neocolonialism through multinationals controlling the production of oil is also inadequate as an explanation. The Arab oil-producing countries were totally incapable of extracting the oil on their own, and had to rely on the scientific and technological know-how and experience of American, British, or Dutch companies. But since the nationalization of many of these hitherto foreign companies, Arab countries have regulated the prices themselves and have become enormously rich.[70]

As Tawfik Hamid, a former Egyptian Islamist, wrote, "No, colo-

---

70 See Adam Bird and Malcolm Brown, "The History and Social Consequences of a Nationalized Oil Industry," June 2, 2005, available at https://web.stanford.edu/class/e297a/VENEZUELA%20OIL%20&%20LAND%20REFORM.htm.

nialism did not spark *jihād*. On the contrary, when Islamic nations were colonized [by the West], Sharia- and Islamist-based crimes tended to drop significantly. In fact, Islamic nations in many respects were more civilized under occupation than they are now; we virtually never heard of suicide bombings or attacks against, or kidnapping of, tourists during that period."[71]

On the other hand, Islamic imperialism destroyed thousands of churches, synagogues, and temples in lands they captured in a most brutal fashion; whole civilizations such as the Pre-Islamic cultures of Iran (Zoroastrians)[72] and the Assyrians were exterminated.

Nor by the Crusades

Ian Richard Netton, Sharjah Professor of Islamic Studies at the University of Exeter, summarizes the Crusades rather narrowly as "[a] series of conflicts which took place in mediaeval times, often in Middle Eastern soil, between Europe and the Muslim East."[73] The European Christians were essentially trying to defend their persecuted fellow Oriental Christians and the Christian holy places such as Jerusalem from Muslims, who had been waging ceaseless *jihād* for several hundred years. The first crusade resulted in the capture of Jerusalem in 1099. But the Crusades were also wars against all European heretics, even unorthodox Christians such as the Cathars.

On the Crusades as an explanation for Islamic terrorism I have already described in *Sir Walter Scott's Crusades and Other Fantasies* (2013) how a new generation of Western scholars of the Middle Ages has been trying to put to right misconceptions that have arisen about the Crusades.[74] As the late Jonathan Riley-Smith, a historian of the Crusades and Dixie Professor of Ecclesiastical History and Fellow of Emmanuel College at Cambridge, has argued, "[M]odern Western public opinion, Arab nationalism, and Pan-Islamism all share perceptions of crusading that have more to do with nineteenth-century European imperialism

---

71 Tawfik Hamid, *Inside Jihād: How Radical Islam Works; Why It Should Terrify Us; How to Defeat It* (Mountain Lake, MD: Mountain Lake Press, 2015), 66.
72 Persia, before the arrival of Islam, was host to another much more ancient religion, Zoroastrianism, founded by Zoroaster, perhaps sometime between the seventh and sixth century BCE.
73 Ian Richard Netton, *A Popular Dictionary of Islam* (Richmond, UK: Curzon Press, 1992), s.v. "Crusades."
74 Ibn Warraq, *Sir Walter Scott's Crusades and Other Fantasies* (Nashville, TN: New English Review Press, 2013), 139–41.

than with actuality."[75]

Muslims in particular have developed "mythistories" concerning the putative injuries received at the hands of the Crusaders. The first point that needs emphasizing is that the Crusades "were proclaimed not only against Muslims, but also against pagan Wends, Balts and Lithuanians, shamanist Mongols, Orthodox Russians and Greeks, Cathar and Hussite heretics, and those Catholics whom the Church deemed to be its enemies."[76]

Second, the Crusades were not "thoughtless explosions of barbarism."[77] Their underlying rationale was relatively sophisticated and elaborated theologically by Christian nations threatened by Muslim invaders who had managed to reach into the heart of Europe, central France in the eighth century and Vienna in the sixteenth and seventeenth centuries. The Crusades were a response to the desecration of the Christian shrines in the Holy Land, the destruction of churches, and the general persecution of Christians in the Near East.

A crusade, to be considered legitimate, had to fulfill strict criteria. "First, it must not be entered into lightly or for aggrandizement, but only for a legally sound reason, which has to be a reactive one." It was, in other words, waged to repel violence or injury and to impose justice on wrongdoers. Never a war of conversion, a crusade was a rightful attempt to recover Christian territory injuriously seized in the past. "Second, it must be formally declared by an authority recognized as having the power to make such a declaration. Third, it must be waged justly."[78]

Crusaders were not colonialists, and the Crusades were not undertaken for economic reasons, as many Western liberals and liberal economists have assumed; most crusaders would have laughed at the prospect of material gain. In fact, crusading became a financial burden as the expenses associated with warfare increased. Crusaders were far more concerned with saving Christendom from Islam, as well as their own souls. The role of penance (an act of mortification or devotion to express repentance for sin, performed voluntarily or imposed by a church official) has often been overlooked when examining crusading thought and practice; many crusaders believed that by enlisting in a crusade they were able to repay the debt their sinfulness had incurred.

---

75 Jonathan Riley-Smith, *The Crusades, Christianity, and Islam* (New York: Columbia University Press, 2008), 79.

76 Ibid., 9.

77 Ibid., 79.

78 Ibid., 11-12.

Nineteenth- and even early twentieth-century Europeans unashamedly used crusader rhetoric and a tendentious reading of crusader history to justify imperial dreams of conquest. For example, after World War I the "French Mandate in Syria generated a wave of French historical literature, one theme of which was that the achievements of the crusaders provided the first chapter in a history that had culminated in modern imperialism."[79] As we shall see, the newly emerging Arab nationalists took nineteenth-century rhetoric seriously.

A second strand in erroneous modern interpretations of crusader history was furnished by European romanticism, manifested, for example, in the novels of Sir Walter Scott. As Riley-Smith summarized:

> The novels [of Scott] painted a picture of crusaders who were brave and glamorous, but also vainglorious, avaricious, childish and boorish. Few of them were genuinely moved by religion or the crusade ideal; most had taken the cross out of pride, greed, or ambition. The worst of them were the brothers of the military orders, who may have been courageous and disciplined but were also arrogant, privileged, corrupt, voluptuous and unprincipled. An additional theme, the cultural superiority of the Muslims, which was only hinted at in the other novels, pervaded the *The Talisman* [1825].[80]

Many believe that modern Muslims have inherited from their medieval ancestors memories of crusader violence and destruction. But as Riley-Smith writes, nothing could be further from the truth.[81] In the Islamic world, by the fourteenth century the Crusades had almost passed out of mind. Muslims "looked back on the Crusades with indifference and complacency. In their eyes they had been the outright winners. They had driven the crusaders from the lands they had settled in the Levant and had been triumphant in the Balkans, occupying far more territory in Europe than the Western settlers had ever held in Syria and Palestine."[82]

The Muslim world began to take a renewed interest in the Crusades in the 1890s, but only through the prism of Western imperialist rhetoric and European romantic fantasies concocted by Sir Walter Scott,

---

79 Ibid., 60.
80 Ibid., 65.
81 Ibid., 68.
82 Ibid., 71.

who encouraged the myth of the culturally inferior crusaders faced with civilized, liberal, modern-looking Muslims. And from Scott the Muslims derived the equally false idea of a continuing Western assault. Many Arab nationalists believed "their struggle for independence to be a predominantly Arab riposte to a crusade that was being waged against them. Since the 1970s, however, they have been challenged by a renewed and militant Pan-Islamism, the adherents of which have globalized the Nationalist interpretation of crusade history."[83]

As a consequence, modern Islamists such as Osama bin Laden often invoke the Crusades: "For the first time the Crusaders have managed to achieve their historic ambitions and dreams against our Islamic umma, gaining control over the Islamic holy places and the Holy Sanctuaries, and hegemony over the wealth and riches of our umma,"[84] and, "Ever since God made the Arabian Peninsula flat, created desert in it and surrounded it with seas, it has never suffered such a calamity as these Crusader hordes, that have spread in it like locusts, consuming its wealth and destroying its fertility."[85] The battle, according to bin Laden, is between Muslims—people of Islam—and "the Global Crusaders."[86]

The idea that Christians—hence all Westerners—continue to wage a Crusade against Islam and Islamic civilization has taken hold of the imagination of all Muslims, not just the Islamic terrorists. This has less to do with historical reality than with Islamist reinterpretation of Crusader history. It rather ingeniously helps Muslims, moderate and extremist alike, to place the exploitation they strongly feel they have suffered historically in a real context, and at the same time to satisfy both their feelings of humiliation (Muslims being defeated and ruled by infidels is the ultimate degradation) and superiority (the Muslims did, after all, drive the Crusaders out of Islamic lands).

---

83 Ibid., 73.
84 Bin Laden, *Messages to the World,* 16; quoted in Riley-Smith, *The Crusades,* 75.
85 Ibid., 59; quoted in Riley-Smith, *The Crusades,* 75.
86 Ibid.

CHAPTER 2
Explanations of Islamic Terrorism

Human Agency, Free Will, and Responsibility

THERE ARE MANY contemporary political commentators and intellectuals who do not accept what seems an obvious starting point in trying to explain the behavior of Islamic terrorists, namely their beliefs, their ideology as laid down in tract after tract, statement after statement, interview after interview, and book after book—books that are the careful work of Muslim scholars of Islam, lavishly sprinkled with quotes from the Koran, which is the very word of Allah, the *hadīth* (the sayings and deeds of Muhammad and his Companions), the *sira* (life of the Prophet), all used to justify their heinous acts, even against civilians, including women, children, and the old.

Western liberals who no longer espouse religious beliefs interpret such behavior as "delusional, perceiving the devout terrorists as suffering from a serious mental illness, or victimized by a rare form of false consciousness originating in their justified grievances and low socioeconomic status," to quote Paul Hollander, historian of many works on communism and its fall and professor emeritus of sociology at the University of Massachusetts, Amherst.[1] These analysts insist that Islamic religious beliefs do not provide any justification or encouragement for barbaric acts of terrorism. We must not, they contend, pay attention to the terrorists' explanations of their motives.

Suddenly these Western pundits seemed to have acquired a deeper

---

[1] Paul Hollander, "Marx and the Koran: The Role of Beliefs and Ideologies in Motivating, Justifying, and Legitimating Political Violence," *Weekly Standard*, February 23, 2015, http://www.weeklystandard.com/marx-and-the-koran/article/850146.

knowledge of Islam than such Islamists as Abdullah Yusuf Azzam, the founder of al-Qaeda, who spent years studying Islam, first at the University of Damascus, where he graduated with a honors degree in Shari'a in 1966, then at the prestigious al-Azhar University in Cairo, where he earned a master's degree, followed by a doctorate in the principles of Islamic jurisprudence.

Thus it was a sign of willful and dangerous ignorance when, speaking at the 2015 World Economic Forum, U.S. Secretary John Kerry refused to take the assertions of the radical Islamists seriously, claiming instead that "it would be a mistake to link Islam to criminal conduct rooted in alienation, poverty, thrill-seeking and other factors."[2]

On January 7, 2015, two Islamists belonging to al-Qaeda's branch in Yemen had stormed into the offices of the French satirical weekly newspaper *Charlie Hebdo* in Paris, killing twelve people and injuring eleven others. (*Charlie Hebdo* had abundantly availed itself of its rights of freedom of expression to satirize Muhammad and Islam.) There were also related attacks in the Île-de-France region, where another five were killed and eleven wounded.

After the massacre "White House press secretary Josh Earnest suggested that 'these are individuals who carried out an act of terrorism, and...later tried to justify that act of terrorism by invoking the religion of Islam and their own deviant view of it.'"[3] This sounds as if the *Charlie Hebdo* terrorists set out to commit a random act of violence, and then, when they realized they needed some justification afterwards, plucked "Islam" out of the air by sheer chance.[4]

Others have refused to hold the terrorists responsible for their acts, laying blame, yet again, firmly on the shoulders of the West. In the January 24, 2015, *New York Times*, Tom Koch, adjunct professor of medical geography at the University of British Columbia, emphasized the socially determined nature of their conduct:

---

[2] Ken Dilanian, "Kerry: Violent Extremism Is Not Islamic," Associated Press, January 23, 2015, https://www.yahoo.com/news/kerry-violent-extremism-not-islamic-170022857--politics.html?ref=gs.

[3] Fred Lucas, "Josh Earnest Says the White House Doesn't Call Terror Attacks 'Radical Islam' Because It's Not 'Accurate,'" *Blaze*, January 13, 2015, http://www.theblaze.com/stories/2015/01/13/josh-earnest-says-the-white-house-doesnt-call-terror-attacks-radical-islam-because-its-not-accurate/; quoted in Hollander, "Marx and the Koran."

[4] Cf. Thomas L. Friedman, "Say It Like It Is," Opinion, *New York Times*, January 20, 2015, http://www.nytimes.com/2015/01/21/opinion/thomas-friedman-say-it-like-it-is.html?_r=0

The tragedy [of the recent murders in Paris] lies...in the decades of military encroachment and colonial expansion that helped to radicalize a religious sect. It lies too, in our culture's failure to integrate new members in an ethos that is inclusive and assures a political space for legitimate complaint....Our tragedy is this collective fatal flaw, which insists on demonizing those we disagree with and turning them into mortal enemies. The question is whether we will react...breeding more terror in our responses, or, instructed in its causes, search for resolution.[5]

Thus Western colonialism, and the failure to integrate immigrants, radicalizes those Muslims who eventually become terrorists. We refuse, it is argued, to listen to their grievances. We demonize them simply because they are different from us.

First, however, colonialism has nothing to do with radicalization; of the nineteen men responsible for the 9/11 terrorists attacks fifteen were of Saudi origin. Saudi Arabia was never colonized by the West; it was de jure colony of the Ottoman Empire.

Second, it is Muslims themselves, and Muslims alone, who refuse to integrate into Western society and its democracies. Muslims may not integrate themselves into a non-Muslim society. It would constitute an act of apostasy. According to many Islamic scholars, it is a Muslim's duty to emigrate from the land of the Infidels to the land of the Believers—the land of Islam. A survey of six hundred U.S. Muslims conducted in June 2015 by pollster Kellyanne Conway revealed that 51 percent agreed that Muslims in America should have the choice of being governed according to Shari'a. Even more alarming, 25 percent of those polled agreed that violence against Americans in the United States is justified as a part of the global *jihād*.[6] In a Senate Judiciary Committee testimony in July 2016, Philip Haney, a founding member of the Department of Homeland Security, reported that mainstream institutional Islam within the U.S. encourages this intolerant Islamic mindset, institutions such

---

5 Tom Koch, "What's Worse Than Sad," Opinion, *New York Times*, January 24, 2015, Sunday Review, http://www.nytimes.com/2015/01/25/opinion/sunday/whats-worse-than-sad.html.

6 As reported by Andrew Bostom, "Shocking Polls Show What U.S. Muslims Think of U.S. Laws," *PJ Media*, July 1, 2016, https://pjmedia.com/blog/shocking-polls-show-what-u-s-muslims-think-of-u-s-laws/.

as the highly influential Assembly of Muslim Jurists of America.[7] Lack of integration in Europe applies almost exclusively to Muslims, and not, for example, to those from Vietnam and Cambodia.

Third, there is the insidious influence of leftist Western intellectuals who have taken over the institutions of higher education, drumming into the malleable minds of young students since the 1960s that all the ills of the world, particularly the Third World, are the sole responsibility of the West. The West is evil, and is the source of all evils in the world, as Susan Sontag once said.[8] If this were true, why would the children of immigrants want to board what James Baldwin once called a "sinking ship"?[9] Such cultural relativism has so sapped our civilizational self-confidence that we in the West are no longer capable of defending Western values. (And as time passes fewer and fewer of the young appear even to know what Western values are, let alone how to defend them.)

Fundamental Differences

Yes, there are differences between the West and the Muslim world, differences of a fundamental kind. Muslims cannot accept a democracy, since that would be to accept that sovereignty lies with the people, and for Muslims sovereignty lies with God alone. Furthermore, Muslims cannot accept to live under man-made laws, only under the Shari'a, which is God-given. The treatment of women and non-Muslims, for example, is clearly defined in the Shari'a. Women have fewer rights (inheritance) than men; they may not marry a non-Muslim; men have the right to beat them.

Another difference involves personal responsibility. Scholars such as Koch in the piece cited above, argue that the perpetrators of terroristic acts have "little choice in the matter." As Hollander explains, Muslim terrorists are

> merely respond[ing] to stimuli they were exposed to, and their prior victimization determined their course of action. Observers like Koch have little discernible interest in the actual motivation of the terrorists, in the roots of their determination to kill, and their apparently clear conscience about

---

7 Ibid.

8 Referred to by George Zilbergeld, *A Reader for the Politically Incorrect* (Santa Barbara, CA: Praeger, 2003), 157.

9 Quoted in *African American Political Thought*, ed. and intro. Marcus D. Pohlmann, vol.6, *Integration vs. Separatism: 1945 to the Present* (London: Routledge, 2003), 6:119.

what most people consider heinous crimes. It is also overlooked that blasphemy is a religious notion, and if the cartoonists were murdered for blasphemies, then the perpetrators were obviously motivated by very strongly felt religious sentiments, as they themselves made quite clear.[10]

So while the "victim" cannot help but act in the way he acts, it seems, the "victimizer" is absolutely free. Hollander again:

> Such explanations of terror entail a selective determinism, a disposition I first noticed in the social criticism of the late 1960s. In this scheme, only the powerful, the top-dogs and victimizers, are capable of making choices and thus can be held responsible for their actions; the underdogs, the victims, the victimized are not in a position to make morally relevant choices as their behavior is determined by brutal social forces. Needless to say, designations of victim and victimizer can be quite subjective and variable, depending on the worldview of those who propose the classification.[11]

Disputes about the motivations of Islamic terrorists are strongly reminiscent of the arguments that took place throughout the existence of the Soviet Union. "Real Marxism has nothing to do with the experiment in the Soviet Union, real Marxism has not been applied" went the claim. This desperate attempt to save Marxism as a viable system was fatally tainted with the Soviet experiment. It was implausible to suggest that Marxism had *nothing* to do with the Soviet systems. And it is similarly argued that Islamic terrorism has nothing to do with Islam. The real Islam, it is claimed, is a religion of peace that respects the rights of women, and so on. But it is actually implausible to suggest that Islam has nothing to do with Islamic terrorism. And I doubt that John Kerry would win the argument against Abdullah Yusuf Azzam that Islam has nothing to do with the terrorists' actions.

Learned Disbelief

There are many scholars who refuse to take *any* aspect of Islamic terrorist belief seriously. Marc Sageman, the government counterterrorism consultant cited in the introduction, asserts that terrorism is not

---

10 Hollander, "Marx and the Koran."
11 Ibid.

"the result of the beliefs and perceptions held by the terrorists."[12] It is no wonder that the U.S. government has failed to learn the "threat doctrine" of the enemy.

Robert Reilly, author of *The Closing of the Muslim Mind* (2011),[13] rebutted Sageman very effectively in a review of *Leaderless Jihād*. Sageman succumbs to the root cause fallacy and tries to "find the 'root cause' of global Islamist terrorism by conducting a ground up exploration of his sample of terrorists." "Ground up" means that Sageman "concentrates on the foot soldiers, and tries to draw his conclusions from his observations of them," and readers learn that "'terrorists rarely execute their operations as a direct result of their doctrines.'...Why, then, do they do it?" Reilly wonders, and "[s]peaking of terrorists in North America and Western Europe," Sageman tells readers they 'were not intellectuals or ideologues, much less religious scholars. It is not about how they think, but how they feel.' Anyone feel like some terrorism?"[14]

"Terrorism is not simply terror," Reilly continues, "some people doing terrible things on the spur of the moment. It is murder advanced to the level of a moral principle, which is then institutionalized in an organization—a cell, a party, or a state—as its animating principle. The very first thing one must understand is the ideology incarnated in the terrorist organization; it is the source of its moral legitimacy. Without it, terrorism cannot exist."[15]

Sageman seems to be aware of some of the Salafi thinkers behind the ideology of current terrorism (the Salafis were ultraconservative Sunni Muslims who wished to restore the pristine Islam practised by their devout ancestors). He mentions Sayyid Qutb twice, Hasan al-Banna once, but never Abul A'la Mawdūdī (more on these figures forthcoming), and because he refuses to acknowledge ideology as a motivating force, the absence of deep analysis of their work is not surprising. To establish the origins and causes of a war, one must refer first to the respective ideologies and principles of the warring factions before interviewing the soldiers in the trenches.

---

12 Sageman, *Leaderless Jihād*, 22.

13 Robert Reilly, *The Closing of the Muslim Mind: How Intellectual Suicide Created the Modern Islamist Crisis* (Wilmington, DE: Intercollegiate Studies Institute, 2011).

14 Robert R. Reilly, "Thinking like a Terrorist," review of *Leaderless Jihād: Terror Networks in the Twenty-First Century*, by Marc Sageman, and *The Mind of Jihād*, by Laurent Murawiec, *Claremont Review of Books* 9, no. 2 (Spring 2009): 31–33, http://www.claremont.org/crb/article/thinking-like-a-terrorist/.

15 Ibid.

When Reilly questioned him on this point at a lecture Sagemen was giving, Sageman told Reilly that "Sayyid Qutb was not relevant because the people in his case studies did not read him." Sageman naively leaves his analysis incomplete, and misses the point entirely. How many rank and file Nazis were aware of the intellectual, putatively biological, and putatively historical underpinnings of Nazi ideology? It is highly unlikely that the ordinary Nazi foot soldier had ever heard of Alfred Rosenberg (1893–1946), a primary creator of the Nazi ideology of racial purity, persecution of the Jews, *lebensraum*, etc., and even less likely that he had read Rosenberg's work. The common Nazi was nonetheless trained to obey and duty-bound to follow the orders of a regime motivated and animated by the ideology created by such thinkers as Rosenberg, Alfred Baeumler (1887–1968), a philosopher and interpreter of Friedrich Nietzsche; Ernst Krieck (1882–1947), a German pedagogue; Herman Schmalenbach (1885–1950), who refined the concepts of *Gemeinschaft* and *Bund*; and Carl Schmitt (1888–1985), a jurist, philosopher, political theorist, and professor of law.

The regime was able to mold the average Nazi soldier to its own image, and train him docilely to carry out its policies. In fact, the Nazi Party successfully persuaded many ordinary citizens of the truth of its Nazi ideology, and was able to turn a hitherto highly civilized nation into barbarians capable of accepting its horrific agenda, and helping to perpetrate unimaginable atrocities. We see a similar pattern in the Islamic world, where the Islamist ideology threatens to attract an ever-growing circle of admirers and activists ready to sacrifice their life for Islam. It is indeed a war of ideas—hence our duty to understand these ideas, ideas of such Islamic ideologues as Hasan al-Banna, Sayyid Qutb, and Mawdūdī, and their roots in Islam, in Islamic theology and Islamic history.

Importance of Ideology as a Motivating Force

British social and political theorist, philosopher, and historian of ideas Isaiah Berlin (1909–1997) often warned of the danger of neglecting ideas and their influence on world events. The arguments in his classic essay, "Two Concepts of Liberty," based on a lecture given in 1958, remain valid and are worth pondering at length:

> [T]here has, perhaps, been no time in modern history when so large a number of human beings, in both the East and the West, have had their notions, and indeed their lives, so deep-

ly altered, and in some cases violently upset, by fanatically held social and political doctrines. Dangerous, because when ideas are neglected by those who ought to attend to them—that is to say, those who have been trained to think critically about ideas—they sometimes acquire an unchecked momentum and an irresistible power over multitudes of men that may grow too violent to be affected by rational criticism.... [I]f professors can truly wield this fatal power, may it not be that only other professors, or, at least, other thinkers (and not governments or Congressional committees), can alone disarm them?[16]

We are similarly engaged in a war of ideas and therefore must come up with better ideas to combat fanatical Islamic terrorists.

Writing in 1966, Marxist Islamologist Maxime Rodinson argued with regard to the Islamic world that "the course of history is, in the last instance, determined by economic and social factors and that ideology plays only a secondary role."[17] Berlin's further observations in "Two Concepts of Liberty" are an implicit reply to Rodinson: "It is only a very vulgar historical materialism that denies the power of ideas, and says that ideals are mere material interests in disguise. It may be that, without the pressure of social forces, political ideas are stillborn: what is certain is that these forces, unless they clothe themselves in ideas, remain blind and undirected."[18]

What were the causes of the horrors perpetrated by Lenin, Stalin, Hitler, Mao, and Pol Pot? They were, in Berlin's view, "not caused by the ordinary negative human sentiments, as Spinoza called them—fear, greed, tribal hatreds, jealousy, love of power—though of course these have played their wicked part," but "by one particular idea. It is paradoxical that Karl Marx, who played down the importance of ideas in comparison with impersonal social and economic forces, should, by his writings, have caused the transformation of the twentieth century, both

---

16 Isaiah Berlin, *Liberty: Incorporating Four Essays on Liberty*, ed. Henry Hardy, 2nd ed. (Oxford: Oxford University Press, 2002), 167.
17 Cited in Rudolph Peters, *Islam and Colonialism* (The Hague: Mouton Publishers, 1979), 6, referring to Maxime Rodinson, Islam and Capitalism, trans. Brian Pearce (London: Allen Lane, 1974), 296ff. Originally published as *Islam et le capitalisme* (Paris: Editions du Seuil, 1966).
18 Berlin, *Liberty*, 167–68.

in the direction of what he wanted and, by reaction, against it."[19]

Berlin continues, "There are men who will kill and maim with a tranquil conscience under the influence of the words and writings of some of those who are certain that they know perfection can be reached."[20] This is an apt and chilling description of the Islamic radicals who are so certain of the rightness of their putatively God-given goals that they are ready to die—and take as many infidels as possible with them.

Soviet Union and Communism

Many explanations of the Cold War, the actions of the Soviet Union, and the collapse of that regime are also framed in such a way that the driving ideology of Marxism-Leninism is sometimes neglected or even denied. Nonetheless, a number of distinguished historians have emphasized the ideological nature of the Soviet phenomenon.

In the introduction to his monumental work, *The Soviet Tragedy: A History of Socialism in Russia, 1917–1991*, for example, Martin Malia, a professor of history specializing in Russia at the University of California, Berkeley, writes:

> This eternal return of utopian hope, breaking through the façade of social-science rigor, brings us back to the premise that the key to understanding the Soviet phenomenon is ideology. It is only by taking the Soviets at their ideological word, treating their socialist utopia with literal-minded seriousness, that we can grasp the tragedy to which it led. The concrete agenda of this book, therefore, is to reassert the primacy of ideology and politics over social and economic forces in understanding the Soviet phenomenon. It is to rehabilitate history "from above" at the expense of history "from below" as the motive force of Soviet development. Finally, it is to resurrect the totalitarian perspective, but in a historical and dynamic, not a static, mode; for it was the all-encompassing pretensions of the Soviet utopia that furnished what can only be called the "genetic code" of the tragedy.[21]

---

19 Isaiah Berlin, "A Message to the 21st Century," acceptance address upon receiving honorary Doctor of Laws, University of Toronto, November 25, 1994, reprinted in *New York Review of Books*, October 23, 2014, http://www.nybooks.com/articles/2014/10/23/message-21st-century/.
20 Ibid.
21 Martin Malia, *The Soviet Tragedy: A History of Socialism in Russia, 1917–1991* (New

Malia returns to the importance of ideas and their consequences: "To produce the distinctive Soviet institutions of Plan, kolkhoz, and Gulag, the illusions of maximalist socialism and the lawlessness of the Leninist Party were indispensable." He continues;

> So once again we return to the primacy of ideology and politics in the Soviet phenomenon. As Solzhenitsyn put the matter with respect to the unique dimensions of the Soviet terror: "The imagination and inner strength of Shakespeare's villains stopped short at ten or so cadavers, because they had no *ideology*....It is thanks to *ideology* that it fell to the lot of the twentieth century to experience villainy on a scale of millions." And Solzhenitsyn's proposition is also valid, and was intended, of course, for Hitler's Final Solution and his camps. But in the Communist case the primacy of ideology holds not just for camps but for the entire Soviet endeavor, from its socioeconomic base to its cultural superstructure.[22] (emphasis in original)

As Malia emphasizes, "[A]ll the basic institutions of the Soviet order... were the creations of ideology; they were nothing less than the Party program set in steel, concrete, and the omnipresent apparat."[23]

Nearly twenty years after the collapse of the Soviet Union and the disintegration of the Communist world, many American intellectuals are in denial, and continue to "applaud and apologize for one of the bloodiest ideologies of human history, and instead of being treated as pariahs, they hold distinguished positions in American higher and cultural life."[24] Eric Foner, DeWitt Clinton Professor of History at Columbia University, was an apologist of communism, and someone who refused to recognize the crimes of Stalin, until Khruschev pointed them out. He is also "an unforgiving historian of America."[25] Unsurprisingly Foner wrote soon after September 11, 2001: "I'm not sure which is more

---

York: The Free Press, 1994), 16.

22 Ibid., 512. Quoting Alexsandr Solzhenitsyn, *The Gulag Archipelago, 1918–1956*, 3 vols. (New York: Harper & Row, 1973–1978), 1:181.

23 Malia, *Soviet Tragedy*, 512.

24 John Earl Haynes and Harvey Klehr, In *Denial: Historians, Communism, and Espionage* (New York: Encounter Books, 2003), 1.

25 John Patrick Diggins, "Fate and Freedom in History: The Two Worlds of Eric Foner," *National Interest*, no. 69 (Fall 2002): 85, cited in Haynes and Klehr, *In Denial*, 40.

frightening: the horror that engulfed New York City or the apocalyptic rhetoric emanating daily from the White House."[26]

A number of apologists of communism, the so-called "revisionist historians," have blamed the United States for the 9/11 attacks, or played the old moral equivalence card. For example, Alan Singer, professor of teaching, literacy, and leadership and program director of graduate programs in social studies education at Hofstra University, has argued that the United States is guilty of far worse crimes than those perpetrated by Islamic terrorists.[27] As John Earl Haynes and Harvey Klehr observe in their *In Denial: Historians, Communism, and Espionage*, "[T]he deeply ingrained anti-Americanism of their intellectual world could not help but make these revisionists view the attack on this country as the secular equivalent of divine retribution."[28]

The Ideology of Nazism

A number of scholars have argued that the ideology of Nazis was the prime motivation for the Holocaust. Yahuda Bauer, professor of Holocaust studies at the Avraham Harman Institute of Contemporary Jewry at the Hebrew University of Jerusalem, is the author of more than forty books on the Holocaust and antisemitism, and a recipient of several awards and honors. In his readily accessible work, *Rethinking the Holocaust* (2001), Bauer argues that from the outset "ideology was the central determinant of the Holocaust."[29] The Nazis considered the Jews a universal devilish element. Pursuing them "was to have been a global, quasi-religious affair, the translation into practice of a murderous ideology"; for the Nazis, "persecution of the Jews was pure, abstract antisemitic ideology in the context of biological racism, and it became a central factor in Hitler's war against the world."[30]

Bauer grants the importance of the bureaucracy, and the impact of economic, social, and political crises, "but without a guiding ideological motivation and justification, mass murder generally, and the intent to annihilate the Jewish people in particular, would have been unthinkable. Ideology is central."[31] And Bauer endorses political scientist and

---

26 Haynes and Klehr, *In Denial*, 49.

27 Cited in ibid.

28 Ibid.

29 Yahuda Bauer, *Rethinking the Holocaust* (New Haven, CT: Yale Nota Bene, 2002), 7, 42, 44.

30 Ibid., 27-28.

31 Ibid., 44.

author Daniel Goldhagen's central point in *Hitler's Willing Executioners: Ordinary Germans and the Holocaust* (1996),[32] which places anti-Semitic ideology at the center of the Holocaust: "I agree with [Goldhagen] rather than those...who emphasize the social stratification in a crisis situation, the political and economic background, and the bureaucratic machinery."[33]

Islam or the Ideology of the Islamic Terrorists

Ideology is also the defining feature of the twentieth century, or perhaps it is more accurate to say that it was the clash of ideologies that characterizes the twentieth century—a period of "ideological frenzy."[34] Communism, socialism, nationalism, fascism, Nazism, etc., mobilized millions to action. Leslie Stevenson, a professor of logic and metaphysics, writes, "A system of beliefs about human nature that is held by some group of people as giving rise to their way of life is standardly called an 'ideology.' Christianity and Marxism are certainly ideologies in this sense."[35] And in this sense, we can just as naturally add Islam to this list.

Thus the ideology of the Islamic terrorists is no exception to this discussion. And despite the theological nature of their beliefs, useful comparisons can be made between Islamic terrorism and the other ideologies of the twentieth century. I argued over ten years ago that one could label the beliefs of the Islamic terrorists—or even Islam, *tout court*—fascist, in a precise way.[36] In that examination I took the fourteen features the late Italian novelist, philosopher, and semiotician Umberto Eco considered to be typical of "Eternal Fascism" (or "Ur-Fascism"), and showed how Islam also satisfied all of those features.[37]

---

32 Daniel Jonah Goldhagen, *Hitler's Willing Executioners: Ordinary Germans and the Holocaust* (New York: Vintage Books, 1996).

33 Bauer, *Rethinking the Holocaust*, 95.

34 I think this phrase originates with American journalist Max Lerner (1902–1992), *Ideas Are Weapons: The History and Uses of Ideas* (New York: Viking Press, 1939), 9—but I am not certain.

35 Leslie Stevenson and David L. Haberman, *Ten Theories of Human Nature*, 3rd ed. (Oxford: Oxford University Press, 1998), 9. Not to be confused with a later edition titled *Twelve Theories of Human Nature*: see Chapter 4, note 1.

36 Ibn Warraq, "Islam, Middle East, and Fascism," in *Virgins? What Virgins?* 255–88. Versions of this article have been floating around the Internet since the late 1990s. One version was published in the *American Atheist* around 2002, and later reposted by *New English Review*, http://www.newenglishreview.org/Ibn_Warraq/Islam,_Middle_East_and_Fascism/.

37 Umberto Eco, "Ur-Fascism," *New York Review of Books*, June 22, 1995, http://www.nybooks.com/articles/1995/06/22/ur-fascism/.

Islam has also been described as totalitarian. Here is an encapsulation of what I wrote in 2008 on this subject: Charles Watson and Georges-Henri Bousquet refer to Islam as a totalitarian system *tout court*, while Bertrand Russell, Jules Monnerot, and Czeslaw Milosz compare Islam to various aspects of communism, while Carl Jung, Karl Barth, Adolf Hitler, Saïd Amir Arjomand, Maxime Rodinson, and Manfred Halpern, among others, point out Islam's similarities to fascism or Nazism (with the latter two terms often used synonymously).[38]

To elaborate, in 1937 Charles Watson, a Christian missionary in Egypt, described Islam as totalitarian by showing how, "by a million roots, penetrating every phase of life, all of them with religious significance, it is able to maintain its hold upon the life of Moslem peoples."[39] The late Georges-Henri Bousquet (d. 1978), a professor of law at the University of Algiers and later the University of Bordeaux and one of the foremost authorities on Islamic law, distinguishes two aspects of Islam he considers totalitarian: Islamic law and the Islamic notion of *jihād*, which has as its ultimate aim the conquest of the world in order to submit it to one single authority.[40]

To quote another great scholar of Islamic law and longtime professor of Arabic at the University of Leiden, Christiaan Snouck Hurgronje—Islamic law has certainly aimed at "controlling the religious, social and political life of mankind in all its aspects, the life of its followers without qualification, and the life of those who follow tolerated religions to a degree that prevents their activities from hampering Islam in any way."[41] The all-embracing nature of Islamic law is apparent in that it does not distinguish between ritual, law (in the European sense of the word), ethics, and good manners. In principle, this legislation controls the entire life of the believer and the Islamic community; it intrudes into every nook and cranny, from (in a random sample) the pilgrim tax to agricultural contracts to the board and lodging of slaves to issuing wedding invitations to the ritual fashion in which to accomplish one's natural needs to the proper treatment of animals.

---

38 Ibn Warraq, "Apologists of Totalitarianism: From Communism to Islam" in *Politcal Violence: Belief, Behavior and Legitimation*, ed. Paul Hollander (New York: Palgrave Macmillan, 2008), 177–91.

39 Charles Watson, *Muslim World* 28, no. 1 (January 1938): 6.

40 Georges-Henri Bousquet, *L'Ethique sexuelle de l'Islam* (1966; Paris: Desclée de Brouwer, 1990), 10.

41 C. Snouck Hurgronje, *Selected Works*, ed. Georges-Henri Bousqet and Joseph Schacht (Leiden: E.J. Brill, 1957), 264.

Islamic law is a doctrine of duties—duties, as Hurgronje explains, "susceptible to control by a human authority instituted by God. However, these duties are, without exception, duties to God, and are founded on the inscrutable will of God Himself. All duties that men can envisage being carried out are dealt with; we find treated therein all the duties of man in any circumstance whatsoever, and in their connections with anyone whatsoever."[42] In *The Practice and Theory of Bolshevism* (1920), British philosopher, historian, and social critic Bertrand Russell wrote:

> Bolshevism combines the characteristics of the French Revolution with those of the rise of Islam....
>
> ...Marx has taught that Communism is fatally predestined to come about; this produces a state of mind not unlike that of the early successors of Mahommet....
>
> ...Among religions, Bolshevism is to be reckoned with Mohammedanism rather than with Christianity and Buddhism. Christianity and Buddhism are primarily personal religions, with mystical doctrines and a love of contemplation. Mohammedanism and Bolshevism are practical, social, unspiritual, concerned to win the empire of this world.[43]

In *Sociologie du Communisme* (1949) Jules Monnerot, a French essayist, sociologist, and journalist, called communism the twentieth-century "Islam."[44] Islam has also been compared more precisely to Nazism and sometimes fascism, terms that are usually used synonymously. For example, in the late 1930s the Swiss psychiatrist Carl Jung was asked in an interview if he had any views on what was likely to be the next step in religious development. He replied, referring to the rise of Nazism in Germany, "We do not know whether Hitler is going to found a new Islam. He is already on the way; he is like Muhammad. The emotion in Germany is Islamic; warlike and Islamic. They are all drunk with a wild

---

42 Ibid., 261.
43 Bertrand Russell, *The Practice and Theory of Bolshevism* (London: George Allen and Unwin, 1920), 5, 29, 114.
44 Jules Monnerot, *Sociologie du Communisme* (Paris: Gallimard, 1949). Translated by Jane Degras and Richard Rees as *Sociology and Psychology of Communism* (Boston: Beacon Press, 1953), 18–22.

god. That can be the historic future."⁴⁵

Karl Barth,⁴⁶ the Swiss Reformed theologian, also writing in the 1930s, reflected on the threat of Hitler and his similarities to Muhammad:

> Participation in this life, according to it the only worthy and blessed life, is what National Socialism, as a political experiment, promises to those who will of their own accord share in this experiment. And now it becomes understandable why, at the point where it meets with resistance, it can only crush and kill—with the might and right which belongs to Divinity! Islam of old as we know proceeded in this way. It is impossible to understand National Socialism unless we see it in fact as a *new Islam*, its myth as a new Allah, and Hitler as this new Allah's Prophet. A prayer for the ruling National Socialism and for its further expansion and increase simply cannot be uttered—unless one wishes to strike his confession in the face and make nonsense of his prayer. But there is one prayer with regard to the ruling National Socialism which may be uttered and ought to be uttered. It may and has to be prayed, in all earnestness, by Christians in Germany and throughout the whole world. It is the prayer which was uttered right into the nineteenth century, according to the old Basel Liturgy: "Cast down the bulwarks of the false prophet Muhammad!"...
>
> ...And there we have it—we stand today, all Europe, and the whole Christian Church in Europe, once again *in danger of the Turks*. And this time they have already taken Vienna and Prague as well. "Thy will be done!" "If I perish then I perish!" They really knew that at the time of the old Turkish menace. They knew it better, knew it with more resignation to the will of God and less querulousness than we today do.⁴⁷ (emphases in original)

---

45 Carl Jung, *The Collected Works*, vol. 18, *The Symbolic Life* (Princeton, NJ: Princeton University Press, 1939), 281.
46 I owe the references to Carl Jung and Karl Barth to Andrew Bostom.
47 Karl Barth, *The Church and the Political Problem of Our Day* (New York: Scribner's, 1939), 43, 64–65.

While serving a twenty-year prison sentence imposed by the Nuremberg tribunal, Albert Speer, Hitler's minister of armaments and war production, wrote a memoir of his World War II experiences. Speer's narrative includes this discussion, which captures Hitler's racist views of Arabs and his effusive praise for Islam:

> Hitler had been much impressed by a scrap of history he had learned from a delegation of distinguished Arabs. When the Mohammedans attempted to penetrate beyond France into Central Europe during the eighth century, his visitors had told him, they had been driven back at the Battle of Tours. Had the Arabs won this battle, the world would be Mohammedan today. *For theirs was a religion that believed in spreading the faith by the sword and subjugating all nations to that faith. Such a creed was perfectly suited to the Germanic temperament.* Hitler said that the conquering Arabs, because of their racial inferiority, would in the long run have been unable to contend with the harsher climate and conditions of the country. They could not have kept down the more vigorous natives, so that *ultimately not Arabs but Islamized Germans could have stood at the head of this Mohammedan Empire.* Hitler usually concluded this historical speculation by remarking, "You see, it's been our misfortune to have the wrong religion. Why didn't we have the religion of the Japanese, who regard sacrifice for the Fatherland as the highest good? The Mohammedan religion too would have been much more compatible to us than Christianity."[48] (emphases added)

The comparison of Islamism with fascism was also put forward by Maxime Rodinson, the eminent French scholar of Islam and by common consent one of the three greatest scholars of Islam of the twentieth century, who pioneered the application of sociological method to the Middle East. As a French Jew born in 1915, Rodinson also learned about fascism from direct experience; his parents perished in Auschwitz. Responding in a long front-page article in *Le Monde* to French philosopher Michel Foucault's uncritical endorsement of the Iranian Revolution, Rodinson targeted those who "come fresh to the problem in an idealistic frame of mind." While admitting that trends in Islamic movements such

---

48 Albert Speer, *Inside the Third Reich* (New York: Macmillan, 1970), 96.

as the Muslim Brotherhood were "hard to ascertain, Rodison stated that "the dominant trend is a certain type of archaic fascism. By this I mean a wish to establish an authoritarian and totalitarian state whose political police would brutally enforce the moral and social order. It would at the same time impose conformity to religious tradition as interpreted in the most conservative light."[49]

In 1984 Said Amir Arjomand, an Iranian American sociologist at SUNY–Stony Brook, also pointed to "some striking sociological similarities between the contemporary Islamic movements and the European fascism and the American radical right....It is above all the strength of the monistic impulse and the pronounced political moralism of the Islamic traditionalist and fundamentalist movements which makes them akin to fascism and the radical right alike."[50]

One scholar I have not discussed before, Malise Ruthven, an Anglo-Irish academic and journalist who focuses on religion, fundamentalism, and especially Islamic affairs, is worth quoting at length.[51] Ruthven points out the debt owed to Marxism and fascism by such thinkers as Sayyid Qutb and Abdullah Yusuf Azzam (discussed later in these pages), though he is careful to use the term "Islamism" and not "Islam" *tout court*. "Qutb's ideas...were 'invisible' adaptations of the revolutionary or political vanguardism to be found in both Bolshevism and fascism," writes Ruthven, however,

> the fascist parallels go deeper than Marxist ones. In his explicit hostility to reason...it is not Marx, grandchild of the Enlightenment, but Nietzsche, an anti-rationalist like the anti-Mu'tazilite al-Ash'ari, whom 'Azzam echoes. The attachment to the lost lands of Palestine, Bukhara and Spain (unlike a rational and humane concern for Palestinian rights) is, like Mussolini's evocations of ancient Rome, nostalgic in its

---

49 Maxime Rodinson, "Islam Resurgent?" *Le Monde*, December 6–8, 1978; quoted in Janet Afary and Kevin B. Anderson, *Foucault and the Iranian Revolution: Gender and the Seductions of Islamism* (Chicago: University of Chicago Press, 2005), 233.

50 Saïd Amir Arjomand, "Iran's Islamic Revolution in Comparative Perspective," *World Politics* 38, no. 3 (April 1986): 383–414.

51 Malise Ruthven, *A Fury for God: The Islamist Attack on America* (London: Granta Books, 2002), esp. 206ff. However, in recent writings, particularly in the New York Review of Books, Ruthven seems to deny such comparisons. Is this a genuine change of opinion, or simply the dead hand of political correctness? Where an earlier generation was afraid of being labelled "Orientalist," the present one is terrified of being accused of "Islamophobia."

irredentism, its "obliteration of history from politics."⁵² The invocation of religion is consistent with the way fascism and Nazism used mythical thought to mobilize unconscious or psychic forces in the pursuit of power—a task made easier in a population sanctified by a millennium of Islamic religious programming. Georges Sorel, sometimes seen as the intellectual father of fascism, declared that "use must be made of a body of images which, by intuition alone, and before any considered analyses are made, is capable of evoking as an undivided whole the mass of sentiments which corresponds to the different manifestations of the war undertaken by Socialism." Mussolini, to whom Sorel in his later years lent his support, saw fascism as "a religious conception in which man is seen in his immanent relationship with a superior law and with an objective Will that transcends the particular individual and raises him to conscious membership of a spiritual society."⁵³ In the same line of thinking Alfred Rosenberg, the Nazi ideologue, stressed the other-worldly, spiritual aspect of Hitler's racial theories: "The life of a race does not represent a logically-developed philosophy nor even the unfolding of a pattern according to natural law, but rather the development of a mystical synthesis, an activity of soul, which cannot be explained rationally."⁵⁴

It would be much too reductive to redefine Islamism as 'Islamo-fascism,' but the resemblances are compelling.⁵⁵

Finally, no less a figure than Sayyid Abu 'l-'Alā' Mawdūdī, one of the major thinkers behind modern Islamist ideology, said that in an Islamic state as envisioned by him, "no one can regard any field of his affairs as personal and private. Considered from this aspect, the Islamic state bears a kind of resemblance to the Fascist and Communist states."⁵⁶

---

52 Mark Neocleous, *Fascism* (Buckingham, UK: Open University Press, 1997), 11.
53 Benito Mussolini, "The Doctrine of Fascism" (1932), in Adrian Lyttleton, *Italian Fascisms: From Pareto to Gentile* (London, 1973), 59–67; cited in Neocleous, *Fascism*, 14. Quoted by Ruthven, *Fury for God*, 206.
54 Neocleous, *Fascism*, p.15.
55 Ruthven, *Fury for God*, 206–7.
56 Syed Abul' Ala Maudoodi, *Islamic Law and Constitution*, trans. and ed. Khursid Ahmad (Chicago: Kazi Publications, Inc., 1993), 262.

CHAPTER 3
Marx, Freud, and Darwin among the Jihādists

Reductionist Views of Islamic Terrorism

FAR TOO MANY writers on the motivation of the Islamic terrorists are reductionist. These writers try to reduce the stated purpose of terroristic behavior to something more basic, more biological, but this leaves them at a loss to account for particular human goals and aspirations. How can the pursuit of ethical, political, religious, aesthetic, or even sporting ideals be reduced to basic biological needs such as survival and reproduction that we share with animals?

Those who argue that the reasons behind the actions of Islamic terrorists lie elsewhere than in the religious texts—which I consider as their primary source—have recourse to any number of theories about human nature. For Marx, "the real nature of man is the totality of social relations" (cf. Maxime Rodinson), and all humans are a product of the particular economic state of human society in which they are born. Freud wished to reduce all human striving to hunger and sexual desire. Darwinian evolution links us inexorably to the animal world, to nature, to genetics, and seems to pose a decisive challenge to our own sense of worth, and to our human values. B.F. Skinner and his radical behaviorism denies free will, and considers all human actions the result of conditioning. Zoologist, ethologist, and ornithologist Konrad Lorenz argues that aggression in humans is innate.[1] And so on.

---

1 Cf. Leslie Stevenson, "Conclusion: A Synthesis of the Theories," in Leslie Stevenson, David L. Haberman, and Peter Matthews Wright, *Twelve Theories of Human Nature*,

Humans are indeed animals, members of the species *homo sapiens*, but we are also persons, rational agents displaying intentionality. We can hold humans, since we have a degree of choice, responsible for our acts, that is, we can ascribe moral responsibility to humans in a way that cannot be ascribed to animals.

Since we humans are rational agents, we can give reasons for our actions, and these necessarily involve our beliefs and values, which can be expressed in terms of concepts engendered in a particular culture. We are undoubtedly products of evolution by natural selection, and have some innate biological drives, but we grow up in a common culture that is as much responsible for creating and molding human nature as our biology. Furthermore, as rational agents we also have individual choices, for which we can be held responsible.

Reductionists, meanwhile, favor a determinist philosophy of human action that does not allow any room for individual choice, freely made. Again, evolution by natural selection has profound implications for human behavior, but so does religion, which imparts values and provides guidance that result in a particular way of living. Religion motivates humans, whose behavior can no longer be explained simply in biological terms. Religion has historically served as a source of values and a guide to action, whether or not we agree with those values and actions, values that are not available otherwise. In other words, values are not a "natural kind," and do not otherwise exist in nature. Values are a human construct.

Importance of Religion in the Middle East

This brings us to religion, and the role of religion in the Middle East and its apparent revival in the last forty years. We return to our previously cited Egyptian sociologist Saad Eddin Ibrahim, who asks "why, in Egypt and the Arab world, people with roughly the same social profile have flocked into militant Islamic movements more readily than they have to into leftist or Marxist groups?" Ibrahim cites four factors that have "tilted the balance in favor of Islamic groups." The first is the ability of the ruling elites to dismiss leftist and Marxist opposition as atheists bent on destroying Islam. The second factor is the comparative failure of socialist or quasi-socialist policies in the Arab world. "The third factor," which is of particular interest to this discussion (I shall return to the fourth later),

---

6th ed. (Oxford and New York: Oxford University Press, 2013), 288–89. Stevenson's observations were immensely helpful in writing this section.

has to do with the deep-rootedness of Islam in the entire Middle East. In Egypt particularly people are said to be quite religious. There is a positive sociocultural sanction to being religious. Even the most avowed liberal or leftist secularist regimes in the area find it necessary and expedient to invoke Islam when they try to institute any major new policy. The point is that for any militant Islamic movement, half its task of recruiting members is already done by socialization and cultural sanctions in childhood. The other half of their task is merely to politicize consciousness and to discipline their recruits organizationally.[2]

In 2005, on the first anniversary of the Madrid bombings that killed 191 people and injured 1800 more, the Club de Madrid, the "world's largest forum" of former heads of state and government and independent nonprofit promoting democracy and international change, organized a conference to discuss the causes of terrorism. Several members who took part in the discussions "wanted to make clear that although economic, political and other causes intertwine with religious ones, the religious element should not simply be reduced to an expression of these other factors. It supplies a significant component of its own." One member urged scholars to "'abandon their reductionism' and respect the fact that 'religion is a body in itself' and a significant factor in violent incidents." Another member argued that "in the case of Al Qaeda and other Islamic groups involved in terrorism, the 'preeminence of the religious factor' is 'undeniable'"[3]

Many liberals and leftists are unwilling to accord religion any role in the events unfolding in the Middle East. Such an attitude merely underlines their lack of imagination, and is condescending at best. As Bernard Lewis wrote in *Islam and the West*,

> Modern Western man, being unable for the most part to assign a dominant and central place in religion in his own affairs, found himself unable to conceive that any other people in any other place could have done so and was therefore

---

2 Ibrahim, "Anatomy of Egypt's Militant Islamic Groups," 26–27.
3 Peter R. Neumann, ed., *Addressing the Causes of Terrorism*, Club de Madrid Series on Democracy and Terrorism, vol. 1 (Madrid: Club de Madrid, 2005), 28, http://www.clubmadrid.org/img/secciones/Club_de_Madrid_Volume_I_The_Causes_of_Terrorism.pdf.

> impelled to devise other explanations of what seemed to him only superficially religious phenomena. We find, for example, a great deal of attention given by eighteenth-century European scholarship to the investigation of such meaningless questions as "Was Muhammad sincere?"...We find lengthy explanations by nineteenth- and early-twentieth-century historians of the "real underlying significance" of the great religious conflicts in Islam among different sects and schools in the past....To the modern Western mind, it is not conceivable that men would fight and die in such numbers over mere differences of religion; there have to be other "genuine" reasons underneath the religious veil....[T]o admit that an entire civilization can have religion as its primary loyalty is too much. Even to suggest such a thing is regarded as offensive by liberal opinion, always ready to take protective umbrage on behalf of those whom it regards as its wards. This is reflected in the recurring inability of political, journalistic, and academic commentators alike to recognize the importance of religion in the current affairs of the Muslim world and in their consequent recourse to the language of left-wing and right-wing, progressive and conservative, and the rest of the Western vocabulary of ideology and politics.[4]

There may also be socioeconomic factors in Muslim political movements that must be taken into account, Lewis goes onto remind us, but in the end, we cannot ignore the centrality of Islam for all Muslims in the Muslim world:

> Whatever the cause—political, social, economic—the form of expression to which Muslims have hitherto had recourse to voice both their criticisms and their aspirations is Islamic. The slogans, the programs, and to a very large extent the leadership are Islamic. Through the centuries, Muslim opposition has expressed itself in terms of theology as naturally and spontaneously as its Western equivalent in terms of ideology....
>
> If, then, we are to understand anything at all about what is

---

4 Bernard Lewis, *Islam and the West* (Oxford and New York: Oxford University Press, 1994), 134–35.

happening in the Muslim world at the present time and what has happened in the past, there are two essential points that need to be grasped. One is the universality of religion as a factor in the lives of the Muslim peoples, and the other is its centrality.[5]

Islam was, then, "not only universal but also central in the sense that it constituted the ultimate basis and focus of identity and loyalty."[6] Religion was a badge of membership uniting those belonging to the group and distinguishing them from those on the outside. Islam provided a far more powerful sense of belonging than language or country. For example, Muslims of Pakistan, though biologically, historically, linguistically, and even in some sense culturally related to Hindus in India, identify with and refer to, with considerable pride, the history and actions of peoples thousands of miles away in present-day Saudi Arabia. Though speaking an Indo-European language, Pakistani Muslims share the same sacred past as Arabs, speaking a Semitic language, Arabic. Transcending national boundaries, Muslims of different countries celebrate one anothers' triumphs and lament one anothers' failures; they exhibit a sense of shared destiny. As one Ottoman minister remarked in 1917, "the Fatherland of a Muslim is wherever the Holy Law of Islam prevails." Islam is the binding and decisive factor.

The importance of religion is further borne out by the number of religious books published in Arab countries. As reported by the Rand Institute, quoting United Nations data, "Religious books constitute 17 percent of all books in Arab countries, in comparison with a world average of approximately 5 percent (United Nations Development Programme, 2003, pp.77–78). The increased sales of religious books may benefit from sponsorship and subsidy of mosques, Islamic foundations, or religious governments, such as that of Saudi Arabia."[7] Subsidies make these religious books cheap, and thus available to poorer people.

---

5 Ibid., 135.
6 Quoted in ibid., 136.
7 Lowell H. Schwartz, Todd C. Helmus, Dalia Dassa Kaye, and Nadia Oweidat, *Barriers to the Broad Dissemination of Creative Works in the Arab World* (Santa Monica, CA: Rand Corporation, 2009), 8–9, http://www.rand.org/content/dam/rand/pubs/monographs/2009/RAND_MG879.pdf.

CHAPTER 4
Islamic Doctrines as Motivating Factors

Like Marxism and Christianity, Islam has

- a background metaphysical understanding of the universe and humanity's place in it
- a basic theory of human nature in the narrower sense of some distinctive general claims about human beings, human society, and the human condition
- a diagnosis of some typical defect in human beings, of what tends to go wrong in human life and society
- a prescription or ideal for how human life should best be lived, typically offering guidance to individuals and human societies[1]

ISLAM, however, is much more all-encompassing and more totalitarian than Marxism or Christianity.

Both religious faith and political ideology, Islam oversees every aspect of a Muslim's life—from what a non-Muslim might consider minor details (such as how to use a toothpick) to larger issues such as prayer, pilgrimage, and marriage. Islam also provides a powerful sense of personal and group identity. Central for all Muslims is the Koran, which is the uncreated word of God and is His inspired Word and Revelation

---

1 Stevenson, Haberman, and Wright, Twelve Theories, 1–2.

as delivered to His Prophet, Muhammad, by the angel Gabriel, or the "Faithful Spirit" (*Rūhu 'l-Amīn*), and sometimes angels in general.

The Koran was revealed over a period of years. The very minimum required to be a Muslim is contained in the profession of faith (*Shahāda*): "There is but one God, Muhammad is the Apostle of God" (*lā ilāha illa'llāh muhammadun rasūlu'llāh*).

Sura 4, Q4. *an-Nisā'*, the Women, 136, addresses all Muslims: "O ye who believe, believe in God and His Apostle and the Book which He hath sent down to His Apostle and the Scripture which He hath sent down formerly. Whosoever denieth God and His Angels and His books and His Apostles and the Last Day hath strayed far from the Truth."

The essential element of true belief for all Muslims is an uncompromising monotheism expressed by the Arabic word, *tawhīd*, "the unity or oneness of God." *Tawhīd* is a central concept, and despite its apparent simplicity leads to complex corollaries, some of which have been further elaborated, as we shall have occasion to see later, by radical thinkers such as Ibn 'Abd al-Wahhāb. First, true belief necessitates *ikhls*, which is the sincere devotion, loyalty, and total allegiance owed to God. Its opposite is *shirk*, sometimes translated as "polytheism" or "idolatry," and is the unforgivable sin of ascribing partners to God. It is the worship of any other being than God; as the Koran tells us, Q4. *an-Nisā'*, the Women, 48: "Verily God forgives not that partners should be set up with Him; but He forgives anything else, to whom He pleases; to set up partners with God is to devise a sin most heinous indeed."

The Koran

The Koran is considered a revelation from God, *ipsissima verba*, the very words of God. The Koran is understood not in an allegorical, analogical, metaphorical, or Pickwickian sense but in a literal sense to be the word of God, and to be obeyed literally. It is a practical manual.

Muslims use the Koran as guide to conduct, both private and public. The Koran gives details of the moral and legal duties of believers; it is the basis of their religious dogma, beliefs, ritual, and one of the sources of their law. The Koran clearly has an exhortatory element; it is not a quiet, meditative tract enjoining private experience of God, but often a robust call to arms—to fight and kill, if necessary, in the name of God, until Islam dominates the world. It is constantly and extensively quoted by the *jihādists*, for all their tenets and ideology are located within its pages.

While there are two or three short verses that enjoin tolerance of non-Muslims (e.g., Q2. *al-Baqara*, the Cow, 256; Q109. *al-Kāfirūn*, the Disbelievers, 1–6), these have been abrogated or canceled by the so-called Sword Verses that enjoin fierce battles against the unbelievers (Q9. *at-Tawba*, the Repentance, 5; see also Q4:76; Q8:12, 15–16, 39–42). Other verses that incite violence against non-Muslims and other religions are abundant.[2]

Jews and Christians are also regarded with much contempt, and Muslims are told not to take them as friends (e.g., Q5. *al-Mā'ida*, the Table, 51). The final verses of the opening chapter of the Koran, the *Fātiha*, which has a central role in Islamic prayer and is repeated at least seventeen times a day, are: "The path of those upon whom Thou hast bestowed favours. Not those upon whom wrath is brought down, nor those who go astray" (Q1. *al-Fātiha*, the Opening: 6–7). Evidently in verse 6, it is those who are on the right path who have been blessed, while verse 7 is interpreted to refer to Jews and Christians, respectively.

Here is the commentary on verse 7 of *al-Qurtubī* (1214–1273), famous for his commentary on the Koran:

> The majority say that those with anger on them are the Jews and the misguided are the Christians. That was explained by the Prophet [pbuh, "peace be upon him"], in the hadith of 'Adī ibn Hātin and the story of how he became Muslim, transmitted by Abū Dāwūd in his *Musnad* and at-Tirmidh in his collection. That explanation is also attested to by the Almighty who says about the Jews, "They brought down anger from Allah upon themselves" (Q2. *al-Baqara*, the Cow, 61; Q3. *āl 'Imrān*, the Family of Imran, 112) and He says, "Allah is angry with them" (Q48. *al-Fath*, the Victory, 6). He says about Christians that they, "were misguided previously and have misguided many others, and are far from the right way" (Q5. *al-Mā'ida*, the Table, 77).[3]

Thus in a sense, Jews and Christians are singled out for admonition several times a day, every day, by all Muslims. Antisemitic sentiments are plentiful in the Koran.[4]

---

2 Q2:216; Q2:221; Q3:28; Q3:85; Q4:101; Q4:144; Q8:39; Q9:14, 17, 23, 28, 29, 36, 39, 41, 73, 111, 123; Q25:52, and so on.

3 *Tafsir al-Qurtubi: Classical Commentary of the Holy Qur'an*, trans. Aisha Bewley (London: Dar al-Taqwa, 2003), 127.

4 E.g., Q2. *al-Baqara*, the Cow, 61; Q4. *an-Nisā'*, the Women, 44–46, 160–61; Q9.

Other elements of belief found in the Koran include a belief in angels (Q2:177), in all the prophets (Q2:177) and their scriptures, and in the Last Judgment (Q2:17). The term *al-ākhira*, meaning "the Hereafter," is mentioned more than a hundred times.

The Hereafter is to be preferred to this life on earth: Q40. *Ghāfir*, the Forgiver, 39: "O my people, surely this present life is but a passing enjoyment, and the Hereafter, is the abode of stability"; Q16. *an-Nahl*, the Bee, 30–31, "the abode of the Hereafter is better"; Q29. *al-'Ankabūt*, the Spider, 64, "And the life of this world is but a sport and a play. And the home of the Hereafter, that surely is the Life, did they but know."

Shari'a Supremacism

While I have largely concentrated on *jihād* in the military sense, as the immediate goals of Islamic terrorists, their ultimate goal is to subjugate the globe to Islam, so that the world is governed by the Shari'a and not, for instance, by the various secular constitutions in the Western world. Muslims cannot accept any other religion or any other constitution.

According to the Koran, Muslims alone possess the absolute truth, and they constitute the best of all nations, as in Q3. *'āl 'Imrān*, the Family of Imran, 109: "And whoever seeks a religion other than Islam, it will not be accepted from him, and in the Hereafter he will be one of the losers." Because Islam is the religion of truth, those not following Islam must be subjugated and made to pay a tax: Q9. *at-Tawba*, the Repentance, 29: "Fight those who believe not in Allah, nor in the Last Day, nor forbid that which Allah and His Messenger have forbidden, nor follow the Religion of Truth, out of those who have been given the Book, until they pay the tax in acknowledgement of superiority, and they are in a state of subjection." Any accommodation with any other creed on a basis of equality is unthinkable, for Islam is destined to prevail: Q9. *at-Tawba*, the Repentance, 33: "He it is Who sent His Messenger with guidance and the Religion of Truth, and that He may cause it to prevail over all religions, though the polytheists are averse." Precisely the same message is given at Q48. *al-Fath*, The Victory, 28, and Q61. *al-Saff*, The Ranks, 9.

Muhammad the Prophet also made it clear that Islam cannot coexist with any other religion, and He dutifully informed his successors that Arabia must be cleansed of Jews and Christians: "There shall be no

---

at-Tawba, the Repentance, 29–31, 34; Q5. *al-Mā'ida*, the Table, 51, 57, 59, 60, 63–64, 66, 70–71, 82; Q33. al-'Ahzāb, Confederates, 26.

two faiths in Arabia" (Imam Malik, *Muwatta*', *hadīth* 1588).[5] The theory and practice of dhimmitude, whereby non-Muslims such as Jews and Christians are termed *dhimmis* and endure various social and legal disabilities, is based on the premise that Muslims are superior to non-Muslims. Most of the canonical *hadīth* collections contain this *hadīth*: "Muhammad the Prophet said: A Muslim should not be killed in retaliation for the murder of a disbeliever."[6] As the Ayatollah Khomeini once put it, "Eleven things are unclean: urine, excrement, sperm, blood, a dog, a pig, bones, a non-Muslim man and woman, wine, beer, perspiration of the camel that eats filth."[7]

To strive to bring the entire world under Shari'a must have seemed an idle dream to Muslims even fifty years ago. Today, there are more than eighty Shari'a courts operating in Great Britain, and a poll in conducted in 2012 found that 40 percent of Muslims in America believe that they should not be judged by U.S. law and the Constitution, but by Shari'a.[8] Various Islamic organizations such as the influential and litigious Council on American-Islamic Relations are working night and day to bring about the compliance of American law. Slowly, Muslims are eroding the Western rights of free speech, as journalists and writers in the West are beginning to practice self-censorship in order not to offend Muslims.

The *Sunna* and Muhammad
The *Sunna*

The *Sunna* plays an important part in Islam, and is a further guide for all Muslims to follow. *Sunna* can be seen as model pattern of behavior. It is also "custom" or "customary behavior." Finally, it is the way

---

[5] Imam Malik, *Muwatta*', trans. Muhammad Rahimuddin, *hadīth* 1588 (New Delhi: Kitab Bhavan, 2003), 371.

[6] Imam Abu Abdullah Muhammad B Yazid Ibn-e-Majah Al-Qazwini, *Sunan Ibn Majah*, trans. Muhammad Tufail Ansari, vol.4, *Book of Blood Money*, *hadīth* 2658, 2659 (New Delhi: Kitab Bhavan, 2008), 4:72. Found also in *Sahīh al- Bukhārī, Book of Blood Money* (ad-diyat), *hadīth* 6915 (Riyadh, Saudi Arabia: Darussalam, 1997), 9:40; and *Sunan Abu Dāwūd, Kitab al-Diyat*, trans. Ahmad Hasan, *hadīth* 4515 (New Delhi: Kitab Bhavan, 1997), 3:1270–71.

[7] Quoted by Bat Ye'or, *The Dhimmi: Jews and Christians under Islam* (London: Associated University Presses, 1996), 396. S.R. (Ayatollah) Khomeini, *Principes, Politiques, Philosophiques, Sociaux et Religieux*, trans. and ed. J.-M. Xaviere (Paris: Libres-Hallier, 1979), 59.

[8] Bob Unruh, "Guess Who U.S. Muslims are Voting For," WorldNetDaily.com, October 30, 2012, http://www.wnd.com/2012/10/guess-who-u-s-muslims-are-voting-for/

Muhammad acted, which is then emulated by Muslims. The *hadīth*, on the other hand, is a tradition or written report, and can be the source material for the *sunna*.

The *Encyclopaedia of Islam* (2nd edition), which is regarded as the most authoritative work of reference on Islam, defines the *sunna* thus:

> Some time after the preaching of Islam had begun, the term *sunna* came to stand for the generally approved standard or practice introduced by the Prophet as well as the pious Muslims of olden days, and at the instigation of al-Shāfiʿī, the *sunna* of the Prophet was awarded the position of the second root (*aṣl*) of Islamic law, the *sharīʿa*, after the Qurʾān...[9]

The opposite of *sunna* is *bidaʿ*, usually translated as "innovation." The *Shorter Encyclopaedia of Islam*, another definitive source, gives the following definition:

> *bidaʿ* is the exact opposite of *sunna*, and means some view, thing, or mode of action the like of which has not formerly existed or been practised, an innovation or novelty. The word became important theologically in the revolt against the precise following of the *sunna* of the Prophet, came thus to indicate all the unrest of new ideas and usages which grew up naturally in the Muslim church, covering dogmatic innovations not in accordance with traditional sources (*uṣūl*) of the Faith, and ways of life different from those of the Prophet. The word, therefore, came to suggest individual dissent and independence, going to the point of heresy although not of actual unbelief (*kufr*). In this development two broad parties showed themselves. One conservative, in the past mostly of Hanbalī and now practically Wahhābī only, taught that the duty of the believer was "following" (*ittibāʿ*)—the sunna understood—and not "innovating" (*ibtidāʿ*). The other accepted the facts of change of environment and condition, and taught, in varying degrees and ways, that there were good and even necessary innovations.[10]

---

9 *Encyclopaedia of Islam*, vol. 9, "San-Sze," ed. C.E. Bosworth et al., 2nd ed. (Leiden: Brill, 1997), s.v. "sunna."

10 *Shorter Encyclopaedia of Islam*, ed. by H.A.R. Gibb and J.H. Kramers on behalf of the Royal Netherlands Academy (Leiden: E.J. Brill, 1953), s.v. "bidʿa."

Muhammad

From our twenty-first century perspective, Muhammad the Prophet was hardly a model of tolerance, kindness, or compassion. Islamic sources contain numerous accounts of his cruelty, hatred of Jews, and intolerance of other religions. Nonetheless, Islamic purists who insist on the *sunna* of Muhammad as a guide to their own behavior are, in terms of doctrine, fully justified.

Here is an instance of Muhammad's cruelty: When some people from the tribe of Ukl, who had reverted from Islam, and while trying to steal some camels had killed a shepherd of camels, were captured. Muhammad ordered their hands and legs to be cut off, their eyes to be branded with heated pieces of iron, and that their wounds not be cauterized till they die.[11] In another instance, Muhammad ordered the torture of a prisoner in order to discover the whereabouts of some hidden treasure, and is recorded as saying, "Torture him until you extract it from him."[12] Muhammad also revived the cruel practice of stoning adulterers to death.[13]

Here are some examples and expressions of Muhammad's hatred of Jews, all taken from the *Life of Muhammad* by Ibn Ishāq (c. 704-c. 767 CE), our earliest and most important source for the life of Muhammad:

- "Kill any Jews that falls into your power," said the Prophet. (p. 369)
- the killing of Ibn Sunayna, and its admiration leading someone to convert to Islam (p. 369)
- the killing of Sallam ibn Abu'l-Huqayq (pp. 482-83)
- the assassination of Ka'b ibn al-Ashraf, who wrote verses against Muhammad (pp. 364-69)
- the raid against the Jewish tribe of the Banu 'l-Nadir and their banishment (437-45)
- the extermination of the Banu Qurayza, between six hun-

---

11 Bukhārī, *The Book of the Punishment of Those Who Wage War against Allah and His Messenger*, trans. M. Muhsin Khan, vol. 8, book 82 of Sahīh, hadīth 794 (New Delhi: Kitab Bhavan, 1987), 519-20.

12 Ibn Hisham, *al-Sira al-Nabawiyya* (Cairo: Mustafa Al Babi Al Halabi & Sons, 1955), 2:328-38; Ibn Ishāq, *The Life of Muhammad*, trans. A. Guillaume (1955; Oxford: Oxford University Press, 1987), 515; *The Victory of Islam*, trans. Michael Fishbein, vol. 8 of *History of al-Tabarī*, 122-23.

13 Ibn Ishāq, *Life of Muhammad*, 266-67; Bukhārī, The Book of Representation (Wakāla, Book 40), trans. M. Muhsin Khan, vol. 3, *hadīth* 2314, 2315 (New Delhi: Kitab Bhavan, 1997), 290..

dred and eight hundred men (pp. 461–69)
- the killing of al-Yusayr (pp. 665–66)[14]

Muhammad also ordered the assassinations of his opponents. For example, the killing of poetess 'Asma' b. Marwan, who had written satirical poems that "vilified Islam and incited people against the Prophet,"[15] is mentioned in Ibn Isḥāq's biography,[16] and described in gruesome detail in *Kitāb al-Tabaqāt* by Ibn Saʿd (c. 784–845 CE),[17] a traditionist and biographer of Muhammad, and *Kitāb al-Maghāzī* by al-Wāqidī (747–823 CE),[18] an important early Muslim historian and judge who was patronized by Harun al-Rashid. Al-Wāqidī's major work, *The Book of Campaigns* (*Kitāb al-Maghāzī*) is an important source on early Islam and the life of Muhammad.

The assassins responsible for the massacre of the cartoonists of the French satirical weekly, *Charlie Hebdo*, on January 7, 2015 (discussed earlier), had Muhammad's example as a guide, and thus Islamic doctrine on their side.

Muhammad's intolerance of other religions is also well-attested in the Islamic sources:

> I was told that the last injunction the apostle [Muhammad] gave [before his death] was in his words "Let not two religions be left in the Arabian peninsula."[19]

A ḥadīth informs us that "The Apostle of Allah said, 'I will certainly expel the Jews and the Christians from Arabia.'"[20]

Hadīth

The hadīth often simply elaborate on and further emphasize

---

14 Ibn Isḥāq, *Life of Muhammad*.
15 *The Life of Muhammad: Al-Wāqidī's Kitāb al-Maghāzī*, ed. Rizwi Faizer, trans. Rizwi Faizer, Amal Ismail, and Abdul Kader Tayob, Routledge Studies in Classical Islam (Milton Park, Abingdon, Oxon, New York: Routledge, 2011), 85. [Henceforth, "*Al-Wāqidī, Life of Muhammad*]
16 Ibn Isḥāq, *Life of Muhammad*, 675.
17 Ibn Saʿd, *Kitāb al-Tabaqāt al Kabīr*, trans. S. M. Haq (New Delhi: Kitab Bhavan, 1972), 2:31.
18 Al-Wāqidī, *Life of Muhammad*, 85–86.
19 Ibn Isḥāq, *Life of Muhammad*, 689.
20 Abū Dāwūd, *Sunan*, trans. Ahmad Hasan, hadīth 3024 (New Delhi: Kitab Bhavan, 1997), 2:861.

certain aspects of Islamic doctrine adumbrated in the Koran, and hinted at in the Sira, the life of Muhammad. *The Dictionary of Islam* gives the following definition for "hadīth":

> All Muslims believe that in addition to the revelation contained in the Qur'ān, the Prophet received the *Wahy ghair Matlū* (literally, "an unread revelation"), whereby he was enabled to give authoritative declarations on religious questions, either moral, ceremonial, or doctrinal. Muhammad traditions are therefore supposed to be the uninspired record of inspired sayings....They are records of what Muhammad did, what Muhammad enjoined, and that which was done in the presence of Muhammad and which he did not forbid. They also include the authoritative sayings and doings of the Companions of the Prophet.[21]

As I shall be examining the *hadīth* on *jihād* further along in this discussion I shall not dwell on it here.

Shari'a

Joseph Schacht (1902–1969), who was, by common consent, a leading Western scholar of Islamic Law, characterized Shari'a in this manner:

> Islamic Law is the totality of God's commands that regulate the life of every Muslim in all its aspects; it comprises on an equal footing ordinances regarding worship and ritual, as well as political and (in the narrow sense) legal rules, details of toilet, formulas of greeting, table-manners, and sick-room conversation. Islamic law is the most typical manifestation of the Islamic way of life, the core and kernel of Islam itself.... [E]ven at the present time the Law...remains an important, if not the most important element in the struggle which is being fought in Islam between traditionalism and modernism under the impact of Western ideas.[22]

---

21 Hughes, *Dictionary of Islam*, s.v. "tradition."
22 Joseph Schacht, "Islamic Religious Law," in *The Legacy of Islam*, ed. Joseph Schacht and C.E. Bosworth, 2nd ed. (Oxford: Oxford University Press, 1979), 392. See also Joseph Schacht, *An Introduction to Islamic Law* (1964; Oxford: Clarendon Press, 1991), 1.

Islamic Law is based on four principles or "roots" (*usūl*, pl. of *asl*): the Koran, the *sunna* of the Prophet, which is incorporated in the recognized traditions, the consensus (*ijmā'*) of the scholars of the orthodox community, and the method of reasoning by analogy (*qiyās*).[23]

Position of Women and Non-Muslims

The position of women under Islamic Law regarding blood-money, evidence, and inheritance is inferior; she is counted as half a man. With regard to marriage and divorce a woman's position is less advantageous than that of a man, and a man has the right to beat his wife. A Muslim woman is not free to marry a non-Muslim. Slavery is recognized as an institution, and the slave is considered both a thing and as a person.

The position of non-Muslims living under Islamic Law is summarized by Schacht: "The basis of the Islamic attitude towards unbelievers (i.e., non-Muslims) is the law of war; they must be either converted or subjugated or killed (excepting women, children, and slaves); the third alternative, in general, occurs only if the first two are refused. As an exception, the Arab pagans are given the choice only between conversion to Islam or death."[24]

Non-Muslims must pay the poll tax (*jizya*) and the land tax (*kharāj*); "they must wear distinctive clothing and must mark their houses, which must not be be built higher that those of Muslims, by distinctive signs; they must not ride horses or bear arms, and they must yield the way to Muslims; they must not scandalize the Muslims by openly performing their worship or their distinctive customs, such as drinking wine; they must not build new churches, synagogues, and hermitages; they must pay the poll-tax under humiliating conditions."[25]

Apostasy is punishable by death. The male apostate from Islam is given three days to return to Islam. If he still refuses, he is killed. The woman who commits apostasy is imprisoned and beaten every three days until she returns to Islam.[26]

In Islamic Law, certain acts are forbidden or sanctioned by punishment in the Koran and have therby become crimes against religion:

> unlawful intercourse (*zinā*); its counterpart, false accusation of unlawful intercourse (*qadhf*); drinking wine (*shurb al-*

---

23 Schacht, *Introduction to Islamic Law*, 60.
24 Ibid., 130–31.
25 Ibid., 131.
26 Ibid., 187.

khamr); theft (*sariqa*); and highway robbery (*qat' al-tarīq*). The punishment laid down for them are called *hadd* (plural *hudud*), Allah's "restrictive ordinances" par excellence; they are: the death penalty, either by stoning (the more severe punishment for unlawful intercourse) or by crucifixion or with the sword (for highway robbery with homicide); cutting off hand and/or foot (for highway robbery without homicide and for theft); and in other cases, flogging with various numbers of lashes.[27]

Beliefs: God and *Tawhīd*

The Encyclopaedia of Islam (2nd ed.) defines *tawhīd* "in the true sense of the term," as "the act of believing and affirming that God is one and unique (*wāhid*), in a word, monotheism." For the Muslim, this means "believing and affirming what is stated by the first article of the Muslim profession of faith: 'there is no other god but God' (*lā ilāha illā llāh*)."[28]

However, as also explained in the *Encyclopaedia of Islam*, over time this term has acquired a much wider significance. Since Islam is uncompromisingly monotheistic, Muslims are sometimes referred to as *ahl al-tawhīd*, the people of *tawhīd*. Throughout history some Islamic groups have claimed that they alone respect the principle of monotheist orthodoxy and thus they alone can be called truly Islamic. Examples include the Mu'tazilīs, who called themselves *ahl al–tawhīd wa 'l-'adl*,[29] and Muwahhidūn, the Almohads, disciples of the *mahdī* (literally, "The One who is Rightly Guided," a figure of great eschatological significance in Islam; his just rule will herald the approach of the end of time) lbn Tūmart (d. 1130),

> a fundamentalist who wished to re-establish what he conceived to be the original purity of the faith by reference to the Koran and the Sunna and so rejected the *taqlīd* which in his day dominated theology in the West. He placed especial stress on the doctrine of *tawhīd*, which to him meant a com-

---

27 Ibid., 175.
28 *Encyclopaedia of Islam*, vol. 9, 2nd ed. s.v. "sunna." *Encyclopaedia of Islam*, vol. 10, "Tā'-U[..]," ed. P. J. Bearman et al., 2nd ed. (Leiden: Brill, 2000), s.v. "*tawhīd*." [The following phrase was later added to the Muslim profession of faith: "And Muhammad is His messenger."
29 Ibid.

plete abstraction or spiritualization of the concept of God, as opposed to *tajsīm*, the literal acceptance of the anthropomorphic phrases of the Koran of which he so often accused the Almoravids.[30]

For certain theologians, *tawhīd* has come to encompass all discussions of God, His existence, and His various attributes. Even broader meanings are understood under *tawhīd*, such as all the "principles of religion" (*usul al-dīn*), and finally, theology in general.[31]

The opposite of *tawhīd* is *shirk*, which can be defined as "the act of 'associating' with God, in other words, accepting the presence at His side of other divinities; it may be translated either literally, by *associationism* or, in more explicit fashion, by *polytheism*."[32] Certain practices (e.g., sorcery, ornithomancy) are denounced as *shirk* in the *hadīth*. Some purist reformers throughout Islamic history have branded as *shirk* such practices as the veneration of saints and worshipping at their tombs:[33]

> *Shirk* is the worst form of disbelief. The treatment to be applied in this world to the "associator" is that prescribed in IX, 5 (the "verse of the sword", *āyat al-sayf*): death, at least if they do not become Muslims (whereas the "People of the Book" are, for their part, allowed to maintain their religion, so long as they pay the *jizya*, IX, 29). In the next world, they will be assuredly consigned to damnation; the Koran states in fact, twice, that God can pardon all sins save one, that of associationism (Q4. *an-Nisā'*, the Women 48, 116).[34]

Commanding Right and Forbidding Wrong

There is one central, distinctive feature of Islamic ethics that is often left out of general surveys of Islam, but is of the utmost importance to understanding the thinking behind various influential modern

---

30 *Encyclopaedia of Islam*, vol. 3, "H–Iram," ed. B. Lewis et al., 2nd ed. (Leiden: Brill, 1971), s.v. "*Ibn Tūmart*."
31 *Encyclopaedia of Islam*, vol. 10, 2nd ed., s.v. "*tawhīd*."
32 *Encyclopaedia of Islam*, vol. 9, "San-Sze," ed. C.E. Bosworth et al., 2nd ed. (Leiden: Brill, 1997), s.v. "*shirk*."
33 Saints are holy men to whom ordinary Muslims the world over pay popular devotion. Muslims also pray to them at the saints' shrines and tombs, asking them to intercede and help them during hard times. This practice was frowned upon by Muslim theologians and reformers.
34 *Encyclopaedia of Islam*, vol. 9, 2nd ed., s.v. "*shirk*."

Islamic ideologues whose writings have not only influenced the Islamic terrorists but also have provided the foundation of their worldview, and have furnished their rationale for action. This principle is as important as the theory and practice of *jihād*, which, on the other hand, has been discussed at great length. In fact, we can regard *jihād* as a special case of the principle of Commanding Right and Forbidding Wrong.

Al-Ghazālī (d. 1111), one of Islam's greatest theologians, a major sufi, and a scholar of Islamic philosophy, defines this specifically Islamic duty thus: "Every Muslim has the duty of first setting himself to rights, and then, successively, his household, his neighbours, his quarter, his town, the surrounding countryside, the wilderness with its Beduin, Kurds, or whatever, and so on to the uttermost ends of earth."[35] As Michael Cook, the greatest modern scholar on the subject, put it, "Of these demanding activities, all bar the first fall under the rubric of 'commanding right and forbidding wrong' (*al-amr bi'l-ma'rūf wa'l-nahy 'an al-munkar*), roughly speaking the duty of one Muslim to intervene when another is acting wrongly."[36]

Like *jihād*, this duty is derived from the Koran, and has been commented and elaborated upon by Islamic thinkers for centuries, right up to today:

> Q3. *al-'Imrān* 104: Let there be one community (*umma*) of you, calling to good, and commanding right and forbidding wrong; these are the prosperers.

> Q3. *al-'Imrān* 110: You were the best community ever brought forth to men, commanding right and forbidding wrong.

Women also have this moral obligation:

> Q9. *at-Tawba* 71: And the believers, the men and the women, are friends one of the other; they command right, and forbid wrong.

---

35 Michael Cook, *Commanding Right and Forbidding Wrong in Islamic Thought* (Cambridge and New York: Cambridge University Press, 2001), 445.
36 For this section, I rely entirely on Michael Cook's two superb and monumental books on the subject: *Forbidding Wrong in Islam: An Introduction* (Cambridge and New York: Cambridge University Press, 2003), which is an epitome of *Commanding Right and Forbidding Wrong in Islamic Thought*. Cook, *Forbidding Wrong*, xi.

There are also numerous traditions of the Prophet that refer to the duty of Forbidding Wrong. However, the Sunni law schools do not cover Forbidding Wrong in their law books, though sectarian scholars among the Zaydīs, Imāmīs, and Ibādīs do. Al-Ghazālī was perhaps the first major Muslim thinker to devote substantial amount of space to this duty in *The Revival of the Religious Sciences* [*Ihyā' 'ulūm al-dīn*], which we shall be examining later in this section.

Forbidding Wrong

For Muslim scholars, Forbidding Wrong was a duty imposed by God—as revealed in the Koran and the traditions. In the Koranic passage cited above (Q3. *al-'Imrān* 104), God is addressing Muslims in general. As Cook explains, the language of here—"let there be"—is clearly prescriptive, "So the obvious reading of the verse is indeed that God is imposing a duty on the Muslims, and this is how it was universally understood."[37] In a *hadīth* Muhammad says: "Whoever sees a wrong, and is able to put it right with his hand, let him do so; if he cannot, then with his tongue, if he can't, then in his heart, and that is the bare minimum of faith."[38]

Since the purpose of the duty is to come to the aid of Islam, it is a duty of believers, not of unbelievers. This was considered by most scholars to be a collective obligation (*fard 'alā 'l-kifāya*). In performing this duty, one must address legally competent persons (thus children and lunatics are excluded).

According to most scholars, Muslims have a duty to command right and forbid wrong, and by "right" they mean *all* that God and His Prophet have commanded, and by "wrong" *all* they have forbidden. Al-Ghazālī has formulated the most comprehensive and influential classification of how wrong is to be forbidden.

By Tongue

He begins forbidding wrong with the tongue, that is the oral mode, of which there are three levels. First, one must inform someone who is acting wrongly out of ignorance, but one must be careful not to humiliate a fellow Muslim. At the second level, one must use exhortation when confronted with someone who knows he is doing wrong. Such

---

37 Cook, *Forbidding Wrong*, 11.
38 Imam an-Nawawi: *Forty Hadith*, trans. Abdassamad Clarke (London: Ta Ha Publishers, 1998), *hadīth* 34. Another edition available at http://ahadith.co.uk/downloads/Commentary_of_Forty_Hadiths_of_An-Nawawi.pdf.

exhortation can include quotations from traditions, stories about pious Muslims, and so on. At the third level, one may be forced to use harsh language with someone who knows he is doing wrong but remains obstinate.

Or Hand

In the case of forbidding wrong with the hand, Al-Ghazālī again has recourse to three levels. The first is physical action that does not involve physical attacks against people. One can, for example, destroy the offending objects (e.g., break a musical instrument,). One can also remove someone from a place where he ought not to be. The second level does involve actual physical violence against the offender. At this level, one may well have to kick and punch the offender, and even use a stick. Arms must only be used as a last resort, and must not lead to public disorder. Finally, at the third level, one may have to collect a band of armed men for assistance, which, of course, could lead to the offender forming his own band of armed men, ending in pitched battles.

As Cook spells out, "[A]ttacks on offending objects are a ubiquitous theme....There are, for example, chess-boards to overturn, supposedly sacred trees to cut down and decorative images to destroy or deface....But the targets that are mentioned again and again are liquor and musical instruments."[39] When the magnificent Buddhas of Bamyan in central Afghanistan were destroyed by the Taliban in March 2001, one Taliban envoy from Afghanistan gave the implausible reason that "the Islamic government made its decision in a rage after a foreign delegation offered money to preserve the ancient works while a million Afghans faced starvation," while more plausibly, "other reports...have said the religious leaders were debating the move for months, and ultimately decided that the statues were idolatrous and should be obliterated."[40] In other words, it was a clear case of Islamic iconoclasm, sanctioned by the very principle under discussion.

The paramount duty for all Muslims is to uphold God's unity, *tawhīd*, which is the fundamental concept in Islam, while its antithesis, *shirk*—associating others with God—is considered *tāġūt*, or idolatry. Any behavior is considered idolatrous that may include the creation of any type of image of the deity, or even other figures of religious sig-

---

39 Ibid., 31.

40 Barbara Crossette, "Taliban Explains Buddha Demolition," *New York Times*, March 19, 2001, http://www.nytimes.com/2001/03/19/world/taliban-explains-buddha-demolition.html.

nificance such as prophets and saints. The creation of images of living things—persons or animals—falls under this definition of idolatrous activity. Thus statues of Buddha constitute idolatry *par excellence.*

Muslim scholars have much debated whether the use of violence in Forbidding Wrong was reserved for the state, or at least needed the permission of the imam, essentially a prayer leader in a mosque, but also someone whose leadership or example is to be followed by the Muslim community. As Cook summarizes, "There were nevertheless a good many scholars who left individuals free to take up arms, and did so without evincing any such concern for the role of the state. This is well-attested among the Muʿtazilites, Zaydīs and Ibādīs. It is also by no means rare among the Sunnīs; thus Abū Ḥanīfa is said to have held that forbidding wrong is obligatory by word and sword, and Ibn Ḥazm gives strong support to recourse to arms where necessary."[41]

Or Heart

Finally, there is the recourse to the heart, which is a purely mental act.

Al-Ghazālī on Emigration

If one lives in a land where wrongdoing prevails, and one does not have the realistic possibility of righting those wrongs, then one's duty is to emigrate.[42] Al-Ghazālī does not endorse this reading, arguing instead that as long as one does not participate in the wrongdoing, one is not obliged to emigrate, which seems a rather unrealistic demand of ordinary Muslims. Nonetheless, al-Ghazālī is relentless in urging Muslims to pursue this Islamic duty, especially if one knows that there is "an evil in the market-place, and are capable of putting a stop to it, then it is your duty not to sit at home, but rather to sally forth to confront evil."[43]

The Zaydī Muʿtazilite Mānkdīm argues that "forbidding wrong has conditions (*sharāʾit*), being obligatory only when they are satisfied."[44] These conditions are: (1) knowledge of law, (2) knowledge of fact, (3) absence of worse side-effects, (4) efficacy, and (5) absence of danger to onself.[45]

As for the condition of danger, "the question for us now is whether

---

41 Cook, *Forbidding Wrong*, 34.
42 Ibid., 39.
43 Ibid., 41.
44 Ibid., 45.
45 Ibid., 46.

in the absence of obligation it is still *good* to proceed. The standard answer is that it is; if you are willing to take risks in God's cause, you will be rewarded. In the limit, this means endorsing the view that someone who is killed forbidding wrong dies the death of a martyr (*shahīd*), and many scholars have no problem with this."[46]

Privacy versus Hidden Sin

Muslim scholars do not have "any single concept equivalent to our notion of privacy; what they have is rather a cluster of related concerns."[47] Cook explains that Muslim scholars do not seem to have

> the notion that certain kinds of behavior are inherently private, and as such immune to public scrutiny. What is protected is not "private life" but rather "hidden sin," behavior that happens not to be public knowledge. It is no business of ours to pry into what is unknown to us, nor to divulge what we innocently stumble upon; but once we know, we are likely to incur some kind of obligation to forbid wrong....The difference between Muslim thinking and that of the modern West is thus not simply that there is no single Muslim concept corresponding to the Western notion of privacy; it is also that the Muslim concepts seem to be of a significantly different kind.[48]

Similarly, this principle also overrides concerns about minding one's own business, as there is "no doctrinal rejection of forbidding wrong based on the principle of minding one's own business."[49]

The Muslim state should be responsible for carrying out this duty. But where the state itself is a wrongdoer, Muslims should speak out publicly to rebuke unjust rulers, many scholars argue, despite the danger to oneself. Al-Ghazālī encourages such rebuke, giving the example of early Muslims who took such risks to fulfill their Muslim duty, "knowing that to be killed in such a case was martyrdom." Al-Ghazālī then quotes seventeen anecdotes "to illustrate their courage and plain speaking. This, he laments, is how things used to be; but today the scholars are silent, or if they do speak out, they are ineffectual, all because of their love of things

---

46 Ibid., 55.
47 Ibid., 57.
48 Ibid., 62-63.
49 Ibid., 94.

of this world."⁵⁰

The Hanafī Muʿtazilite Jassās denounces Sunni traditionists who had a tendency to downplay the duty,

> for holding that injustice and murder may be committed by a ruler with impunity, while other offenders may be proceeded against by word or deed—but not with arms. The point is not, in his view, an academic one. It is these attitudes that have led to the present sorry state of Islam—to the domination of the reprobate, of Zoroastrians, of enemies of Islam; to the collapse of the frontiers of Islam against the infidel; to the spread of injustice, the ruin of countries and the rise of all manner of false religions.⁵¹

This duty is not found in all the classical traditions, but "outright denials of the obligatoriness of forbidding wrong are almost unheard of."⁵² Its importance is underlined in a comprehensive manner by the Indian Hanafī ʿIsmat Allāh of Sharānpur, who was clearly irritated by those who downplay the duty, and the doctrine of some, though not all, Sūfīs, of leaving people in peace:

> For were it pleasing to God to leave people alone, He would not have sent the prophets, nor established their laws, nor called to Islam, nor voided other religions, but would rather have left people to their own devices, untroubled by divine visitations; nor would He have imposed on them the duty of holy war, which involves suffering and death for both Muslims and infidels. He further emphasises that Sūfīs—pantheists included—have made it abundantly clear that they neither practise nor preach an indiscriminate toleration. What is more, distinguished Sūfīs have written on forbidding wrong. Even apart from this, the fact that the prophets were sent to command right and forbid wrong is enough to establish that it is both good and obligatory. In short, if leaving people alone were praiseworthy, then forbidding wrong would not be a religious duty.⁵³

---

50 Ibid., 76.
51 Ibid., 84-85.
52 Ibid., 86.
53 Ibid., 89-90.

Categories of Wrongdoing

As for the kinds of wrongs that Muslims commonly committed, al-Ghazālī's examples are sorted into three categories by Michael Cook: violation of religious norms (e.g., praying faultily), "offense against puritanical norms" (e.g., imbibing liquor, making music, and indulging in improper sexual relations), and "secular" wrongs (e.g., blocking a street).

It is odd that Cook characterizes taking liquor as an offense against "puritanical norms," when imbibing alcohol is quite clearly against the Shari'a, which is incumbent on all Muslims, hence simply an Islamic norm. Cook does refer to drinking alcohol as a common practice in medieval Islamic societies, suggesting that not all Muslims took the Koranic injunction against alcohol seriously. Finally, Cook ends on a very important point: "[T]here is no sign within the secular category of a concern for what we might call social justice."[54] The primary concern for all who insist on the duty to Command Right and Forbid Wrong is to see that Islam is not endangered in any way by laxness among Muslims, from rulers to common people.

Cook shows that "it was common in the early centuries of Islam for rebels to adopt forbidding wrong as their slogan,"[55] examples being "found among the Khārijites, including the Ibādīs, among the Shī'ites, including Zaydīs, and among the Sunnīs, especially the Mālikīs. Some instances of such rebels in the early centuries of Islam are Jahm ibn Safwān (d. 746), in late Umayyad Transoxiana, Yūsuf al-Barm in Khurāsān in 776f., Mubarqa' in Palestine 841f., Ibn al-Qitt in Spain in 901 and an 'Abbāsid who rebelled in Armenia in 960."[56]

Cook's conclusion is that the act of Forbidding Wrong is largely driven by puritanical attitudes, and that "those who participated were members of the religious elite, and above all the scholars....[T]he link between forbidding wrong and rebellion is unproblematically historical."[57]

Forbidding Wrong and Rebellion

There is an inexorable link between Forbidding Wrong and rebellion, and therefore a link that has great importance in light of militant Islam's resurgence in the second half of the twentieth century. Islamic fundamentalists fervently believe in drawing on the Islamic tradition,

---

54 Ibid., 99.
55 Ibid., 81.
56 Ibid., 108-9.
57 Ibid., 110.

which remains profoundly relevant for all Muslims living in the modern world. Thus medieval doctrines of Forbidding Wrong continue to play a vital role in directing the actions of contemporary Islamists.

Educated Sunni Muslims agree that Islam as it has been practised in the last hundred years needs drastic reform, but there is no agreement about what kind of reforms should be enacted. Islamic modernists propose restoring Islam in a way that allows practitioners to continue to live at ease with themselves in the modern world. However, many Muslims see this as a compromise and, in effect, a project to Westernize Islam. Islamic fundamentalists obviously prefer an uncompromising restoration of Islam that shuns omnipresent Western culture. Cook has provided the essential historical link, from groups seeking to apply the Islamic duty of Commanding Right and Forbidding Wrong in order to purify Islam to the modern, violent reform movements.

As I emphasize throughout this book, reform movements, often violent, seeking to restore a pristine Islam have existed since the foundation of the original Muslim community—from movements such as the Khārijities in the eighth century, to movements in Baghdad in the ninth, tenth, and eleventh centuries, to the Qādīzādeli movement in Istanbul in the seventeenth century, which influenced Muhammad ibn 'Abd al-Wahhāb (1703–1792), who founded Wahhābism, the movement named after him in eighteenth-century Najd, in the interior of Arabia, which gave rise to the Saudi state.

Ibn al-Wahhāb, whose ideas are explored in depth in chapter 14, was motivated by purely Islamic concerns such as the elimination of harmful innovations, and he was not afraid to use violence to impose his version of pristine Islam. He would provide inspiration for Islamic fundamentalists worldwide, from India to Indonesia in the East, and Egypt and Iran in the Middle East, as they battled, in their view, the pernicious and ubiquitous influence of Western civilization.

Since Forbidding Wrong is an Islamic practice that tells people what to believe, it reminds us of the profound difference between Islam and Western liberalism. As I have written, under Islam, life is a closed book.[58] Everything has been decided for human beings: the dictates of Sharī'a and the whims of Allah set strict limits on the possible agenda of our lives. In the West, we are free as individuals to choose our goals and determine our path, and to decide what meaning to give to our lives. As Roger Scruton has remarked, "the glory of the West is that life is an

---

58 Ibn Warraq, *Why the West Is Best* (New York: Encounter Books, 2011), 11.

open book."⁵⁹

Both Sayyid Qutb (1906–1966), an Egyptian Islamist and the leading member of the Egyptian Muslim Brotherhood in the 1950s and 1960s (see chapter 19), and 'Ali ibn Hajj (Ali Benhadj or Belhadj, b. 1956), an Algerian Islamist activist, preacher, and cofounder of the Islamic Salvation Front political party, vehemently argue that what the West continues to consider as personal matters are no such thing. It is the duty of observant Muslims to interfere where Islamic laws and custom are being broken. As early as 1961 French Islamologue Louis Gardet (1904–1986) presciently remarked that "forbidding wrong as moral reform (*réforme des moeurs*), though currently held in check by the modern state, was alive in the sentiments of the Muslim people, and could well emerge in favourable circumstances."⁶⁰ Strangely enough, Qutb insisted that one had to establish a true Muslim society *before* one could apply the principle. This, however, was not the position adopted by all Islamic fundamentalists.

When they controlled most of Afghanistan, the Taliban established a department, and later a ministry, for Forbidding Wrong. More notorious are the religious police in Saudi Arabia and Iran, who carry out this duty. For other fundamentalists such as the Ayatollah Khomeini, this duty even overrides the danger condition, and if death occurs to the Muslim trying to forbid wrong, he will have died an honorable death of a martyr.

The Hereafter: Blood and Death, not Life, in Islam

On January 9, 2015, Amedy Coulibaly, hostage-taker and gunman in the Kosher supermarket at La Porte de Vincennes in Paris presented himself to victims in this manner: "I am Amedy Coulibaly, Malian, Muslim. I belong to IS [*État islamique*]. The difference between Muslims and you, the Jews, is that you treat life as sacred. For you, life is too important. As for us, it is death that is sacred."⁶¹ A little later, the young Malian reaffirmed his commitment to Islam in a message sent to his commanders to look after his wife, who, he insisted, must learn

---

59 Roger Scruton, "The Glory of the West Is That Life Is an Open Book," *Sunday Times* (UK), May 27, 2007, http://www.thesundaytimes.co.uk/sto/culture/books/article65281.ece.

60 Cook, *Forbidding Wrong*, 115–16, citing Louis Gardet, *La cité musulmane: vie sociale et politique*, 2nd ed. (Paris: Librairie Philosophique J. Vrin, 1961), 187.

61 Jean Birnbaum, *Un silence religieux: La gauche face au djihādisme* (Paris: Éditions du Seuil, 2016), 14.

Arabic, the Koran, and theology. His hatred of the West resulted, Coulibaly claimed, from its relentless attack on Islamic institutions and values: the caliphate and the Shari'a. To "elevate the words of Allah" and to protect Islam, Coulibaly shot and killed four hostages before he was killed by the police.[62] As former senior international policy analyst with the RAND Coroporation Laurent Murawiec has written, "inseparable... from contemporary Islamic terrorism are the idolization of blood, the veneration of savagery, the cult of killing, the worship of death."[63]

Contempt for Life

That Islamic terrorists embrace death with joy in anticipation of their rewards seems, to non-Muslims, morbid and immoral, for it treats the human life as worthless, expendable. But this disdain for life has been acquired from Islamic history and Islamic texts. The Koran refers to the "Last Day"—*al-yawm al-ākhir*—in some formulation at least forty times,[64] but alludes to the "Hereafter" or the "World to Come"—*al-Ākhirah*—more than a hundred times,[65] often to say that the "Life to Come" is far better than life on Earth, and to heap scorn on those who enjoy living. For example:

- Q2. *al-Baqara*, the Cow, 86: Such are those who have purchased the present life at the price of the world to come.
- Q2. *al-Baqara*, the Cow, 94: Say: If the abode of the Hereafter in the providence of Allah is indeed for you alone and not for others of mankind, then long for death (for you must long for death) if you are truthful.
- Q9. *at-Tawba*, the Repentance / *al-Barā'at*, the Immunity, 38: The enjoyment of the present life, compared with the Hereafter, is a little thing.
- Q16. *an-Nahl*, the Bee, 106-7: Theirs will be an awful doom. That is because they have chosen the life of the world rather than the Hereafter.
- Q87. *al-'A'lā*, the Most High, 16-17: But you prefer the life of world, although the Hereafter is better and more lasting.

---

62 Ibid.
63 Laurent Murawiec, *The Mind of Jihād* (Cambridge and New York: Cambridge University Press, 2008), 21.
64 See Hanna E. Kassis, *A Concordance of the Qur'an* (Berkeley: University of California Press, 1983), 131-32.
65 Ibid., 132-34.

Similar attitudes are expressed in the *hadīth*:

- Sahīh al-Bukhārī: *hadīth* 6413: "Narrated Anas: The Prophet said, 'O Allah! There is no life worth living except the life of the Hereafter.'"[66]
- Sahīh al-Bukhārī *hadīth* 6415: "I heard the Prophet saying, 'A (small) place equal to an area occupied by a whip in Paradise is better than the (whole) world and whatever is in it; and an undertaking (journey) in the forenoon or in the afternoon for Allah's Cause, is better than the whole world and whatever is in it.'"[67]
- Ibn Majah, *Sunan*, book 6, *hadīth* 1571: "It was narrated from Ibn Mas'ud that the Messenger of Allah said, 'I used to forbid you to visit the graves, but now visit them, for they will draw your attention away from this world and remind you of the Hereafter.'"[68]

The Islamic concept of martyrdom is examined in the forthcoming chapter on *jihād*, which includes examples of contempt for this life on Earth, and phrases remarkably similar to those used by modern *jihādists* such as "more eager for death than you are for life," in the history of al-Tabarī in the section on the early Muslim conquests. As for the modern period, there are countless examples to choose from; I share here two, posted in July 2014 on *Palestinian Media Watch*:

> A recorded statement by Hamas Chief of Staff Muhammad Deif, prepared during the current Gaza war, announced: "Today you [Israelis] are fighting divine soldiers, who love death for Allah like you love life, and who compete among themselves for Martyrdom like you flee from death."
>
> Yesterday, Hamas TV also chose to broadcast a statement former Hamas Prime Minister Ismail Haniyeh made in the past: "We love death like our enemies love life! We love Mar-

---

66 *The Translation of the Meanings of Sahīh Bukhārī*, trans. Muhammad Muhsin Khan, *hadīth* 6413 (Riyadh, Saudi Arabia: Darussalam, 1997), 8:233, https://futureislam.files.wordpress.com/2012/11/sahih-al-bukhari-volume-8-ahadith-5970-6860.pdf
67 Ibid., *hadīth* 6415, 8:234.
68 *Sunan Ibn Majah*, trans. Ansari, *hadīth* 1571, 6:397.

tyrdom, the way in which [Hamas] leaders died."⁶⁹

These examples of praise for death, collected on *Jihād Watch*, were posted in 2014:

> A Muslim child preacher taunted those he has been taught to hate most: "Oh Zionists, we love death for the sake of Allah, just as much as you love life for the sake of Satan." *Jihād* mass murderer Mohamed Merah said that he "loved death more than they loved life." Nigerian *jihādist* Abubakar Shekau said: "I'm even longing for death, you vagabond." Ayman al-Zawahiri's wife advised Muslim women: "I advise you to raise your children in the cult of *jihād* and martyrdom and to instil in them a love for religion and death." And as one *jihādist* put it, "We love death. You love your life!" And another: "The Americans love Pepsi-Cola, we love death." That was from Afghan *jihādist* Maulana Inyadullah.⁷⁰

Some may remember the words of the Ayatollah Khomeini, spoken in 1977: "This world is but a passage; it is not a world in which we ought to live….What is called Life in this world is not Life but Death. True Life is that offered only in the Hereafter."⁷¹ And "It is only the Mullahs who can bring the people into the streets and make them die for Islam—begging to have their blood shed for Islam."⁷²

Political analyst and lecturer Amir Taheri, a former editor-in-chief of *Kayhan*, Iran's largest-selling daily newspaper, shares the following startling example of the significance of blood in Islam in his 1987 book, *Holy Terror: The Inside Story of Islamic Terrorism*:

> Pilgrims to the 'waiting room of Paradise' start their guided tour of the Islamic Republic with a visit to the Behesht Zahra (Paradise of Flowers) graveyard south of Tehran. There

---

69 Itamar Marcus, "Hamas: We 'Love Death for Allah,'" *Palestinian Media Watch*, July 31, 2014, http://palwatch.org/main.aspx?fi=157&doc_id=12235.

70 Robert Spencer, "Hamas: 'We Love Death Like Our Enemies Love Life!'" *Jihād Watch*, July 31, 2014, https://www.jihādwatch.org/2014/07/hamas-we-love-death-like-our-enemies-love-life.

71 Quoted in Amir Taheri, *The Spirit of Allah: Khomeini & the Islamic Revolution* (Bethesda, MD: Adler & Adler, 1986), 39.

72 Ibid., 53.

they are invited to stand for a minute's silence in front of the Fountain of Blood, a 4.5 metre-high fountain out of which surges a blood-red liquid, symbolizing, in the words of the guide, the essence of Islam's message.[73]

Finally, consider this quote from Osama bin Ladin, uttered in 1996:

> Since the sons of the land of the two holy places [Saudi Arabia] feel and strongly believe that fighting [*jihād*] against the *kufr* [unbeliever] in every part of the world is absolutely essential, then they would be even more enthusiastic, more powerful, and larger in number upon fighting on their own land... defending the greatest of their [holy places], the noble Kaba....They know that the Muslims of the world will assist and help them to victory. To liberate their [holy places] is the greatest of issues concerning all Muslims; it is the duty of every Muslim in this world. I say to you [U.S. Defense Secretary William Cohen]: These youths love death as you love life.[74]

---

73 Taheri, *Holy Terror*, 114.

74 Rubin, Barry & Rubin, Judith Colp, edd. *Anti-American Terrorism and the Middle East. Understanding the Violence. A Documentary Reader*. (Oxford: Oxford University Press, 2002) 140-41.

CHAPTER 5

JIHĀD: DEFINITIONS, DESCRIPTIONS, AND DISCUSSIONS

I TREAT *jihād* in considerable detail because its theory and practice are central to the whole of Islamic history and Islamic theology, and because it has immediate relevance to the political ideology and acts of contemporary Islamic fundamentalists and terrorists. And yet, many modern Western intellectuals and analysts still deny the centrality of *jihād* as a motivating factor in current Islamist movements. Thus, to drive home the importance of *jihād* I have had recourse to every kind of scholarly evidence available—dictionaries, encyclopaedias, the Koran, *hadīth*, Sira (the Life of Muhammad), the writings of highly regarded Islamic philosophers and theologians, and scholarly works of history.

Definitions of *Jihād*

In his celebrated *Dictionary of Islam* (1885), Thomas Patrick Hughes, a British Anglican missionary who served in British India and was noted for his facility with languages and Islamic scholarship, offers this definition of *jihād*:

> "Lit. "An effort, or a striving." A religious war with those who are unbelievers in the mission of Muhammad. It is an incumbent religious duty, established in the Qur'an and in the Traditions as a divine institution, and enjoined specially for the purpose of advancing Islam and of repelling evil from Muslims.

When an infidel's country is conquered by a Muslim ruler, its inhabitants are offered three alternatives:

(1) *The reception of Islam*, in which case the conquered become enfranchised citizens of the Muslim state.
(2) *The payment of a poll-tax (Jizyah)*, by which unbelievers in Islam obtain protection, and become *Zimmis*, provided they are not the idolaters of Arabia.
(3) *Death by the sword*, to those who will not pay the poll tax.

Sufi writers say that there are two *jihāds*: *al-jihādu 'l-Akbar*, or "the greater warfare," which is against one's own lusts; and *al-jihādu 'l-asghar*, or "the lesser warfare," against infidels.

The duty of religious war (which all commentators agree is a duty extending to all time) is laid down in the Qur'an in the following verses, and it is remarkable that all the verses occur in the al-Madinah Surahs, being those given after Muhammad had established himself as a paramount ruler and was in a position to dictate terms to his enemies.... [Hughes quotes from Q9. *al-Tawba*, the Repentance, 5–6, 29; Q4 *al-Nisā'*, the Women, 76–79; Q2. *al-Baqarah*, the Cow, 214–15; and Q8 *al-Anfāl*, the Spoils of War, 39–42.]

Long chapters in the Traditions are devoted to the subject of *jihād* (see Bukhārī, Sahīh and Muslim ibn al-Hajjāj, Sahīh, Babu 'l- *jihād*).[1]

Hughes continues his discussion of *jihād* with many quotes from the canonical *hadīth*. However, he does not give the precise references for the sources of those *hadīth*. I have diligently tracked them down, and give essentially the same *hadīth*, properly referenced, using the more readily available translations of the Muslim scholars, Muhammad Muhsin Khan, Ahmad Hasan, and Abdul Hamid Siddiqi:

Allāh guarantees that He will admit the Mujāhid in His Cause into Paradise if he is killed, otherwise He will return him to his home safely with rewards and war booty. —Bukhārī,

---

[1] Hughes, *Dictionary of Islam*, s.v. "*jihād*."

Sahīh, *Kitāb al-jihād wa-l siyar.*²

No doubt I wish I could fight in Allah's Cause and be martyred and come back to life again and then again to be martyred and then come back to life once more.³

To guard Muslims from infidels in Allah's Cause for one day is better than the world and whatever is on its surface.⁴

Anyone whose both feet get covered with dust in Allah's Cause will not be touched by the (Hell) fire.⁵

He who equips a fighter in Allah's path has taken part in fighting, and he who looks after a fighter's family when he is away has taken part in the fighting....If any of you looks after the family and property of a warrior, he will receive half the reward of the one who goes forth (in *jihād*). —Abū Dāwūd, *Sunan, Kitāb al-Jihād*⁶

The Holy Prophet said, "This religion will continue to exist, and a group of people from the Muslims will continue to fight for its protection until the Hour [the Day of Resurrection] is established." —Muslim ibn al-Hajjāj, Sahīh, *Kitāb al-Imara*⁷

Whoever is wounded in Allah's Cause—and Allah knows well who gets wounded in His Cause—will come on the Day of Resurrection with his wound having the colour of blood but its smell will be the smell of musk. —Bukhārī, Sahīh⁸

All the sins of a Shahid (martyr) are forgiven except debt. —

---

2 Bukhārī, *Authentic Hadīth: Book of Jihād and Campaigns*, hadīth 2787, 4:47.
3 Ibid., *hadīth* 2972, 4:138; see also *hadīth* 2797, 4:52; *hadīth* 36, 1:73.
4 Ibid., *hadīth* 2892, 4:97.
5 Ibid., *hadīth* 2811, 4:60.
6 Abū Dāwūd, *Sunan, Kitāb al-Jihād*, trans. Ahmad Hasan, *ahādīth* 2503, 2504 (New Delhi: Kitab Bhavan, 1997), 2:695.
7 Muslim ibn al-Hajjāj, *Sahīh, Kitāb al-Imara*, trans. 'Abdul Hamid Siddiqi, *hadīth* 4717 (New Delhi: Kitab Bhavan, 2000), 3:1277.
8 Bukhārī, *Authentic Hadīth*, hadīth 2803, 4:55.

Muslim ibn al-Hajjāj, Sahīh, *Kitāb al-Imāra*⁹

He who dies without having fought or having felt fighting (against the infidels) to be his duty will die guilty of a kind of hypocrisy. —Abū Dāwūd, *Sunan, Kitāb al-Jihād*¹⁰

When you are called (by a Muslim ruler) for *jihād* (holy fighting in Allah's cause), go forth immediately.
The Imam (Muslim ruler) is like a shelter for whose safety the Muslims should fight. —Bukhārī, *Sahīh*¹¹

Descriptions of *Jihād*
Encyclopaedia of Islam, First Edition, 1913

In the first edition (1913) of the *Encyclopaedia of Islam*, D.B. Macdonald, author of the entry on "*djihād*," offers this depiction of "Holy War" (which is reproduced in the *Shorter Encyclopaedia of Islam* (1953):¹²

> The spread of Islam by arms is a religious duty upon Muslims in general. It narrowly escaped being a sixth *rukn*, or fundamental duty, and is indeed still so regarded by the descendants of the Khāridjīs. This position was reached gradually but quickly. In the Meccan Sūras of the Qur'ān patience under attack is taught; no other attitude was possible. But at Madīna the right to repel attack appears, and gradually it became a prescribed duty to fight against and subdue the hostile Meccans. Whether Muhammad himself recognized that his position implied steady and unprovoked war against the unbelieving world until it was subdued to Islam may be in doubt. Traditions are explicit on the point; but the Qur'ānic passages speak always of the unbelievers who are to be subdued as dangerous or faithless. Still, the story of his writing to the powers around him shows that such a universal position was implicit in his mind, and it certainly developed

---

9 Al-Hajjāj, *Sahīh, Kitāb al-Imara*, hadīth 4649, 3:1261.
10 Abū Dāwūd, *Sunan, Kitāb al-Jihād*, hadīth 2496, 2:693.
11 Bukhārī, *Sahīh*, hadīth 2825, 4:67; hadīth 2957, 4:131.
12 *Encyclopaedia of Islam*, vol. 1, "A–D," ed. Th. Houtsma, T.W. Arnold, and R. Basset (Leiden: Brill, 1913), s.v. "*djihād*," by D.B. Macdonald. *Shorter Encyclopaedia of Islam*, s.v. "*Djihād*."

immediately after his death, when the Muslim armies advanced out of Arabia. It is a now a *fard 'ala 'l-kifāya*, a duty in general on all male, free, adult Muslims, sane in mind and body and having means enough to reach the Muslim army, yet not a duty necessarily incumbent on every individual, but sufficiently performed when done by a certain number. So it must continue to be done until the whole world is under the rule of Islam....A Muslim who dies fighting in the Path of Allah (*fī sabīl Allāh*) is a martyr (*shahīd*) and is assured of Paradise and of peculiar privileges there. Such a death was, in the early generations, regarded as the peculiar crown of a pious life. It is still, on occasions, a strong incitement, but when Islam ceased to conquer it lost its supreme value. Even yet, however, any war between Muslims and non-Muslims must be a *jihād* with its incitements and rewards. Of course, such modern movements as the so-called Mu'tazilī in India and the Young Turk in Turkey reject this and endeavour to explain away its basis; but the Muslim masses still follow the unanimous voice of the canon lawyers. Islam must be completely made over before the doctrine of *jihād* can be eliminated.[13]

Encyclopaedia of Islam, Second Edition, 1960–1986

The second edition of the *Encyclopaedia of Islam* (1960–1986) is a highly respected collaborative work of the most eminent Western Islamologists of the twentieth century. It is a monumental work of scholarship, hence its importance. It discusses *jihād*, in part, thus:

In law, according to general doctrine and in historical tradition, the *djihād* consists of military action with the object of the expansion of Islam and, if need be, of its defence....The notion stems from the fundamental principle of the universality of Islam: this religion, along with the temporal power which it implies, ought to embrace to whole universe, if nec-

---

13 D.B. Macdonald's bibliographical references: Th. W. Juynboll, *Handbuch des Islamischen Gesetzes Nach der Lehre der Schafi'itischen Schule Nebst Einer Allgemeinen Einleitung* (Leiden, Leipzig: E.J. Brill, Otto Harrassowitz, 1910), 57, 336 et seq., especially for division of booty; Hughes, *Dictionary of Islam*, 243 et seq.—full on Koran, traditions, and details of Hanafite law; C. Snouck Hurgronje, *Politique Musulmane de la Hollande* (Paris: E. Leroux, 1911), 16 et seq., especially for permanent character of *djihād* in Islam; Māwardī, *Ahkām al-sultānīyya* (ed. of Cairo 1298), 54 et seq.

essary by force....

A religious duty. The *djihād* has the effect of extending the sway of the faith; it is prescribed by God and his Prophet; the Muslim dedicates himself to the *djihād* in the same way that, in Christianity, the monk dedicates himself to the service of God; in the same vein it is said in different hadīths that "the *djihād* is the monasticism of Islam"; the *djihād* is "an act of pure devotion"; it is "one of the gates to Paradise"; rich heavenly rewards are guaranteed for those who devote themselves to it; those who fall in the *djihād* are the martyrs of the faith, etc. A substantial part of the doctrine reckons the *djihād* among the very "pillars" (*arkan*) of the religion, along with prayer and fasting etc. It is a duty which falls upon every Muslim who is male, free and ablebodied. It is generally considered that non-Muslims may be called upon to assist the Muslims in the *djihād*....

Its perpetual character. The duty of the *djihād* exists as long as the universal domination of Islam has not been attained. "Until the day of the resurrection," and "until the end of the world" say the maxims. Peace with non-Muslim nations is, therefore, a provisional state of affairs only; the chance of circumstances alone can justify it temporarily. Furthermore, there can be no question of genuine peace treaties with these nations; only truces, whose duration ought not, in principle, to exceed ten years, are authorized. But even such truces are precarious, inasmuch as they can, before they expire, be repudiated unilaterally should it appear more profitable for Islam to resume the conflict. It is, however, recognized that such repudiation should be brought to the notice of the infidel party, and that he should be afforded sufficient opportunity to be able to disseminate the news of it throughout the whole of his territory

Finally, there is at the present time a thesis, of a wholly apologetic character, according to which Islam relies for its expansion exclusively upon persuasion and other peaceful means, and the *djihād* is only authorized in cases of "self defence" and of "support owed to a defenceless ally or brother." Disregarding entirely the previous doctrine and historical tradition, as well as the texts of the Qur'an and the sunna on the basis of which it was formulated, but claiming, even so, to remain within the bounds of strict orthodoxy, this thesis takes into account only those early texts which state the contrary (v. supra).[14]

Discussions: Modern Scholars on *Jihād*

I have chosen five modern scholars who write unapologetically about the nature of *jihād*, three of whom are Muslim—Majid Khadduri, Fazlur Rahman, and Mustansir Mir—to allay any suspicion that I cite only perhaps biased Western ones.

Majid Khadduri, *War and Peace in the Law of Islam*, 1955 [15]

Majid Khadduri was professor of Middle East studies at the School of Advanced International Studies at Johns Hopkins University, and director of research and education at the Middle East Institute in Washington, D.C.:

---

14 *Encyclopaedia of Islam*, vol. 2, "C–G," ed. B. Lewis, Ch. Pellat, and J. Schacht, 2nd ed. (Leiden: E.J. Brill, 1965), s.v. *"djihād,"* written by E. Tyan. "Dāmād Ef., Madjma' al-anhur, ed. Ahmad b. 'Uthmān, 1328/1910, i, 636ff.; Dardīr, al-Sharh al-Aaghīr, with the gloss of Sāwī, i, 398ff.; Djāhiz, Rasā'il, ed. Sandūbī, Cairo 1933, 57; Farrā', *Ahkām al-sultāniyya*, Cairo, 25ff.; Goldziher, *Schi'itisches*, in *ZDMG*, lxiv, 53iff.; Addison, *The Ahmadiya Movement*, in *Harvard Theological Review*, xxii, iff.; Ibn 'Abidīn, *Radd al-muhtār*, Istanbul 1314/1905, iii, 315 ff.; Ibn 'Abd al-Rahman, *Rahmat al-umma fī 'khtilāf al-a'imma*, Cairo, 294; Ibn Djumā'a, *Tahrīr al-ahkām*, ed. Kofler, (in *Islāmica*, 1934), 349ff.; Ibn Qudāma, *Mughnī*, 3rd. ed. Rashīd Ridā, Cairo 1367/1947, viii, 345ff.; Ibn Taymiyya, *al-Siyāsa al-shar'iyya*, Cairo 1322/1904, 156ff.; Marāghī, *al-Tashri' al-islāmī*, Cairo, 24ff.; Māwardī, *Ahkām al-sultāniyya*, Cairo, 30ff.; Querry, *Recueil de lois concernant les musulmans chiites*, Paris 1871, i, 321; Rashid Ridā, *Khilāfa*, Cairo 1341/1922, 29, 51; Sarakhsī, *Mabsūt*, Cairo, x, 35; Shāfi'ī, *Kitāb al-umm*, Cairo 1903, with the Muzanī gloss, v, 180 if.; Gaudefroy-Demombynes, *Mahomet*, Paris 1957, 578ff.; Draz, *Le droit international publicé et l'Islām*, in *Revue égyptienne de droit international public*, 1949, 17ff.; Haneberg, *Das muslimische Kriegsrecht* (Abh. der kgl. Bayer. Akad. der Wissensch., 1870, philos.-philol. cl., xii. Bd., II. Abt.), 219ff.; Juynboll, *Handbuch 57*, 335ff.; Milliot, *Introd. a L'étude du droit musulman*, Paris 1953, 22, 34; Sa'idī, *al-Siyāsa al-islāmiyya*, Cairo; Sanhoury, *Le Califat*, thesis, Lyon 1925, 146; Strothmann, *Das Staatsrecht der Zaiditen*, Strasbourg 1922, 42ff.; Muh. Shadīd, *al-Djihād fī 'l-Islām*, 1960; 1A, art. Cihād (Halim Sabit Sibay)."

15 Majid Khadduri, *War and Peace in the Law of Islam* (Baltimore: Johns Hopkins University Press, 1955; Clark, NJ: Lawbook Exchange, Ltd., 2006, 2010), 56–57.

The *jihād* may be regarded as a form of religious propaganda that can be carried on by persuasion or by the sword. In the early Makkan revelations, the emphasis was in the main on persuasion. Muhammad, in the discharge of his prophetic functions, seemed to have been satisfied by warning his people against idolatry and inviting then to worship Allah. This is evidenced by such a verse as the following: Q 29 al-'Ankabūt, the Spider 6: "He who exerts himself (*jāhada*) exerts only for his own soul" [*wa-man gāhada fa-'innamā yugāhidu li-nafsihī*], which expresses the *jihād* in terms of the salvation of the soul rather than a struggle for proselytization.[16] In the Madīnan revelations, the *jihād* is often expressed in terms of strife, and there is no doubt that in certain verses the conception of *jihād* is synonymous with the words war and fighting.[17]

The jurists, however, have distinguished four different ways in which the believer may fulfill his *jihād* obligation: by his heart; his tongue; his hands; and by the sword.[18] The first is concerned with combatting the devil and in the attempt to escape his persuasion to evil. This type of *jihād*, so significant in the eyes of the Prophet Muhammad, was regarded as the greater *jihād* [see Ibn al-Humām (d. 1457), *Sharh Fath al-Qadīr* (Cairo, 1898), 4:277]. The second and third are mainly fulfilled in supporting the right and correcting the wrong. The fourth is precisely equivalent to the meaning of war, and is concerned with fighting the unbelievers and the enemies of the faith.[19] The believers are under the obligation of sacrificing their "wealth and lives" [Q61. *As-Saff*, The Row

---

16 Ibid., 56n4: "See Shāfi'ī, *Kitāb al-Umm* (Cairo, A,H,1321), Vol. IV, pp.84–85; 'Abd al-Qāhir al-Baghdādī, *Kitāb Uaūl al-Dīn* (Istanbul, 1928), Vol. I, p. 193; Shaybānī, *al-Siyar al-Kabīr*, with Sarakhsī's Commentary (Hyderabad, A.H. 1335), Vol. I, p. 126."

17 Ibid: "See Q2. *al-Baqara*, the Cow 215; Q9. *at-Tawba*, the Repentance 41; Q 61. *As-Saff*, The Row 11; Q66. *at-Tahrīm*, the Prohibition 9."

18 Ibid 56n6: "See Ibn Hazm, *Kitāb al-Fasl fī al-Milal wa'l-Ahwā' wa'l-Nihal* (Cairo, A.H. 1321), Vol. IV, p. 135; Ibn Rushd, *Kitāb al-Muqaddimāt al-Mumahhidāt* (Cairo, A.H. 1325), Vol.I, p. 259; Buhūtī, *Kashshāf al-Qinā' 'An Matn al-Iqnā'* (Cairo, A.H. 1366),Vol. III, p. 28.

19 Ibid., 57n8: "Ibn Hazm distinguishes between the *jihād* by the tongue and the *jihād* by *ra'y* and *tadbīr* (i.e. reason) and he maintains that the Prophet Muhammad showed preference for reason over the sword. Ibn Hazm, Vol. IV, p. 135."

11: *tu'minūna bi-llāhi wa-rasūlihī wa-tugāhidūna fī sabīli llāhi bi-'amwālikum wa'anfusikum dālikum hayrun lakum 'in kuntum ta'lamūna*] in the prosecution of war.[20]

Fazlur Rahman, *Islam*, 1966

Fazlur Rahman was Harold H. Swift Distinguished Service Professor of Islamic Thought at the University of Chicago:

> The Qur'ān calls upon believers to undertake *jihād*, which is to surrender "your properties and youselves in the path of Allāh"; the purpose of which in turn is to "establish prayer, give *zakāt*, command good and forbid evil"—i.e., to establish the socio-moral order. So long as the Muslims were a small, persecuted minority in Mecca, *jihād* as a positive organized thrust of the Islamic movement was unthinkable. In Medina, however, the situation changed and henceforth there is hardly anything, with the possible exception of prayer and *zakāt*, that receives greater emphasis than *jihād*....Every virile and expansive ideology has, at a stage, to ask itself the question as to what are its terms of co-existence, if any, with other systems, and how far it may employ methods of direct expansion. In our own age, Communism, in its Russian and Chinese versions, is faced with the same problems and choices. The most unacceptable on historical grounds, however, is the stand of those modern Muslim apologists who have tried to explain the *jihād* of the early Community in purely defensive terms.[21]

Mustansir Mir, "*Jihād in Islam*," 1991 [22]

Mustansir Mir is University Professor of Islamic Studies at Youngstown State University, in Youngstown, Ohio:

> The word *jihād* means "determined effort." As a religious

---

20 Ibid., 57n9: "Bukhārī, *Kitāb al-Jāmi' al-Sahīh*, ed. Krehl (Leiden, 1864), Vol.II, p. 199; Abū Dāwūd, *Sunan* (Cairo, 1935), Vol.III, p. 5; Dārimī, *Sunan* (Damascus, A.H.1349), Vol. II, p. 213."

21 Fazlur Rahman, *Islam* (Chicago: Chicago University Press, 1966), 37.

22 Mustansir Mir, "*Jihād* in Islam," in *The Jihād and Its Times*, ed. Hadia Dajani-Shakeel and Ronald A. Messier (Ann Arbor, MI: Center for Near Eastern and North African Studies, University of Michigan, 1991), 113–14.

term in Islam it has a general and special meaning. In its general sense *jihād* stands for any endeavour made in in order to promote the religion of Islam. But the word carries the connotation that the endeavour is made in a situation of struggle or confrontation, the goal being to surmount a hurdle or overcome a difficulty. According to Rāghib, one engages in *jihād* against an outside enemy (*mujāhadat al-ʿaduww az-zāhir*), against Satan (*mujāhadat ash-shaytān*), or against one's baser self (*mujāhadat an-nafs*). In all three types, it can be seen, the goal is to defeat a hostile force or subdue an opponent. In its special sense, *jihād* is equivalent to the first of the three types of confrontation and may be translated "armed action," another term for which is *qitāl*. This, the most familar meaning of *jihād*, is the one we are mainly concerned with here. When the Qurʾān and the Hadīth promise great reward for *jihād*, they are referring primarily to *jihād* in the sense of *qitāl*.

Jihād in Islam is, properly speaking, *jihād fī sabīl Allāh*, i.e., *jihād* "in the way of, or for the sake, of God." This qualifier, frequent in the Qurʾān [for example, 2:154, 2:190, 2:244, 2:246, 2:261, 3:13, 3:157, 3:167, 4:74, 4:76, and so on] seeks to mark Islamic war off from the wars of pre-Islamic Arabia. Arabic had many names for war, but *jihād* was not one of them—it simply meant "to strive, exert oneself, or make an effort." By using this word to denote war, by further limiting it by means of *jihād fī sabīl Allāh*, and by laying down an elaborate set of rules for the conduct of war in all its stages, Islam presents a new understanding of war. According to certain *hādīth*, only that war is *jihād* which is fought not for the sake of booty, glory, or any other personal or selfish ends, but with the intention of serving God and the religion and winning reward in the next world rather than in this [see Abū Dāwūd, *Sunan*, *Kitāb al-Jihād: bāb man yaghzu [wa] yaltamisu d-dunyā*, and *bab man qātala li takū kalimatu llāhi hiya l-ʿulyā*] Moreover, the purpose of *jihād* in Islam is to "establish the Islamic socio-moral order."[23] All this gives to *jihād* an ideological-cum-ethical dimension that is obviously

---

23 Ibid., 124n4: "Fazlur Rahman, *Islam*, 2nd edn. (Chicago & London: University of Chicago Press, 1979) p. 37."

missing from the pre-Islamic practice of war. To say, therefore, that *jihād* was the Arabian raid or razzia Islamized[24] through no more than a "subtle change"[25] that "there was no specifically religious objective"[26] and that the concept was of significance primarily to the individual in that it pictured for him the great reward awaiting the martyr in heaven[27]—to say this is to trivialize the notion of *jihād*, not to say that such a view can hardly explain the gains made—and consolidated—by early Islam.

Rudolph Peters, *Jihād in Classical and Modern Islam*, 1996

Rudolph Peters, a recognized authority on *jihād*, is professor emeritus of Arabic and Islamic studies at the University of Amsterdam, and director of the Netherlands Institute in Cairo, Egypt:

> The Arabic word *jihād* (verbal noun of the verb *jāhada*) means to strive, to exert oneself, to struggle....In the books on Islamic law, the word means armed struggle against the unbelievers, which is also a common meaning in the Koran [which] frequently mentions *jihād* and fighting (*qitāl*) against the unbelievers....Many verses exhort the believers to take part in the fighting 'with their goods and lives' (*bi-amwāli-him wa-anfusihim*), promise reward to those who are killed in the *jihād* (Q3. *āl 'Imrān*, the Family of Imran, 157–158, 169–172) and threaten those who do not fight with severe punishment in the hereafter (Q9. *at-Tawba*, the Repentance, 81–82; Q48. *al-Fath*, the Victory, 16).
>
> Classical Muslim Koran interpretation...regarded the Sword Verses, with the unconditional command to fight the unbelievers, as having abrogated all previous verses concerning the intercourse with non-Muslims....
>
> The doctrine of *jihād*, as laid down in the works on Islamic

---

24 Ibid., 124n5: "W. Montgomery Watt, *Islamic Political Thought* (Edinburgh: Edinburgh University Press, 1968), pp.14–19."

25 Ibid., 124n6: "W. Montgomery Watt, *The Majesty That Was Islam* (London: Sidgwick & Jackson, 1974), p. 32."

26 Ibid., 124n7: "Ibid., p. 33."

27 Ibid., 124n8: "Ibid., p. 34; Watt, Islamic Political Thought, p. 18."

law, developed out of the Prophet and the first caliphs, which is recorded in the *hadīth*. The crux of the doctrine is the existence of one single Islamic state, ruling the entire umma. It is the duty of the umma to expand the territory of this state in order bring as many people under its rule as possible. The ultimate aim is to bring the whole earth under the sway of Islam and to extirpate unbelief: (Q2. *al-Baqara*, the Cow, 193: "Fight them until there is persecution (or: seduction) and the religion is God's (entirely) [*wa-qātilūhum hattā lā takūna fitnatun wa-yakūna d-dīnu li-llāhi*]" and Q8. *al-'anfāl*, the Spoils of War, 39). Expansionist *jihād* is a collective duty (*fard'alā al-kifāya*), which is fulfilled if a sufficient number of people take part in it. If this is not the case, the whole umma is sinning. Expansionist *jihād* presupposes the presence of a legitimate caliph to organize the struggle. After the conquests had come to an end, the legal specialists laid down that the caliph had to raid enemy territory at least once a year in order to keep the idea of *jihād* alive....

Sunnite and Shi'ite theories of *jihād* are very similar. However, there is one crucial difference. The Twelver Shi'ites hold that *jihād* can only be waged under the leadership of the rightful *Imām*. After the Occultation of the last one in 873, theoretically no lawful *jihād* can be fought. This is true for expansionist *jihād*. However, as defence against attacks remains obligatory and the 'ulamā' are often regarded as the representatives of the Hidden Imām, several wars between Iran and Russia in the 19th century have been called *jihād*.
[There are many *hadīth* that sum up] the aims of fighting unbelievers: conversion or submission. In the latter case, the enemies were entitled to keep their religion and practice it, against payment of a poll-tax (*jizya*) (cf. Q9. *at-Tawba*, the Repentance, 29).

Whenever the caliph deems it in the interest of the umma, he may conclude a truce with the enemy, just as the Prophet did with the Meccans at al-Hudaybiyya. According to some law schools a truce must be concluded for a specified period of time, no longer than ten years. Others hold that this not necessary, if the caliph stipulates that he may resume war whenever he wishes to do so. The idea behind it is that the notion of *jihād* must not fall into oblivion.

The most important function of the doctrine of *jihād* is that it mobilizes and motivates Muslims to take part in wars against unbelievers, as it is considered to be the fulfillment of a religious duty. This motivation is strongly fed by the idea that those who are killed on the battlefield, valled martyrs (*shahīd*, plur. *shuhadā'*), will go directly to Paradise. At the occasion of wars fought against unbelievers, religious texts would circulate, replete with Koranic verses and *hadīths* extolling the merits of fighting a *jihād* and vividly describing the reward waiting in the hereafter for those slain during the fighting.[28]

David Cook, *Understanding Jihād*, 2005

David Cook is associate professor of religious studies at Rice University, in Houstson, Texas, and the author of *Studies in Muslim Apocalyptic* (Darwin Press, 2003), *Contemporary Muslim Apocalyptic Literature* (Syracuse University Press, 2005), *Understanding Jihād* (University of California Press, 2005), *Martyrdom in Islam* (Cambridge University Press, 2007), and *Understanding and Addressing Suicide Attacks*, with Olivia Allison (Praeger Press, 2007):

> "Warfare with spiritual significance" is the primary and root meaning of the term as it has been defined by classical Muslim jurists and legal scholars and as it was practiced by Muslims during the premodern period. This meaning is sustained in the standard definition given in the new [2nd] edition of the *Encylopaedia of Islam*.[29]

---

28 Rudolph Peters, *Jihād in Classical and Modern Islam* (Princeton, NJ: Markus Wiener Publishers, 1996), 1–5.
29 David Cook, *Understanding Jihād* (Berkeley: University of California Press, 2005), 2.

CHAPTER 6
JIHĀD: THEORY AND PRACTICE

BY ALL ACCOUNTS, in the early centuries of Islam *jihād* was interpreted in its aggressive, military sense. The Koran encourages the view that the Muslims had God on their side in their war on unbelievers, and were thus assured victory, a fact that played its part in the success of the early Muslim conquests (as a review of primary historical sources in chapter 8 will reveal). The principles adumbrated in the Koran were supplemented by a vast number of reports gathered in great *hadīth* collections, which in turn were used to construct elaborate legal codes of conduct covering all aspects of *jihād*: conquests, prisoners, treatises, truce, etc. The conquests were regarded to be a "confirmatory miracle for Islam,"[1] Cook points out, and "because of the close identification between this miraculous event and the *jihād* ideology that enabled it come about, *jihād* has remained of crucial importance in Islamic culture...and can be brought to the fore...at any time."[2] Familiarity with the theory and practice of *jihād*, therefore, is also essential to understanding the philosophy and practices of modern Islamic fundamentalists groups, who are strictly following in history's footsteps.

While the root of *jihād* means "to strive or exert oneself," in its primary sense it came to mean "warfare with spiritual significance," that is, fighting in a military sense, or armed combat, for the sake of God (*fī sabīl allāh*). The aim of *jihād* is the expansion of Islam, and it is an incumbent religious duty of all able-bodied Muslim males. The goal is to submit the world to Islam, and spread a gospel of unmitigated, uncom-

---

1 Ibid., 30.
2 Ibid., 30-31.

promising monotheism spelled out in the Koran. By its nature *jihād* is a permanent state, and can only fall into abeyance when all of mankind submits to Islam—when the last *Dar al-Harb*, a country that has not yet been subdued by Islam, becomes *Dar al-Islam*, a territory where the edicts of Islam are fully promulgated—where the Shari'a reigns supreme.

Jihād in the Koran

Sura Q9 is the most important chapter of the Koran for the development of the notion of *jihād*. Q9. *at-Tawba*, the Repentance, 111 tells us:

> Allāh has bought from the believers their lives and their wealth in return for Paradise; they fight in the way of Allāh, kill and get killed [*yuqātilūna fī sabīli llāhi fa-yaqtulūna wa-yuqtalūna*]. That is a true promise from Him in the Torah, the Gospel, and the Qur'ān; and who fulfills His promise better than Allāh? Rejoice, then, at the bargain you have made with Him; for that is the great triumph.

This, as David Cook shows, is a contract between God and Muslims: Muslims give their lives to Allah in return for a promise of a place in Paradise.[3] The main subject of Sura Q9. *at-Tawba*, the Repentance is

> the revocation of the immunity granted by God and Muhammad to those tribes that had not converted to Islam prior to this revelation. After the lifting of the immunity, the Muslims must fight the unbelievers: Q9 at-Tawba, the Repentance 5: "Then, when the sacred months are over, kill the idolaters wherever you find them, take them [captive], besiege them, and lie in wait for them at every point of observation [*fa-qtulū l-mušrikīna haytu wagadtumūhum wa-huḍūhum wa-hsurūhum wa-qʻudū lahum kulla marṣadin*]. If they repent afterwards, perform the prayer and pay alms, then release them. Allāh is truly All-Forgiving, Merciful."[4]

Q9:5, known as the "Verse of the Sword," abrogates all other verses on war and peace[5] and sets the tone of hostility toward and domi-

---

3 Cook, *Understanding Jihād*, 9.
4 Ibid., 10.
5 Ibid.

nance over Jews and Christians that runs throughout the Koran, i.e., Q9. *at-Tawba*, the Repentance, 29:

> Fight [*qātilū*] those among the People of the Book [Jews and Christians] who do not believe in God and the Last Day, do not forbid what God and His Apostle have forbidden, and do not profess the true religion [Islam] until they pay the poll-tax out of hand and submissively.

The purpose of *jihād* is to conquer and dominate non-Muslims, hence the importance of this sura, but the entire Koran contains an elaborate "religious justification for waging war against Islam's enemies," and adresses "questions concerning prisoners, the fate and rewards of martyrs, disunity and doubt within the Muslim ranks, and…other issues as well. The Qur'ān even reveals that many Muslims were reluctant to fight [Q2. *al-Baqara*, the Cow, 216; Q9 *at-Tawba*, the Repentance, 38]. The text provides the basis for the doctrine of *jihād* that would result in the great Muslim conquests of the seventh and eighth centuries."[6] The religious nature of *jihād*—"the unifying force of Islam"[7]—must be acknowledged if we are to understand the Muslim conquests, the success of which served, for Muslims, as a sign that God was on their side and as a resounding endorsement of Islam.

Jihād is central to Islam and almost became its sixth pillar, alongside the Five Pillars, or foundations, of Islam, or the Five Foundations of Practice: (1) *Shahāda*, bearing witness that "There is no god but God and Muhammad is the Messenger of God"; (2) *Salat*, the observance of of the five stated periods of prayer; (3) *Zakat*, giving the legal alms once a year; (4) *Sawm*, fasting during the month of Ramadan; (5) *Hajj*, the pilgrimage to Mecca, once in a lifetime. *Jihād* is often seen as the sixth pillar by many Muslims; for the Khārijites, an early seventh-century Islamic sect, it is indeed the sixth pillar.[8] The conquests of holy war were essential in the growth of Islam, from Morocco in the West to India in the East, and all the lands in between, all of which remain Muslim to this day.[9] We shall return to the Muslim conquests in chapter 8.

---

6 Ibid., 11.

7 Ibid.

8 Canadian scholar Andrew Rippin defines *jihād* as, "'striving for the faith', or 'holy war', sometimes seen as a 'sixth pillar'" in the glossary to Muslims: *Their Religious Beliefs and Practices*, 2nd ed. (London: Routledge, 2001), 324.

9 Ibid., 13.

Early Muslim Scholars on *Jihād*

Before examining the six canonical *hadīth* collections that are rich in details concerning the proper waging of *jihād*, let's consider the work of some of the earlier scholars not often discussed in the contemporary literature on *jihād*.

David Cook gives an excellent account of the earliest writers, beginning with 'Abd Allāh Ibn al-Mubārak (d. 797), who was both an ascetic and *jihādist*. He is said to have "made the Pilgrimage and engaged in *jihād* in alternate years."[10] He is alleged to have collected over 20,000 traditions,[11] but also wrote the *Kitāb al-Jihād*, "which documents the evolution of the Muslim conception of warfare during the period of the conquests after Muhammad's death"[12] and contains 262 traditions on *jihād*.[13] Ibn al-Mubārak brings out the spiritual nature of warfare more clearly than the Koran:

> The slain [in *jihād*] are three [types of] men: a believer, who struggles with himself and his possessions in the path of God, such that when he meets the enemy [in battle], he fights them until he is killed. This martyr [*shahid*] is tested, [and is] in the camp of God under His throne; the prophets do not exceed him [in merit] except by the level of prophecy. [Then] a believer, committing offenses and sins against himself, who struggles with himself and his possessions in the path of God, such that when meets the enemy [in battle] he fights until he is killed. This cleansing wipes away his offenses and his sins— behold the sword wipes [away] sins!—and he will be let into heaven from whatever gate he wishes.[14]

Cook is perhaps the first major contemporary scholar to bring out the redemptive character of waging *jihād*. The tradition of Ibn al-Mubārak cited above

> presents *jihād* as spiritualized warfare in the same spirit as

---

10 *Encyclopaedia of Islam*, vol. 3, "H–Iram," ed. B. Lewis et al., 2nd ed. (Leiden: Brill, 1971), s.v. "Ibn al-Mubarak."

11 Ibid.

12 Cook, *Understanding Jihād*, 14.

13 Ibid., 15.

14 Ibid., 14. Cook's reference, 214n9: "Ibn al-Mubarak, *Kitāb al-Jihād* (Beirut: Dār al-Nūr, 1971), 30–31, no. 7."

Qur'an 9 at-Tawba, the Repentance 111. Of the three figures mentioned—the True Believer, the Sinning but Repentant Believer, and the Hypocritical Believer—the second is clearly the most interesting. This Sinning but Repentant Believer seeks to expiate his sins on the field of battle. According to the tradition, the sword, together with the pure intention of the fighter, wipes away the believer's sins. Thus, there is a redemptive aspect to *jihād* that is crucial to understanding its development.[15]

For Ibn al-Mubārak, "Being killed in the path of Allāh washes away impurity; killing is two things: atonement and rank [in heaven]."[16] Ibn al-Mubārak also encourages fighters to wear white so that the blood of their sacrifice is apparent.[17]

Distinguishing several types of fighters, Ibn al-Mubārak is able to bring out the notion of atonement inherent in fighting in the cause of Allah:

> There is a man who fights in the path of Allāh and does not want to kill or be killed, but is struck by an arrow. The first drop of blood from him is atonement for every sin he has committed; for every drop he sheds he gains levels in paradise. The second type of man is one who fights desiring to kill but not to be killed, and is struck by an arrow. The first drop of blood from him is atonement for every sin; for every drop he sheds he gains a level in paradise until he bumps Abraham's knee [on the top level]. The third type of man is one who fights in the path of Allāh desiring to kill and be killed, and is struck by an arrow. The first drop of blood from him is atonement for every sin; he will come to the Day of Resurrection with a drawn sword, [able] to intercede.[18]

Other precanonical collections include the *Kitāb al-Muwatta'* of Mālik b. Anas (d. 796),[19] the imam of the school of law the Mālikīs

---

15 Cook, *Understanding Jihād*, 15.
16 Ibid. Cook is quoting Ibn Al-Mubārak, *Kitāb al-Jihād*, 30, no. 6. Cf. Riley-Smith, *The Crusades*.
17 Cook, *Understanding Jihād*, 15, quoting Ibn al-Mubarak, *Kitāb al-Jihād*, 112, no.137.
18 Ibid., quoing Ibn al-Mubarak, *Kitāb al-Jihād*, 104–5, no. 125.
19 The date of his death, according to the *Encyclopaedia of Islam*, vol. 6, "Mahk-Mid,"

named after him. The *Kitāb al-Muwatta'* is considered the earliest surviving Muslim lawbook, hence its importance to our knowledge of *jihād* in the early days of Islam. Sometimes included in the canonical collection in place of Ibn Majā's *Sunan*, the *Kitāb al-Muwatta'* contains 1720 *hadīth*, and the chapter on *jihād* encourages fighting in the cause of God, discusses martyrs, and examines the spiritual merit of fighting:

> Hadīth 950: The Apostle of Allāh [pbuh] declared, "The Lord stands security for one who fights in His cause and does not start from his house but with the intention of *jihād*, knowing His word to be true that he will be admitted to Heaven or brought back to his house, from where he had issued with reward and booty."[20]
>
> Hadīth 974: The Apostle of Allāh [pbuh] said: "By the Lord Who holds my life, I desired to fight in the cause of the Lord and be killed, to be rendered back to life only to be killed again, again to be rendered back to life and killed."[21]
>
> Hadīth 980: The Apostle of Allāh [pbuh] said, "Undoubtedly, there is nothing better than to be killed in the cause of the Lord."[22]

Al-Awzā'ī (d. 774) also discusses *jihād* in his *Sunan*, but tends to link it to the protection of Islam's frontiers. Ibn Abī Shayba (d. 849), a teacher of Ibn Majā (d. 887 or 889), uses much of the same material as Ibn al-Mubārak, emphasizing "descriptions of heavenly pleasures, conquest and victory, and forgiveness of sins for the martyr."[23] 'Abd al-Razzāq (d. 826), who was the leading scholar of the Yemen, gave much space to division of spoils.

---

ed. C.E. Bosworth, E. Van Donzel, and Ch. Pellat, 2nd ed. (Leiden: Brill, 1991), s.v. "Mālik b. Anas."

20 Mālik b. Anas, Muwatta', *Kitāb al-Jihād*, trans. Muhammad Rahimuddin (New Delhi: Kitab Bhavan, 2003), 198.

21 Ibid., 206.

22 Ibid., 208.

23 Cook, *Understanding Jihād*, 16.

Hadīth on Jihād
Six Canonical Collections

Numerous collections of traditions (*hadīth*) have been prepared by different scholars. Six of these works have obtained canonical standing among Muslims, and recognized by the orthodox Muslim world as authoritative.

Next we come to the six canonical collections (*Kutub al-Sittah* or *Al-Sihāh al-Sittah*) of Sunni Islam, all of which were written in eastern Iran and are extremely important for the development of Islamic practice:

Sahīh al-Bukhārī:	Imām Bukhārī (d. 870)	7397 *hadīth*
Sahīh Muslim:	Muslim ibn al-Hajjāj (d. 875)	9200 *hadīth*
Sunan Ibn Māja:	Ibn Majā (d. 887 or 889)	4000 *hadīth*
Sunan Abu Dāwūd:	Abu Dāwūd (d. 889)	4800 *hadīth*
Jāmi'at-Tirmidhī:	Al-Tirmidhī (d. 892)	3956 *hadīth*
Sunan al-Sughra:	Al-Nasā'ī (d. 915)	5270 *hadīth*

(*Sahīh* means "authentic," "genuine," "valid." *Sunan* is the plural of *sunna*.)

All six hadīth compilations devote considerable space to discussing *jihād* in all its aspects, military and spiritual, and with considerably more detail than found in the Koran.

Bukhārī

Bukhārī's collection of *hadīth* known as *Sahīh*, "The Authentic," is venerated by the Sunnis in a manner second only to the Koran.[24] Bukhārī begins with a chapter on Revelation, followed by a chapter on what constitutes the Islamic faith—the articles of belief, or *kitāb al-Īmān*. Jihād is clearly an article of faith:

> Bāb (chapter) 26. *Al-Jihād* is a part of faith. Hadīth 36: Narrated Abū Hurayra, "The Prophet [pbuh] said, 'Allāh assigns for a person who participates in (holy battles) in Allāh's Cause and nothing causes him to do so except belief in Allāh and in

---

24 *Encyclopaedia of Islam*, vol. 1, "A–B," ed. H.A.R. Gibb et al., 2nd ed. (Leiden: Brill, 1960), s.v., "al- Bukhārī," 1297a: "In time, although criticisms have been made on matters of detail, it [Bukhārī's Sahīh] was accepted by most Sunnis as the most important book after the Kur'ān."

His Messengers, that he will be recompensed by Allāh either with a reward, or booty (if he survives) or will be admitted to Paradise (if he is killed in the battle as a martyr)'. The Prophet [pbuh] added: 'Had I not found it difficult for my followers, then I would not remain behind any Sariya (an army unit) going for *Jihād* and I would have loved to be martyred in Allāh's Cause [*fī sabīl allāh*] and then made alive, and then martyred and then made alive, and then again martyred in His Cause.'"[25] (Parenthetical comments were added by Muhammad Muhsin Khan, the translator; bracketed comments are mine.)

Khan's 1997 translation boasts a seal of approval from several Saudi religious authorities such as Abdul Aziz bin Abdullah bin Baz, the Grand Mufti of Saudi Arabia from 1993 until his death in 1999. Described as the "figurehead for institutional Wahhabism" whose "immense religious erudition and his reputation for intransigence" accounted for his prestige in Saudi Arabia, Ibn Baz "could reinforce the Saud family's policies through his influence with the masses of believers."[26] Thus one presumes that Ibn Baz, and the Saudi government, also endorsed Khan's unequivocal, uncompromising footnote to *hadīth* 36:

Al-Jihād (Holy Fighting) in Allāh's Cause (with full force of numbers and weaponry) is given the utmost importance in Islam and is one of its pillars (on which it stands). By *Jihād* Islam is established. Allāh's Word is made superior. (His Word—*Lā ilāha illalāh*— none has the right to be worshipped but Allāh), and His Religion Islam is propagated. By abandoning *Jihād* (may Allāh protect us from that) Islam is destroyed and the Muslims fall into an inferior position; their honor is lost, their lands are stolen, their rule and authority vanishes. *Jihād* is an obligatory duty in Islam on every Muslim, and he who tries to escape from this duty, does not in his innermost heart wish to fulfil this duty, dies with

---

[25] Bukhārī, *Sahīh, Kitāb al-Īmān, The Authentic Hadīth: Book of Belief (Faith)*, trans. Muhammad Muhsin Khan, *hadīth* 36 (Riyadh, Saudi Arabia: Darussalam, 1997), 1:72–74.

[26] Gilles Kepel, *The War for Muslim Minds: Islam and the West* (Cambridge, MA: Belknap Press, 2006), 186.

one of the qualities of a hypocrite.[27] (Parenthetical comments added by Khan.)

In his three hundred or so *hadīth* on *jihād*, Bukhārī cites the Koran numerous times, beginning the chapter with Q9. *at-Tawba*, the Repentance, 111.[28] This is quoted several times, which is understandable, given its centrality in the development of the religious principle of *jihād*. Here are a few examples:

> Q9. *at-Tawba*, the Repentance, 52: "Say: 'Are you awaiting for us (any fate) other than one of two good things [martyrdom or victory].'"

> Q9. at-Tawba, the Repentance, 38: "O you who believe! What is the matter with you, that when you are asked to go forth in the cause of God [fī sabīli llāhi] [i.e. *jihād*], you cling heavily to the earth? Do you prefer the life of this world to the Hereafter ['āhirati // 'akhirati]? But little is the comfort of this life, as compared with the Hereafter."

Other verses cited include:

> Q33. *al-'Ahzāb*, Confederates, 23: "Of the believers are men who are true to that which they covenanted with Allāh. Some of them have paid their vow by death [in battle, and hence have been martyred], and some of them still are witing; they have not altered in the least."

> Q3. *'āl 'Imrān*, the Family of Imran, 169–71: "Think not of those who are slain in God's way [*qutilū fī sabīli llāhi*]as dead. Nay, they live, finding sustenance in the presence of their Lord. They rejoice in the bounty provided by God. And with regard to those left behind, who have not yet joinedd them [in their bliss], the [martyrs] glory in the fact that on them is

---

27 Bukhārī, *Authentic Hadīth: Book of Belief*, hadīth 36, 1:72.
28 Muhammad Muhsin Khan's translation of Bukhārī that is available online (http://www.theonlyquran.com/hadith/Sahih-Bukhari/?chapter=52&pagesize=0) omits the quote from 9:111. The nine-volume book version, however, includes the quote: "Bukhārī, *Sahīh, Kitāb al-jihād wa –l siyar*, Khan, trans., *Authentic Hadīth: Book of Jihād and Campaigns*, 4:44, hadīth 2787."

no fear, nor have they [cause to] grieve."

Q8. *al-'anfāl*, the Spoils of War, 65: "O Apostle! Urge the believers to fight [*yā- 'ayyuhā n-nabiyyu harridi l-mu'minīna 'alā l-qitāli*]."

More on Jihād from the Canon

Bukhārī and the other canonical traditionists paint a vivid picture of battles, and of the rewards for the martyrs killed in the cause of Allah. Bukhārī *hadīth* 2810 gives the reason for *jihād*, to spread the true word of God, to spread Islam: "A man came to the Prophet (pbuh) and asked, 'A man fights for war booty; another fights for fame and a third fights for showing off; which of them is in Allāh's Cause?' The Prophet (pbuh) said, 'He who fights that Allāh's word be superior, is in Allāh's Cause.'"[29] Thus *jihād* has spiritual significance.

Bukhārī *hadīth* 2946[30] makes it clear that Muhammad has been ordered to fight the people until they admit that there is no God but Allah. Martyrdom is frequently praised, and in Bukhārī *hadīth* 2817 the Prophet is quoted as saying, "Nobody who enters Paradise likes to return to the world even if he got everything on earth, except a martyr who wishes to return to the world so that he may be martyred ten times because of the honor and dignity he receives (from Allāh)."[31]

Anyone shunning the duty to fight unbelievers is accused of hypocrisy and cowardice, and not promised Paradise (Abū Dāwūd, *Sunan*).[32] Other subjects examined include the treatment of prisoners, whether and how women can engage in *jihād*, the proper care of horses, how to use a sword, and arrows, and much more. One point remains clear, Muslims are obligated to fight until all people adopt Islam: "Anas reported the Apostle of Allāh (pbuh) as saying: 'I am commanded to fight men till they testify that there is no god but Allāh, and that Muhammad is His servant and His Apostle, face our *qiblah*, eat what we slaughter, and pray like us.'"[33]

The *hadīth* emphasize what the Koran clearly states concerning the Jews, that fighting the Jews—who must be hunted down and killed since

---

29 Bukhārī, *Sahīh, Kitāb al-jihād wa –l siyar*, Khan, trans., *Authentic Hadīth: Book of Jihād and Campaigns*, 4:59, hadīth 2810
30 Ibid., 4:126, hadīth 2946
31 Ibid., 4:63, hadīth 2817
32 Abū Dāwūd, *Sunan, Kitāb al-Jihād, ahādīth* 2496 and 2497, 2:693.
33 Ibid., *hadīth* 2635, 2:729.

they will hide behind some rocks—is a part of *jihād*. In fact, the Day of Judgement will not arrive until the Muslims fight against the Jews (Bukhārī, *ahadīth* 2925, 2926).

The various *hadīth* collections devote much space to psychological fear as an important component of *jihād*, as indicated in the Koran, Q3.' *āl 'Imrān*, the Family of Imran, 151: "We will cast terror into the hearts of the unbelievers on account of their associating with Allāh [*bi-mā 'ašrakū bi-llāhi*] that for which He sent down no authority."[34] As Cook explains, "The Prophet Muhammad further amplified this idea by noting that God had helped him with a fear (*ru'b* or *mahaba*) that He had sent before the Muslim armies to a distance of a month's journey."[35] According to this idea, all who lived at this distance from the Muslims would feel fear and be defeated even before meeting the Muslims in battle.[36]

The psychological preparation for victory or defeat is another theme of the *hadīth* literature, which contains many references to poetry,[37] flags, and slogans intended to aid the fighters.[38] The most popular slogan—*Allāhu akbar!* ("God is greater!")—is uttered before Muslims advance into battle.[39]

Finally, Cook notes "how closely interrelated Islam and fighting were when the *hadīth* on *hadīth* allow mosques to be put to use as prisons for enemy captives or as storehouses for weapons."[40] Thus, we find in the *Sahīh* of Muslim ibn al-Hajjāj: "It has been narrated on the authority of Abu Hurayra who said: 'The Messenger of Allāh [pbuh] sent some horsemen to Najd. They captured a man. He was from the tribe of Banu Hanifa and was called Thumama b. Uthal. He was the chief of the people of Yamama. People bound him with one of the pillars of the mosque.'"[41]

---

34 Cook, *Understanding Jihād*, 17.

35 Cook's footnote: "E.g. al-Nasa'i, *Sunan* (Beirut, n.d.), VI, pp.3–4; and the examples cited in my 'Muslim Apocalyptic and *Jihād*,' *Jerusalem Studies in Arabic and Islam* 20 (1996), pp. 99–100, n. 120."

36 Cook's footnote: "Al-Bukhari, *Sahih*, IV, pp. 15–16 (nos. 2977–78)."

37 Cook's footnote: "Note how much poetry is cited concerning *jihād* in Muslim, Sahih, V, pp. 168, 186–89, 191–92, and 194–95."

38 Cook's footnote: "Khalil 'Athamina, 'The Black Banners and the Socio-Political Significance of Flags and Banners,' *Arabica* 36, no. 3 (November 1989): 307–26."

39 Cook, *Understanding Jihād*, 17–18.

40 Cook's footnote: "Muslim, *Sahih*, Beirut: Dar Jil, n.d., V, p. 158 [no. 4361]; Abu Da'ud, *Sunan*, Beirut, 1998, III, pp. 31–32 [no. 2673]."

41 Muslim ibn al-Hajjāj, *Sahīh, Kitāb al-Jihād wa'l-Siyar*, trans. 'Abdul Hamid Siddiqi,

The theological construct that we know as the Shari'a, Divine Law, was distilled from the Koran and the thousands of *hadīth* contained in the six canonical collections. There was an attempt to codify the rules governing *jihād*, or warfare in the name of Islam, regulating the manner in which war should be declared, and choices to be offered to the infidels, or polytheistic enemy.[42] Certain rules and principles were already in the Koran, for example, the *khums*, the fifth portion of the spoils of war to be used for Allah, the Prophet, the near of kin, the orphan, and the wayfarer (Q8. *al-Anfāl* 41).

Some Legal Definitions: *Dar al-Islam, Dar al-Harb, Dar al-Sulh*

To regulate the military behavior of the Muslims, legal definitions were established to define where it was permissable to fight, and in what manner. These territories fall into three distinct categories.

Dar al-Islam: a territory where the edicts of Islam are fully promulgated, where the Shari'a reigns supreme. Those who do not embrace Islam are placed under certain disabilities—essentially they become second-class citizens—as long as they are not idolaters. Christians and Jews can worship God according to their own customs; existing churches and synagogues may be repaired, but no new place of worship can be erected. Idol temples, on the other hand, must be destroyed, and idolatry suppressed by force.[43]

Dar al-Harb: a country that has not yet been subdued by Islam, and therefore could be considered a territory in which it is possible, though not necessary, to fight. The second edition of the *Encyclopaedia of Islam* elaborates:

> The *Hadīth*, it is true, traces back the idea of *dār al-Harb* to the Medina period. In any event, the classical practice of so regarding territories immediately adjoining the lands of Islam, and inviting their princes to adopt this religion under pain of invasion, is reputed to date back to the Prophet who invited Caesar and Chosroes (and the Jews) to be converted (al-Bukhārī, *Kitāb al-Jihād*, §§ 147, 148, 149, 151 and *K. al-Maghāzī*, § 416; see also al-Qalqashandī, *Subh*, Cairo 1915, 6, 15). Historically, the invitation to the people of the Yama-

---

hadīth 4361 (New Delhi: Kitāb Bhavan, 2000), 3:1160; also in Abū Dāwūd, *Sunan, Kitāb al-Jihād*, hadīth 2673, 2:741.

42 Cook, *Understanding Jihād*, 19–20.

43 Hughes, *Dictionary of Islam*, s.v. "Daru 'l-Islam."

ma is the prototype (cf. al-Balādhuri, *Futūh*). This traditional concept, which ended by committing the Muslim community (or State) and its princes to war, either latent or openly declared, with all its non-Muslim neighbours (the adjective denoting the latter is *harbī* or, more especially, *ahl al-harb*) is classical and is elaborated in the most widely read law books (e.g., the definitions in the *Kitāb al-Jihād* of the *Durar al-hukkām fī sharh ghurar al-ahkām* of Mullā Khusraw, where the *ahl al-harb* are defined as those who have refused to be converted after being duly invited on the best terms, and against whom any kind of warfare is henceforth permissible in keeping with the rules of *sura* IX).[44]

Dar al-Sulh: "that area with which Muslims had some type of treaty or cease-fire."[45]
Since the ultimate aim of Islam was to bring the entire world under Islamic Law, *dar al-Islam* must always be, at least in theory, at war with *dar al-Harb*. It was Muslim duty to preach Islam by persuasion, and the caliph and the commanders in the field had to offer some limited choices, either accept Islam or pay the poll tax or face continuous warfare. As Majid Khadduri writes,

> the Islamic state was under legal obligation to enforce Islamic law and to recognize no authority even when non-Muslim communities had willingly accepted the faith of Islam without fighting. Failure by non-Muslims to accept Islam or pay the poll-tax made it incumbent on the Muslim State to declare a jihād upon the the recalcitrant individuals and communities. Thus the jihād, reflecting the normal war relations existing between Muslims and non-Muslims, was the state's instrument for transforming dār al-harb into the dār al-Islam.[46]

Islam, in effect, institutionalized "war as part of the Muslim legal system and made use of it by transforming war into a holy war designed to be ceaselessly declared against those who failed to become Muslims....

---

44 *Encyclopaedia of Islam*, vol. 2, "C–G," ed. B. Lewis, Ch. Pellat, and J. Schacht, 2nd ed. (Leiden: Brill, 1965), s.v. "*Dar al-Harb*."
45 Cook, *Understanding Jihād*, 20.
46 Khadduri, *War and Peace in Islam*, 53.

Islam abolished all war except the *jihād* and the jurist-theologians consciously formulated its law subordinating all personal considerations to *raison d'état*, based on religious sanction."[47] (Khadduri cites Ibn al-Humam (d. 1457), Egyptian Hanafi jurist and theologian.)[48]

But we now need to look at how the theory of *jihād* has actually been put into practice. As we shall see, this has had very real consquences for Muslims, and non-Muslims, since it has led to the justification of conquest of many lands, conquests carried out in the name of God, with the express purpose of extending territory where the laws of Islam are fully promulgated.

---

47 Ibid., 53-54.

48 Born in Alexandria and educated in Cairo, Ibn al-Humam lived for some time in Aleppo (Syria). Considered an expert on Sufism, he was appointed head *shaykh* of the Sufi Brotherhood or tariqa of Khanaqah Shaykhuniyyah in Cairo in 1443.

CHAPTER 7

THE GOALS OF *JIHĀD*: APOCALYPSE AND CONVERSION

THE ARABS, coming out of the Arabian peninsula, conquered vast stretches of territory in the Near East and Egypt within thirty years of the death of Muhammad 632 CE, and by the middle of the eighth century they controlled much of North Africa, Spain, Sicily, and lands bordering on India and China. What was the driving force behind the astonishing rapidity of these conquests?

Were they "sustained by a strong belief in the imminent end of the world?"[1] Though the knowledge of the future is God's alone, the Koran is written in an apocalyptic vein, and many verses speak of the Hour being near (Q42. *ash-Shūrā*, Counsel, 17; Q54. *al-Qamar*, the Moon, 1). There is little doubt that it will appear (Q22. *al-Hajj*, the Pilgrimage, 7; Q40. *Ghāfir*, the Forgiver, 54; Q45. *al-Jātiya*, the Kneeling, 32), and when it does it will appear suddenly (Q12. *Yūsuf*, Joseph, 107; Q22. *al-Hajj*, the Pilgrimage, 55; Q43. *az-Zukhruf*, Gold, 66; Q47. *Muhammad*, Muhammad, 18).

The *hadīth* literature, on the other hand, makes a much stronger "connection between the fighting process and the imminent end of the world: 'Behold! God sent me [Muhammad] with a sword, just before the Hour [of Judgment], and placed my daily sustenance beneath the shadow of my spear, and humiliation and contempt on those who oppose me.'"[2] Cook elaborates:

---

1 Cook, *Understanding Jihād*, 23.
2 Ibid., 23. Cook is quoting: Ibn al-Mubarak, *Jihād*, 89–90, no.105. Cook also makes the following references in his footnote: "compare al-Awzaʻi, *Sunan*, p. 360 (no. 1165);

The Prophet Muhammad is portrayed...as a doomsday prophet, sent just before the end of the world to warn those who would heed a warning and to punish those who would not. Here, the process of *jihād*...is one in which the hold of worldly things over the believer is diluted. Because of the impermanence of the soldier's life, and the difficulties of establishing a stable family or gathering substantial possessions, many of the ties that bind people to the world are weakened or even dissolved entirely. When this is taken into consideration, the spiritual significance of *jihād* becomes even more pronounced.[3]

Muslim fighters went into battle fervently embracing the notion of the end of the world, bolstering the courage needed to persist in *jihād*, which numerous *hadīth* and the apocalyptic literature reminded them remained a duty until the Day of Resurrection (Al-Nasā'ī, *Sunan*, vol. 4, book 28, *hadīth* 3591; Abū Dāwūd, *Sunan*).[4] *Jihād*, in general, plays an important role in Muslim apocalyptic literature. "The early Muslims' existence was largely dominated by fighting and conquest, it is hardly surprising to find that their vision of the future just before the end of the world, as well as their vision of the messianic future, was characterized by a state of continuous war."[5]

The *Mahdi*

Muslim messianic thought is dominated by the figure of "the *mahdi*, who will complete those conquests left undone by the early Muslims."[6] As discussed, another goal of *jihād* is spreading Islam via conquest, and *jihād* "created the pre-conditions for conversions, and conversion or proclamation was one of the goals of *jihād*."[7] *Jihād* will continue until conversion occurs—only the scriptuaries, the people of the book, the Jews, Christians, and Sabeans, being exempted, as long as the latter pay a tax and accept a lower social status. Idolaters, polytheists, Hindus, and

---

and Ibn Abi Shayba, *Musannaf*, IV, p. 218 (no. 19, 394); and the discussion in Ibn Rajah, al-Hukm *al-jadira bi-l-idha'a min qawl al-nabi "bu'ithu bi-l-sayf bayna yaday al-sa'a"* (Riyadh, 2002)."

3 Cook, *Understanding Jihād*, 23.
4 Abū Dāwūd, *Sunan*, *Kitāb al-Jihād*, *hadīth* 2478, 2:686–87.
5 Cook, *Understanding Jihād*, 24.
6 Ibid., 24.
7 Ibid., 25.

Buddhists are given a stark choice: convert or die.

While baser motives for *jihād*—such as booty and women— are recognized, many *hadīth* extol the spiritual goals of *jihād*. Already having cited Bukhārī on this subject, two *hadīth* from Abū Dāwūd's *Sunan* suffice:

> 2509: Narrated Mu'adh ibn Jabal: "The Prophet (pbuh) said: 'Fighting is of two kinds: The one who seeks Allāh's favour, obeys the leader, gives the property he values, treats his associates gently and avoids doing mischief, will have the reward for all the time whether he is asleep or awake; but the one who fights in a boasting spirit, for the sake of display and to gain a reputation, who disobeys the leader and does mischief in the earth will not return credit or without blame.'"

> 2510: Narrated Abu Hurayrah: "A man said: Apostle of Allāh, [what of] a man [who] wishes to take part in *jihād* in Allāh's path desiring some worldly advantage? The Prophet (pbuh) said: 'He will not have a reward.'"[8]

The Martyr

A Muslim who blows himself up fighting in the cause of Allāh is not regarded as a suicide bomber, but a *šahīd* (pl., *šuhadā'*), or martyr. In his *Dictionary of Modern Written Arabic* (1974) Hans Wehr gives this definition: "witness; martyr, one killed in battle with the infidels; one killed in action."[9] Edward William Lane in his monumental *Arabic-English Lexicon* (1872), which draws on more than seventy-five Arab lexicographers,[10] gives these definitions:

> *A martyr who is slain in the cause of God's religion;* [S, K;]

---

8 Abū Dāwūd, *Sunan, Kitāb al-Jihād, ahadīth* 2509 and 2510, 2:697.

9 Hans Wehr, *A Dictionary of Modern Written Arabic*, ed. Milton Cowan (Beirut: Librairie du Liban, 1974), s.v. "*šahīd*."

10 For the word *šahīd*, Lane draws on the following lexicographers (given here with Lane's abbreviations in brackets): Ismā'īl ibn Hammād Juwharī (d. 1007), *al-Sahāh* [S]; al-Fīrūzābādī (1329–1414), *Al-Qamus Al-Muhit*[K]; Ahmad Al-Fayumi (d. 1368), *Al-Misbah Al-Munir* [Msb]; al-Anbari, Abu Bakr Muhammad b. Al-Kasim (properly Ibn al-Anbari) (d. 940) [Iamb]; al-Mutarizzī, Burhan al-Din Abu 'l-Fath Nasir (d.1213) *al-Mughrib fi tartib al-Mu'rib* [Mgh]; al-Murtadá al-Husaynī al-Zabīdī (d. 1790), *Tāj al-'Arūs* [TA]; Madjd al-din Abu 'l-Sa'adat al-Mubarak Ibn al-Athir (d. 1210) a*l-Nihaya fi gharib al-Hadīth* [Iath].

[i.e,.] *one who is slain by unbelievers on a field of battle*; [Msb] *one who is slain fighting in the cause of God's religion* [Iath]: so called because the angels of mercy are present with him; [K] because the angels are present at the washing of his corpse, or at the removal of his soul to Paradise [Msb].[11]

The Muslim conception of martyrdom differs from the Christian or the Jewish one. Christian or Jewish martyrs are unwilling to compromise or abjure their faith, but are willing to undergo torture or even death in order to prove their faith. As Cook explains, "Martyrdom in Islam has a much more active sense: the prospective martyr is called to to seek out situations in which martyrdom might be achieved. For example, in 'Abd Allāh b. Al-Mubārak's *Kitāb al jihād*, we find Nawf al-Bikali praying: 'O, God! Make my wife a widow, make my child an orphan, and ennoble Nawf with martyrdom!'"[12] Most often in early Islam, martyrdom meant dying in battle.[13]

Other categories of martyrdom that do not involve war or violence—cases we would categorize as accidents or even illnesses—were added over the centuries, but the jurists of Islam brought the meaning back to the respect accorded to martyrs who died in battle.

The Rewards of Martyrdom
In the Koran

The celebrated delights of Paradise described in the early verses of the Koran are promised to all believers, all Muslims. In later verses, these heavenly pleasures are more "closely associated with being a martyr or dying in battle,"[14] See, for example, Q3. *al-'Imrān* 13–15:

> Already there has been for you a sign in the two armies which met—one fighting in the cause of Allāh [*fī sabīli llāhi*] and another of disbelievers….Fair in the eyes of men is the love of things they covet: Women and sons; Heaped-up hoards of

---

[11] Edward William Lane, *An Arabic-English Lexicon*, part 4 (London: Williams & Norgate, 1872; Beirut: Librairie du Liban, 1968), 1610.

[12] Cook's footnote: "Ibn al-Mubarak, *Jihād*, pp.110–11 (no.135); and see the prayers in al-Wasiti, *Fada'il al-Bayt al-Maqdis* (Jerusalem, 1979), p. 23 (no. 29); Abu Da'ud, *Sunan*, III, p. 21 (no. 2541); al-Tabarani, *Kitāb al-du'a* (Beirut, 1987), III, p.1703 (no. 2015); al-Tirmidhi, *Sunan* III, p. 103 (no. 1704)."

[13] Cook, *Understanding Jihād*, 26.

[14] Ibid., 27.

gold and silver; horses branded (for blood and excellence); and (wealth of) cattle and well-tilled land....Say: Shall I give you glad tidings of things far better than those? For the righteous are Gardens in nearness to their Lord, with rivers flowing beneath; therein is their eternal home; with companions pure (and holy); and the good pleasure of Allāh.

The virtues of the martyrs are extolled; those dying for the cause are always promised just a little more, as at Q3. *al-'Imrān* 169–70: "Think not of those who are slain in Allāh's way as dead. Nay, they live, finding their sustenance in the presence of their Lord; they rejoice in the bounty provided by Allāh. And with regard to those left behind, who have not yet joined them (in their bliss), the (Martyrs) glory in the fact that on them is no fear, nor have they (cause to) grieve."

It is with these promises in mind that the Muslim martyr goes into battle and to his death with equanimity. See Q9. *at-Tawba* 111: "Allāh hath purchased of the believers their persons and their goods; for theirs (in return) is the garden (of Paradise): they fight in His cause, and slay and are slain: a promise binding on Him in truth, through the Law, the Gospel, and the Qur'an: and who is more faithful to his covenant than Allāh? Then rejoice in the bargain which ye have concluded: that is the achievement supreme." Martyrs are promised Paradise at Q. 22 *al-Hajj* 55: "Those who leave their homes in the cause of Allāh, and are then slain or die,—On them will Allāh bestow verily a goodly Provision: Truly Allāh is He Who bestows the best provision."

In the Hadīth

In the *hadīth*, it is faith, sincerity, and intention that count in gaining one's heavenly rewards:

> It has been narrated on the authority of Anas b. Malik that the Messenger of Allāh (may peace be upon him) said: Who seeks martyrdom with sincerity shall get its reward, though he may not achieve it. —*Sahīh Muslim*, Muslim ibn al-Hajjāj, *hadīth* 4694

> Who sought martyrdom with sincerity will be ranked by Allāh among the martyrs even if he died on his bed. —*Sahīh Muslim*, Muslim ibn al-Hajjāj, *hadīth* 4695

And while the sensual aspects of Paradise are often mentioned (for the seventy-two huris, or dark-eyed damsels, see al-Tirmidhī and Ibn Mājā),[15] what matters is pleasing God and the degree of honor attained for oneself and one's earthly family. See, for example, Bukhārī, *hadīth* 2817: "The Prophet said, 'Nobody who enters Paradise likes to go back to the world even if he got everything on the Earth, except a Mujahid who wishes to return to the world so that he may be martyred ten times because of the dignity he receives (from Allāh).'" "It is said that there are one hundred ranks in Paradise [see al-Tirmidhī[16]]," Cook explains, "and that the martyr will achieve the highest among them (ranking only below prophets and other righteous men of God in the hierarchy of Paradise). One of the most important reflections of this spiritual rank is the ability of the martyr to intercede on behalf of Muslims at the Day of Judgment."[17]

This aspect of the martyr's role in spreading Islam was also noted by Edward William Lane in his *Arabic-English Lexicon*, partially cited above: "God and His angels are witnesses for him of his title to a place in Paradise: (Iamb, Mgh, K), or because he is one of those who shall be required to bear witness on the day of resurrection, (K, TA), with the Prophet, (TA)."[18] Al-Tirmidhī also spells out the special privileges the martyr enjoys:

> The Mesenger of Allāh [pbuh] said: 'There are six things with Allāh for the martyr: He is forgiven with the first flow of blood (he suffers), he is shown his place in Paradise, he is protected from punishment in the grave, secured from the greatest terror, the crown of dignity is placed upon his head—and its gems are better than the world and what is in it—he is married to seventy-two wives among the Huri-eyed

---

15 Al-Tirmidhī, Jamī', *The Virtues of Jihād*, trans. Abu Khaliyl, *hadīth* 1663 (Riyadh, Saudi Arabia: Darrusalam, 2007), 3:410. Ibn Māja, *Sunan*, trans. M. Tufail Ansari, *hadīth* 4337 (New Delhi: Kitab Bhavan, 2008), book 37, 5:547–48: "It was narrated from Abu Umamah that the Messenger of Allāh said: 'There is no one whom Allāh will admit to Paradise but Allāh will marry him to seventy-two wives, two from houris and seventy from his inheritance from the people of Hell, all of whom will have desirable vaginas and he will have a male member that never becomes flaccid (i.e., soft and limp)'" (translation slightly modified).

16 Al-Tirmidhī, Jamī', *The Description of Paradise*, trans. Abu Khaliyl, *ahadīth* 2529, 2530, 2531 (Riyadh, Saudi Arabia: Darrusalam, 2007), 4:518–520.

17 Cook, *Understanding Jihād*, 29.

18 Lane, *Arabic-English Lexicon*, part 4, 1610.

of Paradise, and he may intercede for seventy of his close relatives.[19]

The Law Schools on *Jihād*

A great number of law schools existed in the second and third centuries of the Islamic era (the eighth and ninth of the Christian era),[20] but "at this stage no sharp distinction was yet recognized between them. These schools varied from relatively liberal Hanafites and Muʿtazilite jurists—permitting large measures of independent reasoning (*ijtihād*)—to the conservative Zahirite and Hanbalite jurists, who not only restricted ijtihad, but also insisted on a literal interpretation of the Qurʾān and *hadīth*."[21]

By the fourth century of the Islamic era, only four schools of law (madhahib, sing. madhab)—Hanafī, Mālikī, Shāfʿī, and Hanbalī—were recognized (considered orthodox), with the Hanbalīs emerging as the most rigid and intolerant, rejecting *ijtihad* and seeking answers to problems in *hadīth*. Ibn Taymiyya (d. 1328) was a Hanbalī jurist whose teachings, as will be discussed at length, were adopted by ʿAbd al-Wahhāb in the eighteenth century.

As Khadduri explains, the law books of the four schools "became the standard text-books and any attempt to depart from them was denounced as innovation (*bidʿa*). As a result *ijtihād* was gradually abandoned in favor of *taqlīd* (literally, 'imitation') or submission to the canons of the four schools, and the door of *ijtihād* was shut."[22]

Al-Shāfiʿī (d. 820), founder of the Shāfʿī school of law, and considered a founder of the Science of Islamic Jurisprudence or the science of *usūl al-fiqh* (roots or sources of the law), encourages the waging of *jihād*, and then "addresses the payment of the jizya by non-Muslims (Jews, Christians, Sabeans, and others) and the manner in which this tax should be levied and collected....Sections on truces, cease-fires, dealing with rebels, safe-conducts, and disposition of spoils all follow, together with sections describing relations with captured women. All of these

---

19 Al-Tirmidhī, Jamīʿ, *Virtues of Jihād*, hadīth 1663, 3:410.
20 The Islamic era began in 622 CE. Islamic Law developed over a period of years and by the eighth and ninth century of the Christian era, that is, the second and third century of the Islamic era, there were many law schools that interpreted the Koran and *hadīth* and came to rulings about what constituiuted Islamic practice, what was obligatory, what was optional, etc.
21 Khadduri, *War and Peace in Islam*, 35–36.
22 Ibid., 36–37.

discussions presuppose a victorious polity and reflect the confidence of the early Muslims that God would give them victory."[23]

Like Bukhārī, Al-Shāfiʿī in his *Kitāb al-Risāla fī Uṣūl al-Fiqh*, insists that God has imposed the duty of *jihād* on all Muslims, and then quotes extensively from the Koran, particularly sura 9.[24] Al-Shāfiʿī also cites a *hadīth* from Abū Dāwūd's *Sunan* in which Muhammad says, "I shall continue to fight the unbelievers until they say: 'There is no god but God,' if they make this pronouncement they shall be secured their blood and property, unless taken for its price, and their reward shall be given by God.'"[25] Al-Shāfiʿī then summarizes that

> These communications mean that the *jihād*, and the rising up in arms in particular, is obligatory for all-bodied [believers], exempting no one, just as prayer, pilgrimage and [payment] of alms are performed, and no person is permitted to perform the duty for another, since performance by one will not fulfill the duty for another. They may also mean that the duty of [*jihād*] is a collective (*kifāya*) duty different from that of prayer: Those who perform it in the war against polytheists will fulfil the duty and receive the supererogatory merit, thereby preventing those who stayed behind from falling into error.[26]

Hanafī jurist al-Sarakhsī, who lived and worked in Transoxiana in the eleventh century, wrote a thirty-volume legal compendium known as *Kitāb al-Mabsūṭ*, a highly influential work in the genre of *furūʿ*, defined by Hans Wehr as "applied *fiqh*, applied ethics, consisting in the systematic elaboration of canonical law in Islam."[27] As Norman Calder (1950–1998), former senior lecturer in Arabic at the University of Manchester, writes, "[Al-Sarakhsī's] organisation, comprehensive coverage, exploration of *ikhtilāf* [points of dispute], and manipulation of herme-

---

23 Cook, *Understanding Jihād*, 21.
24 Al-Shāfiʿī, *Risāla: Treatise on the Foundations of Islamic Jurisprudence*, trans. Majid Khadduri (Baltimore: The Johns Hopkins University Press, 1961; Cambridge: The Islamic Texts Society, 1987), 82–86. Al-Shāfiʿī quotes, for example, Q9.112, Q9.36, Q9.5, Q9.29, Q9.39–39, Q9.41, Q9.123, but also sura Q4.97 and Q4.88.
25 Abū Dāwūd, *Sunan* (Cairo, 1935), 3:44. Abū Dāwūd, *Sunan*, *hadīth* 2634 (Kitab Bhavan, 1997), 2:729.
26 Al-Shāfiʿī, *Risāla*, 84.
27 Wehr, *Dictionary of Modern Written Arabic*, s.v. "*furūʿ*."

neutical argument, all conduce to make this work a remarkable achievement of juristic literature. It remained a point of reference for the developing *Hanafī furuʿ* tradition till the 19th century."[28]

Calder discusses "the significance of *jihād*, the reasons behind it," in great detail, before considering the relative legal validity of tactics, including the procedure for surrender, how to carry out a siege, and handling captives—who may be killed, who enslaved. He describes many of Muhammad's battles, extracting basic legal principles from each one. In sum, al-Sarakhsi completes what al-Shāfiʿī began and covers the spectrum of waging *jihād* in law. "From this point forward, although individual points continued to be debated, the Muslim method of warfare was set."[29]

A number of legal works works by jurists such as al-Hakim al-Tirmidhī (d. 930) and al-Haythami (d. 1565) also discussed the various sins associated with fighting, further emphasizing *jihād's* "crucial importance for Muslims."[30]

The Spiritual Nature of *Jihād*

The spiritual nature of *jihād* is also underlined by the Koran and in several *hadīths* that emphasize that *jihād* carried out for booty or worldly honors is neither acceptable nor valid.

First, that the phrase "*fī sabīl allāh*," typically translated as "in God's way" (or, perhaps better, as "God's Cause" or "for the sake of God"), appears frequently in the Koran—2:154, 2:190, 2:244, 2:246, 2:261, 3:13, 3:157, 3:167, 4:74, 4:76, etc.)—is significant. As the Koran tells us at Q.61. *As-Saff*, The Row, 4, "Verily, Allāh loves those who fight in His Cause in rows as if they were a solid structure."

Another Koranic verse explains that because the Muslims were fighting in God's Cause against the unbelievers, God helped them win the battle of Badr (Q3. *ʾāl ʿImrān*, the Family of Imran, 13):

> Already there has been for you a sign in the two armies which met—one fighting in the cause of Allah and another of disbelievers. They saw them [to be] twice their [own] number by [their] eyesight. But Allah supports with His victory whom He wills. Indeed, in that is a lesson for those of vision.

---

28 *Encyclopaedia of Islam*, vol. 9, "San-Sze," ed. C.E. Bosworth et al., 2nd ed. (Leiden: Brill, 1997), s.v. "*al-Sarakhsī*."

29 Cook, *Understanding Jihād*, 22.

30 Ibid.

Bukhārī's hadīth 2810 gives an unequivocal reason for *jihād*: "Narrated Abū Mūsa: A man came to the Prophet [pbuh] and asked, 'A man fights for war booty; another fights for fame and a third fights for showing off; which of them is in Allah's Cause?' The Prophet [pbuh] said, 'He who fights that Allah's word [i.e., Allah's religion of Islamic Monotheism] be superior, is in Allah's Cause."[31] Even more decisive is Bukhārī's *hadīth* 2946: "Narrated Abū Hurayrah, Allah's Messenger [pbuh] said, 'I have been ordered (by Allah) to fight ['*uqātila*] against the people till they say *lā ilāha illallāh* (none has the right to be worshipped but Allah), and whoever said *lā ilāha illallāh*, he saved his life and property except for Islamic law, and his accounts will be with Allah.'"[32]

Modern scholars also point out the spiritual nature of *jihād* in opposition to those historians who narrow the causes of *jihād* and the early conquests to socioeconomic conditions. Khadduri, for instance, writes

> The *Jihād* was not a casual phenomenon of violence; it was rather a product of complex factors while Islam worked out its jural-doctrinal character. Some writers have emphasized the economic changes within Arabia which produced dissatisfaction and unrest and inevitably led Arabs to seek more fertile lands outside Arabia. Yet this theory—plausible as it is in explaining the outburst of the Arabs from wihin their peninsula—is not enough to interpret the character of a war permanently declared against the unbelievers even after the Muslims had established themselves outside Arabia. There were other factors which created in the minds of the Muslims a politico-religious mission and conditioned their attitude as a conquering nation.[33]

Cook also observes that "[t]he Prophet Muhammad is portrayed... as a doomsday prophet, sent just before the end of the world to warn those who would heed a warning and to punish those who would not. Here, the process of *jihād*...is one in which the hold of wordly things

---

31 Bukhārī, *Authentic Hadīth: Book of Jihād and Campaigns*, *hadīth* 2810, 4:59. See also al-Hajjāj, *Kitāb al-Imāra*, *hadīth* 4684, 3:1269.

32 Bukhārī, *Authentic Hadīth: Book of Jihād and Campaigns*, *hadīth* 2946, 4:126. See also Bukhārī, *Authentic Hadīth: Book of Belief*, *hadīth* 25, 1:66; and Bukhārī, *Sahīh, Kitāb al-Zakāt*, trans. Muhammad Muhsin, *hadīth* 1399 (Riyadh, Saudi Arabia: Darussalam Publishers, 1997), 2:279.

33 Khadduri, *War and Peace in Islam*, 63.

over the believer is diluted. Because of the impermanence of the soldier's life, and the difficulties of establishing a stable family or gathering substantial possessions, many of the ties that bind people to this world are weakened or even dissolved entirely. When this taken into consideration, the spiritual significance of *jihād* becomes even more pronounced."[34]

We shall return to this discussion of the spiritual nature of the early Muslim conquests.

Greater *Jihād* and Lesser *Jihād*
Non-Canonical Distinction

Modern apologists of Islam tend to emphasize what is actually a nonclassical definition of *jihād*, known as the "greater inner jihād" (*jihād al-akbar*), which is seen as a purely spiritual enterprise, the struggle to overcome one's baser self. Here the original meaning of *jihād* as "struggle" or "striving" is constantly evoked. *Jihād* in the military sense is the "lesser outer *jihād*" (*al-jihād al-asghar*).

There is some justification for this interpretation in the Koran at Q.22 *al-Hajj* 78:

> And strive [*wa-jāhidū*] for Allāh with the striving due to Him [*haqqa jihādihī*]. He has chosen you and has not placed upon you in the religion any difficulty. [It is] the religion of your father, Abraham. Allāh named you "Muslims" before [in former scriptures] and in this [revelation] that the Messenger may be a witness over you and you may be witnesses over the people. So establish prayer and give zakah give alms and hold fast to Allāh. He is your protector; and excellent is the protector, and excellent is the helper.

But as Cook points out, "however much weight is put on this verse, the Qur'an cannot support a reading that would make fighters and noncombatants spiritual equals."[35] Sura 4 *al-Nisā'* verse 95 makes clear there is no equivalence:

> Not equal are those believers remaining [at home]—other than the disabled—and those who fight [*mujāhidūna*] in the cause of Allāh [*fī sabīli llāhi*] with their wealth and their lives.

---

34 Cook, *Understanding Jihād*, 23.
35 Ibid., 32-33.

The Goals of Jihād: Apocalypse and Conversion ∞ 139

Allāh has preferred those who fight [*mujāhidīna*] through their wealth and their lives over those who remain [behind], by degrees. And to both Allāh has promised the best [reward]. But Allāh has preferred those who fight [*mujāhidīna*] over those who remain [behind] with a great reward.

Nonetheless, some early scholars such as Ibn al-Mubārak do talk of *jihād* as a struggle against one's lower soul. But the "greater *jihād*" and "lesser *jihād*" distinction seems to date from the ninth century.

The earliest source that David Cook found for this distinction was in a work by al-Bayhaqi, an Ash'arite scholar, and Shafi'ite in *fiqh*, who died in 1066. His *Kitāb al-zuhd al-kabīr* contains the following tradition: "A number of fighters came to the Messenger of Allāh, and he said: 'You have done well in coming from the "lesser *jihād*" to the "greater *jihād*."' They said, 'What is the "greater *jihād*"?' He said: 'For the servant [of God] to fight his passions.'"[36]

Cook's conclusion is "that it first appears in Bayhaqi (d. 1066), so most likely it is being circulated about a generation or so previously, probably by Sufis who were moving away from the proto-Sufi paradigm of *jihād* (cf. Abd Allāh b. al-Mubārak, who is such a proto-sufi, but does not mention the 'greater *jihād*' in his *Kitāb al-jihād*, circa 790s), and were seeking an alternative line of thinking, and then was popularized by al-Ghazali a generation after al-Bayhaqi."[37] The greater and lesser *jihād* distinction does not appear in any of the canonical *hadīth* collections, however, and while al-Tirmidhī does cite "the fighter is one who fights his passions," as Cook comments in a footnote, "even so, he cites this tradition in the context of the reward of the *murabit* (one who guards the frontier), so it is not entirely without military implications."[38] Clearly the great *hadīth* collectors ruled that the spiritual *jihād* was not a legitimate reading of the meaning of *jihād*.

Here are the conclusions of some modern scholars on the distinction between the greater and lesser *jihād*, and the tradition quoted from al-Bayhaqi:

Reuven Firestone, University of Southern California: "Its

---

[36] Al-Bayhaqī, *Kitāb al-zuhd al-kabir*, ed. 'Amir Ahmad Haydar, no. 373 (Beirut: Dar al-Jinan, 1987), 165.

[37] David Cook, personal communication to author, November, 2015.

[38] Al-Tirmidhī, *Sunan* (Beirut, n.d.), 3:89, no. 1671. Cited in Cook, *Understanding Jihād*, 217n10.

source is usually not given, and it is in fact nowhere to be found in the canonical collections."[39]

Rudolph Peters, University of Amsterdam: "Although this Tradition is quite famous and frequently quoted, it is not included in one of the authoritative compilations."[40]

David Cook, Rice University: "In reading Muslim literature—both contemporary and classical—one can see that the evidence for the primacy of spiritual *jihād* is negligible. Today it is certain that no Muslim, writing in a non-Western language (such as Arabic, Persian, Urdu), would ever make claims that *jihād* is primarily nonviolent or has been superseded by the spiritual *jihād*. Such claims are made solely by Western scholars, primarily those who study Sufism and/or work in interfaith dialogue, and by Muslim apologists who are trying to present Islam in the most innocuous manner possible."[41]

Fazlur Rahman, University of Chicago: "The most unacceptable on historical grounds, however, is the stand of these modern Muslim apologists who have tried to explain the *jihād* of the early Community in purely defensive terms."[42]

Mustansir Mir, University of Michigan: "According to al-Rāghib al-Isfahānī [d. early eleventh century], one engages in *jihād* against an outside enemy (*mujāhadat al-'aduww az-zāhir*), against Satan (*mujāhadat ash-shaytān*) or against one's own baser self (*mujāhadatan-nafs*). In all three types it can be seen, the goal is to defeat a hostile force or subdue an opponent. In its special sense *jihād* is equivalent to the first of the three types of confrontation and may be translated 'armed action,' another term for which is *qitāl*. This, the most familiar meaning of *jihād*, is the one we are mainly concerned with here. When the Qur'ān and the *hadīth* promise

---

39 Reuven Firestone, *Jihād: The Origins of Holy War in Islām* (Oxford: Oxford University Press, 1999), 140.
40 Rudolph Peters, *Jihād: A History in Documents* (Princeton, NJ: Markus Wiener Publishers, 2016), 116.
41 Cook, *Understanding Jihād*, 165–66.
42 Fazlur Rahman, *Islam*, 2nd ed. (Chicago: University of Chicago Press, 1979), 37.

great reward for *jihād*, they are referring primarily to *jihād* in the sense of *qitāl*."⁴³

Renowned classical Islamic philosopher Ibn Taymiyya (mentioned earlier, discussed at length in chapter 12) was also skeptical of the authenticity of this *hadīth*, and quotes suras Q4 and Q9:

> As for the hadīth which is narrated by some in which the Prophet is alleged to have said upon the return of the Muslims from the battle of Tabuk: "We have come back from the minor *jihād* to the major *jihād*." This is a false hadīth, having no origin, and none of those knowledgeable of the words and actions of the Prophet (*sallAllāhu alayhi wa sallam*) have transmitted it. Fighting against the disbelievers is one of the greatest of works. In fact, it is the best thing which a person can volunteer.
>
> Allāh said: Qur'an 4:95–96: "The believers who sit back without any valid excuse are not the same as those who fight in the path of Allāh with their property and their lives. Allāh has preferred those who struggle with their property and their lives over those who sit back by a degree, and to both Allāh has promised good. And Allāh has preferred those who struggle over those who sit back by a great (difference in) reward."
>
> Q9:19–22: "Do you equate providing waters for the pilgrims and maintaining the sacred masjid with those who believe in Allāh and in the last day and struggle in the path of Allāh? They are not equal in the eyes of Allāh, and Allāh does not guide the oppressors. Those who believe and migrate and fight in the path of Allāh with their property and their lives are greater in rank with Allāh, and they are the successful ones. Allāh gives them glad tidings of mercy from Him and acceptance and gardens wherein for them is a permanent bliss. They will stay in it forever, verily with Allāh there is a

---

43 Mir, "*Jihād* in Islam." Abū l-Qāsim Abū l-Husayn ibn Muhammad, known as al-Rāghib al-Isfahānī, *Al-Mufradāt fī Gharīb al-Qur'ān*, ed. Muhammad Sayyid Kīlānī (Egypt: Mustafā al-Bābī al-Halabī, 1381 /1961 impression), 101.

very great reward."[44]

Hundreds of years later, Hasan al-Banna, founder of the Muslim Brotherhood, also dismissed the distinction between the greater and lesser *jihād*:

> The belief is widespread that fighting the enemy is *jihād asghar* (a lesser *jihād*) and that there is a greater *jihād* (*jihād akbar*), the *jihād* of the spirit. Many of them invoke as proof of this the following narration [*athar*]: "We have returned from the lesser *jihād* to embark on the greater *jihād*." They said: "What is the greater *jihād*?" He said: "The *jihād* of the heart, or the *jihād* of the spirit."
>
> Some of them try, by recourse to this, to divert people from the importance of fighting, preparing for combat, and resolving to undertake it and embark on God's way. This narration is not really a *sahih* (sound) tradition: The Prince of Believers in matters of Tradition, Al-Hāfiz ibn Hajar al-'Asqalānī [d. 1449],[45] said in the *Tasdīd al-Qaws*: "It is well known and often repeated, and was a saying of Ibrāhīm ibn 'Abla."[46]
>
> ...Nevertheless, even if it were a sound tradition, it would never warrant abandoning *jihād*, or preparing for it in order to rescue the territories of the Muslims and repel the attacks of the unbelievers. Its meaning is simply that it is necessary to struggle with the spirit so that it may be sincerely devoted

---

44 Ibn Taymiyya, *The Criterion between the Allies of the Merciful and the Allies of the Devil: al-furqān bayna awliyā'ar-rahman wa awliyā' as-shaytān*, trans. Salim AbdAllāh ibn Morgan (Birmingham, UK: Idara Ihya-us-Sunnah, 1993), 52–53, available at: https://shaykhulislaam.files.wordpress.com/2010/12/criterion.pdf.

45 *Five Tracts of Hasan al-Bannā' (1906–1949): A Selection from the Majmū'at Rasā'il al-Shahīd Hasan al-Bannā'*, trans. with annotations Charles Wendell (Berkeley: University of California Press, 1978), 161n49: Ibn Hajar al-'Asqalānī (1382–1449), "a famous historian, theologion, and traditionist, the prolific author of works of hadīth, Islamic Law, Qur'ānic studies, and biography, especially of transliters of hadīth and the early Companions. His best-known works in this genre are multivolumed *Tahdhīb al-Tahdhīb* ['Revision of the Revision'] and *Al-Isāba fī Tamyīz Asmā' al-Sahāba* (Accuracy in Distinguishing the Companions)."

46 Ibid., 155.

to God in every one of its acts. So let it be known.⁴⁷

Abdullah Yusuf Azzam (1941–1989),⁴⁸ a Palestinian who obtained a doctorate in Islamic jurisprudence from al-Azhar in 1973, was fully qualified to write about this *hadīth*, "[It] is in fact a false, fabricated hadīth which has no basis. It is only a saying of Ibrahim Ibn Abi Abalah, one of the Successors, and it contradicts textual evidence and reality.... The word '*jihād*', when mentioned on its own, only means combat with weapons, as was mentioned by Ibn Rushd, and upon this the four Imams have agreed....The implication of '*fī sabīli llāhi* (in the Path of Allāh) is *jihād*, as Ibn Hajar has said."⁴⁹

Military Mysticism: Sufis Soldiers and Jihād

Sufis, the mystics of Islam, are an idealized, mythified group, and thus much misunderstood in the West, where everything peaceful and ecumenical is attributed to them. In fact, the first Sufi order in Islam (founded in the tenth century CE) had a surprising character. Born 1930, former professor of Arabic at Oxford University Wilferd Madelung offers a history:

> The first Sufi order in Iran, and indeed in Islam, was the Murshidiyya or Kāzarūniyya founded by Abū Ishāq al-Kāzarūnī, known as Shaykh-i Murshid (963–1035). Al-Kāzarūnī came from a poor local family in Kāzarūn, west of Shiraz; his grandfather had still been a Zoroastrian. Like Ibn Karrām, he represented an activist asceticism, was a powerful preacher and converted numerous Zoroastrians to Islam. His strictures and aggressive conduct toward the non-Muslims brought him and his followers into sometimes violent conflict with the strong Zoroastrian community backed by the local Būyid authorities. He preached the *jihād* against the infidels, and groups of his followers carried out campaigns

---

47 Charles Wendell's 161n50: Abd al-Rahīm b. Al-Husayn al-Hafiz al-'Irāqī (1325–1404), "a scholar of Kurdish origin who lived most of his life in Egypt. He visited the neighbouring regions for study and research in haith, and was the author of a number of books on Traditions, jurisprudence, the Prophetic biography, and Qur'ānic studies."

48 Imam Abdullah Azzam, "Join the Caravan: Conclusion," *Religioscope*, February 1, 2002, http://english.religion.info/2002/02/01/document-join-the-caravan/.

49 Ibn Hajar al-'Asqalānī (1382–1449), *Fath-ul-Bari*. Unfortunately, Azzam does not give the precise reference.

against the Christians in Anatolia.⁵⁰

In a brilliant section on "Sufi Warriors" in *Understanding Jihād*, Cook points out that many Sufi groups, while promoting the greater *jihād*, "also proclaimed the need for actual fighting and demonstrated the connection between the two....Wherever Sufi groups went, they took both aspects of *jihād* with them."⁵¹

In his classic work on Shiʿism—an important branch of Islam practiced in modern-day Iraq and Iran that differs from Sunni Islam on a variety of matters such as questions of succession, authority and law—Heinz Halm, professor of Islamic studies at the University of Tübingen, gives many examples of Sufi groups that combined the two, such as

> the development of isolated *tarīqas* [Sufi brotherhoods, dervish orders] into militant Shiʿite fighting federations which gained political significance in the 14th century....The earliest example is the *tarīqa* of the Shaykhiyya-Jūriyya which goes back to the 'Pole of the gnostics' (Qutb al-Arifīn) Shaykh-i-Khalīfa (d. 1335) and his successor Shaykh Hasan-i Jūrī (d. 1342). The wandering dervish Shaykh-i-Khalīfa from Māzandarān on the Caspian Sea set himself up as a mystical teacher in the mosque of Bayhaq/Sabzavār (east of Tehran) where he preached the imminent appearance (*zuhūr*) of the Mahdī and urged the Shiʿites to prepare themselves for Holy War.⁵²

(In a Sufi context, a Shaykh is a qualified Sufi, a Sufi master, who is authorized to teach, initiate, and guide aspiring dervishes or novices [*murid*].)

The historically important Safavid dynasty had its origin in the Safaviyya Sufi order founded by Safi ad-din Ardabili (1252-1334). After Safi al-Dīn, the leadership of the Safaviyya passed onto his son Sadr al-Din Musa (1305-1392). The order now became a vigorous proselytiz-

---

50 Wilferd Madelung, *Religious Trends in Early Islamic Iran* (Albany, NY: Persian Heritage Foundation, 1988), 48. Madelung's 48n35: "On al-Kāzarūnī see in general F. Meier, *Die Vita des Scheich Abū Ishāq al-Kāzarūnī in der persischen Bearbeitung von Mahmūd b. ʿUtmān*. Leipzig, 1948."

51 Cook, *Understanding Jihād*, 45.

52 Heinz Halm, *Shiʿism*, 2nd ed. (1991; New York: Columbia University Press, 2004), 70-71.

ing religious movement preaching throughout Persia, Syria, and Asia Minor, while maintaining its Sunni Shafi'ite outlook. The leadership of the order next passed to Sadr ud-Dīn Mūsā's son Khwādja Ali (d. 1429) and in turn to his son Ibrāhīm (d.1429–47). Shaykh Junayd, the son of Ibrāhim, assumed leadership in 1447, and suddenly the history of the Safavid movement changed dramatically. As R.M. Savory, an Iranologist and specialist on the Safavids, wrote, "No longer content with spiritual authority alone, Junayd introduced a miltant note by inciting his disciples to carry on holy war against the infidel."[53]

Halm takes up the story:

> Junayd began to recruit supporters among the nomadic Turcoman tribes whom he commanded as border fighters (*ghāzī*) in the Holy War against the Christian Georgians and the Circassians of the Caucasus. After he fell in battle (1460) his son Shaykh Haydar succeeded him....Haydar too sent his 'representatives' (*khalīfa*) to Turcoman tribes which had linked up with the Safaviyya order and urged them to Holy War against the unbelievers. It is hardly surprising that the character of the order changed substantially under these conditions. Haydar was no longer the traditional Sufi Shaykh who operated in a circle of a dozen adepts; rather he was the leader of a large and powerful force of religious fighters. The word Sūfī increasingly acquired the meaning of "active Muslim."[54]

Or, as the Safavid historian Iskandar Beg Munshī (Eskandar Beg Torkamān Monši, d. ca.1633) put it in *Tārīkh-i 'Alam-ārā-yi 'Abbāsī* ("Haydar Wielded both Spiritual and Temporal Authority"), his history of the reign of Shah Abbas I: "[I]nwardly, following the example of [Sufi] shaykhs and men of God, he walked the path of spiritual guidance and defence of the faith; outwardly, he was a leader sitting on a throne in the manner of princes."[55]

---

53 Roger Savory, *Iran under the Safavids* (1980; Cambridge: Cambridge University Press, 2007), 16.

54 Halm, *Shi'ism*, 75–76. Heinz's footnote appended to "active Muslim" gives the following reference: "H.R. Roemer, 'Die turkmenischen Qïzïlbaš-Gründer und Opfer der safawidischen Theokratie,' *ZDMG* 135 (1985): 227–40."

55 Iskandar Beg Munshī, *Tārīkh-i 'Alam-ārā-yi 'Abbāsī*, trans. R.M. Savory, Persian Heritage Series, ed. Ehsan Yarshater, no. 28, 2 vols. (Boulder, CO: 1978), 31; quoted in Savory, *Iran Under the Safavids*, 18.

It is a similar history in India, where the Sufi order of the Naqshbandiyya-Mujaddidiyya was

> closely associated with Muslim revivalism and conquest. Simon Digby's translation of the *Malfuzat-i Naqshbandiyya*, aptly titled *Sufis and Soldiers in Awrangzeb's Deccan*, illustrates this trend. The major figure of the work, Baba Palangposh, is a local holy man who joins the army of the Mogul rule Awrangzeb (1657-1701) and participates in the campaign to subdue the region of southern India. He witnesses a vision of the Prophet Muhammad's uncle Hamza (slain at the Battle of Uhud in 627, and usually called "the prince of Martyrs") in which Hamza gives Baba Palangposh a sword and says: "Take this sword...and go to the army of Mir Shihab al-Din in the land of the Deccan [southern India]."[56]

Conclusion

While there are hundreds of sources for militant, or lesser, *jihād* in classical Islam—*hadīth* collections, commentaries on the Koran, law books from all the schools of law, and so on—there do not seem to have been any works devoted exclusively to spiritual, or greater, *jihād*. This is clearly a derivative form, since it is not mentioned in any of the canonical collections of *hadīth*. Even the later literature on *jihād* fails to mention "greater *jihād*."

---

56 Cook, *Understanding Jihād*, 46. Cook's 219n40: "Simon Digby, *Sufis and Soldiers in Awrangzeb's Deccan* (New York: 2001), pp. 69-70; other interesting citations can be found on pp. 83-84, 122-23, 216 (where Sufi *murids* are common soldiers in the army)."

CHAPTER 8

MUHAMMAD'S CAMPAIGNS AND EARLY CONQUESTS

ACCORDING TO al-Wāqidī (747–823 CE), a Muslim historian and judge whose major work, *Kitāb al-Maghāzī, The Book of Raids* (or *Campaigns*), is an important source for early Islamic history and the life of Muhammad:

> The Prophet actively participated in twenty-seven raids [*gazawāt*]. He fought in nine of them: Badr, Uhud, al-Muraysī', al-Khandaq, Qurayza, Khaybar, the Conquest of Mecca, Hunayn and al-Tā'if. He directed forty-seven expeditions and performed three *'Umras* [pilgrimage to Meccan Ka'ba undertaken before or after the annual *Hajj* ritual]. Some say that he fought the Banū Nadīr, but God made it a special booty for him. He also fought in the raid of Wādī al-Qurā on his return from Khaybar, when some of his companions were killed. Then he fought in al-Ghāba until Muhriz b. Nadla and six of the enemy were killed.[1]

These campaigns were waged by Muhammad on behalf of Islam. As al-Tabarī (839–923 CE), a major early Islamic historian and exegete of the Koran, put it, "The Messenger of God was commanded to proclaim the divine message which he had received, to declare it publicly to the people, and to summon them to God."[2] Muhammad's wars can

---
1 Al-Wāqidī, *Life of Muhammad*, 5.
2 Al-Tabarī, *The History of al-Tabarī*, trans. W. Montgomery Watt and M.V. McDonald,

be seen as "prototypical *jihād* wars"³ whose religious nature cannot be ignored. Like the conquests, Muhammad's campaigns are grounded in religion, a fact emphasized by Scottish historian W. Montgomery Watt in *Muhammad: Prophet and Statesman*, a biography highly regarded by Muslims: "Thus, whether Muhammad incited his followers to action and then used their wrongs to justify it, or whether he yielded to pressure from them to allow such action, the normal Arab practice of the razzia [raid] was taken over by the Islamic community. In being taken over, however, it was transformed. It became an activity of believers against unbelievers, and therefore took place within a religious context."⁴

Owing to the opposition he had aroused in Mecca, Muhammad eventually left for Medina, where he had a large religious following. Some seventy of his Meccan followers preceded him to Medina. Muhammad's Meccan and Medinan followers came to be known as the Emigrants (*muhājirūn*, those making the *hijrah*) and the Ansār ("Helpers"), respectively.

Watt picks up the story:

> The Emigrants were described as "striving with goods and person in the way of God." They were promoting one of the purposes of the Islamic community in trying to establish a region in which God was truly worshipped. As this character of their activity became clear to the Emigrants, there was no reason why they should not call on the Helpers (Ansār) to share in it. It was God's work, all Muslims should share in it. Besides, the Meccans seem to have been reinforcing the guards on their caravans, and more participants were necessary if the razzias were to be successful. A verse (Q5. *al-Mā'idah* 39) which was probably intended to encourage the Helpers (Ansār) to join the razzia runs: "O believers, fear God...and strive in His way." Thus it was because of the religious character of the Muslim expeditions that the Medinans were invited to share in them.⁵

Watt goes onto analyze the development of the term *jihād* and re-

---

vol. 4, *Muhammad at Mecca* (Albany: State University of New York Press, 1988), 92.
3 Cook, *Understanding Jihād*, 2.
4 W. Montgomery Watt, *Muhammad: Prophet and Statesman* (1961; Oxford: Oxford University Press, 1974), 108.
5 Ibid., 108.

lates it to the religious character of the early conquests:

> This transformation of the nomadic razzia has wider implications than are apparent from the English translations used. The word translated "strive" is jāhada. And the corresponding verbal noun is *jihād* or "striving" which came in the course of time to have the technical meaning of "holy war." The change from the razzia to the *jihād* may seem to be no more than a change of name, the giving of an aura of religion to what was essentially the same activity. Yet this is not so. There was change in the activity which came to be of the utmost importance as time went on. A razzia was the action of a tribe against another tribe. Even if two tribes were very friendly, their friendship might cool, and in a few years a razzia might be possible.
>
> *Jihād*, however, was the action of a religious community against non-members of the community, and the community was expanding. If members of the pagan tribes raided by the Muslims professed Islam, they at once became exempt from further Muslim raids. Consequently, as the Islamic community grew, the raiding propensities of the Muslims had to be directed ever further outwards. It was this "religious" character of the *jihād* which channelled the energies of the Arabs in such a way that in less than a century they had created an empire which stretched from the Atlantic and the Pyrenees in the West to the Oxus and the Punjab in the East. It seems certain that without the conception of the *jihād* that expansion would not have happened.[6]

For Muhammad and the Muslims, the resounding victory against overwhelming odds in the Battle of Badr (March 624) over the Meccans "had a deep religious meaning.... It was a vindication of the faith that has sustained them through disappointment. It was God's...supernatural action on their behalf. The Qur'ān develops this religious interpretation of the event in various passages," and his victory at Badr "came to be regarded as the great deliverance God had effected for the Muslims, comparable to the deliverance he had effected for the Israelites at the Red Sea."[7] The

---
6 Ibid., 108–9.
7 Ibid., 125.

victory for Muhammad was a sign confirming his prophethood.

Muhammad's constant aim, particularly between March 627 and March 628, was to summon all Arabs to Islam.[8] The March 628 signing of the Treaty of Hudaybiyah with the Meccans worked in Muhammad's favor because the religious ideas of Islam continued to hold sway and he was able to attract fresh converts. Also of supreme importance were "Muhammad's belief in the message of the Qur'ān, his belief in the future of Islam as a religious and political system, and his unflinching devotion to the task to which, as he believed, God had called him."[9]

Then, for his greatest expedition in 630 to Tabuk, a town in the Northern Arabian peninsula about 250 miles from Medina, near the Gulf of al-'Aqaba, Muhammad prepared the Muslims by insisting that their participation was a religious duty. "The religious aspect was almost certainly always uppermost in his thoughts," Watt explains, "and the motive which drove him on was the desire to fulfil God's command to spread Islam."[10]

As I have noted throughout this study, Western historians tend to underplay the role of religion in the affairs of the Middle East. "[Many] may feel that the movement of the Arab tribes into the Islamic state was essentially political," Watt observes, but "[t]his is not so....Since the exodus of the Israelites from Egypt religion and politics in the Middle East have always been closely linked...and the fact that a movement had a prominent political aspect has never meant that it was not religious (as it often does in the modern West)."[11]

Many Western Islamologues such as Leone Caetani deny the role of religion in the early Islamic conquests, especially in the seventh and eighth centuries.[12] But Georges-Henri Bousquet rejected this tendency: "I have positive reasons to believe that the religious factor played a far from negligible role in this conquest."[13]

---

8 Ibid., 176.

9 Ibid., 188.

10 Ibid., 222.

11 Ibid., 224.

12 Leone Caetani, *Annali dell'Islam*, 10 vols. (Milano: U. Hoepli, 1905–1926), 2:855–61; and *Studi di Storia Orientale I* (Milano: U. Hoepli, 1911), 364–71. Also see the English translation in Fred Donner, ed., *The Formation of the Classical Islamic World*, vol. 5, *The Expansion of the Early Islamic State* (Burlington, VT: Ashgate, 2008), chap. 1.

13 Georges-Henri Bousquet, "*Queleques remarques critiques et sociologiques sur le conquête arabe et les theories émises àce sujet*," in *Studi Orientalistici in Onore di Giorgio Levi Della Vida* (Roma: Instituto per l'Oriente, 1956), 1:52–60. Also see English translation in Donner, *Expansion of Early Islamic State*, 21.

In a 1956 article Bousquet spelled out his "opposition to the tendency [among scholars]...over the past half-century and more, in reducing the influence of the religious factor" in the Islamic conquests.[14] Bousquet found it remarkable how religious fervor "succeeded in manifesting itself among people who initially joined the ranks for other reasons."[15] Muhammad, according to Bousquet, was responsible for creating "agitation of a religious nature," which "had been favorable to the success of the Muslim armies." How can we set aside the religious motive

> when we read *apud* Zamakhshari, describing the famous battle of the Yarmuk [against the Byzantine forces in August 636]: "the Muslim preachers did not cease to encourage the combatants: Prepare yourselves for the encounter with the houris of the black eyes and for meeting your Lord in the gardens of beatitude, cried Abu Hurayra. And to be sure...never has a day been seen when more heads fell than on the day of Yarmuk." Here we have an account illustrating the classical thesis of religious fanaticism, and belying that of the dessication of Arabia![16]

Scholars such as Sir Thomas Arnold (d. 1930) had argued that the Arab conquests did not have a religious character because the victors had no desire to convert the conquered.[17] But as Bousquet points out, the best example of this was the Crusades, which he characterizes as "the great enthusiasm which aroused western Europe at that time and impelled the Crusaders to rescue the Holy Places, not convert the Muslims, which they never did. Thus the...argument, 'the Arab conquests did not have a religious character, since the victors did not want to convert the vanquished', has no merit, the postulate...being belied by history." Bousquet continues with what I believe is the most compelling part of his argument:

> [I]f we take the history of the first century of the Hegira [i.e, first Islamic century, 622–722 CE] as a whole, we see, at the

---

14 Georges-Henri Bousquet, "*Observations sur la nature et causes de la conquête arabe*," *Studia Islamica* 6 (1956): 37–52. See also Donner, *Expansion of Early Islamic State*, 23.
15 Ibid., 27.
16 Ibid., 28.
17 Thomas Walker Arnold, *The Preaching of Islam: A History of the Propagation of the Muslim Faith*, 2nd ed. (London: A. Constable, 1913), 45–71.

beginning, an inspiration not all influenced by material interests, but assuredly influenced by religious motives, and at the end, a new and characteristically religious civilization, and can anyone deny that what constituted the transition from the one to the other, the conquest, had a religious aspect?...I can grasp well-enough the notion that the tribes, united by Muhammad, were thrown into the attack on the surrounding provinces and subjugated them, surely, solely for non-religious motives. But how, subsequently, could the Muslim civilization have been born? Why did these people not blend into the conquered populations, whose civilization was superior to theirs, like the Barbarians in the Roman west, the Manchus in China? This is what would normally have happened. Certainly, Muslim institutions owed a lot to the surrounding milieu, but they could never have been born if, among the conquerors there had not been men, themselves inspired, like the Prophet, by religious zeal, and having trained disciples, this until the emergence of the first groups of Doctors of Law.[18]

In his highly regarded history, *The End of the Jihâd State: The Reign of Hishām Ibn 'Abd al-Malik and the Collapse of the Umayyads* (1994), Khalid Yahya Blankinship, associate professor of religion at Temple University, argues that many empires, including that of the Muslim Arabs, achieved their greatest reach through military campaigns, and that "expansion became an ideological imperative justified on moral grounds."[19] For Muslims,

this imperative was the establishment of God's rule in the earth, for that was the sole legitimate sovereignty. God's rule was to be established by those kinds of efforts that He had ordained, which included armed struggle in His path. Such armed struggle became known as *jihād* and remained the most salient policy of the caliphate down to the end of the Umayyad rule in 750 C.E. Most significantly, the *jihād* called

---

[18] Bousquet, "*Observations sur la nature et causes*," in Donner, *Expansion of Early Islamic State*, 31.

[19] Khalid Yahya Blankinship, *The End of the Jihâd State: The Reign of Hishām Ibn 'Abd al-Malik and the Collapse of the Umayyads* (Albany: State University of New York Press, 1994).

for a mass mobilization of Muslim manpower that played an important role in the caliphate's success.[20]

Blankinship argues further that the early Muslim successes and "the persistence of the Muslim movement forward on all fronts for nearly a century can only be explained if this basic doctrine of early Muslim ideology is taken into account."[21] Such dedication "required an ideological belief to back it," and for Muslims, "the work of conquest through *jihād* was first for God, second for the reward of the other world for those who sacrificed their property and their lives in God's path, and only third for worldy rewards for God's warriors who survived."[22]

I have repeatedly emphasized the importance of ideology as a motivating force in history, a force that cannot be reduced to a socioeconomic rationale. Blankinship spells out the ideological nature of the early Muslim caliphate:

> More than any polity that had existed before it, the early Muslim caliphate was an ideological state, that is, a state directed toward a single, unified ideological goal. In general, the caliphate's ideology was the religion of Islam or the submission to God's will, as revealed in the Qur'ān to the Prophet Muhammad. Whether or not the Qur'ān contains clear prescriptions for an Islamic state, it is certain that the Prophet himself did in fact establish a charismatic polity based both on the enlightenment of God given to him by revelation, and his own personal leadership. The sole official purpose of this polity was to teach and transmit the ideology of Islam.[23]

Muhammad's demise did not alter this course. "[T]he caliphal state carried on,...finding clear ideological expression...in the doctrine of *jihād*, the struggle to establish God's rule...through a continuous military effort against the non-Muslims until they either embraced Islam

---

20 Ibid., 1.
21 Ibid., 1-2.
22 Ibid., 2; 279n5: "Indeed, a well-known hadith attributed to the Prophet states that the only true *jihād* is that waged to exalt God's word. Bukhari, I, 42–43. Martyrs in the *jihād* are promised paradise, Qur'an, III, 169. And those who fight in God's Path (and survive) are also promised a share of the spoil (*innamā ghanimtum*). Quran VIII, 41."
23 Ibid., 11; 280n1: "Qur'an, IV.59, 64–65, 105; V.44–45, 47–50; Khadduri, [*War and Peace in Islam,*] 8–9, 16–17."

or agreed to pay tribute (jizya) on their persons in exchange for protection." The concept of *jihād* had been applied by the Prophet perhaps as early as Ramadān 1 /March 623. From that time, "the policy of *jihād* constituted one of the main ideological underpinnings for the institution of the caliphate," and since "the struggle to expand Islam's realm had been continuous from the time of the Prophet, there was an obvious need for a central political and military leadership to control and coordinate that effort."[24]

Blankinship is adamant that the emphasis on *jihād* in early Islamic history is well-attested in all the Islamic sources, and even in some non-Islamic ones. The doctrine of *jihād*, as we have discussed, is spelled out in the Koran and elaborated upon in the *hadīth*.[25] *Jihād* is the third most important duty of a Muslim after regular worship and filial piety[26] —or the second after regular worship.[27]

The Ideology of Islam

Early in these pages I called the twentieth century the century of ideology. Blankinship points out a similarity: "In general, the impression one gets from the Qur'an and hadith is of a highly motivated mass ideology directed toward a single goal. Indeed, the ideology of Islam anticipated modern ideologies on its mass appeal and means of creating enthusiasm."[28]

The West was rather shocked when it read Osama bin Laden's 1996 "Declaration of War," particularly the phrase "[the young Muslims] love death as you love life." Here is the context: "Since the sons of the land of two Holy Places [Saudi Arabia] feel and strongly believe that fighting against the unbeliever in every part of the world is absolutely essential....I say to you: These youths love death as you love life. They inherit dignity, pride, courage, generosity, truthfulness....Our youth believe in Paradise after death."[29]

Similarly, years earlier Hasan al-Banna, the founder of the Muslim Brotherhood mentioned earlier in these pages, wrote:

> My brothers! The ummah that knows how to die a noble and

---

24 Ibid., 11.
25 Ibid., 12.
26 Ibid., 14; 282n53: "Bukhari, IV, 17."
27 Ibid., 14; 282n54: "Ibn al-Mubarak, 44."
28 Ibid., 15.
29 Quoted in Rubin and Rubin, *Anti-American Terrorism*, 140–41.

honourable death is granted an exalted life in this world and eternal felicity in the next. Degradation and dishonour are the results of the love of this world and the fear of death. Therefore, prepare for *jihād* and be the lovers of death. Life itself shall come searching after you. My brother, you should know that one day you will face death and this ominous event can only occur once. If you suffer on this occasion in the way of Allah, it will be to your benefit in this world and your reward in the next. And remember brother that nothing can happen without the Will of Allah....You should yearn for an honourable death and you will gain perfect happiness. May Allah grant myself and yours the honour of martyrdom in His way![30]

The Koran, as we have considered at length, encourages Muslims to love the life to come, as in Q9 *at-Tawba*, The Repentance, 38: "O you who have believed, what is [the matter] with you that, when you are told to go forth in the cause of Allah, you adhere heavily to the earth? Are you satisfied with the life of this world rather than the Hereafter? But what is the enjoyment of worldly life compared to the Hereafter except a [very] little." And these sentiments, this philosophy, are, as we have also discussed, continuously repeated in the Koran, *hadīth*, and in the primary Arabic sources for the early Islamic conquests. It is to these sources we now turn, after a brief note on their nature.

Fred Donner, distinguished professor of Near Eastern history at the University of Chicago, makes the following observation:

> [M]ilitary action was a central part of this process of expansion, so much so that most scholars who have studied the expansion have referred to it as the "Islamic Conquest" or the "Arab Conquest." This emphasis on conquest, often neglecting other aspects of the expansion, may be in part a reflection of the Islamic sources themselves, which have a special genre of *futūh* literature the object of which was to relate how the many towns and districts of this vast empire came to be part

---

30 English Translation of *Maj'muaat Rasail* (the complete works) Imam Hasan al-Banna," vol. 10, "*al-Jihād*," https://thequranblog.files.wordpress.com/2008/06/_10_-al-jihād.pdf, epilogue, full text available at *The Quran Blog—Enlighten Yourself*, June 7, 2008, https://thequranblog.wordpress.com/2008/06/07/english-translation-of-majmuaat-rasail-the-complete-works-imam-hasan-al-banna/

of it. Actually, however, the word *futūh* does not mean "conquest," although it is often so translated; its use in relation to the expansion is probably to be associated with the Qur'ānic use of the term to mean a favor or act of grace granted by God to His faithful believers (cf. Q2: 76 and many other passages). The implication being made by the purveyors of the *futūh* literature, then, was that the Muslims' domination of these territories was legitimate because they were literally something bestowed upon them by God.[31]

Here, once again, the religious nature of the "conquests" is emphasized.

Al-Tabarī, in his monumental universal history, *Ta'rikh al-rusul wa'l-mulūk*, offers many details concerning the early Islamic conquests. Khālid ibn al-Walīd, the Muslim commander under orders from the caliph Abū Bakr, reached al-Hīrah, whose nobles came to meet him with Qabīsah the governor. Khālid said to him, "I call you to God and to Islam. If you respond to the call, then you are Muslims: You obtain the benefits they enjoy and take up the responsibilities they bear. If you refuse, then [you must pay] the jizya. If you refuse the jizyah, I will bring against you the tribes of people who are *more eager for death than you are for life*. We will then fight you until God decides between us and you" (emphasis added).[32] A little later, Khalid repeats the threat with a slight variation: "then we will bring against you a people who love death more than you love drinking wine."[33] Abu Bakr, the caliph, exhorts Khālid to fight the Persians, and "prefer the matter of the afterlife to this world so that you may obtain the benefits of both, and do not prefer this world lest you be denied both."[34]

'Umar, the second caliph, before sending him off to war in Iraq says to Sa'd: "Know that fear of God consists of two things: being obedient to Him and avoiding rebellion against Him. One obeys Him by hating this world and loving the hereafter; one hates Him by loving this world and hating the hereafter."[35]

Again during the caliphate of 'Umar, Al-Mughirah b.Shu'bah says to his Persian adversary Rustam, "If you kill us, we shall enter Paradise,

---

31 Donner, *Expansion of Early Islamic State*, xviii.

32 *The History of al-Tabarī*, vol. 11, *The Challenge to the Empires*, trans. Khalid Yahya Blankinship (Albany: State University of New York Press, 1993), 4.

33 Ibid., 6.

34 Ibid., 48.

35 Friedman, *Battle of a-Qadisiyya*, 9.

if we kill you, you shall enter the Fire,"³⁶ while the Muslim commander Zuhrah b. Hawiyyah al-Tamīmī says to Rustam, "We do not come to you looking for things of this world, our desire and aspiration is the hereafter."³⁷ Throughout the volume covering the events of the caliphate of 'Umar, al-Ṭabarī repeats the sentiments expressed by Muslim commanders and fighters, that they are fighting for the cause of Allah and value only the Hereafter, all the while extolling the virtues of martyrdom,³⁸ epitomized in this final example:

> The Muslims have prepared themselves for battle. Tonight be the first among the Muslims to reach God and to [engage in] holy war. Because whoever is the first tonight will receive his reward accordingly. Compete with the [other] Muslims for martyrdom and accept death cheerfully. This will more effectively save you from death, if you wish to live, and if not, then it is the hereafter which you wish to attain....Compete with each other [in risking] your children and wives. Do not fear being killed, because being killed is the aspiration of the noble and the destiny of the martyrs.³⁹

Al-Ṭabarī also had the main figures in his history express how much they have been helped by God in their battles against the unbelievers. God honors the religion of Islam by granting them victory after victory: "Then God granted victory to the Muslims who vanquished the enemy in a glorious manner," "Then God defeated them [unbelievers] through him [a Muslim]," and many variations on this phrasing.⁴⁰

---

36 Ibid., 32.
37 Ibid., 64.
38 Ibid., e.g., 38, 50, 75, 81, 84, 87, 88, 138, 167.
39 Ibid., 119.
40 *The History of al-Ṭabarī*, vol. 13, *The Conquest of Iraq, Southwestern Persia, and Egypt*, trans. Gautier H.A. Juynboll (Albany: State University of New York Press, 1989), 188–89; 175. See also vol. 11:102, 104, 126,129, 164, 171, 211; and vol. 12:61, 131, 134, 145, 149, 171, 177, and so on.

CHAPTER 9

THE FIRST TERRORISTS? KHĀRIJITES, VIOLENCE, AND THE DEMAND FOR THE PURIFICATION OF ISLAM OF ITS UNPIOUS ACCRETIONS

IN 1966 FAZLUR RAHMAN wrote that the radical spirit of the Khārijites, the early seventh- century movement in Islam, without necessarily an overt influence "has been relived not only in certain outstanding individuals in medieval Islam but in relatively recent movements inspired by radical idealism such as the Wahhābīs in the 18th century, and in a more moderate spirit and more recently the Muslim Brotherhood in the Arab Middle East." Rahman also notes a certain "similarity of the Khārijite ideal with certain aspects of the doctrine of the radical Islamic movement, the Jamā'at-i Islamī, in Pakistan."[1]

In 1973, Arab intellectual Mahmūd Ismā'īl argued that the Khārijites rejected foreign cultures in order to preserve the Islamic identity and culture of the early Muslim community. Similarly, modern Islamic fundamentalist movements were fighting against the aggressive intrusion of Western culture threatening to dilute and corrupt Islamic society. Just as the Khārijites condemned and rebelled against the political and religious authorities in early Islam, so modern fundamentalists critiqued and rose up against Arab governments they considered un-Islamic.[2]

---

[1] Rahman, *Islam*, 2nd ed., 170.
[2] Mahmūd Ismā'īl, *al-Harakāt al-sirrīyah fī al-Islām: ru'yah 'asrīyah* (Secret Movements in Islam: Modern View) (Bayrūt: *Dār al-Qalam*, 1973), 14f., cited in Hussam S.Timani,

In a 1927 volume of the first edition of the *Encyclopaedia of Islam*, Giorgio Levi Della Vida, an Italian Jewish linguist, described the actions of the Khārijites thus: "the extreme fanaticism of the [Khārijites] at once manifested itself in a series of extremist proclamations and terrorist actions."[3] The *Encyclopaedia's* second edition retained Levi Della Vida's article—quote intact.[4] Distinguished Islamologist W. Montgomery Watt, writing in *The Formative Period of Islamic Thought* (1973), also described the Azraqites, a Khārijite subgroup, as "terrorists."[5] I shall return to the Azraqites shortly.

Who were the Khārijites? The most appropriate starting point for any discussion of the Khārijites is the murder of the caliph 'Uthmān in 656 in Medina. As Watt puts it, "The Kharijites," who came into being because of this event, "claimed continuity with the revolutionary bodies responsible for the murder, though the precise nature or importance of the continuity is not obvious."[6]

After 'Uthmān's murder, various groups of disgruntled Muslims proceeded to Medina to air their grievances. Some complained that 'Uthmān had given certain individuals land grants in Iraq that should have been held in trust for Muslims. Others alleged that 'Uthmān had given lucrative governorships to members of his clan. The third grievance was religious: it was claimed that 'Uthmān had failed in certain cases to carry out penalties prescribed by the Koran.

On their own, these grievances seem insufficient to explain the violence against 'Uthmān. Watt, though puzzled at first, finally arrives as his customary socioeconomic plus anthropological explanation. Underlying all these grievances was the complete change of life of former nomads, the Bedouins: going from the freedom of the desert to the unbearable constraints imposed by a powerful bureaucracy led to spiritual and social crisis. Watt concludes that "the root of the problem was the new economic, social and political structure in which they [the malcontents] found themselves."[7] However, Watt's interpretation, as we shall

---

Modern Intellectual Readings of the Kharijites (New York: Peter Lang, 2008), 94–95.

3 *Encyclopaedia of Islam*, vol. 2, "E–K," ed. M. Th. Houtsman, A.J. Wensinck, and T.W. Arnold (Leiden: Brill, 1927), s.v. *"Khāridjites,"* by Giorgio Levi Della Vida.

4 *Encyclopaedia of Islam*, vol. 4, "Iran–Kha," ed. by E. van Donzel, B. Lewis, and Ch. Pellat 2nd ed. (Leiden: Brill, 1978), s.v. *"Khāridjites,"* by Giorgio Levi Della Vida.

5 W. Montgomery Watt, *The Formative Period of Islamic Thought* (Edinburgh: University of Edinburgh Press, 1973), 21.

6 Ibid., 9.

7 Ibid., 12.

see later, is challenged by Wellhausen, who sees a religious- that is, an Islamic- motive in their actions.

After 'Uthman's death the Muslims in Medina appointed 'Ali caliph. However, he was not universally recognized. He had not punished those responsible for the murder, and had even shown sympathy for the rebels. Many withdrew from Medina, having rejected 'Ali. While in Syria,

> Mu'āwiya, who was governor and related to 'Uthman, also refused allegiance to 'Ali. There was a third group which was led by Muhammad's widow, 'Ā'isha, and which openly challenged 'Ali's legitimacy, and rose up against him. 'Ali was able to defeat this group at the battle of the Camel in December, 656. 'Ali now felt confident and marched against Mu'āwiya, and confronted him at Siffin. After some minor skirmishes, a probably apocryphal story tells us that some religious-minded men in Mu'āwiya's army went out to 'Ali's men with copies of the Koran tied to their lances, which seems to have been a way to suggest that the dispute should be settled by a judgement according to the Koran.[8]

Levi Della Vida argues that the majority of 'Ali's men accepted the proposal either because they were tired of war or because the *qurrā'*, the Koran readers, "hoped that there would emerge from this Koranic judgment the justification of the furious campaign they had conducted against 'Uthman which had ended in the latter's assassination."[9]

The warring armies withdrew and arbitration took place. But some among the supporters of 'Ali, after reaching agreement with Mu'āwiya, protested vehemently against submitting the dispute to human tribunal above divine word. They shouted out "judgment belongs to God alone" (*lā hukm illā li-llāh*). Soon after, several thousand men withdrew to the village of Harūrā', near Kufa. Despite some concessions from 'Ali, there was a second withdrawal of three or four thousand men to an-Nahrawān, when it was clear that the arbitration was going to take place after all.

Levi Della Vida describes the next phase in the development of the Khārijit movement and simultaneously characterizes the Khārijites in this manner:

---

8 Ibid., 13.
9 *Encyclopaedia of Islam*, vol. 4, 2nd ed., s.v. "*Khāridjites.*"

The extreme fanaticism of the Khawāridj at once manifested itself in a series of extremist proclamations and terrorist actions: they proclaimed the nullity of 'Ali's claims to the caliphate but equally condemned 'Uthman's conduct and disclaimed any intention of avenging his murder; they went farther and began to brand everyone infidel and outside the law who did not accept their point of view and disown 'Ali as well as 'Uthman. They then committed many murders, not even sparing women. Little by little the strength of the Kharidji army grew by the accession of other fanatical and turbulent elements, including a number of non-Arabs, attracted by the principle of equality of races in the faith that the Khawaridj proclaimed. 'Ali, who had so far tried to avoid dealing with the rebels...was obliged to take steps to avert the growing danger. He attacked the Khawaridji in their camp and inflicted a terrible defeat on them in which Ibn Wahb and the majority of his followers were slain (battle of al-Nahrawan, 17 July 658). But the victory cost 'Ali dear. Not only was the rebellion far from suppressed and was prolonged in a series of local risings...but 'Ali himself perished by the dagger of the Kharidji 'Abd al-Rahman b. Muldjam al-Muradi, the husband of a woman whose family had lost most of its members at al-Nahrawan.[10]

The Basic Doctrine of the Khārijites

The slogan of the Khārijites, "No judgment but God's" (*lā hukm illā li-llāh*), is taken by Watt to mean any rule laid down in the Koran must be applied: humans cannot make their own decisions on questions already settled by God. But the late Patricia Crone, who was Andrew W. Mellon Professor in the School of Historical Studies at the Institute for Advanced Study, is not all certain that is what the Khārijites meant: "[T]his is too banal to explain the programmatic nature of the slogan."[11] Crone and Michael Cook in their work *Hagarism* have another explanation, as does Gerald Hawting, emeritus professor of the history of the Near and Middle East at the School of Oriental and African Studies in London.[12] Perhaps the Khārijites meant that they did not want any gov-

---

10 Ibid.
11 Patricia Crone, *God's Rule—Government and Islam: Six Centuries of Medieval Islamic Political Thought* (New York: Columbia University Press, 2004), 54.
12 Gerald R. Hawting, "The Significance of the Slogan 'lā hukma illā lillāh' and the Ref-

ernment. That also seems unlikely, except perhaps in the case of the Najdiyya, as shall be discussed.

The Khārijites believed that 'Uthmān had broken some clear prescriptions of the Koran, thus there was no need for arbitration regarding the legitimacy of 'Uthmān's killing. 'Ali was equally to blame for not following the clear Koranic prescription to fight oppressive parties as found in Q49, *al-Hujurāt*, the Dwellings, 9, in 'Ali case's failing to continue his fight against Mu'awiya.

Nietzsche once suggested that fanaticism follows most naturally, not from doubt, but certainty, as with the Khārijites, who operated on the premise that their party is right, their opponents are wrong, and it is their duty to fight them. Watt summarizes:

> A verse (Q7. *al-'A'raf*, the Heights 85) said "be patient until God judges between us"; and this was taken to mean that they were patiently to continue to fight until God gave them victory, as He was bound to do in the end. In all this there is no suggestion of a doubt or uncertainty being resolved by the outcome of a battle. To the Kharijites the judgement of God is clear and already known, and it only remains to carry it out, so far as this is work for human agents.[13]

Also implied in "no judgement but God's" is the idea of a righteous community, "which knows the divine law and practises it, and which opposes communities and individuals which either do not know or do not practise the law."[14] The grave sinner is a person who does not forbid what God and His messenger have forbidden, and is thus excluded from the community as an unbeliever. This kind of declaration or judgment is known as *takfir*, which is defined as "to declare someone a *kāfir* or unbeliever," a very serious charge indeed, since "apostasy" is punishable by death.[15]

Some of the principles of the Khārijites can be inferred from the meaning of "Kharijite," an "anglicized form representing the Arabic *Khawārij* or *Khārijiyya*," which may be described as a plural and a col-

---

erences to the 'Hudūd' in the Traditions about the Fitna and the Murder of 'Uthmān," *Bulletin of the* (University of London) *School of Oriental and African Studies* 41, no. 3 (1978): 453.

13 Watt, *Formative Period*, 15.

14 Ibid.

15 *Encyclopaedia of Islam*, 2nd. ed., vol. 10, "Tā'-U[..], s.v. "*takfir*."

lective noun respectively....[D]erivatives of verb *kharaja*, 'go out,'" The word can be understood in various ways," Wyatt explains, "of which four are relevant to the explanation of the name 'Khārijites.'" They are those who

- "'went out' or 'made a secession' from the camp of 'Ali"
- "went out from among the unbelievers 'making the Hijra to God and His messenger' (Q4. *an-Nisā*', the Women, 100), that is, breaking all social ties with the unbelievers"
- "have 'gone out against' (*kharaja 'alā*) 'Ali in the sense of rebelling against him"
- "go out and take an active part in the *jihād*, in contrast to those who 'sit still'; the two groups, and the concepts of *khurūj*, "going out", and *qu'ūd*, "sitting still," are contrasted in the Koran (e.g. Q9. *at-Tawba*, the Repentance, 83)"[16]

All of these have been employed at some point by various Khārijite individuals. For instance, the fourth sense is prominent in the doctrines of the radical Ibn al-Azraq. Those striving to separate themselves from a group they considered unrighteous thought of their "secession" in the second sense. 'Ali and the Umayyad caliphs were perhaps justified in seeing the Khārijites as "rebels," in the third sense. In fact, 'Ali is reported by al-Tabarī to have used the term "*khārija*" in the sense of "rebel band."[17] Thus while government circles and other opponents of the Khārijites used khawārij to mean "rebels" or "bands of rebels," their sympathizers used it to mean "activists."

Khārijite doctrine developed over time, but one thing remained clear, the Khārijites were from the beginning, in the words of German biblical scholar and Orientalist Julius Wellhausen, "the true sons of Islam."[18] In *The Religio-Political Factions in Early Islam* (1901) Wellhausen writes:

> They were in earnest about their conception of the Theocracy and introduced nothing strange or peculiar to it....They had only principles, but these were always well-known to the

---

16 Ibid.
17 Watt, *Formative Period*, 16, citing al-Tabarī, i.3372.
18 Julius Wellhausen, *The Religio-Political Factions in Early Islam* (Amsterdam: North-Holland Publishing Company, 1975), 17. Originally published as *Die religiös—politischen Oppositionsparteien im alten Islam* (Göttingen, 1901).

people, and attracted supporters without their seeking them. However, the ones who actually took part in the subsequent action were always very few in number. They constantly took in new recruits. When the flame was stamped out in one area, it would burst out again elsewhere without visible communication. Tension reigned everywhere and was ready to explode. This is an indication of how deeply ingrained it was in the nature of Islam and the Theocracy.[19]

Wellhausen is adamant that the Khārijites "do not emerge from Arabism," as Watt has argued, "but from Islam, and their relation to those virtuosi of Islamic piety, the Koran readers, formally resembles that of the Jewish Zealots to the Pharisees. However, there remains the material difference that the Zealots fought for the fatherland, but the Kharijites only for God."[20]

Furthermore, the actions of the Khārijites exemplify the Koranic principle of Commanding Right and Forbidding Wrong. "In the Theocracy," Wellhausen explains,

> piety generally has a political slant, and this is so to the greatest extent amongst the Kharijites. God forbids His people to keep silent if His commandments on earth are abused. Not only must they personally do good and avoid doing evil, but they must see to it that this happens in all cases....Public action against injustice is the duty of the individual. He must express his convictions by word and deed. While this principle is common to all Muslims, to act recklessly upon it at all times is characteristic of the Kharijites.[21]

Cook correctly summarizes that the duty of Forbidding Wrong is "regularly associated with Kharijite political activism."[22]

Islam scholar Wilferd Madelung also sees Khārijite activism as a consequence of this principle duty in Islam:

> Although the formula [commanding right and forbidding wrong] could be interpreted to refer to the preaching of faith

---

19 Ibid., 17–18.
20 Ibid., 20.
21 Ibid.
22 Cook, *Commanding Right and Forbidding Wrong*, 393.

in God and the precepts of Islam to the infidels and to the *jihād* in order to reduce them to obedience (see Tabarī, *Tafsīr*, ed. M. M. Šāker, Cairo, 1374-/1955-, VI, pp. 90ff., XIII, p. 165), it came soon to be understood primarily as a duty of Muslims to induce their fellow Muslims to live and act in accordance with the Koran and the religious law and to refrain from acts objectionable under the *šarī 'a*. In particular, the Khārijites proclaimed it as a slogan in their censure of the unlawful and unjust conduct of the Muslim rulers and of the Muslim community at large supporting them, justifying their armed revolt and struggle to enforce adherence to the divine law.[23]

As noted earlier, the Khārijites refused the title of believer to anyone who had committed a mortal sin, regarding him as *murtadd* (apostate). Khārijite extremists, represented by the Azraqites, pronounced that anyone who becomes an infidel in this way can never regain entry into the faith and should be killed, along with his wives and children, for apostasy.[24] In fact, all non-Khāriji Muslims are considered apostates. This is "the principle of *isti'rād* (religious murder)," Levi Della Vide notes, which was "applied from the beginning of the Khariji movement, even before it had been formulated in theory, and which found its completest application during the war of the Azraqis."[25] Referring to five Arab lexicographers, Lane's *Arabic-English Lexicon* includes this usage for *isti'rād*: "The Kharijee slays men in any possible manner, and destroys whomsoever he can, without inquiring respecting the condition of anyone, Muslim or other, and without caring whom he slays."[26] Much more current, Wehr's *Dictionary of Modern Written Arabic* gives this definition, among several others: "to proceed ruthlessly; to massacre without much ado (*hum*, the enemy)."[27]

Later History of the Khārijites

The Khārijites were able to survive partly due to raids in the countryside, where their philosophy allowed them to pillage and kill

---

23 *Encyclopaedia Iranica* (www.iranicaonline.org/), s.v. "Amr be Ma'rūf," by Wilferd Madelung.
24 *Encyclopaedia of Islam*, vol. 4, 2nd ed., s.v. "Khāridjites," by Giorgio Levi Della Vida.
25 Ibid.
26 Lane, *Arabic-English Lexicon*, part 5, 2006, col. 3.
27 Wehr, *Dictionary of Modern Written Arabic*, s.v. "isti'rād."

non-Khārijites as enemies. Their Islamic roots must not be forgotten; the Khārijites fervently believed that the body politic and society itself should be based on the Koran and Koranic principles.

On the death of the caliph Yazid in 683 'Ubayd-Allah ibn-Zayid, the governor of Basra, lost control of various Khārijite and Shī'ite factions. The people of Basra had decided to support Ibn-az-Zubayr, who was in Mecca claiming the caliphate. A number of Khārijites had come to Mecca to give their assistance to Ibn-az-Zubayr. He, however, was not sympathetic to their cause. Led by Ibn-Al-Azraq, a group of Khārijites then returned to Basra to oppose Ibn-az-Zubayr's appointment. Ibn al-Azraq's forces were defeated, but he and some of his followers retreated to an eastern province, where the Zubayrid army eventually caught up with them. Ibn al-Azraq was killed in 685, but the Azraqites "continued under other leaders as a body of rebels and terrorists," recounts Watt. "Wherever they were strong enough and the opponents weak... pillage, arson and massacre became the order of the day, and none were exempt except those who actively supported the Azraqites."[28] It was left to the redoubtable al-Hajjaj, the new governor of Iraq, to wipe out the last Azraqites in 698.

Watt describes Ibn al-Azraq's development of the Khārijite philosophy as influenced by the notion of group solidarity. Ibn al-Azraq accepted the original Khārijite slogan "No judgement but God's!" and its implication that the body politic must be based on the Koran, which in his understanding meant that those "who 'sat still' and did not 'go out' or actively associate themselves with the group prosecuting the struggle against the unbelievers were themselves breaking a divine command and therefore unbelievers."[29] In other words, those who did not engage in *jihād* against the infidels were unbelievers. Thus it appeared that the Azraqites were the only true Muslims, and that all other persons could be lawfully robbed or killed. This, Watt writes, "was the religious justification of their terrorism."[30] Such a rigid, exclusionary system of thought of course resulted in the Azraqites being in state of potential and perpetual war with all other Muslims.

This "applied also to the wives and children of non-Azraqite Muslims," Watt continues, "since by their conception of group solidarity the families of unbelievers were also unbelievers":

---

28 Watt, *Formative Period*, 21.

29 Ibid., 22.

30 Ibid.

Because when they encountered other Muslims they questioned them about their beliefs, the word *isti'rād*, which properly means "questioning," came to connote "indiscriminate killing" of theological opponents. Before joining the Azraqites, too, a test (*mihna*) was made; and this is said to have consisted in giving the candidate a prisoner to kill. If the man complied, he would be more closely bound to the Azraqite body, since, especially if the man killed was of his own tribe, he would have broken existing ties, and would be dependent on the Azraqites for "protection." This test, however, may have been an occasional rather than a regular practice.[31]

The Significance of the Khārijite Movement

The fundamental principle for the Khārijites was that the Islamic community must be based on the Koran. Watt is convinced that without the Islamic and political activism of the Khārijites, ordinary Muslims may well have allowed the caliphate to become a secular Arab state.[32] The Khārijites emphasized that "membership of the Islamic community presupposed some minimum standard of belief and conduct."[33] This communalistic way of thinking had the consequence that for the Khārijites ultimate salvation or damnation was linked with membership in the group. Watt calls a community so conceived a "charismatic community":

> Its charisma is that it is capable of bestowing salvation on those who become members of it. It possesses this charisma because it has been divinely founded (through the revelation given by God to Muhammad) and because it is based on and follows the divinely given rule of life or *Sharī'a* (which has been developed from the Koran and the example of Muhammad)....[I]t is through belonging to the community that a man's life becomes meaningful. The community is the bearer of the values which constitute meaningfulness, and so transmits some of this meaningfulness to the members.[34]

While the Shī'ites placed a great emphasis on the charismatic char-

---

31 Ibid.
32 Ibid., 35.
33 Ibid.
34 Ibid., 36.

acter of the leader, the Khārijites placed it on the community, and therein, according to Watt, lies their true significance. "While the Kharijites thought that this charisma was attached to their small sect-community, one result of their striving was that the Islamic community as a whole (or at least the Sunnite part of it) came to regard itself as a charismatic community. Much of the strength and solidarity of the Islamic community today comes from the belief of the Sunnite Muslims in its charismatic character."[35]

Their view of the caliphate is another aspect of the Khārijites' political and religious theory that remains influential. It is the duty of all believers to proclaim and even depose the imam who has strayed from the right path, hence the Khārijites' abandonment of 'Ali after his acceptance of arbitration in the seventh century. For the Kharijites, there was only one criterion of eligibility for the office: merit, without considerations of descent. "Any free male, adult Muslim of sound body and mind was eligible as caliph, whatever his origins. Slaves were excluded from consideration (contrary to what is often stated), so were women."[36] Elected by the community, as Crone explains, the caliph

> retained his position for as long as he retained his superior merit. He was God's deputy on earth, at least according to Ibadis, and he was entitled to unquestioned obedience as long as this was the case. If he erred, the believers should ask him to repent, and mend his ways. If he refused to resign of his own accord, the believers were obliged to depose him by force and, if necessary, kill him, this being how they had dealt with 'Uthman. Their account of 'Uthman endorsed the lawfulness indeed the obligatory nature, of rebellion and tyrannicide.[37]

This vision of the Khārijite is essentially anti-authoritarian. But is it democratic? Crone gives a nuanced answer: "[T]he balance of power is in the community's favour, and for this reason they were described as 'democratic.' But for the Ibadis the imam represented God, not the people, who merely had to obey. But since it was the people (in the form of the scholars) who decided whether he represented God or not, it was

---

35 Ibid.
36 Crone, *God's Rule*, 57.
37 Ibid., 58.

in practice through them rather than him that God displayed His will."[38]

Ethical principles of the Khārijites show a similar puritanism; they demand "purity of conscience as an indispensable complement to bodily purity for the validity of acts of worship."[39] For example, the Khārijites rejected Sura Yusuf of the Koran (Q12 Yusuf) as too worldly and frivolous to be the word of God. On the other hand, they did not allow stoning for adulterers, since it is not mentioned in the Koran, and did not recognize the *hadīth* justifying such a punishment as authentic.

The political activism of the Khārijites, who were described by both Watt and Della Vida as "terrorists", represents a model to be followed for many contemporary Islamic terrorists. The Khārijites were pursuing an Islamic goal derived from the Koran, and they saw themselves as members of a privileged community singled out by Allah Himself.

---

38 Ibid., 59.
39 *Encyclopaedia of Islam*, vol. 4, 2nd ed., s.v. "Khāridjites."

CHAPTER 10
Sahl ibn Salāma, Barbahārī, and *Bidʿa*: Religious Violence in Ninth- and Tenth-Century Baghdad

MODERN-DAY ISLAMIST groups and organizations did not emerge *ex nihilo* in the 1970s but from an Islamic cultural matrix, a tradition they could draw upon with legitimacy. Their political structures and, above all, the origins of their ideology are located in the founding texts of Islam, the Koran, the *hadīth* and *sunna*, and the *Sira*, the life of the Prophet.

How do we know this?

Many Islamists tells us openly, developing and spreading their ideas via the news media and the Internet. For example, admiration is frequently expressed for Ibn Taymiyya, the medieval Islamic Hanbali theologian who has been mentioned in these pages. Here is how one Western scholar, Ignaz Goldziher, a founder of the modern scientific study of Islam, has described the influence of Ibn Taymiyya:

> In the age immediately following [his death in 1328], the salient theme of theological literature was whether he had been a heretic or a devout zealot of the *sunna*. His handful of followers surrounded his memory with a nimbus of holiness, and his opponents were soon appeased and brought to a more favorable view of him by the lasting impression of earnest religiosity that the writings of the dead enthusiast made on them. For four centuries his influence was latent but

felt. His works were read and studied. In many Islamic milieus they were a mute force that from time to time released outbreaks of hostility to *bid'a* [innovations].¹

Not just the works of Ibn Taymiyya, but the precepts of Islam, especially, the notion of *jihād*, which, as has been mentioned, almost became the sixth pillar of Islam, were a latent force, running like a crimson river underground, only to resurface with a bloody roar from time to time when the surrounding strata could no longer restrain its flowing rage. Thus, long before the arrival of Ibn Taymiyya in the early fourteenth century, periods of religious-social unrest erupted.

Al-Ma'mūn came to power in 813 in Iraq after a civil war in which he defeated his brother, the previous Caliph al-Amīn.² But he had great difficulty establishing his authority, especially in the province, and had to contend with many rebellions. Some of al-Ma'mūn's opponents were Shī'ites laying claim to the caliphate, such as al-Hasan al-Harashi, whose rebellion was followed by a rebellion by Nasr ibn Shabath, and yet another, in 814–816 in Kufa, led by Ibn Tabataba. As Ira M. Lapidus, emeritus professor of Middle Eastern and Islamic history at the University of California at Berkeley, explains, "The rally cry of this rebellion was 'al-Rida' and "*amal bil-kitāb wal-sunna*'—'the chosen one' and 'action in accord with the [holy] book and the tradition (*sunna*).'"³

When law and order collapsed in Baghdad, there was some popular organization to resist the looting and general banditry. For instance, Khālid al-Daryūs, a concerned citizen, called upon his neighbors and the people of his quarter to fight: "Using the religious slogan, *amr bil-ma 'rūf wa-nahy 'an al-munkar* [Commanding Right and Forbidding Wrong], Khālid mobilized volunteers called *mutawwi'a* to defend themselves against the bandits."⁴ As German Islamic scholar Josef van Ess has indicated, this religious slogan "became identified more or less with political independence and with the self-government of small social groups."⁵

---

1 Ignaz Goldziher, *Introduction to Islamic Theology and Law*, trans. Andras and Ruth Hamori (Princeton, NJ: Princeton University Press, 1981), 241.

2 For this section on Baghdad under al-Ma'mūn, I rely entirely on Ira M. Lapidus, "The Separation of State and Religion in the Development of Early Islamic Society," *International Journal of Middle East Studies* 6, no. 4 (October 1975): 363–85.

3 Ibid., 370.

4 Ibid., 372.

5 Josef van Ess, "*Une lecture a rebours de l'histoire du mu'tazilisme*," *Revue des études*

"Religious themes were even more explicit in a similar defense led by Sahl ibn Salāma al-Ansārī," one of the people from Khurasan who resided in of Baghdad's al-Harbiyya quarter and

> wore a copy of the Koran around his neck and called on the people to "Command the good and forbid the evil." He appealed to his neighbours, to the people of his [quarter], and to a larger audience including the Banū Hāshim, the Caliphal family, and to the people of high and low rank. While Sahl organized his followers and marched through the streets and suburbs to keep order and stop the protection rackets, his movement went beyond resistance to banditry. Sahl signed his supporters into a dīwān, or registry, required that they uphold the Koran and the *sunna*, *'amal bil-kitāb Allah wa-sunnat nabīyihi*, and pledged them to take an oath of allegiance to him to oppose whosoever opposed the Koran and *sunna*. Beyond resistance to banditry Sahl envisaged allegiance to a higher principle which justified opposing even the Caliph and the state authorities if they failed to uphold Islam. On this point he and Khalid al-Daryush parted ways. Khalid wished to mobilize the people to maintain order, but would not oppose the Caliphal authority which he regarded as intrinsically legitimate, while Sahl preached that allegiance to the Koran and sunna superseded obedience to authorities who were compromised by failure to uphold Islam.[6]

Sahl evidently posed a serious threat to al-Ma'mūn, and his religious claims became more explicit when he adopted the slogan, *lā tā'a lil-makhlūq fī ma'siyat al-khāliq*, "No obedience to the creature in disobedience of the Creator," which, Lapidus explains, was "an open allusion to the conflict, as he saw it, between God's will and Caliphal authority."[7] Sahl was easily captured in his quarter in Baghdad (in approximately 817), imprisoned, released, and, when he recognized al-Ma'mūn as a legitimate caliph, was given a pension by the latter.

Sahl's slogan, "Command the good and forbid the evil," Lapidus writes, "sums up the demand for a righteous society, a community of the just living in accord with God's law." But the caliphs beginning with

---

islamiques 47, no. 1 (1979): 68.

6 Lapidus, "Separation of State and Religion," 372.

7 Ibid., 373.

al-Ma'mūn claimed that only they and their officials known as *muhtasibs* were responsible for commanding good and forbidding evil. Popular preachers, however, held that it was incumbent on all Muslims to see that the holy law was adhered to, and applied. "Thus, Sahl's slogan embraces a conception of Islam in which every Muslim was obliged not only to obey the legal, moral, and ritual teachings of Islam, but also to prevent their gross violation by others."[8]

Sahl's ambitious goal went beyond the need for self-protection from bandits:

> [H]e tried to mobilize the latent religious sentiment which made each Muslim personally responsible for a just society. Sahl was appealing to a sentiment akin to the sentiment for *jihād*, or holy war—indeed his volunteers were called *mutawwiʿa*, as were the volunteers for frontier duty and for holy war against Byzantium. Sahl was appealing to a sentiment which reached beyond the boundaries of Caliphal government to an essentially communal conception of Islam. In this respect [this] vigilante movement embodied a revolutionary conception of the structure of Muslim society.[9]

The slogan "No obedience to the creature in disobedience of the Creator" also expressed a radical position. It was originally used by the Khārijites to justify their resistance to caliphal authority. Ibn al-Muqaffaʿ (c. 720-756), an Arabic author of Persian origin who was among the first translators into Arabic literary works of the Indian and Iranian civilizations, discusses the slogan and makes it clear that, in his opinion, while no obedience is due a ruler in violation of religious precepts, he must be obeyed in political matters in general. "A sacrilegious command is not binding, but it does not dissolve the authority of the ruler."[10]

Finally, *ʿamal bil-kitāb Allah wa-sunnat nabīyihi* had been used by the ʿAbbāsids themselves in the Khurasan in their revolt against Umayyad rule. Sahl's use of it "placed him in the revolutionary tradition of Khurasan and of the precedents set by the ʿAbbāsid *daʿwa* itself." Sahl's movement is descended from the earlier movement, "which overthrew Umayyad rule in the name of religious ideals." Thus, the real significance of Sahl's movement, which was more than a peace-keeping device or

---

8 Ibid., 376.
9 Ibid.
10 Ibid., 377.

struggle for power in an unsettled political situation, is that "it revive[d] the religiously inspired political activism which had already replaced one dynasty with another and which now opposed its own creature in the name of basic religious principles."[11]

"Fanatical Terrorism" and Barbahārī

Ibn Hanbal (d. 855) was rather apolitical, and his attitude is described by Michael Cook as "relative quietism." And yet, by the tenth century "Hanbalite violence was rampant on the streets of Baghdad. This muscular Hanbalism was already noted by Goldziher, who spoke caustically but aptly of an evolution from an *ecclesia pressa* to an *ecclesia militans*, with a penchant for 'fanatical terrorism.'"[12]

This new style of Hanbalite politics is linked to the life of Barbahārī (d. 941). The supporters of Hanbali theologian Barbahārī were often involved in bloody confrontations with his adversaries in the streets of Baghdad.[13] Barbahārī wrote a profession of faith, *Kitāb al-Sunna*, which is

> a polemic work denouncing the multiplication of suspect innovations (*bid'a*) and energetically enjoining a return to the precepts of the "old religion" (*dīn 'atīq*), as it was understood at the time of the first three Caliphs, before the schism which followed the assassination of 'Uthman b. 'Affan and the succession of 'Alī b. Abī Tālib.

Barbahārī condemned, as would Ibn Taymiyya, "the pernicious deviations that result from the personal and arbitrary use of reasoning (*ta'wil; ra'y; qiyās*) in the domain of religious beliefs." And again Ibn Taymiyya would follow Barbahārī's example in reminding believers of their duty to obey all established authority except where disobedience to God is involved. He condemned all attempts at armed revolt (*khurūdj bi 'l-sayf*),

---

11 Ibid., 378.

12 Cook, *Commanding Right and Forbidding Wrong*, 116, citing Ignaz Goldziher, "Review of Walter M. Patton, *Ahmed Ibn Hanbal and the Mihna*," in *Zeitschrift der Deutschen Morgenländischen Gesellschaft*, Bd. 52 (1898), 158.

13 The entire section on Barbahārī is dependent on Henri Laoust's entry in the *Encyclopaedia of Islam*, vol.1, "A–B," ed. H.A.R. Gibb et al., 2nd ed. (Leiden: Brill, 1960), s.v. "al-Barbahārī."

considering in fact that the re-establishment of the Law should be effected by appeal to public opinion, by the duty of missionary preaching (*da'wa*), of enjoining the Good (*amr bi 'l-ma'rūf*) and of proffering good counsel (*nasīha*). This re-establishment of the Law, in a world in which Islam had split up into numerous sects, was incumbent especially on the 'people of the *hadīth*', on the *ahl al-sunna wa 'l-djamā'a*, whose triumph God had definitely assured. True to his doctrine, al-Barbahārī conducted so vigorous a personal action against *bid'a* and against the sects (*firqa*), especially against Mu'tazilism and Shī'ism, that he was at times accused of entertaining political ambitions.[14]

But as Henri Laoust, late Professor of Islamic Sociology at the Collège de France, reminds us, "[A]l-Barbahari's influence is to be discovered behind several popular demonstrations and insurrections which broke out in Baghdad between 921 and 941. He was not unconnected with the opposition encountered by al-Tabari, who, in 309, was invited by the *wazir* 'Alī b. 'Isā to come to discuss with his Hanbali opponents points of doctrine which separated them and who, in 310, had to be buried at night in his own house because of the hostility of the mob."[15]

There was another violent confrontation that resulted in much bloodshed in 929 in Baghdad, over the interpretation of a verse in the Koran, Q17. *al-'Isrā'*, the Night Journey, 79: "Perchance thy Lord will send thee to a sojourn worthy of praise (*maqām mahmūd*)." "Al-Barbahari's disciples maintained that this was to be interpreted as meaning that on the Day of Resurrection, *God*, would seat the Prophet on His throne, whilst, for their adversaries, who followed the doctrine of al-Tabarī and Ibn Khuzayma, this was merely a question of the great intercession (*shafā'a*) of the Prophet in favour of believers culpable of grave faults on the Day of Judgement."[16]

Further demonstrations by Barbahārī's supporters followed, the agitation reaching its apogee in 935, when Hanbalis began "looting shops, intervening in commercial transactions to impose the prescriptions of the Law, attacking the wine-sellers and singing-girls, smashing musical instruments, pushing their way into private dwellings and denouncing to the Prefect of Police any man found in the street with a

---

14 Ibid.
15 Ibid.
16 Ibid.

woman, not being her *mahram* [any relative a Muslim is not allowed to marry]."[17]

The caliphal authorities banned Barbahārī's supporters from meeting and teaching and the Muslims from praying behind an imam following the Hanbali doctrine. Barbahārī's supporters refused to settle down, and "a decree by the Caliph al-Rādī was issued in 923, condemning Hanbalism and excluding it from the Muslim community," and "accus[ing] it of developing an anthropomorphist theodicy (*tashbīh*) and of forbidding the visiting of the tombs of the great imams (*ziyārat al-qubūr*). This condemnation only prevented Hanbali demonstrations for a while."[18]

Barbahārī's supporters continued their violent demonstrations in 939 under the amirate of Badjkam. Despite the efforts of the police, Barbahārī' was able to escape into hiding, although his lieutenant Dallā' was captured and executed. The situation worsened in 940, when Badjkam had the mosque of Barāthā, demolished under the Caliph al-Muqtadir as a hotbed of Shī'ism, rebuilt.

When Kurdish robbers assassinated Badjkam in 941, the Hanbalis celebrated with much noise, attempting to demolish the rebuilt mosque and attacking the commercial and banking district. Some of the Hanbalis were arrested, and the Shī'ī mosque was placed under guard.

Barbahārī died in April 941 and was buried where he had been hiding. His influence continued to grow among his Hanbali contemporaries. One of his disciples was Sharif Abū Dja'far al-Hāshimī (d. 1078), who was behind several violent popular demonstrations against *bid'a*. Another disciple, Ibn Batta al-'Ukbarī (d. 997), who had met Barbahārī several times, wrote two professions of faith—his '*aqīda* —that greatly influences two important scholars: qādī Abū 'lā b. al-Farrā' (d. 1066) and Ibn Taymiyya. As Laoust points out, there is a direct line from early Hanbali polemicists such as Barbahārī to Ibn Batta, who

> through his doctrinal work and his sermons, belongs to the great tradition of Hanbali polemic which was practised, during the century following the death of the founder of the school, by the *shaykh* 'Abd Allah (d. 903), Abū Bakr al-Khallāl and Barbahārī. Like them, he denounced and forbade all the blameworthy innovations (*bid'a*), which he considered had come to debase the religion founded by the Prophet, in the

---

17 Ibid.
18 Ibid.

field of dogma as well as in those of worship, law or morals. His severity concerning *bid'a* was such that he refused to distinguish, not only between good and bad *bid'as* but also between small and great. He saw as the only means of salvation a return to the primitive religion (*dīn 'atīq*) exactly as it had been formulated during the lifetime of the Prophet and of the first three caliphs, Abu Bakr, 'Umar and 'Uthmān.[19]

From Ibn Batta to Ibn Taymiyya the line proceeds to Birgili, Qādīzāde, and to Ibn 'Abd al-Wahhāb and the modern Islamists.

---

[19] *Encyclopaedia of Islam*, vol. 3, "H–Iram," ed. B. Lewis et al., 2nd ed. (Leiden: Brill, 1971), s.v. "Ibn Batta," by Henri Laoust.

CHAPTER 11
RELIGIOUS VIOLENCE IN BAGHDAD BETWEEN 991 CE AND 1092 CE

AFTER BARBAHĀRĪ, Hanbalite activism continued during the Buyid period, a major Shīʿite dynasty in mediaeval Islamic history that flourished in Persia and Iraq between 945 and 1055. Buyid Baghdad witnessed many clashes between the Sunni and Shīʿite populations. But as Michael Cook emphasizes, "Confrontation between Sunnis and Shīʿites did not, of course, end with the passing of the Buyids; it is enough to note that it remained a feature of the politics of Baghdad to the fall of the ʿAbbasid caliphate [with the sack of Baghdad in 1258]."[1]

Baghdad was shaken by numerous violent incidents of a religious character between 991 and 1092.[2] The accession of al-Qādir (991–1031), brought a new resolution to defend the *Sunna* and to reestablish the authority of the caliph. At the foundation of House of Science (*Dār al-ʿilm*), sometimes considered the first madrasa established to serve the defence of Shīʿism, the caliph replied by inaugurating a new *khutba* (sermon) mosque in the Harbīya quarter.

Serious disturbances broke out in 998, when the Shīʿites of Baghdad were celebrating with particular fervor the solemn ceremonies of *al-ʿāshūrā*ʾ on the 10 *muharram* and Ghadīr Khumm on 18 *dhūʾl-hijja*.[3]

---

1 Cook, *Commanding Right and Forbidding Wrong*, 118.
2 In this section I depend upon Henri Laoust, "Les Agitations Religieuses à Baghdad aux IVe et Ve Siècles de l'Hegire," in *Islamic Civilisation 950–1150*, ed. D.S. Richards (Oxford: Oxford University Press, 1973).
3 Shīʿa Muslims commemorate *Al-ʿāshūrāʾ* as a day of mourning for the martyrdom of Husayn ibn Ali, Muhammad's grandson, who was massacred with a small group of family and companions at the Battle of Karbala on 10 Muharram 61 AH (October 10,

The Sunnis reacted by replying to these Shī'ite ceremonies with two ceremonies of their own: visiting the grave of Mus'ab b.Zubayr on 18 *muharram*, which commemorated the victory of Mus'ab over the rebellion of al-Mukhtār; and celebrating the festival of the Day of the Cave (*yawn al-ghār*), an episode in the life of Muhammad when he and Abu Bakr escaped from their enemies by hiding in a cave.[4]

The public disturbances provoked by celebrating these ceremonies finally ended in 1002, in an armed confrontation in the streets of the capital between the so-called *'ayyārūn*[5] of the two parties: the party of 'Alī and the party of al'Abbās. The public celebration of all these festivals had to be forbidden the following year.

Sunni and Shī'ite clashed again in 1007, this time over the status of the version of Koran according to Ibn Mas'ūd versus the version according to 'Uthman. It seems to have started with the looting of the Shī'ite mosque of Barāthā, in response to attacks on two of the most prominent Shafi'ites, the qadi Abū Mahammad al-Akfānī and Shaykh Abū Hāmid al-Isfarā'inī. A commission set up by the caliph concluded that Ibn Mas'ūd's recension of the Koran constituted an inacceptable alteration of the Koranic text.[6]

During the night of April 24-25, 1008, a Shī'ite in Karbala publically cursed "the man who had burnt the *Mushaf* [of Ibn Mas 'ūd]," which was obviously aimed at the Caliph 'Uthmān, whom Shī'ites reproached for having dispossesed Imām 'Alī, having persecuted 'Abd Allāh b. Mas'ūd, and having had burned all the recensions of the Koran that differed from his own. The caliph had the blasphemer arrested and executed. In the ensuing riots, and during which the Fātimid al-Hākim was cheered, Shaykh Abū Hāmid al-Isfarā'inī had to flee from his home, and Shaykh al Mufīd, the spokesman of the Twelver Shī'ias, was sent into exile.

---

680 CE).
Ghadīr Khumm refers to the appointment, according to Shī'a Muslims, of Ali ibn Abi Talib as his successor by the Prophet Muhammad. Sunni Muslims do not believe that the Prophet Muhammad appointed a successor in Ghadīr Khumm, or anywhere else.
4 Laoust, "Les Agitations," 170.
5 *Ayyār*, a noun literally meaning "vagabond," applied to members of medieval *futuwwa* (*futūwa*) brotherhoods and comparable to popular organizations; irregular fighters or class of warriors who dominated Baghdad during this period of lawlessness, often imposing taxes on roads and markets, burning wealthy quarters and markets, and looting the homes of the rich. For several years (1028–1033), Al-Burjumi and Ibn al-Mawsili, leaders of the *'ayyārūn*, ruled the city because of governmental instability.
6 Laoust, "Les Agitations," 171.

The intervention of the caliph and the Buyid Emir, at the request of the leading citizens of Baghdad, brought some balm to the situation; and the popular preachers of the two parties, who had been forbidden to hold their meetings in public places, were able to resume their activities—as long as they abstained from inciting riots by their sermons.[7] After a brief lull, the violence resumed between 1015 and 1017.

Once again, Sunni and Shī'ite were at the center of the discord. The vizir Fakhr al-Mulk brought a measure of calm by allowing the Shī'ites to celebrate *al-'āshūrā'*. In 1016, the violence incidents became even more frequent. Fires whose origin remains mysterious broke out in Karbala, in the mausoleum of Imām al-Husayn, in diverse sanctuaries of Baghdad, and in the Great Mosque of Sāmarrā. The three great mosques of Mecca, Medina, and Jerusalem were also plundered.

Al-Qādir's main worry was his struggle against pernicious doctrines, especially those that threatened the caliphate. In 1017,

> [he] demanded that the Hanafi juriconsults who had shown some sympathy with Mu'tazilism make an act of penitence; at the same time he forbade the teaching of Mu'tazili and Shi'i doctrines. Then, in 1018, he had a reading given in the palace of the text called the *al-risāla al-qādiriyya*, a profession of faith defining the the official doctrine which also conformed to the ideas of the Men of Old [Salaf]. Inspired by Hanbalite ideas, this text condemned not only Shi'ism in all its forms but also Mu'tazilism and even Ash'arism, which was denounced for taking a stance that was a dangerous compromise with Mu'tazilism, and put forward the veneration of the Companions as a genuine obligation.[8]

During the last years of his caliphate, al-Qādir consolidated his gains in the cause of Sunnism. He had read out aloud from his palace three letters: the first denounced Mu'tazilism, the second attacked the doctrine of the "created Koran," and the third proclaimed the superiority of the early caliphs, and affirmed the obligation of Commanding Right and Forbidding Wrong.[9] To ease tension, al-Qādir had the preacher at the mosque of Barāthā dismissed because of his extreme pro-Shī'ite

---

7 Ibid.

8 *Encyclopaedia of Islam*, vol. 4, "Iran–Kha," ed. by E. van Donzel, B. Lewis, and Ch. Pellat 2nd ed. (Leiden: Brill, 1978), s.v. "Al-Kādir Bi'llāh," by Dominique Sourdel.

9 Ibid.

sermons.

The disturbances did not cease during the reign of al-Qādir's successor, al-Qa'im. If anything, they became more frequent. As the chief of the 'ayyārūn, Al-Burjumi inspired, in Laoust's words, "a veritable terror," and his crimes added to the Turkish militia's lack of discipline. Such was the chaos and agitation that the pilgrimage caravan was not able to depart. There were riots in 1045 and 1047, when Jews and Christians were also targeted. In 1048, no pilgrimage caravan was able to set off because of the violence.

In 1049 the Sunnis and Shī'ites were at it again; the two communities barricaded themselves in their quarters of the city. Occasional apparent reconciliations were brief, and violence broke out between the two once again in Baghdad in 1051. Tombs were violated, and some Shī'ites even thought of violating the tomb of Ibn Hanbal, but were persuaded not to do so. The year 1053 witnessed more Sunni-Shī'ite violence. That same year, Tughril Beg officially condemned Ash'arism.

The policies of Nizām al-Mulk (d. 1090), the minister of the Seljuk Sultans Alp Arslan and Malik Shah, were favourable to Ash'arism, Shafi'ism, and Sufism, which contributed to a renewal of the disturbances. However the inauguration of Nizām al-Mulks's college, known as the Nizāmīya, was vigorously opposed by both the Hanifites and Hanbalites. Popular agitation of a serious kind erupted, evidence of the tension that existed within the Sunnite schools and the unpopularity of Nizāmian and Seljukite policies.

Religious agitation continued in Baghdad during the reign of Malik-Shah (1072–1092). Two great facts dominate the history of Baghdad during this time: first, the often violent confrontations between the Hanbalites and Ash'arites, and later, a renewal of the conflict between the Sunnis and Shī'ites.

Michael Cook gives an account of Hanbalite activism in the Seljuq period in Baghdad. There is the example of Ibn Sukkara, a prominent Sharīf, who raided two groups near the caliphal palace, smashing musical instruments and pouring out liquor. In 1072, a younger Hanbalite scholar, Abu Sa'd al-Baqqāl (d. 1112), came across a singing-girl who had been performing for a Turk. He grabbed her lute and cut its strings. She complained to the Turk, who retaliated by raiding Abū Sa'd's home. Sharīf Abū Ja'far (d. 1077), a typical Hanbalite activist with a considerable following, defended the mosque of the Hanbalites during the 1077 Hanbalite-Ash'arite riots, "routing the attackers with barrage of mud bricks."¹⁰ When the caliph tried to make peace, Abū Jaʿfar replied that conflicts of doctrine could not be patched up like conflicts of interests.

In 1078, the conflict between the two groups renewed. As Cook writes, "These hostilities between Hanbalism and Ashʿarism continued into the following century and beyond."¹¹ The older Hanbalite conflict with the Muʿtazilism also continued unabated. While the Hanbalites were no longer in awe of the state, they nonetheless sought its cooperation in the duty of Forbidding Wrong, asking the caliph to take measures against brothels, prostitutes, and liquor-sellers. The caliph did his best to comply.¹²

The Hanbalites were emboldened by the fact that there were, by the eleventh century, far more Hanbalites than Shīʿites in Baghdad. The state was perceived as being weaker than in the past, but there was also an understanding that "a certain bond was established between the Hanbalites and the caliphate: they needed each other in the face of local Shīʿites and alien military rulers."¹³

There was also a changed attitude among the Hanbalites to state employment, something that had been shunned by Ibn Hanbal. Personal debt forced his son to take a position as a judge, and Hanbalite scholars now had more extensive dealings with the court. Abu Muhammad al-Tamīmī (d. 1095), for example "enjoyed a career as a courtier and diplomat,"¹⁴ and then there is the example of Ibn al-Jawzī (d. 1201), the preacher who was a "favourite of caliph and populace alike."¹⁵ He was given executive powers in 1176 "to mount a crackdown on manifestations of extreme Shiʿism (*rafd*); the operation was to include the permanent imprisonment of offenders, and the demolition of their homes."¹⁶

The intellectual curiosity of the Hanbalite theologian Ibn ʿAqīl (d. 1119) would lead him into much trouble. "Before the death of his teacher Abu Yaʿla in 1066, he had already frequented the study circles of Muʿtazili masters, had delved into the study of *kalām*, vigorously condemned by Hanbalism, and had become interested in the writings of the great mystic of *wahdat al-shuhūd*, al-Hallāj."¹⁷ Ibn ʿAqīl was first attacked

---

10 Cook, *Commanding Right and Forbidding Wrong*, 118–20.
11 Ibid., 120.
12 Ibid., 121.
13 Ibid., 122.
14 Ibid., 124.
15 Ibid., 127.
16 Ibid.
17 *Encyclopaedia of Islam*, vol. 3, 2nd ed., s.v. "Ibn ʿAkīl," by George Makdisi.

in 1069 for such transgressions, and had to go into hiding between 1068 and 1072. In 1072, under pressure from Abū Ja'far, Ibn 'Aqīl read his public retraction, repudiating his own earlier writings on al-Hallāj, and the Mu'tazilites.

Abū Ja'far, the persecutor of Ibn 'Aqil, Henri Laoust tells us, was "a successor in spirit of Barbahari and Ibn Batta" who "distinguished himself…by the energetic drive he brought to bear in support of the Hanbali credo and the restoration of the authority of the 'Abbasid Caliphate. We see him then at Baghdad taking command of a series of popular uprisings against Mu'tazilism and Sufism; in 1068 against the teaching of at the Nizamiyya;…in 1071 against various forms of corruption;…finally in 1076 against Ibn al-Qushayri who, in his teaching at the Nizamiyya, had taken up again against Hanbalism the old charge of anthropomorphism (*tashbih*)."[18]

Violent confrontations erupted between the supporters of Ibn al-Qushayri and those of Abu Ja'far. In 1077, new disturbances broke out, and the expulsion of the ringleaders brought about some calm. Unrest reignited in 1082, when a Hanbalite scholar attacked the Nizamiya and exhorted his listeners to destroy it. He was caught, flogged, and imprisoned. Another incident occurred in 1083, when the partisans of a certain al-Bakri, who had been appointed to give sermons at the Nizamiya, plundered the house of one of the sons of Abū Ya'lā, making off with one of his works. When given the work, al-Bakri publicly accused Abū Ya'lā of unbelief. That same year al-Bakri gave a sermon in which accused the Hanbalites of unbelief. Stones were thrown, but the caliph managed to restore order.

In the following years incidents multiplied. There were bloody skirmishes in 1085 between the Sunnis and Shi'ites, leaving many dead. The visit of Malik-Shah and Nizam to Baghdad calmed things down, but the disturbances resumed in 1088, followed by even more serious riots in 1089, which left, according to Ibn al-Jawzi, more than two hundred dead. The Shi'ites were accused of hating Islam and its Law. Between 1091 and 1095 there were a series of violent deaths.[19] The riots leaving hundreds dead confirm that religiously inspired terrorism, far from being a twentieth-century phenomenon, was present throughout the tenth eleventh, twelfth, and right up to the thirteenth century in the Islamic world, especially in large cities such as Baghdad.

---

18 *Encyclopaedia of Islam*, vol. 3, 2nd ed., s.v. "Hanabila," by Henri Laoust.
19 Laoust, "*Les Agitations*," 184.

CHAPTER 12
Ibn Taymiyya

THE MAY 1983 *Encounter* contained "Ibn Taymiyya: Father of the Islamic Revolution: Medieval Theology & Modern Politics," history scholar Emmanuel Sivan's report on a dangerous influence on contemporary Muslim youth:

> What has been called "the hottest literary property" in the Arab world today (particularly in Egypt) is the work of a 14th-century theologian, Ibn Taymiyya. Six months before President Sadat's assassination, his ruling Party's weekly, *Mayo*, singled out Ibn Taymiyya (together with his major contemporary disciple) as the most pervasive and deleterious influence upon Egyptian youth. From him they learned that "violence and seizure of power are justified by Islamic law and tradition"—and that fellow Muslims, be they Sunnis (orthodox, i.e., not Shiite heretics) could become the target of a "holy war in the cause of Allah." No wonder, *Mayo* concluded, the proliferating Muslim Associations at the universities, where Ibn Taymiyya's views prevail, have been spawning various terrorist groups.[1]

More recently, Yahya Michot, a Belgian Muslim professor of Islamic studies and staunch admirer of Ibn Taymiyya, had this to say in his entry in *The Princeton Encyclopaedia of Islamic Political Thought* (2013): "The writings of this major independent Sunni mufti, theologian, and

---

1 Emmanuel Sivan, "Ibn Taymiyya: Father of the Islamic Revolution: Medieval Theology & Modern Politics," *Encounter* 69, no. 5 (May 1983): 41.

activist of the Mamluk period influenced various reformist and puritanical developments in later Muslim societies. Often misinterpreted, they remain central in modern Islamist ideology and Muslim recourse to violence."[2]

Early Life and Education

Taki al-Din Ahmad Ibn Taymiyya, born in Harran (modern southeastern Turkey) in 1263, was a Hanbalī theologian and juriconsult, known to his many admirers as "Shaykh al-Islam." He and his family fled the Mongols and settled in Damascus in 1269. He would spend his entire life in the Mamluk sultanate (Syria, Egypt, Palestine, and the Hijaz), and died in prison in Damascus in 1328.

Ibn Taymiyya studied law with his father and Shams al-Din 'Abd al Rahman al-Maqdisi (d. 1283). He also briefly studied Arabic grammar and lexicography under Su¬layman ibn 'Abd al-Qawi al-Tuft (d. 1316), and eventually was able to master Sībawayhī's seminal grammar of the Arabic language, *Al-Kitāb*. Ibn Taymiyya was qualified to issue legal opinions by the age of twenty, and succeeded his father at his death in 1283 as professor of *hadīth* and law at Dar al-Hadith al-Sukkariyah, a Sufi monastery and college of *hadīth*. In 1285, Ibn Taymiyya began teaching Koranic exegesis at the Umayyad mosque and in 1292 went on pilgrimage to Mecca, a journey that provided much material for his first treatise, *Manāsik al-hajj*, in which he denounced a certain number of *bid'as* or innovations in the ritual of the pilgrimage,[3] even though it meant going against the opinion of Ibn Qudama, the great Hanbalite scholar.[4]

The greatest influence on Ibn Taymiyya's doctrinal education was the Koran, which had an "an all-encompassing and active" hold over him.[5] Ibn Taymiyya wrote a forty-volume commentary (no longer extant) on the Koran while in prison. He also mastered the *hadīth*, but it was the *Musnad* of Ahmad ibn Hanbal that he preferred above all other

---

[2] Yahya Michot, "Ibn Taymiyya," in *The Princeton Encyclopaedia of Islamic Political Thought*, ed. Gerhard Bowering (Princeton, NJ: Princeton University Press, 2013), 238.

[3] *Encyclopaedia of Islam*, vol. 3, "H–Iram," ed. B. Lewis et al., 2nd ed. (Leiden: Brill, 1971), s.v. "Ibn Taymiyya," by Henri Laoust. George Makdisi, "Ibn Taymiyah," *Islamic Philosophy Online*, May 13, 2003, updated September 6, 2007, http://www.muslimphilosophy.com/it/itya.htm.

[4] Henri Laoust, "*La Biographie d'Ibn Taimīya d'après Ibn Katīr*," *Bulletin d'études orientales* 9 (1942–1943): 117.

[5] Henri Laoust, *Essai sur les doctrines sociales et politiques de Takī-d- Dīn Ahmad b. Taimīya* (Cairo: Imprimerie de l'Institut Français d'Archéologie Orientale, 1939), 73.

works. And after the Koran and *hadīth*, it was Ahmad ibn Hanbal and his disciples who played the most important part in Ibn Taymiyya's intellectual and doctrinal development.[6] He did not follow the traditions blindly, however, and found Bukhārī and Muslim less than rigorous, claiming that many of the traditions in Bukhārī, for example, were of dubious authenticity.

Clash with Authorities and Imprisonment

Ibn Taymiyya's first clash with the authorities took place in 1293, at the time of the affair of 'Assāf al-Nasrānī, a Christian accused of having insulted the Prophet. According to Ibn Kathir, the authorities asked Ibn Taymiyya to give an Islamic legal verdict (*fatwa*). He accepted and delivered his *fatwa*, which called for the death penalty, arguing that anyone insulting the Prophet, even a Muslim, ought to be killed. Though the public approved of Ibn Taymiyya's verdict, the governor of Syria tried to resolve the situation by asking 'Assāf to convert to Islam, to which he agreed. Ibn Taymiyya refused to accept this outcome, and together with his followers protested outside the governor's palace demanding 'Assāf's death. This intransigence and defiance led to Ibn Taymiyya's imprisonment. While in prison, Ibn Taymiyya wrote his first important work, *al-Sārim al-maslūl 'alā shātim al-Rasūl* (*The Drawn Sword against Those Who Insult the Messenger*).[7]

Ibn Taymiyya was imprisoned six times and spent a total of six years in prison because of his beliefs and views on matters of jurisprudence. Michot contends that the real reasons for his incarceration were the "doctrines and practices prevalent among the powerful religious and Sufi establishments, an overly outspoken personality, the jealously of his peers, the risk to the public order due to this popular appeal and political intrigues."[8] Michot explains how Ibn Taymiyya's involvement in public affairs antagonized the authorities:

> Actively taking it upon himself to implement the religious duty to command right and forbid wrong, he is said to have, among other things, shaved children's heads, led an anti-debauchery campaign in brothels and taverns, struck an atheist with his hand before [the atheist's] public execution,

---

6 Ibid., 79.

7 Makdisi, "Ibn Taymiyah." See also *Wikipedia*, s.v. "Ibn Taymiyyah," last modified, January 14, 2017 https://en.wikipedia.org/wiki/Ibn_Taymiyyah.

8 Michot, "Ibn Taymiyya," 239.

destroyed a supposedly sacred rock in a mosque, conducted attacks on astrologers, and obliged deviant Sufi shaykhs to make public acts of contrition and to adhere to the sunna. He not only exhorted to *jihād* on various occasions but also personally took part in some expeditions and battles.[9]

Ibn Taymiyya's Character

His difficult character is well-summarized in Donald Little's classic article, "Did Ibn Taymiyya Have a Screw Loose?" which cites Ibn Taymiyya's supporters such as al-Dhahabī (d. 1339), a pro-Hanbalī Shāfiʿī, and al-Hādī (d.1343–44), a member of his Hanbalī *madhab*:

> Accounts of Ibn Taymiyya's public activities offer abundant proof for other of al-Dhahabī's observations, in particular those regarding Ibn Taymiyya's pride, impetuosity, obstinancy, intolerance, and tactlessness. Examples of such behavior are readily available from secondary sources, and we need only recall such episodes as his rash confrontations with Mongol officials,[10] his boldness in preaching *jihād* to the Mamluk sultan against the Mongols,[11] his destruction of a holy relic attributed to the Prophet,[12] his daring expose of the charlatanism of the Rifāʿī dervishes,[13] his presumptuousness in releasing his follower al-Mizzī from prison,[14] his refusals to obey the Mamlūk authorities,[15] his tactless denunciation of the Copts when all the other *ʿulamāʾ* saw the wisdom of silence.[16] So single-minded was his devotion to religious principles, so intolerant of idleness and vanity, that, according to Ibn ʿAbd al-Hādī, he converted the prison in which he was incarcerated in Egypt into an institute of religious study and

---

9 Ibid.
10 Laoust, *"Biographie d'Ibn Taimīya,"* 123–24.
11 Ibid., 127.
12 Ibid., 133; Hasan Q. Murād, "Mihan of Ibn Taymiya: A Narrative Account Based on a Comparative Analysis of Sources" (master's thesis, McGill University, 1968), 80.
13 Laoust, *"Biographie d'Ibn Taimīya,"* 135–36, and *Essai*, 126–27; Murād, "Mihan of Ibn Taymiya," 80–82.
14 Laoust, *"Biographie d'Ibn Taimīya,"* 137; Murād, "Mihan of Ibn Taymiya," 89.
15 Laoust, *"Biographie d'Ibn Taimīya,"* 139–41, 153, and *Essai*, 133–34, 144–45; Murād, "Mihan of Ibn Taymiya," 92, 94–95, 106–7.
16 Laoust, *Essai*, 141–42; Murād, "Mihan of Ibn Taymiya," 101–2.

devotion, turning the inmates away from chess and trictrac to prayer!¹⁷ Even when he was marching through the streets of Cairo on his way to what his followers saw as certain assasination, he could not resist stopping briefly to kick over a backgammon board when he spied two men playing a game outside a black-smith's shop!¹⁸

...Although he was obviously a great and brilliant man whose main virtues were courage, piety, self-denial, and vast knowledge, he also had the faults which al-Dhahabī named, the chief ones being a violent temper (which, admittedly, he learned to control), intolerance of human imperfection, and stern inflexibility. All of these qualities, both good and bad, made him an exceptional person, set apart from his fellow *'ulamā'* including al-Dhahabī himself, who were molded from softer clay.¹⁹

Call to *Jihād*

Ibn Taymiyya became professor of Hanbali jurisprudence at the Hanbaliyya madrasa in Damascus in 1296. That same year the Mamluk sultan al-Adil Kitbugha was deposed by his vice-sultan, Al Malik al-Mansur Lajin, who soon after, wishing to launch an expedition against the Christians of Armenian kingdom of Cilicia, asked Ibn Taymiyya to call the Muslims to *jihād*. As Laoust relates, Lajin found a propagandist in Ibn Taymiyya, whose doctrine of *jihād*, perfectly legitimate from the point of view of *Shari'a*, could be used to serve the cause of Islamic Imperialism of the Mamluks.²⁰ Ibn Kathir records that in July 1298 Ibn Taymiyya gave a rousing speech calling for holy war to a large crowd at the mosque of the Umayyads, evoking the rewards reserved for the martyrs. All these efforts, however, would end in failure.²¹

In 1299, Ibn Taymiyya wrote his profession of faith, *al-Hamawiyya al-kubrā*, which was very hostile to the rationalistic or speculative form

---

17 Muhammad b. Ahmad b. 'Abd al-Hādī (d. 744/1343), *Al-'Uqūd al-durriyya min manāqib Shaykh al-Islām Ahmad b. Taymiyya* (Beirut: Dār al-kutub al-'ilmiyya, n.d), 288.
18 Ibid., 269.
19 Donald P. Little. "Did Ibn Taymiyya Have a Screw Loose?" in *Studia Islamica*, No. 41 (1975; Paris), 107-108.
20 Laoust, *"Biographie d'Ibn Taimīya,"* 120.
21 Ibid.

of Sunnite theology of Ash'arī and to *kalām* (scholastic theology). His enemies accused him of anthropomorphism (*tashbīh*, attributing human characteristics or behavior to a god, animal, or object) and summoned him before the Hanafī *qādī*, Jalāl al-Dīn Ahmad al-Rāzī (d. 745/1344-5). Ibn Taymiyya refused, on the grounds that this *qādī* did not have the proper jurisdiction in matters of dogma. "After a private meeting, held in the house of the Shafi'i qādī, Imām al-Dīn 'Umar al-Qazwīnī (d. 699/1299-1300), at which the Hamawiyya was studied, Ibn Taymiyya, whose replies are said to have been judged satisfactory, was troubled no further."[22]

For some modern scholars, Ibn Taymiyya is "an inveterate anthropomorphist" who "interpreted literally all the passages in the Koran and tradition referring to the Deity."[23] Ibn Battūta, who described Ibn Taymiyya as having "a screw loose," claimed that he saw Ibn Taymiyya "preaching to the people from the *minbar* [the pulpit from which the Friday sermon is preached by the mosque imam] and admonishing them. Amongst other things in his address he said 'Verily, God descends to the sky over our world in the fashion of this descent of mine', and stepped down one step of the minbar."[24] Ibn Taymiyya wrote in the *al-'Aqīda al-Wāsitiyya* (Principles of Islamic Faith):

> Part of the belief in Allah is the belief in how He has described Himself in His Book (the Qur'an) and in how His Messenger Muhammad (peace be upon him) has described Him. Believe without distorting or denying and without questioning or shaping; Rather, believe in Allah, The Exalted: "There is none like Him; He is the All-Hearer, the All-Seer." (Q42. *ash-Shūrā*, Counsel, 11) Do not deny Him the way He has described Himself; Do not change words from their context; Do not disbelieve the names of Allah and His Signs.[25]

---

22 *Encyclopaedia of Islam*, vol. 3, 2nd ed., s.v. "Ibn Taymiyya," by Laoust.
23 *Encyclopaedia of Islam*, vol. 2, "E-K," ed. M. Th. Houtsman, A.J. Wensinck, and T.W. Arnold (Leiden: Brill, 1927), s.v. "Ibn Taimīya," by M. Ben Cheneb.
24 Ibn Battūta, *The Travels of Ibn Battuta, A.D. 1325-1354*, trans. by H.A.R.Gibb (Delhi: Munshiram Manoharlal Publishers, 1999), 1:136. It is difficult to see how Ibn Battūta could have witnessed what he said he witnessed in August 1326, when in fact Ibn Taymiyya was in prison in July 1326 until his death in September 1328.
25 Sheikh Al-Islam Ahmad Ibn Taimiyah, *Principles of Islamic Faith* (Al-'Aqidah Al-Wasitiyah), trans. Assad Nimer Busool (Skokie, IL: IQRA' International Educational Foundation, 1992), http://www.islamicweb.com/beliefs/creed/wasiti/taimiyah_1.htm.

In 1300, Ibn Taymiyya worked with the Mamluks once again when he joined their expedition against Nusayris (*Nusayrīyya*), or as they are also known, the Alawites, a sect founded by Ibn Nusayr in the ninth century in the Lebanese mountains thought to have collaborated with the Mongols and their Shia allies. Ibn Taymiyya considered them dangerous heretics:

> These people named "Al-Nusayriyyah," and other groups from among the Qarāmita [Carmathians] and Bātiniyya [i.e., Ismā'īlīs], are greater disbelievers than the Jews and Christians. Nay, they are greater disbelievers than most of the *mushrikīn* (polytheists from other than *Ahl al-Kitāb*), and their harm to the *Umma* of Muhammad, [pbuh], is greater than the harm of the disbelievers who are in war with Muslims,...[f]or they present themselves in front of ignorant Muslims as supporters and advocates of *Ahl al Bayt*, while in reality they do not believe in Allah, or the Messenger, or the Book, or [Allah's] orders, or prohibitions, or reward, or punishment, or Paradise, or Fire....Rather, they take the words of Allah and His Messenger, known to the scholars of Muslims, and they interpret them based on their fabrications, claiming that their interpretations are "hidden knowledge" ("*ilm al-bātin*")....They have no limit in their unbelief....Their aim is repudiation of Islamic Beliefs and Laws in every possible way, trying to make it appear that these matters have realities that they know.[26]

During the Mongol invasion of 1300, led by the Ilkhan Ghazan and supported by the Mamluk amir Qibjaq, Ibn Taymiyya served at Damascus as a leader of the resistance party. Through discussions with Ghazan and his commanders, Ibn Taymiyya was able to obtain the release of a certain number of Muslim and non-Muslim prisoners.[27] When the Mongols renewed their attacks, he was asked to exhort people to the *jihād* and went to Cairo in January 1301 to plead with the Mamluk sultan Muhammad b. Qalawun to intervene in Syria. Ibn Taymiyya was present at the victory over the Mongols, of Shakhab, near Damascus in

---

26 ASHĀBULHADEETH, "Ruling on the Nusayri/Alawi Sect," Shaykh-ul-Islaam Ibn Taymiyyah, August 13, 2009, https://shaykhulislaam.wordpress.com/2009/08/13/ruling-on-the-nusayrialawi-sect/.
27 Michot, "Ibn Taymiyya," 239.

1303, "where he had been instructed to issue a fatwā on the dispensation from the duty of fasting for those who were fighting."[28]

Concern for Commanding Right and Forbidding Wrong

Ibn Taymiyya was very concerned with Commanding Right and Forbidding Wrong, an Islamic duty that suited his activist temperament, but got him into constant trouble with the authorities. As Little indicates, "It is Ibn Taymiyya's distinction that he opposed by word and deed almost every aspect of religion practiced in the Mamluk Empire."[29] And yet, as Michael Cook points out, underlying these confrontations "was a structural disposition to cooperate with the state, and it is cooperation rather than confrontation that is the keynote of his political thought."[30] In fact, Ibn Taymiyya wrote a short treatise on the Islamic duty of Forbidding Wrong. It was aimed at the widest possible audience.

For Ibn Taymiyya, this duty

> is what God's revelation is all about, and it is closely linked to the duty of holy war. Like holy war, it is a duty by which all are obligated until someone actually undertakes it; it is thus a collective duty (*'alā 'l-kifāya*), rather than one incumbent by its nature on each and every individual. At the same time, no one is exempt from the scope of the duty. It is to be performed in the three modes specified in the Prophetic tradition: with the hand, with the tongue and in (or with) the heart. The emphasis is on civility (*rifq*)....One must possess the knowledge requisite to distinguish right (*ma'rūf*) from wrong (*munkar*). The benefit (*maslaha*) secured by performing the duty must outweigh any undesirable consequences (*mafsada*)—a consideration which rules out attempts to implement it through rebellion. One must nevertheless be prepared to display endurance (*sabr*) in the face of adverse reactions. The obligation also turns on one's having the power (*qudra*) to act.[31]

What is remarkable about the discussion of this duty is Ibn Tay-

---

28 *Encyclopaedia of Islam*, vol. 3, 2nd ed., s.v. "Ibn Taymiyya," by Laoust.
29 D.P. Little, "Religion under the Mamluks," *Muslim World* 73, no. 3-4 (October 1983): 180.
30 Cook, *Commanding Right and Forbidding Wrong*, 150.
31 Ibid., 152-53.

miyya's utilitarianism. "In his major work on politics" Ibn Taymiyya indicates that "in cases where costs and benefits have to be weighed, the proper course is secure the greater benefit by sacrificing the lesser, and to avert the larger cost by accepting the smaller," Cook explains. "Likewise in his work on the office of censor (*hisba*), he stresses that one's duty is limited to taking the best course of action open to one; in real life, this will usually mean choosing the greater of two goods, or settling for the lesser of two evils....[T]he utilitarian idiom of costs and benefits, with its brushing aside of moral absolutes, is a strikingly pervasive feature of his political thought."[32]

Ibn Taymiyya also sees this largely as the responsibility of those in authority: it is the duty of "the scholars (*'ulumā'*), the political and military grandees (*umarā'*), and the elders (*mashāyikh*) of every community (*tā'ifa*)" to command right and forbid wrong "vis-à-vis the common people subject to their authority (*'alā 'āmmatihim*)."[33] Later on, Ibn Taymiyya adds kings (*mulūk*) and state functionaries (*ahl al-dīwān*) to those in authority, as well as anyone who has a following (*matbū'*). "Each one of them should order and forbid what God has ordered and forbidden; each person subject to their authority should obey them in obedience to God, though not in disobedience to Him. This emphasis on the role of constituted authority in forbidding wrong is attested elsewhere in Ibn Taymiyya's works; indeed he considers it to be the purpose of all state power to carry out the duty."[34] Since the successful performance of the duty is obviously dependent on having the power to execute it, it is natural that it is those in authority who should perform the duty.

Ibn Taymiyya is equally pragmatic in his political philosophy; political morality consists in doing one's best: "anyone in a position of authority who does this in good faith has done his duty, and is not to be held responsible for what he lacks the power to achieve."[35] The ruler's duty is to find the best man for the job in making an appointment to a public office, even if undesirable consequences ensue because of his choice. "[A]ll forms of political authority have the blessing of the holy law (*sharī'a*) and all public offices are religious offices (*manāsib dīniyya*)."[36]

Unlike Ibn Hanbal, Ibn Taymiyya does not feel unease over the

---

32 Ibid., 154.
33 Ibid., 155.
34 Ibid.
35 Ibid., 156.
36 Ibid.

exercise of political power. He argues that people "fall into three groups with respect to their attitudes towards political power. The first group holds...that there can be no such thing as political morality; so opts for politics without morality. The second shares the premise, but opts for morality without politics. The third group is...the one that gets it right, avoiding the extreme positions of the other two by rejecting their shared premise."[37]

However, Ibn Taymiyya elaborates on the second, moralistic, group, and develops arguments that have a direct bearing on twenty-first century discussions of his influence on Islamic terrorists. According to Ibn Taymiyya, there are *quietist* moralists and *activist* moralists:

> The quietist moralist, for all his uncompromising righteousness, is characterized by a certain timidity or meanness of spirit. This failing can lead him to neglect a duty the omission of which is worse than the commission of many prohibited acts; it can equally lead him to forbid the performance of a duty where this is tantamount to turning people aside from the way of God....The activist moralist believes it to be his duty to take a stand against political injustice, and to do so by recourse to arms; thus he ends up fighting against Muslims in the manner of the Khārijites.[38]

Ibn Taymiyya's Anti-Mongol *Fatwas*

The principal objective of Ibn Taymīyya's three *fatwas* was to determine the status of the soldiers fighting, at the end of the thirteenth and the beginning of the fourteenth century, in the Mongos and Mamluk armies. Ghāzān Khān, ruler of the Mongol Empire's Ilkhanate division 1295–1304, and most of his soldiers were converts to Islam. What is more, among the Mongol ranks were Mamluk prisoners being forced to fight against their Muslim brothers. If the Mongols were Muslims like the Mamluks, then what was the status of the Mamluk soldier who refused to fight? What was the status of the Mamluk soldiers who had voluntarily joined the Mongols?[39]

Large areas of territory were now under Mongol rule. It was no

---

37 Ibid., 157.
38 Ibid.
39 Denise Aigle, "The Mongol Invasions of Bilād al-Shām [Syria] by Ghāzān Khān and Ibn Taymīyah's Three 'Anti-Mongol' Fatwas" *Mamluk Studies Review* 11, no. 2 (2007): 97, http://mamluk.uchicago.edu/MSR_XI-2_2007-Aigle.pdf.

longer possible, as in the past, for Muslims to leave the conquered regions and emigrate to Muslim lands. When the city of Mardin fell to the Mongols, for example,

> Ibn Taymiyya was asked whether the city was considered to be *Dar al-Harb* (abode of war) or *Dar al-Islam* (abode of Islam). He replied that the Muslims of Mardin were still Muslims and should not be accused of hypocrisy or condemned for residing in a city under non-Muslim rule, but by the same token maintained that they should not render any obvious aid to their Mongol overlords. As to the question of whether Mardin was *Dar al-Harb* or *Dar al-Islam*, Ibn Taymiyya answered: "It is not accorded the status of *Dar al-Islam* in which the laws of Islam are in force, because its armies are Muslims, nor does it have the status of Dar al-Harb whose inhabitants are infidels, but it falls into a third category: the Muslim in it acts according to the level that he is able, and fights outside [presumably the Mongols] on behalf of the *sharī'a* of Islam according to what he is able."[40]

As David Cook points out, this statement divorces the individual Muslim from the Muslim state, since it envisages the possibility that Muslims and their rulers might not be in religious accord. For Ibn Taymiyya, a Muslim fights for the victory of Islam and upholds its laws, but the Mongols were fighting with the aid of a coalition of troops consisting of Christian Armenians, Georgians, still pagan Mongols, and both Shi'ites and Sunni Muslims, among others. Therefore, they could not be considered to be fighting for Islam: "the Mongols were infidels and false Muslims; they were even more dangerous and must be fought on a more consistent basis than other obvious infidels (such as Christians)."[41]

Unusual for Ibn Taymiyya, he was prepared "to identify the quality of a given person's Islam with that person's being willing to fight for Islam. Since the Mongol Muslims' primary loyalty was to the larger Mongol state, and not to any Islamic state, they were non-Muslims according to the formulation of Ibn Taymiyya."[42] He compares the fighting against

---

40 Ibn Taymiyya, *Majmū'at Fatāwā* (Cairo: n.d.) 28:240–41; cited by Cook, *Understanding Jihād*, 64.
41 Ibn Taymiyya, *Majmū'at Fatāwā*, 28:410–67, esp. 413–16, and 28:501–8, 589–90; cited by Cook, *Understanding Jihād*, 65.
42 Cook, *Understanding Jihād*, 65.

the Mongols to the Prophet's battle against the Confederates described in the Koran at Q33. al-'Ahzāb, Confederates/the Allies. For Ibn Taymiyya, there was no difference between the two coalitions because both were defined by their hatred of and desire to crush Islam.[43]

Groups to Be Fought

One of Ibn Taymiyya's major concerns was to fight those who rebelled against legitimate authority. Then there were those who failed to live up to their Islamic religious duties, such as performing the five canonical prayers, "the payment of legally-required tax (*al-zakāt*), fasting (*al-sawm*), and the pilgrimage to Mecca (*al-hājj*)," as well as those who did not "take part in *jihād* against the infidels (*al-kuffār*) in order to make them submit and pay the poll-tax (*al-jizyah*)....Those who engage[d] in adultery (*al-zinā*) and the consumption of fermented drinks (*al-khamar*)" were to be "harshly repressed as they contravene the divine order" and "fall into the category of offences canonically disapproved in the Quran (*hudūd Allāh*). Also amongst the groups that must be fought" were those who did not "order good and forbid evil (*al-amr bi-al-ma'rūf wa-al-nahy 'an al-munkar*), since for Ibn Taymīyah this duty is another form of *jihād*."[44]

In his second Mongol *fatwa,* Ibn Taymiyya extends his list of groups that must be fought to include "those who deny the free will of God (*al-qadar*), his decree (*al-qadā'*), his names and his attributes, as well as those who display innovation (*al-bid'ah*) contrary to the Quran and Sunnah, those who do not follow the path of the pious forebears (*al-salaf*), and an entire assemblage of Muslim religious movements...Ibn Taymīyah considered deviant with regard to scriptures and to the consensus (*al-ijmā'*) of scholars in the religious sciences."[45] Essentially, any community or group that causes disorder is to be fought since disorder is to be feared more than death, and any public manifestations of heresy must be dealt with even more harshly than silent heresy.

In order to justify *jihād* against the Muslim invaders, Ibn Taymiyya constantly referred to the Koran and the *Sunna* of the Prophet, as revealed in the *hadīth*, and turned to events from the early years of Islam to serve as paradigms:

Ibn Taymīya links those rebels, who introduced sedition into

---
43 Ibid., 65-66.
44 Aigle, "Mongol Invasions of Bilād al-Shām," 98.
45 Ibid.

the Islamic community in its early years, with the events taking place in his time. Islam, after six centuries of undivided supremacy, was being shaken by these new Muslims whose political ideology permitted them to strike deals with Christians, the heretical sects of Islam, and the Shi'ah. Ibn Taymīya's principal grievance with the Mongols of Iran was their collusion with—in his view—all these infidels. He uses this as the basis for justifying *jihād* against those who declare that it is permitted "to kill the best of the Muslims."[46]

Ibn Taymiyya presents the Egyptian sultans as the champions of Islam, and best placed to fight the Mongols. The Muslim community had been weakened by disunity and the lack of participation in *jihād* against various groups, from the Franks to the sectarian movements. "Ibn Taymīyah saw Ghāzān Khān's claims over the holy places, as well as those of Öljeitü at a later stage, as a grave danger for Sunni Islam, and for this reason he argued in favor of the Mamluk regime."[47]

After gaining knowledge of Mongol political ideology, Ibn Taymiyya reproached the Ilkhans for fighting to achieve a people's submission rather on behalf of Islam: "Whoever enters into their obedience of the Age of Ignorance (*al-jāhilīyah*) and into their infidel way (*al-kufrīyah*) is their friend (*sadīquhum*), even if he is an infidel (al-kāfir), a Jew, or a Christian. Whoever refuses to submit is their enemy (*'adūwuhum*), even if he were to be one of the prophets of God."[48] And he vehemently rejects their political theocracy since the Mongols had deviated from the laws of Islam (*khārijūn 'an sharā'ī al-Islam*) and maintained their ancient beliefs from the Age of Ignorance. Ibn Taymiyya explains their deviant theology: "It is that the Tatars believe grave things about Chinggis Khan. They believe that he is the son of God, similar to what the Christians believe about the Messiah (*al-masīh*).[49]

The problem lay with the Mongols' conception of law, radically at variance with Islamic Law:

> Chinggis Khan had conceived a law, the *yāsā*, according to "his reason (*'aqlihi*) and his own opinion (*dhihnihi*)." On this basis Ibn Taymīyah develops an argument that the Mongols

---

46 Ibid., 102.
47 Ibid., 111-12.
48 Ibid., 112, quoting Ibn Taymiyya, *Majmū' Fatāwa*, 28:525.
49 Ibid., 113-14, quoting Ibn Taymiyya, *Majmū' Fatāwa*, 28:521-22.

were guilty of blameworthy innovation (*al-bid'ah*): "He has caused men to leave the ways of the prophets in order to take up that which he has innovated: his way of the Age of Ignorance (*sunnat al-jāhilīyah*) and his infidel law (*sharī 'ati-hi al-kufrīyah*)."⁵⁰ With this reasoning, Ibn Taymīyah argues against the Mongols' political system. The Ilkhans' Islam, according to Ibn Taymīyah, exposes the Muslim religion to a grave risk because in it the rational (*al-'aqlī*) had replaced the legal (*al-shar'ī*).

The Mongols of Iran were promoting a modern Islam: they advocated religious freedom and claimed to follow the *yāsā*, the law established by Chinggis Khan. In other words, although they had converted to Islam, the Mongols did not comply with the principles of Islamic law.⁵¹

Innovations, Heresies, and Religious Minorities

As noted above, in 1296 Sultan Lajin enlisted Ibn Taymiyya to rally the Muslims to conduct *jihād* against the Armenians of Cilicia, and in June 1300 Ibn Taymiyya joined the expedition to Kasrawan in the Lebanese mountains to battle Shī'ites who were accused of having collaborated with the Franks and the Mongols. This operation immediately followed a massacre of some Sunnis, instigated by, according to Syrian historians, Christian Armenians and Georgians. But Ibn Taymiyya suspected that the Shī'ites were behind the massacre.⁵² In April 1303 he was present at the victory of Tell-Šaqhab over Ghāzān, when he issued a *fatwa* exempting the combatants from fasting during the month of Ramadān, so that they could conserve their strength to fight the Mongols. Availing himself of the precedent set by Muhammad, who had done the same during the conquest of Mecca, Ibn Taymiyya went so far as to condemn the fast if it risked weakening the fighters, thereby compromising the success of the struggle for the triumph of Islam.⁵³

Ibn Taymiyya's spent his last fifteen years in Damascus. His polemical zeal led him to denounce violently all those whom he suspected of introducing innovations into Islam, including the Šāfi'tes, Aš'arites,

---

50 Ibn Taymiyya, *Majmū' Fatāwa*, 28:523.
51 Aigle, "Mongol Invasions of Bilād al-Shām," 116.
52 Alfred Morabia, "*Ibn Taymiyya: Dernier grand théoricien du Ğihād médiéval,*" Bulletin d'études orientales, Mélanges offerts a Henri Laoust, tome 2, 30 (1978): 90.
53 Ibid.

Zindīqs, heretics, and Sufis suspected of having succumbed to antinomianism, monism or esotericism. He equally gave opinions that contradicted those accepted by *all* the Sunni schools.[54]

In July 1326, Ibn Taymiyya was imprisoned in the citadel of Damascus on the order of the Sultan, following Ibn Taymiyya's vehement condemnation of visits to the graves of prophets and saints. He remained in the citadel more than two years, where he died on September 26, 1328. His funeral was followed by a big crowd of Damascenes. Ibn Taymiyya was buried in the cemetery of the Sufis, where, ironically, his tomb was much visited and venerated.[55]

More Innovations [56]

Ibn Taymiyya's opposition to the Mongols was total. While he was ready to admit unconditionally into the heart of the Muslim community those People of the Book who had converted to Islam, Ibn Taymiyya remained irreducibly hostile to the Ilkhans when they converted. He denounced their Islam as suspect, even hypocritical; he reproached them for keeping an equal balance between all the faiths, of having benefited from the support of the Christians and Shī'ites to make sure of their triumph, of having suppressed the caliphate, of not being of a rigorous orthodoxy, and above all, of contributing to the breakup of the united front of the Muslim Community.

Ibn Taymiyya adhered to a long Hanbalite tradition of loyalty to the established powers, in virtue of Q4. *an-Nisā'*, the Women, 59: "O you who believe, obey Allah and obey the Messenger and those in authority from among them," which he interpreted as an alliance between the rulers and the *'ulamā'*. Ibn Taymiyya believed that Religion and State were indissolubly linked. Without the power to constrain (*šawka*) available to the State, religion declines and collapses. Without the discipline of the Revealed Law, the State becomes a tyrannical organization.[57]

The Mongols presented a real threat to the Mamluks, however, and they had even gained the sympathy of some Syrian nobles. Alfred Morabia suggests that Ibn Taymiyya saw the struggle between the Mamluks and the Mongols as a showdown between different politico-religious

---

54 Ibid., 91.

55 Ibid.

56 I have leaned heavily on Alfred Morabia's classic paper, "*Ibn Taymiyya: Dernier grand théoricien du Ğihād médiéval,*" for this section, which is largely a free paraphrase of pages 91 and following.

57 *Encyclopaedia of Islam*, vol. 3, 2nd ed., s.v. "Ibn Taymiyya," by Laoust.

worldviews leading to two possible outcomes: (1) the alliance of military and religious leaders defending the purity of Islam, true to the vision of Muhammad and his companions, leading to piety, stability, and a united *umma* (community); or (2) moral chaos with the triumph of innovations and intellectual speculation, leading to the decay of Islam.[58]

His hatred of the Mongols was equaled by his hatred of innovations, in which Ibn Taymiyya saw the spiritual death of Islam, and the insidious triumph of impiety: "The more an innovator works at being original, the further he distances himself from God."[59] He devoted a five hundred-page work to pronouncing his anathemas on the innovations (*bidaʿ*) introduced into Islam by imitating the People of Hell, that is all non-Muslims.[60] In this tome, Ibn Taymiyya denounced, one by one, the excesses of Sufism, non-Arab customs, the philosophers, the *kalām* (philosophical theology),[61] the abusive use of *qiyas* (analogy), monasticism, and the traditions of the Bedouins (Ibn Taymiyya had utter contempt for the coarseness of nomads, singling out Arab Bedouins, Armenians, Kurds, and Tartars).[62] Elsewhere, he showed a similar disdain for the populace,[63] the de-Arabisation of Muslims, the celebration of Christian and Persian festivities, associating with unbelievers, the absence of rigor among scholars, the celebration of *Mawlid* (the anniversary of the Prophet's birth) and *ʿĀšūrāʾ*,[64] pilgrimage to Jerusalem (more on

---

58 Morabia, "Ibn Taymiyya," 92.

59 Laoust, *Essai*, 223.

60 Ibn Taymiyya, *Iqtidāʾ al-sirāt al-mustaqīm li-mukhālafat ashāb al-jahīm* (Cairo, 1950); also ed. ʿIsām Fāris al-Harastāni & Muhammad Ibrāhīm al-Zaghlī (Beirut: Dār al-Jīl, 1993).

61 *Encyclopaedia of Islam*, vol. 3, "H–Iram," ed. B. Lewis et al., 2nd ed. (Leiden: Brill, 1971), s.v. "*ʿilm al-kalām*":
the discipline which brings to the service of religious beliefs (*ʿaqāʾid*) discursive arguments; which thus provides a place for reflexion and meditation, and hence for reason, in the elucidation and defence of the content of the faith. It takes its stand firstly against "doubters and deniers," and its function as defensive "apologia" cannot be over-stressed. A fairly common synonymous term is *ʿilm al-tawhid*, the "science of the Unity (of God)," understood as concerned not merely with the divine unity but with all the bases of the Muslim faith, especially prophecy.

62 Ibn Taymiyya, *Iqtidāʾ al-sirāt*, 146–47.

63 A.N. Poliak, "Les révoltes populaires en Égypte à l'époque des Mamelouks et leur causes economiques," *Revue des Études Islamiques* 8 (1934): 255.

64 "Tenth day of Moharram, the first month of the Islamic calendar; for Sunnis it is a day on which fasting is recommended, and for Shiʾites a day of mourning for the martyrdom of Imam Hosayn." *Encyclopaedia Iranica*, http://www.iranicaonline.org/, s.v. "*ʿĀšūrāʾ*."

Jerusalem shortly), worship of the Rock within the walls of the mosque of ʿUmar,[65] the veneration of the graves of Muhammad and his Companions (Ibn Taymiyya reckons it far more meritorious to follow their example than to gape at their relics), astrology, and resorting to other intercessors than the Prophet (a practice he violently denounced in *al-Furqān bayn awliyā' Ar-Rahmān wa awliyā' aš-Šaytān*).[66] Ibn Taymiyya untiringly took up his refrain: Muslims should always ensure they are distinguishable from the Infidels, as Muhammad himself had taught. In what constitutes the specificity of the Believer (Muslim) is his desire not to resemble non-Muslims in anyway.[67]

Furthermore, Ibn Taymiyya attacked Greek philosophy and its Muslim representatives such as Ibn Sinā and Ibn Sabʿīn, asking, "Does not philosophy lead to unbelief? Is it not for a great part the cause of the different schisms which have been produced in the bosom of Islam?"[68]

Sufis and Shīʿites

Ibn Taymiyya did not mince words regarding the Sufis and the Shīʿites. He considered both groups "people of innovations and whims" (or "heresies," literally "passions," *ahl al-bidaʿ wa l-ahwā'*). In many ways, Ibn Taymiyya resembles Ibn al-Jawzī (al-Ǧawzī) (d. 1200), an earlier Hanbali preacher, traditionist and juriconsult, whom Ibn Taymiyya greatly admired.[69] Like Ibn al-Jawzī, Ibn Taymiyya found the mystical movement unsound, full of deviations contrary to the Faith.

His attitude towars the Sufis was ambivalent. Ibn Taymiyya reproached Sufi practices that took the place of worship rendered to Allah and His Messenger and denounced the Sufi principle of tolerance, founded on syncretic and interconfessional tendencies. There was abso-

---

65 Ibn Taymiyya concedeed that this rock was an object of veneration for Jews and Christians, but insisted that Muslims should not imitate them. Furthermore, it was dishonest to claim that a footprint of the Prophet or his turban was inside the mosque.
66 Taymiyya, *Criterion between Allies*.
67 Morabia, "Ibn Taymiyya," 92.
68 *Encyclopaedia of Islam*, vol. 2, s.v. "Ibn Taimīya," by Cheneb.
69 "Ibn al-Jawzī attacked all sorts of heresies in his robust polemic *Talbīs Iblīs*, "in which he attacks not only the various sects more or less outside Sunnism (*khawārij, rawāfid, muʿtazila, falāsifa, bātiniyya*, etc.), but also, within Sunnism, all those whom he considered responsible for having introduced into the dogma or the law of Islam innovations which were to be condemned (*bidʿa*): *fuqahā'*, traditionists, statesmen and, above all, *sūfiyya*, among whom men such as Abū Tālib al-Makkī, al-Qushayrī and al-Ghazālī, with many others, are vigorously attacked." *Encyclopaedia of Islam*, vol. 3, 2nd ed., s.v. "Ibn Taymiyya," by Laoust.

lutely no place in Ibn Taymiyya's philosophy for ecumenical sentimentality. To say, "What does it matter as long as the divergent paths lead to worship of the same Lord?" was a betrayal of God, but Ibn Taymiyya's greatest reproach was that such contemplative exercises led the faithful to disengage, and abandon the *jihād*: "To those who prefer fasting, the vigils, the silence, the solitude and other similar practices, we should say that *jihād* is far more demanding. It is, in fact, self-sacrificing (self-giving), exposing oneself to death. In it is embodied the meaning of the term asceticism, which implies the renunciation of all worldly temptations."[70]

Ibn Taymiyya often verbally attacked individual Sufis for various reasons—for example, he accused Shaykh Muhammad al-Khabbāz of antinomianism—as well as whole groups. Ibn Taymiyya wrote to the *shaykh* Nasr al-Din al-Manbidji, the spiritual director of Baybars al-Djashnikir and one of "the most prominent members" of the Ittihādiyya, who were supporters of Ibn al-'Arabi (d. 1240–41), "a letter which was courteous, but nevertheless firmly condemned the monism of Ibn al-'Arabi."[71] As Henri Laoust explains, Ibn Taymiyya "refers to knowing and having reflected on the works of many of the *Sufiyya*…and mentions also having allowed himself to be deluded, in his youth, by the *Futūhāt* of Ibn al-'Arabi…before discovering how subtly heretical they were." Nonetheless, he "never condemned Sufism in itself, but only that which he considered to be, in the case of too many Sufis, inadmissible deviations in doctrine, ritual or morals, such as monism (*wahdat al-wujūd*),[72] antinomianism (*ibāha*) or esotericism (*ghuluww*)."[73]

Still, Ibn Taymiyya had the temerity to attack the most famous Sufi of all, al-Ghazāli (d. 1111), and his philosophical views as expressed in *Munqidh min al-Dalāl and Ihyā' 'ulūm al-dīn*, which "contains a large number of apocryphal hadiths." Ibn Taymiyya declared, "The Sufis and the Mutakallimūn are from the same valley (*min wādin wāhid*)."[74]

For the Shī'tes, often referred to as *Rawāfid* or *al-Rāfida*, Ibn Taymiyya nursed an implacable hatred—though he spared the Zaydites,

---

70 Ibn Taymiyya, *al-Jawāb al-Sahīh li-man baddala dīn al-Masīh* (Cairo: Matba'at al-Nīl, 1905), 4:113–14; quoted by Morabia, "Ibn Taymiyya," 93n42.
71 *Encyclopaedia of Islam*, vol. 3, 2nd ed., s.v. "Ibn Taymiyya," by Laoust.
72 Ibn Taymiyya wrote a treatise, *Ibtāl wahdat al-wujūd* (*The Bankruptcy of Oneness of Existence*); monism seems to be equated with pantheism, which for him would be an unacceptable innovation.
73 Ibid.
74 *Encyclopaedia of Islam*, vol. 2, s.v. "Ibn Taimīya," by Cheneb.

who, unlike the *Rawāfid*, admitted the legitimacy of the caliphates of Abu Bakr and 'Umar.[75] Ibn Taymiyya considered the *Rawāfid* far more dangerous than the Jews and Christians since they worked treacherously and insidiously from within the community. Their theodicy was corrupted by borrowings from Judaism and Christianity, and they had always shown a culpable indulgence towards the minorities, freeing them, in violation of the Law, that is, the *Shari'a*. So Ibn Taymiyya insisted on leading a pitiless and relentless holy war against them.

He was determined to conduct this fight on the doctrinal and military levels. He denounced the Shi'ite heresy, and proposed to constrain all its followers, all innovators, to perform an act of contrition, under penalty of death. In his treatise on the *hisba*, Ibn Taymiyya called for the death penalty for the public good: "When execution is the only way in which a man can be stopped from going about causing mischief, then he may be put to death: such are the divider of the Muslim community and the preacher of innovations in the Religion....In the *Sahīh* we find these words ascribed to the Prophet, on him be peace: 'If homage is paid to two caliphs, then kill the second of the two.'"[76]

Ibn Taymiyya's participation in expeditions against the Nusayrīs of Kasrawān have already been discussed. In 1317 in the region of Jabala, another Nusayrī farmer uprising (of likely religious and economic origin) goaded Ibn Taymiyya to write ferociously against them. After their savage repression by the Mamluks, Ibn Taymiyya wrote several *fatwas* concerning the Nusayrīs, who should be forced to convert to Islam for their own good, and for the good of the Muslim community.[77] As he asserted in the *Iqtidā'*: "The real Faith consists in, not only in adoration of the sole Creator, but, equally, in worshipping Him in conformity with His prescriptions."[78]

"Praise be to God," Ibn Taymiyya wrote in one *fatwa*: "These [Nusayrīs] should be fought as long as they resist, until they accept the law of Islam." They spring

---

75 Morabia, "Ibn Taymiyya," 93n43.

76 Sahīh Muslim, *Kitab Al-Imara (The Book on Government)*, trans. Abdul Hamid Siddiqui, no. 4568 (Delhi: Kitab Bhavan, 2000), 3:1243–44. "Narrated Abu Sa'id al-Khudri: The Messenger of Allah (peace_be_upon_him) said: When oath of allegiance has been taken for two caliphs, kill the one for whom the oath was taken later."

77 See Yaron Friedman, *The Nusayrī-'Alawīs: An Introduction to the Religion, History and Identity of the Leading Minority in Syria* (Leiden and Boston: E.J. Brill, 2010).

78 Ibn Taymiyya, *Iqtidā'*, 451.

from the worst heretical people guided by the devil, they are from the worst *murtaddūn* [apostates]; their fighters should be killed and their property should be confiscated.... They do not pray the five prayers, they do not fast during Ramaddān, nor do they carry out the pilgrimage. They do not pay *zakāt* (alms), and they do not admit that it is an obligation. They permit [drinking] wine and other prohibited things. They believe that 'Alī is God; they recite: "I testify that there is no other God but Haydara the transcendent the esoteric / and that there is no veil but Muhammad the righteous the faithful / and that there is no path to him but Salmān the powerful." Even if they do not reveal their extremism, and do not declare that this liar is the expected *mahdī*, they should be fought....they should be compelled to obey Islamic law; if they refuse they must be killed....Those who lead them astray should be put to death even if they show regret....so, without any doubt, this devil [the Nusayrī *mahdī*] must be killed. God knows better.[79]

Ibn Taymiyya's attitude toward the People of the Book[80] was contemptuous. He firmly believed that these stubborn scripturaries needed to be ostracized. They still did not understand the virtue of the Religion of Truth, as the Koran indicates at Q9. *at-Tawba*, the Repentance / *al-Barā'at*, the Immunity, 33: "He it is Who sent His Messenger with guidance and the Religion of Truth [*dīni l-haqqi*], that He may cause it to prevail over all religions, though the polytheists are averse." (Almost the same words appeared at Q48. *al-Fath*, the Victory, 28, and Q 61. *As-Saff*, The Row/ The Ranks, 9.)

Jew, Christians, and *Ahl Dhimmi*

Judaism and Christianity were also false ways. Imperfect and incomplete, they could not assure the happiness of their adherents and their respective Law was only revealed in a limited sense (*muqayyad*), in anticipation of the arrival of Muhammad, who brought the Final and

---

79 Ibn Taymiyya, *al-Fatāwā al-kubrā*, (Cairo: Dār al-Kutub al-Hadītha, 1966), 3:513–14; quoted by Friedman, *The Nusayrī-'Alawīs*, 194.

80 "This term initially referred to the Jews and Christians whose scriptures like the Torah and the Gospel were completed in Muslim belief by Islamic revelation of the Qur'an. The term was later broadened to cover adherents of other religions like Zoroastrianism." Netton, Popular *Dictionary of Islam*, s.v. "People of the Book."

Absolute (Unlimited) Law (*mutlaq*).[81] Muhammad had reproached the Jews for their pride, stubbornness, and rigorism, and the Christians for their culpable Laxism and aberrations, because they had deformed Jesus's teachings.[82] Ibn Taymiyya sought to eliminate this imperfect monotheism, which he saw as an insult to the Revelation's truthfulness and a constant pernicious incitement to error for faithful Muslims. Ibn Taymiyya wrote that the servile imitation of Jews and Christians resulted in the degradation of Muslim customs and ethics, therefore the Lord, angered by His community, sent as punishment the Turks, who were responsible for a heretofore unseen destruction.[83] And because the minorities did not hide their sympathy for the heretical sects, they must be persuaded to find the right path of the Muslim mission.

However, Ibn Taymiyya did not call for forced conversion or persecution, but to apply, in all its rigor, the laws concerning the *dhimmis* (second-class citizens), as defined by the jurists basing themselves on the Pact of 'Umar. For Ibn Taymiyya, the religious minorities benefited from a protected status only insofar as it was in the interest of the Muslim community; otherwise, the authorities were acting legally in exiling the minorities, as 'Umar did when he threw out the Jews and Christians from the Arabian peninsula.

But Ibn Taymiyya was not content to let things take their course. Rather, he harangued the authorities to apply rigorously the discriminatory measures, as in the case of the Christian who insulted the Prophet. He also wrote pamphlets against the maintenance or building of synagogues and particularly of churches.[84] When the Mamluks closed the churches in Cairo in 1301, Ibn Taymiyya wrote *Mas'alat al-Kanā'is*, a *fatwa* denying that "there is any injustice in the closing of the churches," and arguing "that the consensus of the Companions, the Successors, the four legal Sunni schools and other early jurists is that the ruler would be justified in demolishing every church in Muslim territory conquered by force (*ard al-'anwa*), which includes Egypt, Iraq, and Syria, if he so wished."[85] And since the Pact of 'Umar, which defined the rights of non-Muslims, was written after the time of the Companions, it had no

---

81 Ibn Taymiyya, *al-Jawāb al-Sahīh*, 3:261; referred to by Morabia, "Ibn Taymiyya," 93.
82 Ibid., passim.
83 Ibn Taymiyya, *Iqtidā'*, 118–19.
84 *Encyclopaedia of Islam*, vol. 2, s.v. "Ibn Taimīya," by Cheneb. See also, Ibn Taymiyya, *Mas'alat al-Kanā'is*, Paris Bibliothèque Nationale, no. 2962, ii.
85 *Christian-Muslim Relations: A Bibliographical History*, ed. David Thomas, vol.4, 1200–1350, ed. David Thomas and Alex Mallet (Leiden: E.J. Brill, 2009), 857.

legal standing.

In terms of doctrine, Ibn Taymiyya adopted an even more intransigent position than his Hanbalī predecessor Ibn Qudāma with regard to the Zoroastrians, the poll tax and its imposition on the monks and priests who had taken a vow of poverty, and the tax to be collected in an unpleasant manner. Ibn Taymiyya demanded, incessantly, the total and irrevocable eviction of all non-Muslims occupying a position of responsibility in political and military life. And, if he forbade the killing of women, children, priests, the old, and "protected" infirm, Ibn Taymiyya did not hesitate to affirm:

> To worship what provokes disapproval and divine wrath is of a totally different order of seriousness than to abandon oneself to the lustful appetites forbidden by the Lord. That is the reason why associationism [*shirk*, worshipping another besides God, polytheism] is considered a hideous crime far more serious than adultery. That is equally the reason for which *jihād* against the Possessors of the Books or Scripture is more meritorious than the one conducted against the idolators. Also the believer [Muslim] killed by the Scriptuaries [People of the Book] deserves a double celestial compensation.[86]

The Great Regenerator of *Jihād*

Morabia considers Ibn Taymiyya the great regenerator of the doctrine of *jihād*. Not content to reuse fixed formulas dating back centuries, he placed the idea of "fighting for the cause of Allah" at the center of his activities, making it the essence of religion. Morabia names Ibn Taymiyya "the Bard of the Golden Age of *Jihād* "—defensive, doctrinal, ethical, and realistic enough to grasp that an offensive *jihād* against enemies who are too powerful was pointless.[87]

It was not the right time to extend Islam's domain by force of arms. Hence Ibn Taymiyya's recourse to a defensive *jihād*[88]—fighting Islam's internal enemies: heretics, rebels, and those who sow discord and scan-

---

86 Ibn Taymiyya, *Iqtidā'*, 192.
87 Morabia, "Ibn Taymiyya," 95.
88 Ibn Taymiyya, *al-Siyāsa al-shar'iyya fī iAlāh al-rā'ī wa-al-ra'iyya*, (*Le Traité de droit public d'Ibn Taimīya*), trans. Henri Laoust (Beruit: Institut français de Damas, 1948), 17.

dal.⁸⁹ Hence the greater urgency for the duty of Commanding Right and Forbidding Wrong, with the goal of constructing a society devoted to the service of God. Ultimately, *jihād* is "one of the most meritorious undertakings there is"[90] and "the best form of voluntary service a man can consecrate to God"[91] that consolidates the activities carried out in the interest of the Islamic *umma*.

Because all public functions are only intended as fraternal correction and as a duty to the moral apostolate, and because *jihād* is the prerogative of Islam alone, it is the proof of Islam's superiority over the other religions.[92] In fact, an essential element of Christianity, and focus of reproach for Ibn Taymiiya, is its refusal to engage in war.[93] He also rejects the tradition espoused by some mystics on the subject of the greater *jihād* versus the lesser *jihād*:

> As for the hadīth which is narrated by some in which the Prophet is alleged to have said upon the return of the Muslims from the battle of Tabuk: "We have come back from the minor *jihād* to the major *jihād*." This is a false hadīth, having no origin, and none of those knowledgeable of the words and actions of the Prophet (pbuh) have transmitted it. Fighting against the disbelievers is one of the greatest of works. In fact, it is the best thing which a person can volunteer.
>
> Allāh said: Qur'an 4:95–96: "The believers who sit back without any valid excuse are not the same as those who fight in the path of Allāh with their property and their lives. Allāh has preferred those who struggle with their property and their lives over those who sit back by a degree, and to both Allāh has promised good. And Allāh has preferred those who struggle over those who sit back by a great (difference in) reward."[94]

Ibn Taymiyya had no desire to impose Islam on the heathens, since they presented no threat to Islam, but the same could not be said of the

---

89 Ibid., 74ff., 90, 122, 130–33.
90 Ibid., 72.
91 Ibid., 125.
92 Ibid., 178.
93 Ibn Taymiyya, *al-Jawāb al-Sahīh*, 3:299–300.
94 Ibn Taymiyya, *Criterion between Allies*, 52–53.

heretics, who were to be repressed by all means necessary, including arms, and forced back to the right way of Sunni orthodoxy for their own good: "To punish a man who neglects his duties or commits a prohibited action is the supreme aim of *jihād*; fighting him being the collective duty of the whole community as the Koran and the hadith make clear."[95]

Ibn Taymiyya's works are anchored in the society of his times. His propensity to preach *jihād* should be seen against the background of Mamluk activism against the Mongols, the Franks of Cyprus, the Armenians of Cilicia, and the Shīʿite heretics.[96] But he put too much passion into condemning innovations (*bidaʿ*) and extolling the return to the pious teachings of the Elders or Ancestors (*aslāf, sing. salaf*) to allow himself to contradict his predecessors. Without daring to cross the line, and including *jihād* among the fundamental principles (*usūl, sing. asl*) of the Religion, he gave fighting in the cause of Allah the most enthusiatic praise possible. Ibn Taymiyya made the divine institution of fighting, along with prayer, the essential elements of Islam: "It is for this reason that most of the hadith of the Prophet concern prayer and *jihād*. When he went to the bedside of someone ill, the Prophet used to say: 'O Lord, heal your slave so that he can, take part in prayer for You, and for You, vanquish an enemy.'"[97]

Jihād, for Ibn Taymiyya, is superior to pilgrimage, although the latter is a recognized pillar of Islam.[98] "Every community has its devotional (*siyāha*) journeys," Ibn Taymiyya wrote, "those of my community consists in the *jihād* in the way of God":

> Here we have a subject of very wide implications. Among all the obligations, there is none whose rewards and merit are so often glorified as *jihād*. And this is easy to understand why. The benefit of *Jihād* is general, extending not only to the person who participates in it but also to others, both in a religious and a temporal sense. Second, *jihād* implies all kinds of worship, both in its inner and outer forms. It indicates love of God, sincerity, trust in God, a total surrender, a desire for resignation, asceticism, the mention of the name of God, and all other kinds of acts of worship, that no other act of worship

---

[95] Laoust, *Le Traité*, 73.
[96] Morabia, "Ibn Taymiyya," 96.
[97] Laoust, *Le Traité*, 19.
[98] Ibid., 125.

implies.[99]

Whoever opposes the realization of *jihād* ought to be fought:[100]

> Anyone who excludes the People of the Book from [the list of] the enemies who must be fought, is himself, an infidel.[101]

> Each man is assured of meeting death. That obtained in fighting for the faith is the most beautiful, the easiest, and the only one that offers the sublime alternative of triumph here on earth or happiness in the Hereafter.[102]

For Ibn Taymiyya, all must contribute to the success of *jihād*—but worldly attractions are not to be despised. Muslim princes must make combatants in the cause of Allah the first beneficiaries of the spending of the State.[103] One must not hesitate in giving satisfaction to those whose hearts we wish to rally by political expediency.[104] The Muslim finding himself in the Land of the Infidels has the right to practice *kitmān* (*taqīya*, legal duplicity and tactical submission), so reviled when the Shi'ites make use of it. Finally, the booty is an essential resource:

> [T]he infidels render their persons with which they no longer serve Allah, and their goods, which do not help to serve Allah, legitimate to the faithful believers (Muslims) who serve Allah and to whom Allah restitutes their due: thus one restitutes to man the heritage of which he had been deprived; even if he has not yet taken possession of it.[105]

The duty of *jihād* implies the acceptance of state guardianship— the only means to assure the observation of the celestial prescriptions. And Ibn Taymiyya, who could scarcely disguise his admiration for the intransigent piety and activism of the Khārijites, reproaches them nonetheless for calling for rebellion against unworthy leaders. More realistic,

---

99 Ibid., 127.
100 Ibid., 128.
101 Ibn Taymiyya, *al-Jawāb al-Sahīh*, 2:257.
102 Ibid., 4:266–67; Laoust, *Le Traité*, 127–28.
103 Laoust, *Le Traité*, 47.
104 Ibid., 49.
105 Ibid., 35-36.

he returns often to a saying of the Prophet—"Allah can reinforce His religion through perverse men"[106]—and argues that the interest of the community can override moral scruples.

Faith in Islamic lands always demanded the evidence and commitment of the believer in relation to the Creator and his brothers in religion. Insofar as under its multiple forms *jihād* has been the most remarkable instrument of this evidence and commitment, Ibn Taymiyya— ferocious attacker of desertion, cowardice, and abstention—imposed himself as the herald of the "fight in the cause of Allah." And all the more easily, since he lived during a time when religious tepidity and compromise reigned.[107]

While the theses of Ibn Taymiyya were adopted only to the extent that they were consistent with the interests of the moment, they have never ceased to exercise a latent yet distinct influence on Islamic fundamentalists. And Islamic history has demonstrated that *jihād*, even when it seems to be asleep, is capable of dazzling revivals, when its danger, rightly or wrongly, is once again perceived.

---

106 Ibid., 12.
107 Morabia, "Ibn Taymiyya," 98.

CHAPTER 13
THE QĀDĪZĀDELI MOVEMENT IN SEVENTEENTH-CENTURY ISTANBUL

THERE WERE A number of violent fundamentalist movements in the Islamic world, particularly in Baghdad, in the preceding centuries that bore a close resemblance to the one examined in this chapter. In Islamic history, not all pietists and pirs were for leaving people in peace. For example, the duty of Commanding Right and Forbidding Wrong was enthusiastically endorsed by the sixteenth-century Ottoman pietist Birgili (also al-Birgiwī, Birgewī, Birgivi, Birkawī, Birgiwī, al-Birgawī, d. 1573), who also extolled martyrdom, arguing that the duty was even more binding than *jihād*.[1] According to the *Encyclopaedia of Islam*, Birgili, "Like Ibn Taymiyya, set himself firmly against all innovation in order to protect the sacred law, and no considerations of rank would cause him to connive at any non-observance of the faith. Towards the end of his life he even made the journey from Birgi to Istanbul to advise the grand vizier Mehmed Pasha about the rectification of some irregularities which he had observed. Birgewī, an utter fanatic in religious matters, would not abide the slightest deviation from the *sharīʿa*."[2]

Birgili inspired the violent puritan Istanbul-based Qādīzādeli movement (1620–1680), during which simple smoking infractions, for example, often resulted in execution by "dismemberment, impaling, or hanging."[3] Birgili was popular throughout the Muslim world; his

---

1 Cook, *Forbidding Wrong*, 91.

2 *Encyclopaedia of Islam*, vol. 1, "A–B," ed. H.A.R. Gibb et al., 2nd ed. (Leiden: Brill, 1960), s.v. "Birgewī."

3 Simeon Evstatiev, "The Qādīzādeli Movement and the Revival of Takfīr in the Otto-

works were commented upon and much discussed.⁴ Scholars such as Rudolph Peters⁵ and Barbara Flemming⁶ suggest that the activities of the Qādīzādelis may well have influenced the Wahhābī movement in the Arabian peninsula in the eighteenth century.⁷ Works attributed to Birgili are extremely popular among Salafī and Wahhābī groups to this day.⁸

Birgili devoted most of his time to teaching and writing in the remote town of Birgi, near Izmir. Though living a fairly simple, pious life, Birgili was always mindful of his Islamic duty to revive and protect the *sunna* of the Prophet by Commanding Right and Forbidding Wrong, and furthermore, he insisted that others do the same.⁹

His followers relied on his two important works: *Risale-i Birgili Mehmed* (also known as *Vasiy(y)etname* or *Ilmihal of Birgili*), written in Turkish between 1562 and 1563, and *al-Tarīqa al-Muhammadiyya*, or *Tarikat*, written in Arabic and completed in 1572.

The *Risale* was "a catechism of fundamentals in simple Turkish prose,"¹⁰ which perhaps explains its wide dissemination and popularity. In this work, Madeline Zilfi, a scholar cited earlier in these pages, explains,

> [Birgili] adduced proofs from the Koran, from the traditions of the Prophet, and from the writings of the patriarchal authorities to designate "the straight path." He addressed such subjects as the scriptures, the prophets, miracles and saints, those whose lot is heaven or hell; the portents of Judgment Day; those things that are by holy law enjoined, permissible, neutral, abominable, or forbidden; love of grandeur, lying, stubbornness, and other hallmarks of the unethical life; pa-

---

man Age," in *Accusations of Unbelief in Islam: A Diachronic Perspective on Takfīr*, ed. Camilla Adang et al. (Leiden: Brill, 2015), 221.

4 Ibid., 222.

5 Rudolph Peters, *"Islamischer Fundamentalismus: Glauben, Handeln, Führung,"* in *Max Webers Sicht des Islams: Interpretation und Kritik*, ed. Wolfgang Schlucter (Frankfurt: Suhrkamp, 1987), 217–42.

6 Barbara Flemming, *"Die vorwahhabitische Fitna im osmanischen Kairo, 1711,"* in *Ord. Prof. İsmail Hakkı Uzunçarşili'ya Ar-mağan* (Ankara: Türk Tarih Kurumu, 1976), 55–65.

7 Referred to by Evstatiev, "Qādīzādeli Movement."

8 Evstatiev, "Qādīzādeli Movement," 230.

9 Madeline C. Zilfi, "The Qādīzādelis: Discordant Revivalism in Seventeenth-Century Istanbul," *Journal of Near Eastern Studies* 45, no. 4 (October 1986): 260.

10 Ibid., 261.

tience, generosity, piety, and other ethics; the proper rearing of children; conditions under which women may venture outside their homes; kinds and occasions of prayer; and the nature and substance of innovation.

Zilfi goes on to compare Birgili's *Risale* to his *Tarikat*, which was

> intended for more learned audiences. Its treatment of the issues taken up in the "Risale" was more elaborate, with more space given to the canonical authorities underlying Birgili's positions. In common with fundamentalists before and since, Birgili "attached no importance to custom and usage."[11] That is, the fact that the community had embraced a particular practice could not compensate for the lack of a Koranic or hadith-based authority.[12]

The Qādīzādeli movement itself is named after Qādīzāde Mehmed b. Mustafa (d. 1635), a fiery Friday mosque preacher who railed against the introduction of *bidaʿ* (innovation) into Islam, particularly by Sufis. The message of his sermons and those of fellow like-minded preachers "more than once between 1630 and 1680...erupted into bloody confrontations not only on the streets, but within the sacred precincts of the mosque."[13]

In seventeenth-century Istanbul, the conflict was between "holy law-defined 'orthodoxy' and the methods and claims of Sufism, Islamic mysticism."[14] This conflict recalled those that have arisen throughout Islamic centuries. Though the Sufis bore the brunt of the attacks, both rhetorical and physical, the dispute essentially existed between Qādīzādeli puritanism and the pragmatism of the *ulama* decision makers, who allowed for the necessity of some innovations. Qādīzādelis were against popular Islam and Sufis in particular.

Qādīzāde Mehmed

Born in 1582 in the western Anatolian town of Balikesir, Qādīzāde

---

[11] Ibid., 261n47: "Katib Chelebi, *The Balance of Truth*, p. 60; Birgili, *Tarikat-i Muhammediyye Tercümesi* (trans. from Arabic into Turkish by Celal Yildirim), Istanbul, 1981, pp. 34–41."

[12] Ibid., 261.

[13] Ibid., 251.

[14] Ibid., 252.

Mehmed studied under Birgili, then made his way to Istanbul, where he became a professional mosque preacher ("the path of sermon and admonition"). Though at first attracted to Sufism, Qādīzāde rejected its "emotionalism" and pursued the more austere path of preaching. He was appointed preacher at the Sultan Selim I mosque because of his "gifts of expression and grace of delivery."[15]

In 1631, Qādīzāde was promoted to Aya Sofya, the imperial mosque, where he began to preach a kind of fundamentalist ethic, "a set of doctrinal positions intended to rid Islam of beliefs and practices that had accumulated since the era of the Prophet Muhammad's Medina. Qādīzāde's sermons, and the infecting style of his delivery, infused new life into centuries-old dialectic between innovation and fundamental, 'orthodox', Islam."[16]

Zilfi underlines the fact that the fundamentalism of Birgili and Qādīzāde should be seen against the backdrop of the Islamic community's ongoing problematic relationship with its own history, which is liable to resurface at any given moment in the Islamic community:

> The lasting appeal of the fundamentalist ethic has its origins in the relationship of the Islamic community to its own past, to the austerity and righteousness of the epoch of the Prophet and the patriarchs of the faith. While the original Islamic community at Medina has provided Sunni Islam with perhaps its most compelling memory, the memory has been a painful one. Every age since that of the One True God's revelation to His last Prophet necessarily means a dreaded distancing from the ideal practice of the faith. With time come changes and deviations. Whether large or small, matters of ritual or dress or social ceremony, differences are inherently consequential for a faith that holds all human activity to be a sacred concern. Innovation, for Qādīzāde and his followers, as well as for their spiritual guides from the Islamic past, represented a falling away that threatened the salvation of the community. According to a Prophetic tradition (Turkish, *hadis*; Arabic, *hadith*) repeated by the orthodox down through the centuries, "every innovation is heresy, every her-

---

15 Ibid., 252n7: "*Katib Çelebi, Fezleke-i Tarih*, 2 vols. (Istanbul, 1286/1870), vol. 2, p. 64; Bursali Mehmed Tahir, *Osmanli Müellifleri*, 3 Vols. (Istanbul, 1972–75), vol. 1, p. 173; Nevizade Atai, *Zeyl-i Şakaik*, 2 vols. in 1 (Istanbul) pp. 602–3, 759."
16 Ibid., 253.

esy is error, and every error leads to hell."[17] In a salvationary sense, far from healing all wounds, time is itself wounding.[18]

One main contention was that the Islamic injunction to Command Right and Forbid Wrong was obligatory for all Muslims. The Qādīzādelis were activists who campaigned in mosques, urging Muslims to intervene and fulfill this religious obligation. They condemned those who insisted that the Prophet Muhammad's parents and all who had died before the divine revelations had died as believers, or believed in the immortality of the Prophet al-Khadir, or referred to Islam as "the religion of Abraham." They also condemned the writings of the mystic Ibn al-Arabi (d. 1240), especially the Sufi notion of "Unity of Being" (*wahdat al-wujūd*), which smacked of pantheism. As much as the pilgrim visiting a tomb to pray for divine intercession, reading Ibn al-Arabi was an innovation and sinful, and the guilty must be stopped since this behavior endangered the faith and the community.

Qādīzādeli violence "was directed against the Sufis. Individual Sufi masters were denounced and beaten, and their lodges vandalized, often at the instigation of Qādīzādeli preachers. In Qādīzāde Mehmed's day, and in part at his urging, Sultan Murad IV shut down taverns and coffeehouses and outlawed tobacco and wine. In the 1630s Murad had a number of taverns destroyed, and thousands of smokers were executed for defying his ban on tobacco."[19]

Sultan Murad did not have any particular quarrels with the Sufis, however, and actually had strong personal ties to certain Sufi orders. He left the Sufi lodges to themselves and the Qādīzādelis made more headway under Murad's successor, Ibrahim I (1640–1648) and in the first years of Mehmed IV (1648–1687), when they obtained a *fatwa* condemning Sufi excesses, particularly their music and dancing.

This second wave of Qādīzādeli activism ended in 1656, when many of their ringleaders were arrested and banished to Cyprus. A third and final wave of confrontations began with "Vani" Mehmed (d. 1685),

---

17 Ibid., 254n10: "Ignaz Goldziher, *Muslim Studies*, ed. S. M. Stern (London, 1967–1971), Vol. 2, pp. 34–35; for similar condemnations, see also ibid., pp. 28ff."

18 Ibid., 253.

19 Ibid., 257n22: "Mustafa Naima, *Tarih-i Naima*, 6 vols. (Istanbul, 1280/1863-64), Vol. 3, pp.160-64, 168-72, 179; Katib Çelebi, *Fezleke-i Tarih*, 2 vols. (Istanbul, 1286/1870), vol.2, p. 154; Paul Rycaut, *The History the Turkish Empire from the year 1623 to the Year 1677*, 2 vols. in 1 (London, 1680), vol. 1, pp. 52, 59, 71, 79; Antoine Galland, *De l'Origine et du progrez du café* (Caen. 1699); Dimitrie Cantemir, *The History of the Growth and Decay of the Othman Empire*, trans. N. Tindal (London, 1734), p. 246."

a scholar and preacher at the Lala Mustafa Pasha mosque in Erzurum, who was hostile to the ecstatic wing of Sufism. He managed to have at least one dervish lodge destroyed near Edirne, publicly denounced Sufis for disobedience to the Shariʻa, and had the public performance of Sufi music forbidden. Later, the the sale and consumption of wine was forbidden on pain of death wherever a mosque existed. Vani's influence ended with the Ottoman defeat at Vienna in 1683.

Qādīzādeli Influence

Turning now to whether the Qādīzādelis had an influence on the Wahhābīs, historian Simeon Evstatiev points out that both "movements were the product of very different social, political, and cultural local contexts but…shared a pattern of understanding what the demands of 'true belief' were and what an authentically Islamic orthodox creed should mean for Muslims."[20] Evstatiev argues for "continuity rather than rupture between the ideas promoted by its adherents and other revivalist strands in Islamic history," for example, "their struggle for a *sharīʻa*-minded reform brought about through reviving the beliefs and practices of the first Muslim generations…seems not to have been entirely new; such trends appeared not only in earlier Islamic experience in general but also in the earlier Ottoman intellectual and religio-political experience."[21] In other words, what these movements—one in a seventeenth-century urban setting, the other in the heart of eighteenth-century Arabia—for the purification of Islam share is their understanding of Islam.

"[T]he Qādīzādeli movement was one of the culminations of an already existing trajectory in Islamic history," Evstatiev emphasizes.[22] The Qādīzādelis admired Ibn Taymiyya; his "appeal for the eradication of blasphemous practices and unbelief"[23] resonated within the rank and file. Islamic history is full of such movements, and this was a part of a wider call for a return to the Koran and the *Sunna*, a rejection of heretical innovations, and the aggresive reassertion of *tawhīd*—an uncompromising monotheism that was in danger from *shirk*, polytheism, or more stricly attributing partners to God, and thus by extension, practising idolatry.

---

20 Evstatiev, "Qādīzādeli Movement," 213.
21 Ibid., 214.
22 Ibid., 215.
23 Ibid., 228.

Influence of Ibn Taymiyya

Contradictory opinions exist regarding the influence of Ibn Taymiyya on Birgili, Qāḍīzāde, and the Qāḍīzādelis generally. Khaled El-Rouayheb, James Richard Jewett Professor of Arabic and of Islamic Intellectual History at Harvard, has argued that the "views of Birgiwi and Kadizadeli followers may have been rooted, not in the thought of [Hanbalī] Ibn Taymiyya, but an intolerant current within the Hanafī-Māturīdī school, represented by such scholars as 'Alā' al-Dīn al-Bukhārī (d. 842/1438), who famously declared both Ibn 'Arabi and Ibn Taymiyya unbelievers."[24] However, in *Tarikat* Birgili contends that the visitation of graves is forbidden, an opinion close to those of Ibn Taymiyya and his student Ibn al-Qayyim.

Second, Saudi researcher Sultān Ibn 'Abd Allāh al-'Arrābī has claimed that Birgili, fearful of being rejected and suppressed by the Ottoman religious establishment, borrowed directly from Ibn Taymiyya and Ibn al-Qayyim, but without acknowledgment: "Accordingly, al-Birgiwi borrowed from Ibn Taymiyya, including whole passages from his *fatāwā*, but in doing so, he was 'just very slightly modifying them' (*bi-ta-Asrruf yasīr jiddan*)."[25]

There is another work that was once attributed to Birgili, *Ziyārat al-qubūr* (*On the Visitation of Graves*), which is very popular among Salafī and Wahhābī religious groups. Probably authored by an admirer of Birgili's, Ahmad al-Rūmī al-Aqhizārī (d. 1631 or 1634), this treatise begins with an explicit mention of Ibn al-Qayyim, which surely indicates Ibn Taymiyya and Ibn al-Qayyim's importance to and influence on Birgili and his admirers.

As for Qāḍīzāde Mehmed, he is said to have "expressed his political views through an expanded translation of Ibn Taymiyya's *al-Siyāsa al-shar 'iyya* into Ottoman Turkish, entitled *Tācü 'r-resā'il ve minhācü l-vesā'il*, which he presented to Sultan Murad IV."[26]

---

24 Khaled El-Rouayheb, "From Ibn Hajar al-Haytamī (d. 1566) to Khayr al-Dīn al-Ālūsī (d. 1899): Changing Views of Ibn Taymiyya among non-Hanbalī Sunni Scholars," in *Ibn Taymiyya and His Times*, ed. Yossef Rapoport and Shahab Ahmed (Oxford: Oxford University Press, 2010), 304.

25 Evstatiev, "Qāḍīzādeli Movement," 232, quoting Sultān Ibn 'Abd Allāh al-'Arrābī, "*Dāmighat al-mubtadi 'īn wa-kāshifat butlān al-mulhīdīn. Al-Imām Muhammad b. Bīr 'Alī Iskandar al-Birgiwī: Dirāsa wa-tahqīq*," (master's thesis, Jāmi 'at Umm al-Qurā, Mecca 1425/2004), 114.

26 Ibid., 228n81.

CHAPTER 14
Ibn ʿAbd Al-Wahhāb and Eighteenth-Century Renewal and Reform

The Eighteenth Century

AS I HAVE sought to emphasize throughout this work, the late twentieth-century resurgence of Islamic fundamentalism should be considered against the background of "a long tradition of special emphasis on the need for purification and revival of strict adherence to the 'fundamentals' of the faith."[1] While I concentrate here on eighteenth-century movements that have decisively influenced and "provided a significant foundation for renewalist movements of the modern era,"[2] the thrust of my entire argument is that something deep within Islam encourages activism. As the late Palestinian-American philosopher Ismail R. al-Faruqi, who was widely recognized as an authority on Islam and comparative religion, put it, "Islam teaches not only that the realization of the good is possible in this world but that to bring it about here and now is precisely the duty of every man and woman."[3] In the words of Nehemia Levtzion and John O. Voll, authors of *Eighteenth Century Renewal and Reform in Islam*, "Renewal and reform are important dimensions of the historical experience of Muslims. An important part

---

1 Nehemia Levtzion and John O. Voll, eds., *Eighteenth-Century Renewal and Reform in Islam* (Syracuse, NY: Syracuse University Press, 1987), 6.
2 Ibid.
3 Ismail R. al-Faruqi, *Islam* (Niles, IL: Argus Communications, 1979), 13, cited by Levtzion and Voll, Eighteenth-Century Renewal, 6.

of the mission of believers is the implementation of God's revelation in the actual conditions of human society....[R]eform is at the heart of the faith and action of every Muslim."[4]

Many activist movements of renewal and reform took place in the Islamic world during the eighteenth century, and even where these did not occur, the intensification of Islamic identity created the necessary conditions for later revivalism. But eighteenth-century movements should be seen as continuous "with both earlier and later movements of Islamic resurgence."[5] For instance, there is direct continuity between the Wahhābi movement and the present-day Saudi state.

Eighteenth-century growth and intensification of Islamic identity took places in areas of the Islamic world where it seemed threatened by the apparent self-assertion of non-Muslims in society. Whereas in the past Muslims lived in symbiosis with members of other religions, the new reformists sought to separate Muslims from non-Muslims. They felt that far too many "Muslims" had acquired decidedly un-Islamic practices such as tomb worship and seeking intercession from dead saints. These practices were enough for militant reformers to brand such putative Muslims as nonbelievers—the act of *takfir*—a very serious charge, since an apostate must eventually be executed, since *jihād* can only be waged against infidels.

Like all reform efforts, the Islamic movements challenge prevailing conditions in society, when Islam is no longer practiced in a manner that the reformers find satisfactory. Eighteenth-century reform movements "stressed the authenticity of the Islamic tradition in more exclusivist rather than inclusivist terms."[6] This was a reaction against what reformers believed were too many compromises made to accommodate other traditions and religions. This gave the reformist movement a puritanical rigor: "The 'resurgences' of Islam that have been seen in the modern era have tended to have a 'fundamentalist' tone...in keeping with the tone of renewalism at the beginning of the modern era when Western influences become more important in many parts of the Islamic world."[7]

Rudolph Peters on Fundamentalism and a Religious Riot in Eighteenth-Century Cairo

Let's take a closer look at how these movements operated. Here is

---

4 Levtzion and Voll, *Eighteenth-Century Renewal*, 6.
5 Ibid.
6 Ibid., 19.
7 Ibid.

an account of a religious riot that occurred in eighteenth-century Cairo from a scholar mentioned in these pages, Rudolph Peters.[8] In "The Battered Dervishes of Bab Zuwyala" Peters writes generally about Islamic fundamentalism as his account sheds historical and ideological light on our examination of the Qādīzedili movement in seventeenth-century Istanbul.

"One of the most important motivating factors behind eighteenth-century Islamic renewal and reform is undoubtedly Islamic fundamentalism," Peters opens. "By its very nature, fundamentalism is activist and militant and tends therefore to produce movements and organizations aimed at implementing the Islamic ideals."[9] He then describes a short-lived fundamentalist movement among Turkish soldiers in Egypt, who in their religious fervor attacked dervishes (members of a mystical order) performing Sufi rituals, which the soldiers considered un-Islamic.

In October 1711, a Turkish student of religion (*softa*) and some companions took up lodgings in the Muyyad Mosque. They sat together to study the treatise of Birgili (discussed in the previous chapter as a major influence on the Istanbul Qādīzadeli movement). The *softa* then began giving sermons that became more and more popular, and his audience grew.

His sermons made these claims:

> Miracles of saints cease after death and accounts of miracles performed by them after their death therefore are false.

> It is false that some saints can see the Well-Preserved Tablet,[10] and anyone holding such an opinion is an unbeliever. Since even prophets cannot see the Well-Preserved Tablet, how could it be possible for saints to be able to do so? [The *softa* also denied that Prophet had ever seen the Well-Preserved Tablet.]

> It is not permissible to burn candles and oil lamps at the

---

8 Rudolph Peters, "The Battered Dervishes of Bab Zuwyala: A Religious Riot in Eighteenth-Century Cairo," in Levtzion and Voll, *Eighteenth Century Renewal*, 93–115.

9 Ibid., 93.

10 The Well-Preserved Tablet is a tablet in heaven on which is to be found the original text of the Koran. It is mentioned in the Koran in Sura Q85, *al-Buruj*, The Mansions of the Stars, 22.

tombs of saints, and those who kiss their thresholds and tombs are feared to be unbelievers. All Muslims must put an end to this practice.

It is obligatory for Muslims to destroy cupolas built over graves (*tekkes*), like the Gulseni and the Mevlevi *tekke*, and over the tombs of saints.

The *tekkes* contructed for the dervishes must be abolished, and the dervishes living there must be ejected, their places must be taken over by students of religion, and the *tekkes* thereafter be converted into madrasas [schools of Islamic instruction].

It is forbidden to visit in groups Imam Shāfiʻī and other tombs during the nights before Saturday in order to perform public *dhikrs*. [Literally, "remembrance," "recollection," "mention." In Sufism, this term has acquired a technical sense of "litany," in which the name of God or formulae like "God is Most Great" (*Allāhu Akbar*) is repeated in either a high or low voice, and often linked to bodily movement or breathing. The *dhikr* is often one of the most important activities of a sufi.][11]

It is forbidden and an act of polytheism (*shirk*) that a band of ignoramuses among the groups that during the nights of Ramadan are to be found near Bab Zuwayla (Demirkapu) shout and jump until midnight on the pretense of performing a *dhikr*. It is incumbent upon the *qādī* and others to stop them, for a person who fails to forbid what is abominable (*al-nahy an al-munkur*) will be punished in the Hereafter.[12]

The Turkish *softa*'s followers lay in ambush for the dervishes holding a *dhikr*, and attacked them after evening prayer with swords and

---

11 Ian Richard Netton, *A Popular Dictionary of Islam*, (Richmond, Surrey, UK: Curzon Press 1992), s.v. "*Dhikr*."
12 Peters, "Battered Dervishes," 94–95. Peters is relying on three sources: Ahmad Shalabi, "*Awdah al-isharat fi-man tawalla Misr min al-wuzara wa-l-bashat*"; Yusuf al-Mallawani, "*Tuhfat al-ahbab bi-man malak Misr min al-muluk wa-l-nuwwab*"; and Muhammad b.Yusuf al-Hallaq, "*Tarih-I Misr.*"

cudgels. The dervishes were severely beaten and chased from Bab Zuwayla. Some people went to Shaykh Ahmad al-Nafrawi, and informed him of what the *softa* had said. The Shaykh got together with the *'ulamā'* of the Hanafites and Shafiites to issue a *fatwa* that tried to refute the *softa's* arguments. As Peters writes,

> That our Turkish *softa* was a radical is beyond dispute. His radicalism was of a religious kind and appears in his fierce stance vis-à-vis certain popular Sufi rituals and saint veneration. It is significant that he and his friends had been studying a treatise by Birgili, a popular author well-known for strict views on these matters. These attitudes are typical of fundamentalist Islam, by which I mean those trends in Islam that emphasize the transcendence of God versus His imminence, the authenticity of religious experience as based on the revelation (direct and indirect, i.e., Quran and *hadith*), unity of religious experience, and finally, the basic equality of all believers in the face of God.[13]

Peters then makes an important observation: "As a rule, fundamentalism is action-oriented; it wants to change the world by subjecting it to fundamentalist ideals. Central to fundamentalist thought is the claim that the gate of *ijtihād* [the exercise of independent judgment unfettered by case law or precedent] is not entirely closed."[14]

Clearly the Turkish *softa* wanted to put to an end a number of customs deemed un-Islamic, action either the authorities or individual Muslims must take. Appealing to the Muslim duty of Commanding Right and Forbidding Wrong, the *softa's* sermons were effective: the crowds came under his control and attacked the dervishes holding a dhikr at Bab Zuwayla.

His followers were mainly Turkish soldiers serving during the civil war of 1711, which pitted regiments of Janissaries against Janissaries, regiments of the Azaban against Azaban, and so on. Three months of fighting had left nearly 4000 dead. As Peters notes:

> In these troubled times the soldiers must have been responsive to religious calls implying a break with the past and offering a clear and simple way to salvation. During the fight-

---
13 Ibid., 100.
14 Ibid.

ing the people of Cairo had attributed the calamity that had befallen them to their own impiety and sinfulness, and these soldiers may have had similar feelings. So, when a preacher showed them a new way of being pious—a departure from their habitual, mystical religiosity or indifference to religion—which, because of its active and practical character appealed to their soldierly temperament, many must have felt attracted to it. And more than attracted; they identified with the movement to the extent that that they were willing to risk their lives.[15]

The Turkish *softa*'s subsequent reaction to the fatwa was violent. He inveighed against the *'ulamā'*, calling them unbelievers, which implied that they should be declared apostates and eventually killed. He urged the crowd to follow him to the *qādī askar* (principle judge),[16] where thing got out of hand when the crowd seemed to threaten the *qādī*, a high ranking Ottoman official. Finally, the military authorities had to step in to restore order.

Peters sums up the significance of this short-lived movement: the sermonizing student's "ideas and actions were rooted in Turkish *softa* radicalism and a brand of Turkish fundamentalism that went back via Birgili Mehmed, to Ibn Taymiyya and Ibn Qayyim al-Djawziyya," and offers a wider and familiar conclusion:

> The trend that I have labelled fundamentalism—and that for equally good reasons may be called revivalism—has its roots deep in Islamic history. Over the centuries, fundamentalist opinions have been expressed by Islamic scholars. Time and again, fundamentalist movements of protest arose arguing that religion had become corrupted and that they wanted to purify it by going back to the revealed sources and ridding it of unwarranted accretions. These movements often had a militant and activist character because they wished to change the world and subject it to the values of a pure and unadulterated Islam based on *tawhīd*, the recognition of God's unity and uniqueness, and the *sunna*, the ideal standard of behav-

---

15 Ibid., 104.

16 The two highest-ranking *qādīs* of the Ottoman judiciary. As senior members of the royal court, they supervised judicial affairs, heard legal cases, oversaw legal matters of the military-administrative personnel, and handled campaign duties.

ior set by the Prophet Muhammad.[17]

And Peters unequivocally states that the fundamentalist movements cannot be linked to Western expansion:

> It is true that Egypt had, to some extent, been affected by the shift in trade routes due to the rise of Western commercial capitalism. Yet, it is impossible to relate the events I have mentioned to these economic changes.[18]

The Birth of Wahhābism

Before beginning with the founder of Wahhābism, Ibn 'Abd al-Wahhāb, I should like to offer some background details. Wahhābism was born in the mid-eighteenth century in Najd (also "Nejd"), the central region of Saudi Arabia, which consisted of the regions of Riyadh (Riyād), al-Qassim (al-Qazīm), and Hā'il. An indigenous religious reform movement that arose in an area long considered a religious and cultural backwater, Wahhābism was not an anticolonialist movement. In fact, the first Wahhābis were unaware of the "speed and depth of contemporary English and French intrusion into far-off Muslims territories."[19] Nor was it nationalist, and did not borrow anything of its central beliefs from the West. As Michael Crawford, an independent consultant who writes on the Middle East explains, Wahhābism "was a pre-modern movement that arose before the most serious Western threat materialized against Islamic lands on the Mediterranean or in India. It can present itself today, as it has always done, as an authentic Islamic response to contemporary challenges."[20] Saudi Arabia itself was never colonized by the West, though it was theoretically part of the Ottoman Empire in the early eighteenth-century, especially Hijaz, with its holy cities of Mecca and Medina, and the interior Najd region only nominally so.

In periods of disorientation and change Muslims looked for solutions in their own cultural and religious heritage, where they found a greater sense of purpose and belonging, and a renewed, reassuring Islamic identity. The Wahhābis were primarily concerned with the moral and religious well-being of Muslims in their corner of the world.

---

17 Peters, "Battered Dervishes," 109-10.
18 Ibid., 110-11.
19 Michael Crawford, *Ibn 'Abd al-Wahhāb* (London: Oneworld Publications, 2014), 7.
20 Ibid., 13.

Najd and the Hanbalī Tradition

Given the importance of the Hanbalī school to the development of the ideas of Muhammad Ibn 'Abd al-Wahhāb, it is worth pointing out that Najdi scholars had followed the Hanbalī rite long before the advent of Wahhābism. Unfortunately, our knowledge of these scholars does not commence before the sixteenth-century. Ahmad ibn 'Atwa (d. 1541) is the first name handed down to us.

Ibn 'Atwa studied in Damascus, attending lectures on Islamic jurisprudence by several Hanbalī scholars such as Shihāb al-Dīn Ahmad ibn 'Abd Allāh al-'Askarī. On his return to the Najd, Ibn 'Atwa became a respected authority on the Hanbalī tradition and rite, and taught such later scholars as Ahmad ibn Muhammad ibn Musharraf. He issued many *fatwas* and wrote two works of *fiqh* (sources of the law). Our sources indicate there were seven other such scholars during the sixteenth century, and by the seventeenth century most Najdi towns seemed to have their own *qādīs* (judges), all of them Hanbalīs.[21]

The scholars of Najd were also in touch with prominent Hanbalites in Egypt and Syria. Shaykh Manzūr al-Buhūtī, for example, was an Egyptian scholar with several Najdi students, notably 'Abd Allah ibn 'Abd al-Wahhāb, who became the *qādī* of al-'Uyayna until his death in 1646. Another Egyptian scholar at al-Azhar, Mar'ī ibn Yūsuf, a celebrated Hanbalī, "sent a copy of his work, *Ghāyat al-Muntahā* [*The Utmost Limit*], to the scholars of Najd, giving his regards to two of them, Khamīs ibn Sulaymān and Muhammad ibn Ismā'īl."[22] The latter had students who later gained some renown, including 'Abd Allah ibn Dhahlān, who became the *qādī* of Riyadh and teacher of several well-known scholars, including Ahmad al-Manqūr and Muhammad al-'Awsajī. He died of the plague that reached the region in 1687.[23]

Perhaps the greatest Najdi scholar of the seventeenth century was Sulaymān ibn 'Alī, the grandfather of Muhammad ibn 'Abd al-Wahhāb.

On the whole, these Najdi scholars concentrated solely on jurisprudence. This is understandable because the main purpose of education in this region was to prepare scholars to carry out the duties of a judge in towns. One exception was 'Uthmān ibn Qā'id, who studied under 'Abd Allah ibn Dhahlān, who traveled to Damascus before settling in Cairo, where he died in 1685. He wrote several works, the most significant of

---

21 'Abd Allāh Sālih al-'Uthaymīn, *Muhammad ibn 'Abd al-Wahhāb: The Man and His Works* (London and New York: I. B. Tauris, 2009), 20–21.
22 Ibid., 21.
23 Ibid.

which, *Najāt al-Khalaf fī "tiqād al-Salaf* (*The Salvation of Successors in the Belief of their Predecessors*), concerns "the beliefs of contemporary Muslims" and shows Ibn Dhahlān's "conviction that there should be a return to the practices of the early age of Islam."[24]

During the first half of the eighteenth-century more than twenty scholars are mentioned in Muslim history books as flourishing in the Najd, some writing on jurisprudence, others acting as judges.

Pre-Wahhābi Beliefs and Practices

Over time many questionable beliefs and innovations had been added to Islamic practices. This included, for example, the widespread belief that dead saints could intercede for the living before God, which lead many Muslims to construct buildings and arches over the graves of pious persons and visit such tombs, almost in pilgrimage. They would circumambulate the tombs, praying to the saints to plead on their behalf, in conviction that the saints could ward off evil and bring about good. Pre-Islamic practices such as the veneration of certain rocks and trees were also revived.

These practices were clearly idolatrous, and are described in some detail by Wahhābi scholars such as ibn Bishr (1795–1873), who wrote that the Najd in particular had been much corrupted by them:

> Polytheism was widespread in the Najd and elsewhere. It was common for trees and rocks to be invested with supernatural powers; tombs were venerated and shrines were built about them; and all these were regarded as sources of blessing and objects of vows. The people sought refuge from the jinn, made sacrifices to them and put food for them in the corners of their houses, believing that by so doing they would cure their sick relatives, bring good and prevent evil. Moreover, swearing by beings other than God, and similar forms of major and minor polytheism were widely practiced.[25]

Another scholar encouraged by the Saudi ruler was the chronicler Ibn Ghannām (d. 1811), who described the state of Najd before Wahhabism as one of ignorance, *jahiliyya*, a term made famous by Sayyid Qutb (d. 1966) much later.

---

24 Ibid., 22.
25 Uthmān ibn Bishr, *'Unwān al-Majd fī Ta'rīkh Najd* (*Token of Glory: On the History of Najd*) (Beirut, 1967), 16; cited in al-'Uthaymīn, *Muhammad ibn 'Abd al-Wahhāb*, 23.

Muhammad Ibn al-Wahhāb (1703–1792)

Muhammad Ibn al-Wahhāb was born in al-'Uyayna in 1703 into a family of religious notables in the Najd. His father was a *qādī* and his first teacher. A quick learner, Ibn al-Wahhāb memorized the Koran by the age of ten. He also studied *tafsir* (exegesis, interpretation, and commentary on the Koran), *hadīth,* and *madhhab* (school of law; in Ibn al-Wahhāb's case, jurisprudence of the Hanbalī school).

Ibn al-Wahhāb seems to have made a pilgrimage to Mecca, probably just before his marriage at the age of twelve.[26] After the pilgrimage, he went on to Medina, where he came under the influence of Shaykh 'Abd Allah ibn Ibrāhīm ibn Sayf. Back home in al-'Uyayna, he deepened his knowledge of Islam reading works on *tawhīd*.

Ambitious, Ibn al-Wahhāb was determined to travel to extend his knowledge under renowned scholars. He returned to Mecca and Medina, where he renewed his acquaintance with Ibn Sayf and joined the circle of Muhammad Hayāt al-Sindī. An admirer of Ibn Taymiyya, Ibn Sayf was from al-Majma'a, a small town in the Najdi region of Sudayr and recognized that the Najd was in need of spiritual reform.

One day Ibn Sayf asked Ibn al-Wahhāb, "Do you want to see the weapon that I have prepared for al-Majma'a?" When the young man said yes, Ibn Sayf brought him to a house where many books were stored and said, "This is the weapon I have prepared." As Russian scholar Alexei Vassiliev put it, "Ibn 'Abd al-Wahhāb hinted thereby that his Medina teacher had prepared an 'ideological weapon' to combat the beliefs that were widespread in his oasis."[27]

Ibn al-Wahhāb also learned much from Muhammad Hayāt, who "was opposed to *taqlīd* (imitation) commonly accepted by the followers of the four Sunni schools, advocating instead *ijtihād* (independent legal or doctrinal judgment). On the other hand, he was so opposed to innovation that he seems to have considered those who practiced such to be similar to the idolaters, applying to them Qur'ānic verses concerning the pagans of the Prophet's time."[28]

Ibn al-Wahhāb's stay in Medina was important to his intellectual development for three reasons, for his (1) introduction to Ibn Taymiyya's works, (2) association with Muhammad Hayāt al-Sindī, and (3) vehement denunciation of *bida'* (innovations), specifically the idolatrous practices among visitors of the Prophet's tomb. His admiration for Ibn

---

26 Al-'Uthaymīn, *Muhammad ibn 'Abd al-Wahhāb*, 30.
27 Alexei Vassiliev, *The History of Saudi Arabia* (London: Saqi Books, 2000), 65.
28 Al-'Uthaymīn, *Muhammad ibn 'Abd al-Wahhāb*, 33.

Taymiyya led him to travel to Damascus, which remains an active center of Hanbalī thought.

It is probable that Ibn al-Wahhāb travelled widely at this period in his life, spending time as well in Basra, Baghdad, Kurdistan, Hamadan, Isfahan, Qom, Aleppo, Jerusalem, Cairo, and once again, Mecca. He seems to have returned to the Najd in the 1730s and began preaching. After his father's death in 1740, Ibn al-Wahhāb returned to his birthplace, probably in 1742. Soon after his arrival, he made an alliance with 'Uthmān, the chief of al-'Uyayna, and set out to end all idolatrous practices by cutting down trees, demolishing the shrine of the Companions of the Prophet, and destroying the tombs. Our sources agree that "within a comparatively short time" after Ibn al-Wahhāb's arrival

> the spectacle of all idolatrous practices in the district had been removed. Nothing could have been more effective, it was claimed, in convincing the untutored people of what the true Islamic faith was and in making them abandon their superstitious belief...than the demonstration of their inability to do any harm against those who destroyed them. These activities were, in fact, the practical declaration of the beginning of the Wahhabi movement.[29]

Like many Hanbalīs, Ibn al-Wahhāb was very critical of Sufis, which may have been the source of their disagreements just before his father's death. His father may have had links to the Qadiri Sufi order, but Ibn 'al-Wahhāb made no distinction between the idolatrous practices of the masses and "the sober mystic orders such as the Qadiris or Naqshbandis. For him they all traded in some form intercession with God which he saw as placing the intercessor on a par with God, a practice he equated with polytheism."[30] Ibn 'Abd al-Wahhāb had firsthand knowledge of the mystic fraternities in Basra, and his attitude to Sufism was in keeping with the views of Ibn Taymiyya.

He was also intellectually indebted, however, to Ibn Qudama (d. 1223), another Hanbalī ascetic and juriconsult, whose works *al-Mughnī* and *al-'Umda* had great authority in the Najd in the early eighteenth century. Ibn Qudama had a surprisingly soft spot for mystics and mysticism, which was confirmed by his condoning of Ibn 'Akīl's veneration for the great mystic al-Hallāj. But like many Hanbalīs, Ibn Qudama was

---

29 Ibid., 43.
30 Crawford, *Ibn 'Abd al-Wahhāb*, 28–29.

very critical of Ibn 'Akīl's excessive rationalism—an intellectual trait that Ibn 'al-Wahhāb also acquired.[31] Later on the Wahhābis softened their attitude toward the Sufis, seeing no incompatibility of Wahhābism and Sufism. Some Sufis established personal links to the Al Sa'ud, the ruling royal family of Saudi Arabia.[32] "On the conquest of Mecca Shaykh 'Abd Allah, son of Ibn 'Abd Al-Wahhāb, even declared acceptable Sufi orders that observed orthodoxy and orthopraxy (as interpreted by the Wahhabis)."[33]

In 1744 (it is estimated), Ibn al-Wahhāb was pressured to leave al-'Uyayna for al-Dir'iyya, where he had the fateful meeting with Muhammad ibn Sa'ūd, the ruler with whom he eventually signed a pact whereby all religious matters would be left to Ibn al-Wahhāb and all military and political issues to Ibn Sa'ūd, with both agreeing to bring all the peoples of the peninsula back to the true principles of Islam, purified of its impure accretions. This pact marked the beginning of the first Saudi state.

Influences and Some of His Doctrines

In addition to Ibn Taymiyya, Ibn al-Wahhāb was influenced by Ibn Qayyim al-Jawziyya, Ibn Qudama, and earlier writers in the Hanbalī tradition such as 'Abd Allah (d. 903) and Abu Bakr al-Khallāl (d. 924). On innovations, as discussed above, the Wahhābis adopted the conservative attitude of the Hanbalītes. Ibn al-Wahhāb condemned all forms of innovation, and rejected the views of those who maintained that a *bid'a* could be praiseworthy. Also in line with Hanbalī thought, he was very hostile to the sects he considered incompatible with Sunnism: Shi'a, Mu'tazila, Khawārij. He denounced all forms of scholastic theology (*kalām*) and considered heretical or schismatic various Sufis who had introduced all sorts of innovations.

For Ibn al-Wahhāb, Shi'ism was one of the greatest sources of corruption threatening the true religion:

> Hostility to Shi'a was natural for Hanbalīs. Their doctrinal

---

[31] *Encyclopaedia of Islam*, vol. 3, "H–Iram," ed. B. Lewis et al., 2nd ed. (Leiden: Brill, 1971), s.v. "Ibn Kudāma al-Makdisī," by George Makdisi.

[32] The House of Sa'ud has thousands of members. It is composed of the descendants of Muhammad bin Saud, founder of the Emirate of Diriyah, known as the First Saudi state (1818–91), and his brothers, though the ruling faction of the family is primarily led by the descendants of Ibn Saud, the modern founder of Saudi Arabia.

[33] Crawford, *Ibn 'Abd al-Wahhāb*, 86.

approach rested heavily on Prophetic traditions transmitted by Companions. The Shi'a believed many of these took the wrong side of the dispute with the Caliph 'Ali and discounted them as unreliable or worse. In early Wahhabi demonology the Shi'a were archetypical associationists and deserved particular condemnation for attributing special powers or aspects of divinity to 'Ali and his offspring. They were among the enemies of God and the Prophet. Anyone who doubted their unbelief was himself an unbeliever.[34]

Ibn al-Wahhāb used the abusive term *"Rāfidite"* ("rejectors" or "abandoners") for all Shi'as, "because they had deserted Abu Bakr and 'Umar or according to another explanation, because they considered the revolt of Zayd ibn 'Alī in Kufa 740 to be unrighteous."[35]

Ibn al-Wahhāb first encountered the Shi'as in Basra, and found their practices incompatible with true Islam. He accused them of having introduced polytheism into Islam, and held it against them that they rejected all the caliphs except 'Ali and regarded many of the Prophet's Companions as apostates. They were all guilty of *taqiyya* (dissimulation) and such practices as temporary marriage (*mut'a*). They were worse than the Jews and Christians in their excesses.

Wahhābi hostility toward the Shi'a manifested itself in 1802, when Wahhābi forces attacked Karbala, a town sacred to the memory of all Shi'a since the massacre of al-Husayn b. 'Ali in 680. J.B.L.J. Rousseau, the consul-general of France in Iraq until 1816, describes the gruesome events:

> We have recently seen a horrible example of the Wahhabis' cruel fanaticism in the terrible fate of [the mosque of] Imam Husayn....12000 Wahhabis suddenly attacked Imam Husayn; after seizing more spoils than they had ever seized after the greatest victories, they put everything to fire and the sword....Old people, women and children— everybody died at the barbarians' sword....[I]t is said that whenever they saw a pregnant woman, they disemboweled her and left the foetus on the mother's bleeding corpse. Their cruelty could not be satisfied, they did not cease their murders and blood flowed like water. As a result of the bloody catastrophe, more

---

34 Ibid., 86-87.
35 Halm, *Shi'ism*, 39.

than 4000 people perished.[36]

In a letter to Muhammad ibn 'Īd, Ibn al-Wahhāb once said that his doctrines were based on four points:

1. The interpretation of *tawhīd* ["the unity or oneness of God"];
2. The demonstration of what polytheism [*shirk*] actually is and the denunciation as infidels of those who, in spite of knowing full well that monotheism is the religion of God and His Prophet, not only hate it but deter people from it and fight against those who support the Prophet in its cause;
3. The denunciation, [as unbelievers (*takfir*)] too, of those who know what polytheism is and realize that the Prophet was sent to combat it, and yet persist in praising it and arguing that the people who practice it, because they are the vast majority (*al-sawād al-a'zam*), are not in error;
4. Finally, sanctioning warfare [which is a divine commandment] against such as these so that the true religion remains exclusive to God alone.[37]

But as 'Abd Allāh Sālih al-'Uthaymīn points out, it is essentially the first point that is cardinal. The other three parts are its logical consequences.[38]

Tawhīd

Most of Ibn al-Wahhāb's works are fairly short, full of quotations from the Koran and hadīth, written in a plain, concise manner. His first major work was probably *Kitab al-Tawhīd* written sometime between 1734 and 1742, in which Ibn al-Wahhāb "sets out his teaching in the line of the strictest Hanbalī doctrine."[39]

---

36 J.B.L.J. Rousseau, *Description du Pachalik de Bagdad Suivie d'une Notice Historique sur les Wahabis* (Paris: Treutel & Würtz, 1809), 7:261f.; quoted in Vassiliev, *History of Saudi Arabia*, 97.
37 Al-'Uthaymīn, *Muhammad ibn 'Abd al-Wahhāb*, 114, citing Husayn ibn Ghannām, *Ta'rīkh Najd al-Musmmā Rawdat al-Afhām li-Murtād Hāl al-Imām wa-Ta'dād Ghazawāt Dhawī 'l-Islām*, 2 vols. (Cairo, 1949), 1:107.
38 Ibid., 114.
39 *Encyclopaedia of Islam*, vol. 3, "H–Iram," ed. B. Lewis et al., 2nd ed. (Leiden: Brill, 1971), s.v. "Ibn 'Abd al-Wahhāb," by Henri Laoust.

The *Kitab al-Tawhīd* is divided into sixty-seven chapters.[40] Under each chapter heading, Ibn 'Abd al-Wahhāb collects Koranic verses and traditions supporting his views. These are followed by quotations from the Companions of the Prophet or their immediate successors, with occasional reference to scholars such as Ibn Taymiyya. He gives 125 hadīth: eighteen derived from Muslim, six from Bukhārī, thirty-one from both, seven from Ibn Hanbal, and seventeen by Ibn Hanbal and others. The rest are related by other traditionists such as Ibn Maja, al-Tirmidhī, and Abu Dāwūd.

Central to Ibn al-Wahhāb's thought was an uncompromising monotheism—*tawhīd* (the oneness of God)—the recognition of which was the first duty of all Muslims, even before prayer. (As a reminder, the opposite of *tawhīd* is *shirk*, which is often translated as "polytheism.")

The Wahhābis divide tawhīd into three kinds:

1. *Tawhīd al-rubūbiyya* (Unity of Lordship)
2. *Tawhīd al-asmā' wa-A-sifāt* (Names and Attributes)
3. *Tawhīd al-ilāhiyya* (Unity of Godship) or t*awhīd al-'ibāda* (Unity of Worship)

Tawhīd al-rubūbiyya is defined as the assertion of the unity of God in His actions, such as to believe and confess that He alone is the Creator, the Provider and Disposer of the universe. Allied to *tawhīd al-rubūbiyya* is the principle of predestination and the will of the created. (However, it seems doubtful that the Wahhābis have resolved the contradictions implied in such a view.)

Tawhīd al-asmā' wa-A-sifāt is to believe and affirm all the Names and Attributes of God found in the Koran and the *hadith*, which must be accepted without any kind of modification in word or meaning. There are no similarities between the Attributes of God and mankind, even when it might seem so. For example, God says, "That He may punish the hypocrites, men and women, and the pagan men and women, who have an evil opinion of Allah. A circle of evil is around them; Allah is Angry with them, Curses them and has prepared for them an evil end" (Q48. *al-Fath*, the Victory, 6).

Tawhīd al-ulūhiyya[41] or ***Tawhīd al-'ibāda*** is "the acknowledgement that God alone should be the addressee of prayers, supplications,

---

40 Al-'Uthaymīn indicates sixty-nine chapters, whereas Crawford gives sixty-seven chapters.

41 However, 'Abd Allāh Sālih al-'Uthaymīn gives "*ilāhiyya*."

and sacrifices, and other forms of worship. There were no other Gods or mini-Gods who could act as intermediaries or intercessors."[42] Wahhābis wished to emphasize that the prophets did not call upon their people merely to believe that God was the sole Creator and Lord, but also wanted worship to be devoted to Him alone.[43]

For Ibn al-Wahhāb, even nonbelievers (*kuffar*) subscribe to *tawhīd al-rububiyya*, calling it the unbelievers' Oneness (*Tawhīd al-kuffar*): "Unbelievers, especially Christians, include those who worship God night and day. They are ascetics in this world and give in alms what they receive from it, isolating themselves from people in a monastery. Nonetheless they are unbelievers, enemies of God and destined for perpetual fire because of their belief in Jesus and other saints."[44]

Ibn al-Wahhāb was equally severe with Muslims who observed all the precepts and requirements of Islam and yet prayed to a being or object other than God. These Muslims would face the same fate, such conduct "render[ing] their lives, property, and wives forfeit, regardless of whether they observed *tawhīd al-rububiyya*. It was *tawhīd al-uluhiyya* that brought the believer into true Islam. Anything worshiped in place of God was an idol (*taghut*)."[45]

According to Ibn al-Wahhāb, God created the *jinn* and mankind so that they would worship Him alone—monotheism being the first duty of all mankind. The prophets had been sent to their peoples to remind them to fulfil this obligation; once fulfilled they would receive a reward: "Anyone who fully observes the *tawhīd* will enter heaven without undergoing trial"—on the Day of Judgment.[46] *Jihād* is legal against those who refuse to join Islam and oppose its representatives.[47] Muhammad the Prophet commanded the Muslims to take part in *jihād* in Allah's cause.

All believers must be vigilant lest they slip into polytheism. This happens when people seek blessings from trees, stones, shrines of saints, etc. And no sacrifices to God should be made where other sacrificial acts are practiced, for this, too, may lead to polytheism. Help and protection must not be sought from anyone but God. Intercession from dead saints is forbidden. Magic is prohibited; anyone found practicing it deserves

---

42 Crawford, *Ibn 'Abd al-Wahhāb*, 29.
43 Al-'Uthaymīn, *Muhammad ibn 'Abd al-Wahhāb*, 120.
44 Ghannām, *Ta'rīkh Najd al-Musmmā Rawdat*, 1:177; quoted in Crawford, *Ibn 'Abd al-Wahhāb*, 29.
45 Crawford, *Ibn 'Abd al-Wahhāb*, 29
46 Quoted in al-'Uthaymīn, *Muhammad ibn 'Abd al-Wahhāb*, 79.
47 Ibid.

the death penalty.⁴⁸ A Muslim must not seek worldly reward for religious acts.⁴⁹

"Belief in predestination is obligatory and anyone who denies this or doubts it will have his good deeds rejected by God and he will enter hell."⁵⁰ Creating statues and pictures is forbidden, for in doing so, man is imitating God and His creation; all such works must be destroyed.

For Ibn 'Abd al-Wahhāb, there is never a question of neutrality concerning *tawhīd*. You are for it or you are against it, there is no third way: "What is there beyond the truth but error?"⁵¹

Nowhere is Ibn 'Abd al-Wahhāb's activism more evident than when he insisted that it was not enough for a Muslim to know of the Oneness of God; renunciation of polytheism does not guarantee entry into heaven. This knowledge must be acted on:

> There is no dispute that *tawhīd* must be in the heart, on the tongue and by deed. If there is any deficiency in this, a man is no Muslim. If he knows *tawdīd* and does not act on it, he is an unbeliever (*kafir*) and disobedient [to God], like the Pharaoh, Devil and such like. Many of the people make this mistake, saying this is the truth and we understand and witness it as such but cannot practice it because the people of our town allow only those who agree with them, and other such excuses….Practising *tawhīd* is an outward activity, and he who does not understand and believe it in his heart is a hypocrite worse than an outright infidel.⁵²

Finally, there is no place in Ibn al-Wahhāb's formulation for personal devotion or private piety. As Michael Crawford explains it:

> A Muslim had not only to recognize and practise *tawhīd* in his or her own personal life and activities but to demonstrate adherence in the public space by objecting to the polytheism of others. The battle with unbelievers was not abstract or distant. Unbelief was real and all around. One had to be able to

---

48 Ibid., 80.
49 Ibid., 81.
50 Ibid., 82.
51 Crawford, *Ibn 'Abd al-Wahhāb*, 56.
52 Muhammad Rashid Rida, ed., *Majmū'at al-Tawhīd al-Najdiyya* (Riyadh: Al-Amana al-'Amma, 1999), 120–21; quoted in Crawford, *Ibn 'Abd al-Wahhāb*, 57.

recognize it and denounce and contest it. The true believer could not stand aside and absolve him- or herself of the responsibility to interfere by saying that the people's condition was known to God and it was for Him to resolve. Every Muslim had to be both activist and interventionist.[53]

Takfir and Qitāl

Bernard Haykel, professor of Near Eastern studies and director of the Institute for Transregional Study of the Contemporary Middle East, North Africa and Central Asia at Princeton University, summarizes Ibn 'al-Wahhāb's view on *takfir* and *qital* (armed action), drawing out the disturbing implications of such a position:

> According to Ibn 'Abd al-Wahhāb, to be considered a Muslim, it is not sufficient to declare oneself a believer by, for instance, uttering the creedal statement (*shahāda*); one must also actively deny, in both speech and acts, all beliefs and forms of polytheistic worship. Not to share activist Wahhabi beliefs and praxis or to plead ignorance of the requirements of the faith will result in one being considered an infidel. Furthermore, Ibn 'Abd al-Wahhāb, as well as a number of his descendants...insisted that a Muslim show loyalty and friendship to fellow believers and evince hostility toward unbelievers. This doctrine, known as *al-walā' wa-l-barā'* [loyalty and disavowal], has embedded in it the potential for political activism, even violence, against individuals or a political order that is deemed un-Islamic.[54]

Haykel goes on to note that the Wahhābis were not known for "recognizing the Ottoman state as Islamic and therefore legitimate," but instead "considered it and the lands it controlled the abode of unbelief. The Wahhabi practice of *takfir* and waging war (*qitāl*) on other self-described Muslims led many scholars, including some Hanbalīs and members of Ibn 'Abd al-Wahhāb's immediate family, to condemn the movement and its teachings."[55] However, it is clear that it was these very aggressive doctrines that were responsible for the eventual success of the

---

53 Crawford, *Ibn 'Abd al-Wahhāb*, 57.
54 Bernard Haykel, "Ibn 'Abd al-Wahhāb, Muhammad (1703–92)," *Princeton Encyclopaedia of Islamic Political Thought*, 231.
55 Ibid.

Wahhābis, in alliance with Muhammad ibn Saʻud, in founding a state.

Ibn al-Wahhāb made the doctrine of *al-walā' wa-l-barā'* one of the three fundamentals of true religion, along with the two basic forms of *tawhīd*.[56] This had obvious consequences for his views on excommunication of unbelievers (*takfir*), and emigration (*hijra*). He went from disengagement to hostility towards polytheists, declaring that "a person's Islam is not sound even if he practises *tawhīd* of God and deserts polytheism unless he is hostile to polytheists and declares to them his hostility and hatred."[57] Again, a true Muslim made the necessary distinction between friends and enemies. "There could be no two valid confessions in the same religion."[58] This emphasis on loyalty obviously created great tension, and isolated the Wahhābis, who were ever wary of hypocrites. Such a Manichaean view of life evidently "placed most Muslims of his era on the wrong side."[59]

The later Wahhābis decided that pronouncing *takfir* of whole settlements was indiscriminate and unacceptable. Such pronouncements entailed the obligation of waging *jihād* against them, an unjust state of affairs if these settlements contained pious Muslims. Ibn al-Wahhāb's definition of a Muslim was too strict. Following the example of Ibn Taymiyya, he designated anyone who did not pronounce *takfir* of an infidel an infidel.

Then there was the question of *hijra*, which traditionally meant the physical migration to the land of Islam (*dar al-Islam*) from territory where unbelief predominates (*dar al-kufr* or *dar al-harb*). Ibn al-Wahhāb felt that life in towns was full of dangers of contamination by polytheism, and so encouraged emigration to Wahhābi territory. But this was not always possible or realistic for many true Muslims.

Jihād

Always plainspoken, Ibn al-Wahhāb "acknowledged that force was integral to tawhīd and required 'unsheathing of the sword'"[60] As

---

56 Crawford, *Ibn ʻAbd al-Wahhāb*, 58.
57 Rida, *Majmūʻat al-Tawhīd al-Najdiyya*, 140; quoted in Crawford, *Ibn ʻAbd al-Wahhāb*, 59.
58 Crawford, *Ibn ʻAbd al-Wahhāb*, 59.
59 Ibid., 61.
60 Muhammad Ibn ʻAbd al-Wahhāb, *Muʻallafāt al-shaykh al-imām Muhammad ibn ʻAbd al-Wahhāb*, including *al-Rasāʼil al-Shakhsiyya* (RS), and *al-ʻAqīda* (2 parts), *ʻAqīda, al-Fiqh* (Fiqh), and *MukhtaAar Sīrat al-Rasūl* (Sira), ed. ʻAbd al-ʻAzīz Zayd al-Rūmī et al. (Riyadh: Jāmiʻat al-Imām Muhammad b. Suʻūd al-Islāmiyya, 1978), *ʻAqīda*, 1:284; quoted in Crawford, *Ibn ʻAbd al-Wahhāb*, 69.

the Koran tells us at Q8. *al-'anfāl*, the Spoils of War / Voluntary Gifts, 39: "so that there should cease to be civil strife (fitna) and all religion should belong to God." If it was agreed that death was the punishment for doubting or contesting one of the bases of Islam, "how could it not be the penalty for repudiating tawhīd, which was the very foundation of the religion."[61] Furthermore, since God had "ordered *jihād* by word and deed against the unbelievers and hypocrites, the believer had no choice but to wage it."[62] As was emphasized in many classical *hadīth*,[63] though the obligation to wage *jihād* was absolute, it had to be engaged in for serving God, and not for booty.[64] Ibn al-Wahhāb, too, was very critical of those who wavered or hung back. On one occasion, when the people of one settlement who had initially agreed to wage war with the Saudis but then declined to fight a neighbouring town, he accused them of "preferring the ephemeral to the eternal, and selling pearls for dung and goodness for evil."[65]

In classical Hanbalī law, before declaring *jihād* on non-Muslims, Muslims had to summon them formally to Islam, that is, to convert. Thus, when it came to dealing with ignorant Bedouins the Wahhābis tried to educate them in the precepts of Islam. Only when the Bedouins rejected the summons to Islam would *jihād* be waged upon them. But if there were fellow Muslims already familiar with the Koran and *sunna* in he community, then *jihād* from the outset was considered legitimate. "Once the Wahhabi campaign had been running for some years," Crawford writes, "Ibn 'Abd al-Wahhab probably regarded every Najdi as on notice of the Koranic proofs, whether or not he or she accepted them."[66]

Ibn al-Wahhāb was the first to denounce the local holy men and their followers as non-Muslims; in this blanket *takfir* he refused to distinguish among the holy men, saints, and Sufis. His opponents responded by excommunicating the Wahhābis, which lead to their persecution. Though the Wahhābis could at this point legitimately claim that their

---

61 Rida, *Majmū'at al-Tawhīd al-Najdiyya*, 117; quoted in Crawford, *Ibn 'Abd al-Wahhāb*, 69.

62 Ghannām, *Ta'rīkh Najd al-Musmmā Rawdat*, 1:189; quoted in Crawford, *Ibn 'Abd al-Wahhāb*, 69.

63 For example, Bukhārī, *Authentic Hadīth: Book of Jihād and Campaigns*, hadīth 2810, 4:59.

64 Ghannām, *Ta'rīkh Najd al-Musmmā Rawdat*, 1:159, 178; quoted in Crawford, *Ibn 'Abd al-Wahhāb*, 69

65 Ibn 'Abd al-Wahhāb, *al-Rasā'il al-Shakhsiyya*, 293; quoted in Crawford, *Ibn 'Abd al-Wahhāb*, 69–70.

66 Crawford, *Ibn 'Abd al-Wahhāb*, 70.

jihād was defensive, "it was a conflict precipitated by Ibn ʿAbd al-Wahhāb's own ideology and actions. His doctrines and ambitions were destined, even intended, to turn the struggle between Wahhabis and their opponents into violent confrontation."[67] According to Ibn Bishr, Ibn al-Wahhāb declared an offensive *jihād* on towns that refused to convert when summoned by him.[68]

Normally, it was the ruler who declared offensive *jihād*. Since Wahhābism did not acknowledge any "boundary to the regime of godliness," Ibn al-Wahhāb had, in effect, launched a war

> that could end only in complete victory or annihilation. This was the inexorable outcome of Ibn ʿAbd al-Wahhāb's doctrines. They were calculated to split the Islamic community and precipitate a struggle between Wahhabis and anti-Wahhabis. The dogma of *tawhīd* defined the cause; the doctrine of association with believers and disassociation from unbelievers secured loyalty; the concepts of primary and secondary *takfīr* singled out the enemy; emigration (*hijra*) helped marshall the forces; and *jihād* was the necessary, if violent, expedient for achieving God's will.[69]

The Bedouin

Abou El Fadl, Omar and Azmeralda Alfi Distinguished Professor of Law at the UCLA School of Law, has written what Michael Crawford described as "a classic misreading of Wahhabism": "Wahhabis have always equated the austere cultural practices of Bedouin life with the one and only true Islam."[70] In fact, Crawford explains, Wahhābism was a phenomenon of the small towns and settlements of Najd. Ibn al-Wahhāb had a particularly low opinion of contemporary Najdis, who "relied on customary law and practice, not the shariʿa" and "drew their smattering of religion from their forefathers and handed traditional beliefs and practices down the generations....The Bedouin bore the brunt of

---

67 Michael Crawford, "The Daʿwa of Ibn ʿAbd al-Wahhāb before the Al Saʿūd," *Journal of Arabian Studies* 1, no. 2 (2011): 159–60.

68 Uthmān ibn Bishr, *ʿUnwān al-Majd fī Taʾrīkh Najd*, 1:45–46, 48; quoted in Crawford, *Ibn ʿAbd al-Wahhāb*, 70.

69 Crawford, *Ibn ʿAbd al-Wahhāb*, 71.

70 Khaled M. Abou El Fadl, *The Great Theft: Wrestling Islam from the Extremists* (New York: HarperOne, 2007), 47; quoted in Crawford, *Ibn ʿAbd al-Wahhāb*, 77.

Ibn 'Abd al-Wahhāb's opprobrium as the epitome of ignorance."[71] In this situation, the Al Sa'ud were ideally placed to build coalitions; "their detribalized, settled nature...helped make them an effective instrument for driving a campaign that challenged the Bedouin life-style and primacy of tribal allegiances among the Bedouin and some of the settled communities."[72]

Ibn al-Wahhāb held that the true Islam was found in the settled populations, which preserved the Koran and followed the Shari'a, whereas the Bedouins were traditionally hostile to the villagers and ignored the provisions of the Shari'a on marriage and divorce, property, and inheritance. According to Ibn al-Wahhāb, the Bedouin had declared *takfir* on the Koran and the whole religion.[73] He considered them infidels because they ignored the Holy Law, preferring customary law, attitudes, and beliefs that took them beyond Islam.[74]

It was a logical step for Ibn al-Wahhāb to issue a fatwa declaring the Bedouin infidels—it simply was not enough for a Bedouin to recite the profession of faith to be considered a Muslim.[75] This *takfir* led to much opposition, even among the settled elements, since it risked their viability and cohesion. In the last years of the eighteenth century, the Saudis eventually coopted the Bedouin, who played an important part in Saudi military successes, not to mention the massacre of Karbala of 1802, and who were also responsible for the savagery at the taking and sacking of Taif in 1803.[76]

Ijtihād and Taqlīd

According to Ibn 'al-Wahhāb and his followers, God ordered people to obey and worship Him and follow the teachings of the Prophet. God did not make it obligatory to obey anyone else. A strict adherence to the Koran and tradition is sufficient to resolve any disputes between Muslims. Ibn al-Wahhāb's followers therefore will refer to other scholars as long as they support Wahhābi views. And while they adhere to the Hanbalī school in questions of *furū'* (that is, apart from *usul al-fiqh*— roots of jurisprudence, the other major genre of juristic literature, *furu'*

---

71 Crawford, *Ibn 'Abd al-Wahhāb*, 77.

72 Ibid., 78.

73 Ibn 'Abd al-Wahhāb, *Sira*, 39; quoted in Crawford, *Ibn 'Abd al-Wahhāb*, 79.

74 Ghannām, *Ta'rīkh Najd al-Musmmā Rawdat*, 1:159,178; quoted in Crawford, *Ibn 'Abd al-Wahhāb*, 79.

75 Ibn 'Abd al-Wahhāb, *Sira*, 44; quoted in Crawford, *Ibn 'Abd al-Wahhāb*, 80.

76 Crawford, *Ibn 'Abd al-Wahhāb*, 81–82.

al-fiqh—branches of jurisprudence, which is constituted primarily by rules-positive law),⁷⁷ the Wahhābis are ready to reject their own madhhab if it is not in accordance with the Koran and Tradition.⁷⁸

The Wahhābis do not reject *ijmāʿ* (the consensus of Muslim community or of a local group of jurisprudents in a particular generation),⁷⁹ finding it a binding source of the Shariʿa, but argue that anything that conflicts with the Koran and Tradition, even when practiced by a majority of the people, is not accepted: "Sound *ijmāʿ* cannot be contradictory to the texts of the prime sources."⁸⁰

As for *ijtihād*—the exercise of independent judgment unfettered by case law or past precedent⁸¹—the Wahhābis reject two views they consider extreme: "that it is always and in every case, allowed, and…that it is not permitted to anyone at the present time. Thus, although they do not allow it in all questions, they equally reject the idea that the doors of *ijtihād* have finally been closed."⁸²

Taqlīd literally means "imitation," but it also carries the more technical sense of an uncritical dependence on past precedent and law as expounded by the law schools. Ian Richard Netton compares this sense with the concept of case law. *Taqlīd* is usually contrasted with *ijtihād*.⁸³ According to Ibn al-Wahhāb, it is not obligatory for Muslims to follow anyone in Islam except the Prophet: "The Four Imams [founders of the four schools of law] warned against unquestioning imitation even of themselves, and enjoined their followers to abandon their views if they were found in conflict with the Koran and the tradition, or when other, sounder opinions were advanced."⁸⁴

Imāma

The *imamate*, that is, the caliphate, was not an important doctrinal matter for the Wahhābis. Nonetheless, al-Wahhāb believed that obedience to rulers was obligatory, "even if they are oppressive or sinful," and "their commands should be followed as long as they do contradict the

---

77 Norman Calder, "Law, Islamic philosophy of" Islamic Philosophy Online, 1998, http://www.muslimphilosophy.com/ip/rep/H015.htm
78 Al-ʿUthaymīn, *Muhammad ibn ʿAbd al-Wahhāb*, 139.
79 Netton, *Popular Dictionary of Islam*, s.v. "*Ijmāʿ*."
80 Al-ʿUthaymīn, *Muhammad ibn ʿAbd al-Wahhāb*, 140.
81 Netton, *Popular Dictionary of Islam*, s.v. "*Ijtihād*."
82 Al-ʿUthaymīn, *Muhammad ibn ʿAbd al-Wahhāb*, 142.
83 Netton, *Popular Dictionary of Islam*, s.v. "*Taqlīd*."
84 Al-ʿUthaymīn, *Muhammad ibn ʿAbd al-Wahhāb*, 142.

rules of religion, affirming that their call for *jihād* should be willingly met."[85] But rulers also had their duties, and "should seek to prevent crimes against religion and society, to work for the protection of Muslims, and to strive for the spread of Islam through *jihād*. In short, the aim of the ruler should be to make the word of God reign and reveal itself in all aspects of life, both religious and secular."[86]

Political power was needed not for its own sake, but in service of religion, and a ruler had to uphold *tawhīd* and Shari'a and forbid *bid'a*. A ruler who did not follow the Koran and the *sunna* became a *taghut*—an idol.

Commanding Right and Forbidding Wrong

Forbidding wrong, Michael Cook informs us, was not a prominent concern for al-Wahhāb,[87] though he occasionally referred to it. There are two passages in his writings where he does dwell on it to a certain extent.

In his letter to the Wahhābis of Sudayr, Ibn al-Wahhāb emphasizes the importance of tact in the performance of the duty, for it must not give rise to any kind of schism in the community. A ruler should not be reproved in public. In the second passage, Ibn al-Wahhāb relates Forbidding Wrong to the struggle against polytheism[88] and notes that in earlier times it was scholars, not rulers, who performed this duty. Crawford argues that Commanding Right and Forbidding Wrong was a well-established Islamic concept "that Ibn 'al-Wahhāb endorsed and which today is reflected in the activities of the Saudi 'religious police' (*mutawwi'in*)."[89]

However, I believe Cook seriously underestimates Ibn al-Wahhāb's commitment to intervention when he urges commanding *tawhīd* and forbidding *shirk*. He may not have formally dealt with this duty, but his beliefs and, above all, his actions were founded on the principle that one must not stand idle as polytheism triumphs (see my discussion on *tawhīd*). As Crawford points out, throughout his life Ibn al-Wahhāb showed moral and physical courage in putting his principles into action, such as when he refused to be silenced in Basra and Huraymila and he took charge of destroying the tomb and mosque at al-Jubayla, despite popular hostility, in al-'Uyayna.

---

85 Ibid., 144.
86 Ibid., 145.
87 Cook, *Commanding Right and Forbidding Wrong*, 169.
88 Ibid., 170.
89 Crawford, *Ibn 'Abd al-Wahhāb*, 93.

For Ibn al-Wahhāb, the duty to practice and enforce *tawḥīd* clearly overrode allegiance to family, tribe, and country. Nor did fear of losing friends or status justify neglecting this duty.⁹⁰ And while he was concerned with enforcing religious norms, Ibn al-Wahhāb was "more interested in major doctrinal infractions than everyday sinning."⁹¹ This is why, Crawford relates, Ibn al-Wahhāb "employed the traditional language of commanding right and forbidding wrong relatively infrequently in his formal writings. The dynamic concept of *tawḥīd* in action exerted more ideological and polemical force."⁹² Ibn al-Wahhāb endorsed public intervention, but he did not know how best to organize communal enforcement itself. Aware of the dangers of excessive zeal in applying interventionism, he feared strife—communal solidarity overrode any rigorous enforcement that might lead to disunity.

The theme of Commanding Right and Forbidding Wrong was taken up more formally by later Wahhābi scholars. For example, 'Abd al-Rahmān ibn Hasan (d. 1869) argues that religious and worldly affairs cannot be fulfilled without the application of this principle. The prophets were sent to enjoin good—the greatest good being monotheism—and to forbid wrong, such as polytheism. This includes *jihād*, without which the word of God would not reign. His son 'Abd al-Latīf ibn 'Abd al-Rahman (d. 1876) agrees and "mentions that this principle is obligatory for the Muslim community, as well as being one of its best qualities. Everyone should try to apply it according to his ability; for the Prophet says that he who sees an objectionable act should oppose it either by force or by words. If he cannot do either, he must at least hate it."⁹³ In 1926 in Saudi Arabia the Committee for Commanding Right and Forbidding Wrong (*Hay'at al-amr bi'il ma 'rūf wa'l-nahy 'an al-munkar*) was established and went about trying to stamp out various vices from sodomy to drinking alcohol. It has proven to be a very controversial institution.⁹⁴

Ibn al-Wahhāb: Other Writings

Works by Ibn 'Abd al-Wahhāb "include compilations of hadith, some abridgements, especially of works by Ibn Taymiyya and Ibn al-Qayyim, an abridged and extended biography (*sira*) of the Prophet, and some Koranic exegesis (*tafsir*)....His books were grounded in a narrow,

---

90 Ibid., 58.
91 Ibid., 94.
92 Ibid.
93 Al-'Uthaymīn, *Muhammad ibn 'Abd al-Wahhāb*, 146.
94 Cook, *Commanding Right and Forbidding Wrong*, 191.

dogmatic literalist tradition hostile to speculative theology (*kalam*). They inclined to interpretative authoritarianism, embodied a strongly prescriptive approach. They lacked the intellectual virtuosity of those Hanbalīs he admired so much (especially Ibn Taymiyya, Ibn al-Qayyim, and Ibn Qudama) and even the range and nuance of some of his opponents."[95] His successors tried to redress these limitations, without success since they were unable to go much beyond the confines of his thought.[96]

Real Causes and Aims of Wahhābism

In view of my thesis that Islamic fundamentalism has a long history, and that the propensity to violence is embedded in the core principles of Islam and thus was not engendered by poverty, colonialism, and socioeconomics, I must point out that Wahhābism is a classic example of the resurgence of Islamic activism and has nothing to do with nationalism or anticolonialism. As Crawford writes:

> Wahhabism...was a pre-modern movement that arose before the most serious Western threat materialized against the Islamic lands on the Mediterranean or in India. It can present itself today, as it has always done, as an authentic Islamic response to contemporary challenges.[97]

On the whole, Ibn al-Wahhāb did not concern himself with non-Muslims. The European powers played no significant role in the Middle East during his formative years. There were no Christian or Jewish minorities in the Peninsula, and their status in Islamic law as *dhimmis* (second-class citizens) was not under dispute. Ibn al-Wahhāb's "attention and venom were reserved first for the enemies within his own religious and cultural tradition, then for fellow Muslims of different backgrounds."[98]

Crawford also emphasizes that "[s]ocial justice is not a strong theme in early Wahhabi writings and thought."[99] Ibn al-Wahhāb's main concern was establishing a state of godliness. And while the Wahhābi doctrine of the brotherhood of believers did attract the poor to the

---

95 Crawford, *Ibn ʿAbd al-Wahhāb*, 50–51.
96 Ibid.
97 Crawford, *Ibn ʿAbd al-Wahhāb*, 13.
98 Ibid., 115.
99 Ibid., 104.

movement, Ibn al-Wahhāb himself was distrustful of the populace, fearing its susceptibility to polytheism and sedition. Ibn al-Wahhāb would have found "social justice" difficult to reconcile with his principle of absolute obedience to the tyrannical ruler. "In the main, he showed little apparent interest in social issues."[100]

Nor was Ibn al-Wahhāb concerned with state formation and thus furnished no ideas for government apart from his insistence that all Muslims obey a ruler unconditionally. Nonetheless, Wahhābism provided the ideological glue that fostered the emergence of a state—a regime of godliness committed to defending and promoting Islamic values.

Critiques of Wahhābism and the Ikhwān

Syed Ameer Ali (1849–1928), a liberal British Muslim and one of the founding members of the All India Muslim League, published in 1891 *The Life and Teachings of Mohammed: Or, The Spirit of Islam*, a comprehensive life of Muhammad and the political and cultural history of Islam. Ameer Ali wrote that although the Azraqites, a (previously discussed) Khārijite subgroup, were destroyed by Hajjāj ibn Yusuf, "their sanguinary, fierce, and merciless doctrines found expression nine centuries later in Wahhabism." Like the followers of Ibn al-Azraq,

> the Wahhabis designate all other Muslims as unbelievers, and permit their despoilment and enslavement. However commendable their revolt against the anthropolatrous usages in vogue among the modern Muslims, their views of religion and divine government, like those of the *Ikhwān* of the present day in Najd, are intensely morose and Calvinistic, and in absolute conflict with progress and development.[101]

Much to the dismay of liberal Muslims like Ameer Ali, Ibn Saʻūd recaptured the Holy Cities in the Hijaz for Wahhābism between 1924 and 1925. And the entire Islamic world was alarmed when the Wahhābis set about destroying tombs and shrines beloved of thousands of pious Muslims—acts that precipitated anti-Wahhābi polemics.

The Saudis did their best to counter this by garnering the support of religious reformists in Egypt, Iraq, and elsewhere. One such intellectual reformer was Rashid Rida (1865–1935), who popularized Wahhābi

---

100 Ibid., 105.
101 Syed Ameer Ali, *The Life and Teachings of Mohammed: Or, The Spirit of Islam* (London: W.H. Allen & Co., Ltd., 1891), 527.

ideas in the 1920s and 1930s. The Saudis banned the term "Wahhābism" and began calling their brand of Islam "Salafism."

The precise circumstances of the emergence of the Ikhwān (the Brethren) movement are unknown. It may have been Ibn Sa'ūd or the Wahhābi *'ulamā'* who set out to tame nomadic tribesmen, weaning them away from idolatry and educating them in the doctrines of Islam. In the end, the Wahhābis created a monster: the Ikhwān became zealous, even extremely violent, intolerant religious warriors motivated by religious idealism rather than allegiance to Ibn Sa'ūd, who, finally, had to crush them.[102]

Ibn al-Wahhāb's contempt for the Bedouins and their education into Islam has been discussed. Ibn Sa'ūd was, in a sense, carrying out this mission to Islamisize the nomads. He achieved it by founding settlements known as *hijra* ("place of emigration") populated by emigrants. Here the term emphasized a religious purpose—to emigrate from the abode of idolatry to the abode of Islam. Emigration "remained a central part of Wahhabi polemic in the nineteenth century, when ulama argued against travel to and residing in idolatrous lands."[103]

To be a true Muslim while living among and under the authority of infidels and idolaters was considered impossible due to constant pressure to conform—"assimilate," in modern parlance—to their manners and customs. Emigration was, hence, a duty. Consider the example of the early Muslims, who were compelled to emigrate from Mecca to Medina in the seventh century. The *hijra* was a perfect way to "assemble the nomads in settlements of belief and assimilate then to Wahhabi religious practice."[104]

The *hijra* was thus a camp of concentrated religious indoctrination:

> Along with removal of a tribal section to the hijra, the sections's sheikh went to Riyadh for instruction in Wahhabi tenets while ulama taught the tribesmen in the hijra. The settled Bedouins' first exposure to formal Islamic tenets thus came directly and exclusively from Wahhabi teachers. The hujar also had religious zealots, called mutawwi'a, to enforce

---

102 David Commins, *The Wahhabi Mission and Saudi Arabia* (New York: I.B. Tauris, 2006), 80.
103 Ibid., 81–82.
104 Ibid., 82.

public morality and punctual observance of prayer.[105]

Among other texts, they studied a short "catechism" by Ibn al-Wahhāb.

The Ikhwān became known for ferocity in battle; they regularly killed male captives, and on occasion women and children. "The pretext for such slaughter was the Ikhwān's notion that the nomads they fought, particularly from 1912 to 1919, had to convert or be put to death."[106] They frequently attacked tribes and oases they considered religiously lax, and wanted the forced conversion of the Shi'a. Clash with Ibn Sa'ūd was inevitable, since he was far more flexible in his political dealings with the British in Iraq. Some Ikhwān tribesmen rebelled in 1927. Ibn Sa'ūd with the help of the British defeated them in 1929.

On Ibn Sa'ūd's death in 1953, he was succeeded by his son Sa'ūd, who proved to be a weak and ineffective ruler. Sa'ūd's brother Prince Faysal ousted him in 1964, and restored some order in the kingdom while facing challenges from the secular nationalist trend in the Middle East in the early 1970s. But King Faysal had invested in a policy of Islamic solidarity, which helped turn the tide in the region in favor of religious ideologies:

> He founded new global Islamic institutions in the Hijaz to contest secular, nationalist dogmas and in tandem further Salafi beliefs and Saudi interests. The Muslim World League and the World Assembly of Muslim Youth, founded in 1962 and 1972 respectively, proved valuable instruments of Saudi and Wahhabi influence. So too were Islamic educational institutions such as the Islamic University of Medina (founded in 1961), to which Saudis welcomed foreign students. As its oil revenues grew, Saudi Arabia assumed a new role as leader of the Islamic world and spread Wahhābism actively overseas not only in Islamic countries but in Islamic communities in the West.[107]

When King Faysal, in a gesture of Islamist solidarity, gave refuge to Muslim Brothers escaping Gamal Abdel Nasser's persecution in Egypt in the 1960s, little did he understand that he was helping to introduce violent ideas into his kingdom. King Faysal merely saw the Muslim

---

105 Ibid.
106 Ibid., 85.
107 Crawford, *Ibn 'Abd al-Wahhāb*, 125.

Brothers as fellow Islamists resisting Western cultural influence—but the Muslim Brotherhood had different strategic aims, and worked with a different set of concepts, many developed by Sayyid Qutb.[108]

The Influence of Wahhabism

One cannot exaggerate the influence of Wahhabism on revivalist movements throughout the Islamic world. For instance, the Algerian shaikh, Muhammad Ibn Ali as-Sanūsi established a theocratic state in southern Libya and equatorial Africa "in protest against the secularist laxity of the Ottoman Sultans; and the Mahdist brotherhood was organized by Muhammad Ahmad as the instrument of revolt in eastern Sudan against Turco-Egyptian rule and its European agents. Even in such distant regions as Nigeria and Sumatra, Wahhabi influence contributed to the outbreak of militant movements."[109]

Here I should like to give a brief account of Wahhabi influence in India, beginning with the Fara'idiyya (or as it is known in the Indian Subcontinent, the Fara'izis). The Fara'idiyya was a movement of a religio-social character reacting against the loss of Muslim political supremacy, and the power of both Hindu and Muslim landowners over the Muslim masses. It was founded by Hajjī Sharī'at Allāh, who was born in Eastern Bengal at an uncertain date (possibly in 1781[110]). At a young age, he went to Mecca where he seems to have stayed twenty years. It is again unclear when he returned to India, as three different dates are given in the sources, 1807, 1822, 1828. As the *Encyclopaedia of Islam* tells us, "If we accept the latest date, it is unquestionable that Sharī'at Allāh was in touch with the Wahhābī reformers in Mecca. A specific Wahhābī influence is in no sense indispensable for an understanding of the orientation of Sharī'at Allāh's activities in Bengal, which are to be explained above all by the contrast he so vehemently resented between a certain type of Islam in his own country and the "Arab" Islam of the Prophet's native land; mutatis mutandis, other Muslim reformers in India (beginning with Shah Wall Allah of Delhi himself) had had the same experience."[111] He may well have studied at al-Azhar University in Cairo before returning to Bengal.

---

108 Ibid., 126.
109 H.A.R. Gibb, *Modern Trends in Islam*, (New York: Octagon Books, 1975), 27.
110 According to Kenneth W. Jones, *Socio-religious Reform Movements in British India* (Cambridge: Cambridge University Press. (*The New Cambridge History of India*, III.1), 1989), 19.
111 *Encyclopaedia of Islam* 2nd Edn., Vol. 2, s.v. FARĀ'IDIYYA (A.Bausani), 783 b.

Sharī'at Allāh's main message was one of religious purification, since the popular beliefs of Bengali Muslims had strayed far from the purity of early Islam. He wanted a return to the *farā'id*, "the obligatory religious duties", such as the profession of faith, the daily prayers, fasting during the month Ramadan, paying the zakat poor tax, and pilgrimage to Mecca. Like Ibn 'Abd al-Wahhab, Sharī'at Allāh stressed the principle of *tawhīd*, and denounced *bida'*, innovations, and *shirk* (polytheistic practices and beliefs). As Alessandro Bausani sums up, "besides various para-Hindu customs, he rejected the celebration, with funerary lamentations and special ceremonies, of the martyrdom of Husayn at Karbalā', the pomp and ceremonial that had been introduced into the very simple, austere rites of Muslim marriage and burial, the offering of fruit and flowers at tombs, etc.; moreover, he prohibited the use of the mystical terms *pir* and *murid* ("master" and "disciple"), which at that time conveyed an almost Brahmin-like implication of total devotion of the disciple to his spiritual master, out of keeping with the sturdy Islamic tradition, and instead proposing the two terms *ustādh* and *shāgird* (also Persian, but more "secular"); the initiation ceremony common to the various Muslim confraternities, the *bay'a*, [oath of allegiance] was also prohibited and replaced by a simple statement of repentance (*tawba*) and a changed life made by the *murīd* (or *shāgird*). Another significant precept of Sharī'at Allah was the prohibition of communal prayers on Fridays or feastdays, based on the exclusion of British India from the *dār al-Islām*."[112]

Militant and united, the Fara'izis faced opponents in eastern Bengal challenging those Muslims who wished to continue to practice Islam as it was then. They also considered Hinduism a threat since it was, for them, a fountain of polytheism and evil innovations. By 1831 there were disturbances as factories were burnt, and the Muslim peasants refused to pay their Hindu landlords, who had also demanded money for various Hindu festivals. After the death of Sharī'at Allāh, his son Muhammad Muhsin, better known as Dūdhū Miyān [1819-1860] took over the organization of the movement, focusing on both political and religious issues. There were serious clashes as Dudhu Miyan told his followers that they should not pay taxes, as from the point of view of the *Sharī'a* they had no legitimacy. The British arrested Dudhu Miyan, who was then convicted, but released him in 1847 when the conviction was set aside by the High Court in Calcutta. The sons of Dudhu Miyan took over after his death, and eventually began cooperating with the British.

---

112 Ibid., 784 a.

Finally, as Kenneth Jones says, "The Fara'izis had succeeded in redefining Islamic belief and practice among many of the Muslim peasants of eastern Bengal."[113]

Born in West Bengal, Titu Mir [1782-1831](also known as Sayyid Mīr Nithār 'Alī) studied Arabic, Persian and various Islamic subjects at the local madrasa. He became a wrestler before beginning work for local Hindu landowners. Titu Mir was imprisoned briefly for defying feudal power. In 1822, on pilgrimage, Titu Mir met Sayyid Ahmad Brelwi in Mecca, when the latter initiated him into the *Tariq-i Muhammadiyya*. Henceforth, back in India, Titu Mir began campaigning in favour of a purified Islam along the lines of what Sayyid Ahmad Brelwi and Sharī'at Allah preached. Titu Mir was able to exploit the discontent of peasants who were oppressed by the zamindars, or landowners, both Hindu and Muslim. Titu Mir and his growing mass of followers "attacked a village within the estate of one of the landowners, slaughtered a cow in a public place and defiled the village [Hindu] temple with its blood. Open warfare between Titu Mir and the zamindars followed and Titu Mir did not hesitate to attack Muslim zamindars hostile to his movement."[114] These acts were deliberate and intended to outrage Hindus, and to "terrorise both Muslim and Hindu communities."[115] After a series of skirmishes that left dozens dead, an armed confrontation with the British authorities eventually led to Titu Mir constructing a bamboo fort that was demolished by the artillery of the East India Company, and Titu Mir, together with a large number of his followers, was killed on 19 November 1831.

The two movements, the Fara'izi and that of Titu Mir, were not, as Banerjee explains, just "peasant struggles for economic amelioration. Religious fanaticism was a prominent feature in both cases, and coercion and violence were necessary off-shoots. The raids on the establishments of Hindu zamindars were sometimes accompanied by desecration of idols. Orthodox Muslims who refused to accept the Wahabi version of Islam were subjected to coercion. [A British] officer…observed: 'They consider it justifiable to compel other Mahomedans to become of their sect by violence or constant acts of annoyance'. Titu Mir had a similar

---

113 Kenneth W. Jones, *Socio-religious Reform Movements in British India* (Cambridge: Cambridge University Press. (The New Cambridge History of India, III.1), 1989), 22.
114 Peter Hardy, *The Muslims of British India* (Cambridge: Cambridge University Press, 1972), 57.
115 Charles Allen, *God's Terrorists: The Wahhabi Cult and the Hidden Roots of Modern Jihād* (Cambridge, MA : Da Capo Press, 2006), 93.

programme."¹¹⁶ Both the Fara'izis and Titu Mir declared that India was *dar al-harb*, hence *jihād* was obligatory, until India became *dar al-Islam*.

---

116 A.C. Banerjee, *Two Nations. The Philosophy of Muslim Nationalism* (New Delhi: Concept Publishing Company, 1981), 68.

CHAPTER 15
Sayyid Abu 'l-'Alā' Mawdūdī

MAWDUDI'S IDEAS did not emerge in a vacuum but were in line with the thought of earlier Indian Muslim philosophers who greatly influenced him.

Thirteenth and Fourteenth Century India Under Islamic Rulers

As early as the thirteenth century, thinkers like Nur-ud Din Mubarak Ghaznavi, working at the court of Sultan Iltutmish [ruled 1211-1236] set the aggressive tone of Islamic presence in India. Nur-ud Din elaborated the doctrine of *Din Panahi* [protection of religion], by which Islam had to be defended from the defiling Hindus who were idolaters who must be kept in their place, and insulted, disgraced, dishonoured and defamed.[1] Ziauddin Barani [Diyā al-Dīn Baranī: 1285-1357] who was an Indian jurist, historian, political thinker, writer, and a companion of Sultan Muhammad b. Tughluq [1309 –1388], wrote a *Fürstenspiegel*, a Mirror of Princes, akin to Machiavelli's *The Prince*, the *Fatāwā-yi Djahāndarī*, in order to educate the *de facto* rulers of the day, the sultans, in their duty towards Islam in an age of corruption. Barani advises sultans to enforce the *sharī'a*, to curb unorthodoxy (especially speculative philosophy, *falsafa*), to degrade the infidel, who must be treated harshly.[2] The Sultans must fight like the Prophet until all people affirm that "there is no God but Allah." It is the duty of Muslim rulers to overthrow infidelity, uproot it completely, and apply the Holy Law,

---

1 A.C. Banerjee, *Two Nations: The Philosophy of Muslim Nationalism*, (New Delhi: Concept Publishing Company, 1981), 11.
2 *Encyclopaedia of Islam* 2nd. Edn., Vol. I .1036a. s.v. Baranī, Diyā al-Dīn.

the Sharia on all.³ Firuz Shah Tughlaq (1309 – 1388), the Turkic Muslim who reigned over the Sultanate of Delhi (1351-1388) carried on the intolerant tradition of the early invaders, and believed that by extirpating Hinduism wherever possible he served God.⁴

Shaykh Ahmad Sirhindī and the Sixteenth Century

When the Mughal emperor Akbar [reigned 1556-1605] manifested general tolerance of all religions, the Muslim religious class, the *'ulamā'*, were not at all amused. As a result, there were a number of Islamic Revivalist Movements, some of which included a belief in the coming of a Messiah, who would sweep away all the corruption and inaugurate an era of piousness, a true, pristine Islam. One of the first to launch such a revival movement was Shaykh Ahmad Sirhindī⁵ [1564-1624], later known as *Mujaddidi Alf-i Thānī* (the Renovator of Islam). For Sirhindi, the *sunna* and *Sharī'a* remain the most important components of Islamic culture. Despite being a member of the Naqshbandi order of the Sufis, Sirhindi insists that Sufi experience is inferior to the *Sharī'a*, because *Sharī'a* "is based on incontrovertible proof, while Sufi experience is a result of fallible speculation only....Any Sufi experience that is rejected by the *Sharī'a* is heresy."⁶ Sirhindi denounces all innovations, even so-called good innovations (*bid'a hasanah*). He does not approve of certain customs introduced by some Sufi orders, such as music (*samā'*), dancing (*raqs*) singing (*naghmah*), and ecstatic sessions (*wajd, tawājud*).⁷ Sirhindi also attacked the Shi'a in a most violent and bitter manner in his *Epistle on the Refutation of the Shi'is*, arguing that it was his duty to denounce heretical ideas wherever they appear.⁸

Like many fundamentalists, Sirhindi has no tolerance for philosophers, since he believed that "the human intellect is incapable of under-

---

3 Mohammad Habib, *The Political Theory of the Delhi Sultanate*, (Allahbad: Kitab Mahal, 1961), 46-47.
4 Vincent A. Smith, *The Oxford History of India*, (Delhi: Oxford University Press, 1981 [Ist edn. 1919]), 258-259.
5 Also spelt: Sirhandi (Ayesha Jalal, *Partisans of Allah: Jihād in South Asia* (Cambridge, MA: Harvard University Press, 2008),), and Sarhindi (Q. Ahmad, *Wahabi Movement in India* (Calcutta, 1966).
6 Yohanan Friedmann, *Shaykh Ahmad Sirhindi, An Outline of His Thought and a Study of His Image in the Eyes of Posterity* (Montreal: McGill-Queen's University Press, 1971), 41.
7 Ibid., 68.
8 Ibid., 51.

standing properly the nature of God without prophetic assistance."[9] But this rejection of the philosophers also "leads him to an equally indignant rejection of their [the philosophers] natural sciences. Their geometry, astronomy, logic, and mathematics are useless as far as the hereafter is concerned and fall therefore within the category of 'inconsequential things' [mā lā ya'nī]."[10] He even discourages the reading of popular literature.[11]

Sirhindi also launched a vicious attack on Hinduism, and believes all Hindus, since they were guilty of *shirk*, must be humiliated whenever possible. Sirhindi stood for a ruthless suppression of innovations, and wrote, "It is therefore enjoined upon every Muslim to wage a regular crusade against all innovations."[12] As Ayesha Jalal points out, he was "a firm believer in the need to use state power to enforce Islam" and Sirhindi coined the slogan, "*Shariat* [*Sharī'a*] can be fostered through the sword."[13] Sirhindi argues one should adhere to the Prophet's sunna and to the *sharī'a*, which was most comprehensive and "the essence of all heavenly books was included in the Koran. Hence all those who pinned their faith on the *Sharī'a* were superior to all peoples and nations who did not. He condemned the study of philosophy and the beliefs of the Mutazilas and their followers, in most emphatic terms."[14]

Shāh Walī Allāh and the Eighteenth Century

Shāh Walī Allāh [1703-1762] is best remembered for his efforts to restore Muslim rule to India, ending with his appeal to the Afghan ruler Ahmad Shah Abdali to invade India, destroy the Hindu Marathas.

Shāh Walī Allāh was in the Hijāz between April 1731 and the end of June, 1732, a period of fourteen months. Shāh Walī Allāh (born 1703) and Ibn 'Abd al-Wahhab (born 1702) both studied in Medina over the same period and with at least one teacher in common. We know that Muhammad Hayāt al-Sindī [also written Hayyā al-Sindī] was Ibn 'Abd al-Wahhab's teacher, and had an important influence on him. When

---

9 Ibid., 53.
10 Ibid., 54.
11 Ibid.
12 Saiyid Athar Abbas Rizvi, *Muslim Revivalist Movements in Northern India in the Sixteenth and Seventeenth Centuries*, (New Delhi: Munshiram Manoharlal Publishers Pvt. Ltd. 1965), 256
13 Ayesha Jalal, *Partisans of Allah. Jihād in South Asia* (Cambridge, MA: Harvard University Press, 2008), 31-32.
14 Saiyid Athar Abbas Rizvi, *Muslim Revivalist Movements*, 255.

Shāh Walī Allāh came to Arabia, he studied hadith under Muhammad Hayat's teacher, Abū 'l-Tāhir Muhammad ibn Ibrāhīm al-Kūrānī.[15]

The central element in Shāh Walī Allāh's vision of the restoration of the true Islam was the emphasis on the textual sources of Islam, the Koran and the *hadith*. In his *Hujjat-Allah al-bāligha*, Shāh Walī Allāh tells us that the Sharī'a was the "*fitrat*"[16] or natural disposition or original qualities of mankind and, "as the last in the cycle of divine laws, was the guardian of the best interests of mankind. The Islamic *Sharī'a* was destined to dominate the world and crush all undesirable elements. All misinterpretations which entered it were removed by a renewer whom God raised up at the end of each century."[17] Islam was superior to all other religions, and especially to Hinduism. *Jihād* was central to Islam, which could not have been so successful without it. Shāh Walī Allāh deplored the way *jihād* had been interpreted as defensive. Rizvi paraphrases Shāh Walī Allāh's doctrine as spelled out in his *Hujjat-Allah al-bāligha*: "The modern interpretation of *jihād* or Islamic holy war over-emphasized its defensive character. To the *'ulamā'*, *jihād* was the *fard kifāya* (collective duty) and it remained a duty as long as Islam was not [the] universally dominant religion in any area. According to Shāh Walī Allāh the mark of the perfect implementation of the *Sharī'a* was the performance of *jihād*... Force, said the Shah, was the much better course-Islam should be forced down the throats like bitter medicine to a child. This, however, was only possible if the leaders of the non-Muslim communities who failed to accept Islam were killed; the strength of the community reduced, their property confiscated and a situation was created which led to their followers and descendants willingly accepting Islam."[18]

Shah Wali-Allah's political ideas were influenced by Sunni theo-

---

15 John Voll, "Muhammad Hayyā al-Sindī and Muhammad ibn 'Abd al-Wahhab: An Analysis of an Intellectual Group in Eighteenth-Century Madīna" in *Bulletin of the School of Oriental and African Studies* (University of London), Vol.38, No. 1 (1975), 39.

16 Cf., Koran: Q30 *al-Rūm*, The Romans, 30: So direct your face toward the religion, inclining to truth. [Adhere to] the fitrah of Allah upon which He has created [all] people. No change should there be in the creation of Allah. That is the correct religion, but most of the people do not know.

17 Saiyid Athar Abbas Rizvi, *Shah Wali-Allah and His Times* (Lahore: Suhail Academy, 2004), 281.

18 Shah Wali-Allah, *Hujjat-Allah al-baligha*, Urdu translation by Abū Muhammad 'Abd al-Haq Haqqānī (Karachi: Asahhal-Mutābi', n.d.) II.480. Summarized in Saiyid Athar Abbas Rizvi, *Shah Wali-Allah and His Times* (Lahore: Suhail Academy, 2004), 285-286.

rists such as al-Mawardi (d.1058), al-Ghazali (d.1111), and particularly Ibn Taymiyya (d.1328), whose ideas on innovations were especially important for him.

Shah Wali Allah ascribes at least three objectives to *jihād*[19]: First, to extend the boundaries of right guidance;[20] second, to fight criminality; and finally to combat idolators. Like earlier Muslim thinkers of India cited above, Shah Wali Allah showed implacable hatred for non-Muslims in general, and Hindus, in particular, often encouraging, and exulting in, the destruction of Hindu temples.

Apart from advocating *jihād*, Shah Wali Allah was fierce and consistent in his attack on innovations, many of which had crept into Muslim practice from Hindu and Shi'ite festivals and customs such as Muharram. Muslims were also neglecting prayers, and the payment of *zakat*. As for praying at the tomb of Khwaja Mu'in al-Din Chisti at Ajmer, and other similar tombs, Shah Wali Allah considered such practices as no better than idol worship. In fact, according to the Shah, anyone who prayed to the dead for their needs was a sinner.

When he called for equity, justice and moderation, Shah Wali Allah only saw these principles through Muslim eyes—in other words non-Muslims and Shi'ites were not considered worthy of similar treatment as if equal to Muslims.

Sayyid Ahmad Brēlwī [1786-1831]

Sayyid Ahmad Brēlwī, [also Syed Ahmad Barelwi; Sayyid Ahmad Shahid, or Shah Syed Ahmad or simply, the Sayyid] was born in 1786 in Rai Bareilly, N. India. In 1804 in Delhi, he became the disciple of the divine Shāh 'Abd al-'Azīz [died 1823], the eldest son of Shāh Walī Allāh. He was initiated, in 1807, into the mystic (Sufi) tradition of Islam. In 1807, he went back to Bareilly where he got married, and then in 1810 he left for Tonk in Rajasthan where he served for seven years in the army of Nawāb Amīr Khān. But when the Nawab of Tonk made an alliance with the British, Sayyid Ahmad left, much disillusioned since he had dreamt of recreating an Islamic state, thereby restoring Islamic supremacy, and re-establishing a purified Islam.

Sayyid Ahmad Brelwi initiated several members of Shah Wali Allahs' family into the sufi orders, and they became his disciples. Between 1818 and 1819, Sayyid Ahmad Brelwi made extensive missionary tours

---

19 J.M.S. Baljon, *Religion and Thought of Shāh Walī Allāh Dihlawī 1703-1762* (Leiden: E.J. Brill, 1986),186.
20 Shah Wali Allah, *al-Khayr al-Kathīr* (Arabic) (Maktaba al-Qāhira, 1974), Khizāna 6.

of northern Indian cities, when along the way his disciples 'Abd al-Hayy and Shah Ismail gave fiery speeches denouncing degenerate Muslim practices like the visitations of graves. A riot broke out when the Sayyid's meetings were banned by the authorities. They set off again on their missionary tours in April 1819.

The Sayyid and his disciples often discussed both *jihād* and *hajj* in their private assemblies.[21] The Sayyid and his disciples went on missionary tours to persuade Muslims to go on *hajj*, an Islamic obligation which had been almost forgotten as there were many contradictory *fatwas* floating around absolving Muslims from this duty. Finally in July 1821, the Sayyid set out from Rai Bareilly with a party of 400. Along the way, "they preached against *bida'* (innovations) and commended strict adherence to the puritanical rules of the *Sharī'a*. ...In Banaras some of the Sayyid's Sunni disciples destroyed several hundred *ta'zīyas*[22] and used the wood and paper as fuel to cook the party's food."[23] The net result was to exacerbate relations between the Sunnis and Shias generally, even in places where hitherto they had lived together amicably. And yet, the Sayyid's party attracted a large number of converts to their cause.

The Sayyid and his party reached Mecca in May 1822. Even in the Hijāz, the Indian Muslim pilgrims tried to eradicate non-Muslim practices. In August 1822, the Sayyid obtained a pledge from his followers to fight *jihād*.[24] They left Mecca in July 1823, arriving back in April, 1824 in Rai Bareilly, where he stayed for one year and ten months devoting his thoughts to *jihād* and its preparation.

Here it would be appropriate to discuss just where and when the Sayyid acquired his doctrines and views which resemble the ideas of Ibn 'Abd al-Wahhab. The Sayyid's ideas are to be found in the *Sirāta l-Mustaqīm* which was compiled at Delhi in 1817-1818, in other words before his pilgrimage to Mecca, which he finally reached in May, 1822. But Najdi Wahhabi ideas were already known by this time to Muslim intellectuals in India.[25] Rizvi also points out that though the *Jihād* Movement was planned by Sayyid Ahmad, 'Abd al-Hayy, and Isma'il Shahid *before* their departure on hajj, "the fame of the Wahhabi wars in Mecca and

---

21 Saiyid Athar Abbas Rizvi, *Shah 'Abd al-'Aziz*, 480.
22 In South Asia this term refers specifically to the Miniature Mausoleums (imitations of the mausoleums of Karbala, generally made of coloured paper, wood, and bamboo) used in ritual Shi'te processions held in the month of Muharram.
23 Saiyid Athar Abbas Rizvi, *Shah 'Abd al-'Aziz*, 481.
24 Ibid., 484.
25 Ibid., 498.

Medina strengthened the determination of the Sayyid and his party to fight *jihād* with the help of the North-West Frontier tribes."[26] The *'ulama* of the Hijāz had considerable influence on their Indian counterparts. Finally, Dr Peter Hardy points out that "Arabian Wahhabism no doubt helped turn Sayyid Ahmad's thoughts towards an active military *jihād*, though precedents were not wanting in India itself for reforming brotherhoods to become military brotherhoods, as in the militant Raushaniyya movement on the north-west frontier in the sixteenth century, and indeed in Sikhism."[27]

As Banerjee argues, "Wahabism [sic] in India was derived from two sources, one internal, the other external: the philosophy of Shah Wali Allah and the teachings of Ibn 'Abd al-Wahhab."[28] Islam was no longer in a dominating position in India after the decline and fall of the Moghul Empire; India was no longer *Dar al-Islam* but again a *Dar al-Harb*, and Islam had been slowly but surely corrupted by non-Islamic traditions and customs. "Total reform of the corrupt variety of Islam and *jihād* against non-Muslim rule were the needs of the age. Shah Wali Allah's works provided sanction for the ambitious programme."

"But," continues Banerjee, "the basic lessons on lifting Islam from the corrupting innovations or heresies (*bida'*) were drawn from the doctrines of Ibn 'Abd al-Wahhab and-- from the long term point of view-- from the Kharijites through the Azraqites. Wahabism [sic] actually represented a special type of Pan-Islamism."[29]

For the Sayyid, many innovations were dangerously close to denying God's Unity, innovations such as prostrating oneself before the tomb of a saint. Making a circuit round tombs is also illicit since that is a ceremony retained only for the *Ka'ba*. Asking for the intercession of Saints is a way to deny one's fate which has been already decided upon by God.

The Sayyid also takes the Shias to task for corrupting the beliefs of the ordinary Sunni believer, particularly in their estimations of the relative merits of the first Caliphs. Other abuses result from the ceremonies regarding the Muharram. There are also countless superstitions that have grown over the years such as astrology—they must all be jettisoned.

The *Sirat al-Mustaqim* discusses, in considerable detail, *jihād*

---

26 Ibid., 523.

27 Peter Hardy, *The Muslims of British India* (Cambridge: Cambridge University Press, 1972), 53.

28 A.C. Banerjee, *Two Nations: The Philosophy of Muslim Nationalism*, 57.

29 Ibid., 58.

whose benefits are considered universal, and beneficial not only to believers but sinners and hypocrites. "The special benefits of *jihād* that accrue to the martyrs of the true faith, the Muslim ghazis, mighty rulers and brave warriors are indescribable. *Jihād* enables spiritualistic Sufis to rise to the position of eminent saints (*wilāyat*) by simple spiritual exercises. *Jihād* enables the 'ulamā' to disseminate the true faith and to promote an increase in religious education....The association of infidels with pious Sunnis and the promotion of Islamic customs and administrative laws may induce infidels to become Muslims. Those who are killed fighting against the Muslims also benefit because their death reduces the time they would have remained adamant in their infidelity and therefore the burden of their punishment grows lighter. Their families also benefit for they become the slaves of the Muslims and their association with them may prompt them to embrace Islam."[30]

On his return to India in 1239/1824, he began to make active preparations for a *jihād* or religious war. The ultimate object of his reformist movement was to overthrow the rule of the British and the Sikhs and restore Muslim dominion in India. First he had to dislodge the Sikhs from the Punjab.[31] Sayyid Ahmad set out from Rae Bareilly in January 1826 on a long circuitous journey of several thousand miles. The Sayyid's first act was to send an ultimatum to Ranjit Singh. The Sayyid gained an early victory over the Sikhs in December 1826, and he was joined by neighbouring Pathan chiefs, including sardars of Peshawar. In early 1827 he was formally elected Imam or *khalifa*, and assumed the title of Amir al-Mu'minin (Commander of the Faithful). While many of the tribesmen were clearly delighted with the booty acquired after the first two battles, the Sayyid made it clear that his aim "was to obey God and to promote the interests of Islam. Were the important rulers to accept Islam, he (the Sayyid) would be their whole-hearted well-wisher. ...He had no interest in booty or in ruling the territory but had been asking Muslims to fight against the infidels for Islam's sake."[32]

In May 1831, at Balakot on the Kaghan river, in an area where he was trying to enlist the local chiefs against the Sikhs in Hazara and Kashmir, Sayyid Ahmad, Shah Ismail and nearly six hundred of his followers were killed."[33]

---

30 Saiyid Athar Abbas Rizvi, *Shah 'Abd al-'Aziz*, 506-507.
31 *Encyclopaedia of Islam* 2nd Edn. Vol.1, 282a-282b, s.v. "Sayyid Ahmad Brēlwī."
32 Saiyid Athar Abbas Rizvi, *Shah 'Abd al-'Aziz*, 488-489.
33 Peter Hardy, *The Muslims of British India* (Cambridge: Cambridge University Press 1972), 52.

The significance of Sayyid Ahmad Brelwi's *Jihād* Movement must not be misunderstood. It is certainly wrong to think that once he had driven out the British from India, the Sayyid intended to hand over supreme power to the Indian heads of states and non-Muslims. This is to misunderstand totally the Sayyid's life mission, and the spirit and purpose of his movement. "He would never have allowed an Indian secular, or a united Hindu-Muslim, rule which did not make Islam or Islamic law predominant and where the control of the states or the sovereign authority was not in Islamic hands. His letters themselves are clear evidence against this popular myth. In fact, the Sayyid's *jihād* was designed to destroy both the Sikhs and the British and to make India a *dar al-Islam*. Those Hindu heads of state who helped him were guaranteed their throne and a *dhimmi* (protected subjects [and essentially inferior]) status; the future for the others in the Sayyid's *dar al-Islam* was bleak. By no stretch of the imagination [was] his *jihād* a war for Indian independence."[34]

Ayesha Jalal makes a similar assessment. It was in Balakot that Sayyid Ahmad and Shah Ismail, "quintessential Islamic warriors in South Asian Muslim consciousness, fell in battle against the Sikhs on 6 May 1831. Considered to be the only real *jihād* ever fought in the subcontinent to establish the supremacy of the Islamic faith…".

Balakot has become even more important as a symbol of Islamic *Jihād* in recent times. As Jalal explains: "Balakot's association with the idea and practice of *jihād* in South Asia was reinforced in the 1990s, when militant groups set up training camps in its environs to prepare for their campaign against Indian security forces stationed in predominantly Muslim Kashmir. For these militants, Sayyid Ahmad and Shah Ismail are great heroes, whose *jihād* their admirers wish to emulate, to redress what they perceive as current injustices."[35] It is not just militants that extolled *jihād*: "[T]he most gifted Muslim thinkers and poets of India were evidently influenced by the movement and wrote feelingly about Sayyid Ahmad's martyrdom, along with that of Shah Ismail in Balakot on 6 May 1831."[36]

As symbols, the Martyrs of Balakot have taken on an enormous amplitude and significance that cannot be exaggerated. "The *Shahnamah-i-Balakot* is an extended laudatory poem on the movement

---

34 Saiyid Athar Abbas Rizvi, *Shah 'Abd al-'Aziz*, 535.
35 Ayesha Jalal, *Partisans of Allah: Jihād in South Asia* (Cambridge: Harvard University Press, 2008), 2.
36 Ibid., 61.

by a Pakistani poet [Alim Nasiri]. Writing across the great divide of 1947, Maulana Husain Ahmad Nadwi notes in his foreword that the hallowed blood shed on that famous battlefield still runs in the veins of the Muslim community (millat). This is because Sayyid Ahmad Shahid and Maulana Ismail Shahid's movement blended Ahmad Sirhindi's ideas on Sunni reform and the elimination of bid'a (innovation) with Shah Wali Allah's *jihād* movement. The party of six hundred or so selfless Muslim mujāhidīn who fought in the rugged terrain of the northwest frontier along with tens of thousands of Pathan tribesmen ushered in the spring of Islamic culture and civilization. It is their deeds that have kept alive the spirit of *jihād* in Muslim society to this day in the shape of various Muslim organizations and movements."[37]

Meanwhile the poet himself, Alim Nasiri, goes into raptures over the peaks of the mountains surrounding Balakot coloured by the blood of the martyrs of Balakot. Another modern writer, Khwaja Abdul Wahid, sings the praise of the *mujāhidīn* who have kept the light of Islam burning despite betrayals.[38]

Sayyid Abu 'l-'Alā' Mawdūdī

Sayyid Abu 'l-'Alā' Mawdūdī was born in Aurangabad, South India, in 1903 into a distinguished family from Delhi that traced its lineage to the great Sufi saints of the Chishti order. His father Hasan was determined not to give his son a Western education, and thus Mawdūdī was educated in Urdu, Persian, Arabic, law, and *hadīth* through private tutors. He imbibed Western science, however, and learned English and mathematics at an Islamic academy influenced by Sayyid Ahmad Khan's modernism. In 1919, Mawdūdī left for Delhi where he acquired even greater knowledge of Western science, history, and philosophy. Mawdūdī came into contact with *Jam'iyyat-i 'Ulamā'-i Hind* (JUH, founded in 1919 at the hight of the Khilafat movement by "clerics" from Deoband and the Lucknow seminaries), of whose journal, *al-Jam'iyyat*, he became editor. He left the JUH because of their alliance with Congress (i.e. The Indian National Congress Party, a secular political party founded in 1885), and left Delhi for Hyderabad in 1928.

At first Mawdūdī was attracted to some aspects of Western culture, but now came to the conclusion that the reason for the Muslims' decline was the corruption of Islam partly by Western culture, and to propagate "pure" Islam he founded the Urdu journal, *Tarjumanul Qur'an*, in 1932.

---

37 Ibid., 62-63.
38 Quoted by Ayesha Jalal, 62-63.

By the 1930s, Mawdūdī had a clear vision of his plan:

> I should first break the hold which Western culture and ideas had come to acquire over the Muslim intelligentsia, and to instil in them the fact that Islam has a code of life of its own, its own culture, its own political and economic systems and a philosophy and an educational system which are all superior to anything that Western civilisation could offer. I wanted to rid them of the wrong notion that they needed to borrow from others in the matter of culture and civilisation.[39]

It was in Hyderabad that Mawdūdī fully developed his views on the corruption of Islam "by centuries of incorporation of local customs and mores that had obscured that faith's veritable teachings," writes University of San Diego assistant professor of political science Seyyed Vali Reza Nasr. "Salvation of Muslim culture and the preservation of its power lay in the restitution of Islamic institutions and practices after they had been cleansed of the cultural influences that had sapped Muslims of their power."[40]

But "Mawdudi's revivalist position was radical communalism as it articulated Muslim interests and sought to protect their rights, and demanded the severance of all cultural and hence social and political ties with Hindus in the interests of purifying Islam."[41] Mawdūdī created an Islamic ideology to counter especially the Western ideologies of socialism and capitalism. He viewed "Islam as a holistic ideology similar to western ideologies. His notion of Islamic ideology, one of the most prolific and systematic articulations of its kind, has been most influential in giving shape to Islamic revivalism as a distinct reading of Islam, its history, and its purpose across the Muslim world."[42]

Mawdūdī was critical of both the Congress and the All India Muslim League, which he saw as being secular, calling it a "party of the pagans." As the Muslim League had no agenda for a Sharī'a state, Mawdūdī

---

39 Sayyid Abul Ala Maudoodi, "Twenty-Nine Years of the Jamaat-e-Islami," *Criterion* 5, no. 6 (November–December 1970): 45; quoted in *Encyclopaedia of Islam*, vol. 4, "Iran–Kha," ed. by E. van Donzel, B. Lewis, and Ch. Pellat, 2nd ed. (Leiden: Brill, 1978), s.v. "Mawdūdī, Sayyid Abu 'l-a'la," by F.C.R. Robinson.

40 Seyyed Vali Reza Nasr, "Mawdudi and the Jam'at-i Islami: The Origins, Theory and Practice of Islamic Revivalism" in *Pioneers of Islamic Revival*, ed. Ali Rahnema, Studies in Islamic Society (London: Zed Books Ltd., 1994), 2.

41 Ibid., 103.

42 Ibid., 105.

despaired for the future Pakistan, dubbing it an "infidel state of Muslims."⁴³ It was against this background that in 1941 Mawdūdī founded his *Jamā'at-i Islāmī* (JI), Islamic party. After the Partition of India in 1947,⁴⁴ the *Jamā'at-i Islāmī* split into an Indian party and a Pakistani party.

Mawdūdī along with 385 members opted for Pakistan, but his ambitious goal was "Allah's Government" (*hukūmat-i ilāhiyya*) or a true "Islamic State." Shari'a and the belief in monotheism was central to all Muslims:

> In *Qur'an ki Char Bunyadi Istelahen* (Four Fundamental Concepts of the Qur'an), he reinterpreted words such as *ilāh* (God), *rabb* (Lord), *'ibādat* (worship), and *dīn* (religion) to argue that the Qur'an obliged Muslims to establish a state based on divine sovereignty and simultaneously reject, or rather dethrone, *jāhiliyyat*, the embodiment of human sovereignty. This approach also informs Mawdudi's multi-volume commentary on the Qur'an, *Tafhīm al-Qur'ān* (begun in 1942 and completed in 1972), which finds a coveted space on the bookshelves of many Muslims who are not Islamists.⁴⁵

Despite his hatred of the secular West, Mawdūdī often used Hegelian and Marxists analyses in his own philosophy to show that history since the seventh century has been a battle between Islam and *jāhiliyyat*, with secular democracy as the ultimate expression of *jāhiliyyat*. He advised his followers not to vote in elections for a secular, democratic state.⁴⁶ But an Islamic state could not function properly until society was already thoroughly Islamicized. For example, *hudud* (pl. of *hadd*, "boundary," "limit," "stipulation," or "restriction" laid down by God) punishments as prescribed in the Koran could only be implemented when the people were "fully aware of the teachings of Islam and would have no excuse for not following the *Sharī'a*." Thus an Islamic State "should not be the enforcer of the *Sharī'a* but the implementor of the

---

43 Irfan Ahmad, "Mawdudi, Abu al-A 'la (1903–1979)," *Princeton Encyclopaedia of Islamic Political Thought*, 334.

44 In 1947, India was partitioned into two political entities to provide a homeland for Muslims. The state of Pakistan was created for Muslims.

45 Irfan Ahmad, "Mawdudi, Abu al-A 'la (1903–1979)," *Princeton Encyclopaedia of Islamic Political Thought*, 334.

46 Ibid.

will of the people. Ideally, popular will should demand implementation of the *Sharī'a*, unburdening the state and legitimizing its rule."[47]

But Mawdūdī's primary concern was to establish an Islamic State where sovereignty lies with God, not the people. Therefore, as Reza Nasr points out,

> He dwelt less on socio-economic problems such as population growth, economic inequalities, and social injustice. He believed that these problems were not real issues of concern, for they were symptoms of the absence of an Islamic order and reflections of the failure of western ideologies. They would disappear once the state and society were Islamized [sic], so Muslims were best advised not to dwell on these issues but to focus on establishing and managing the Islamic state.[48]

As for minorities in an Islamic State, Islamic law already had clearcut rules governing *dhimmis* or non-Muslims, second-class citizens subject to a special tax and other social disabilities. The role of women was also spelled out in the Shari'a. How could claims that an Islamic State would be democratic be sustained alongside such views? Mawdūdī "remained unapologetic":

> He argued that the Islamic state was an ideological one, and the preservation of its ideological purity was therefore the condition sine qua non for its survival and development. Extended rights for minorities would undermine the Islamic state as they would diffuse its ideological vigilance. Therefore limiting their rights to those of zimmis in Islamic law was a matter of national security and self-preservation.[49]

In 1953, Mawdūdī campaigned against Zafar'ullah Khan, Pakistan's Ahmadi Foreign Minister, and demanded that the Ahmadiyya, a religious movement, be classified as a non-Muslim minority.[50]

---

47 Reza Nasr, "Mawdudi and the *Jam'at-i Islami*, 107.
48 Ibid., 108.
49 Ibid., 109.
50 The Ahmadiyya was founded in 1889 by Mirza Ghulam Ahmad (1835–1908). The Ahmadiyya are often persecuted by other Muslims because Ghulam Ahmad made a number of claims, including being a recipient of revelation. Orthodox Muslims reject

Mawdūdī also clearly did not accord women a sociopolitical role equal to men. Fearing that greater interaction of the sexes would lead to immorality and undo the Islamic State, he "comes close to characterizing women as an insidious force whose activities ought to be regulated and restricted before they could wreak havoc."[51] Mawdūdī wrote: "God has prohibited the unrestricted intermingling of the sexes and has prescribed *purdah* [a word of Persian origin meaning the religious and social practice of female seclusion]" recognizing "man's guardianship of woman," for Muslims must guard against "that satanic flood of female liberty and licence which threatens to destroy human civilization in the West."[52]

By 1992 the *Jamā'at-i Islāmī* of Pakistan had grown 7,861 members, and 357,229 sympathizers. Their great emphasis has been on education. JI sees itself as an *umma*, a virtuous Muslim community that demands each member to reforms all aspects of his life to conform to Islamic standards as defined by the party. JI wishes to change society in accordance with Mawdūdī's vision. "In political terms," Reza Nasr writes, "the Jamā'at-i Islāmī's organizational model has performed the function of a vanguard party in the struggle for Islamic revolution."[53] But the overall aim has always been to train a vanguard of Islamic elite to oversee the revival of Islam on a national level, to encourage the existing, inherent religious activism in Islam to push Pakistan toward complete Islamisization.

In newly-created Pakistan, Mawdūdī was in constant trouble with the authorities. He served time in prison and was even sentenced to death (later annulled) for participating in anti-Ahmadi agitation. Mawdūdī was also uwelcome under the military regime of General Ayub Khan (1958–1969), who tried modernize Pakistan without Islam. Mawdūdī's candidates did not win many seats in various elections. He vehemently opposed the government of Zulfiqar Ali Bhutto (d. 1979), who espoused a form of socialist populism, and Mawdūdī formed a movement for the installation of *nizām-i mustafā* (Prophetic Order).[54]

During the 1950s, Mawdūdī travelled widely outside Pakistan, of-

---

this notion as blasphemy; for them Muhammad is the last of the Prophets to have received a revelation.
51 Reza Nasr, "Mawdudi and the *Jam'at-i Islami*," 110.
52 Syed Abul A'la Maududi, *Political Theory of Islam* (1960; Lahore: Islamic Publications Ltd., 1980), 27.
53 Reza Nasr, "Mawdudi and the *Jam'at-i Islami*," 113.
54 Ahmad, "Mawdudi," 334.

ten visiting Saudi Arabia, where he helped establish and run Medina's Islamic university and the World Muslim League, but he never neglected Islamic matters in Pakistan such as the Muslim Family Laws Ordinance of 1961 or the Ahmadiyya question. JI anti-Bhutto protests played a part in the July 1977 military coup that brought General Muhammad Zia al-Haq (d.1988) to power. Zia al-Haq was quick to grant some kind of legitimacy to the Prophetic Order movement, and even accorded Mawdūdī the "status of senior statesman, one whose advice was sought by the new leadership of the country and whose words adorned the front pages of the printed media."[55] However, Mawdūdī died in 1979 in Buffalo, New York, seeking medical attention from the very people he despised, the infidels. Over a million people were said to have attended his funeral in Lahore.

Zia al-Haq earnestly undertook the Islamization of Pakistan, and the JI enjoyed unprecedented success and political influence, its leaders holding important government offices, including cabinet portfolios. "The party's views were reflected in government programmes. The party played a direct role in the Islamization of the country, as well as in articulating state policy, especially concerning the Afghan war and the government's reaction to provincialist and ethnic tendencies."[56] Nonetheless, in the 1985 election, the JI won only ten seats to the National Assembly and thirteen seats to the various provincial assemblies.

Despite electoral failures, the JI "had become a powerful political force with significant social and cultural influence"[57] and remains so, thanks to its organizational abilities. Mawdūdī was "amongst the most influential" of Muslims of the twentieth century who felt "that the answer to western domination need not be formulated in terms of nationalism and secularism but in terms of Islam. Himself inspired by Ibn Khaldun, Shah Walī Allah, Muhammad Iqbal and Hasan al-Bannā' he has influenced...leaders of Islamic movements in Egypt, Syria and Iran to many ordinary Muslims throughout the Islamic world."[58]

Mawdūdī's Beliefs

For Mawdūdī, God alone is sovereign. Man goes astray when he accepts sovereigns other than God and Shari'a is an all-embracing guide for mankind because it is God-given, being derived from the Koran, the

---

[55] Reza Nasr, "Mawdudi and the *Jam'at-i Islami*," 118.
[56] Ibid., 119.
[57] Ibid.
[58] *Encyclopaedia of Islam*, vol. 4, 2nd ed., s.v. "Mawdūdī, Sayyid Abu 'l-a'la."

Sunna, and the *hadīth*. Islam does not recognize national boundaries, and thus the state ruled by God's laws would be universal. The ruler can be chosen by the people, who are imbued with the principles of Islam, but the ruler must govern by God-given laws. The legislature, too, can be chosen by the people, but legislation is "by interpretation, by analogy, by inference, and, in that area of human affairs about which the Shari'a is silent, by independent judgement." All people must submit to the Law, being God-given, and the sole function of the state is to implement this law. "Islamic norms exist not merely to be followed by Muslims on their personal initiative and in their individual lives but to be put into effect through the coercive power of the state."[59]

Mawdūdī was convinced that only the Islamic State could guarantee an effective means of living according to Islamic norms. The people, being extraordinarily ignorant of true Islam, had to be educated in what this meant. Given his family background and admiration for Shah Walli Allah (1703–1762) and Ahmad Sirhindi (1564–1624), Islamic scholars of India who were sympathetic to Sufis and Sufism), Mawdūdī was surprisingly hostile to the Sufis, who "appeared to him to be especially egregious in violating 'true' Islam" and "went so far as to range Sufi asceticism alongside atheism and polytheism."[60]

Mawdūdī's major contribution was

> to have transformed Islam into an ideology, an integrated and all-embracing system. He aimed to set out the ideal order of the time of the Rightly-Guided Caliphs. The outcome is the most comprehensive statement of the nature of the Islamic state in modern times, and one which, while conjuring an ideal from the past, has been shaped by contemporary concerns and modes of thought. His exposition, as might be expected from a man who was primarily a theologian, is strong on general principles but weak on detail.[61]

Clearly aware of the Islamic revival tradition in India, Mawdūdī was heavily influenced by the example of Shaykh Ahmad Sirhindi and Sayyid Ahmad Shahid, and considered that "his authority emanated

---

59 Roxanne L. Euben and Muhammad Qasim Zaman, *Princeton Readings in Islamist Thought: Texts and Contexts from al-Banna to Bin Laden* (Princeton, NJ: Princeton University Press, 2009), 81.
60 Ibid.
61 *Encyclopaedia of Islam*, vol. 4, 2nd ed., s.v. "Mawdūdī, Sayyid Abu 'l-a'la."

from the tradition of Ibn Taymiyyah and Shah Wali Allah."[62] Mawdūdī appealed to the tradition of the mujaddid as a model of religious leadership. As Reza Nasr notes, "Since Sirhindi's time, generations of Muslim figures of authority have drawn on his tradition of renewal and reform of Islam to revive the faith. Much like them, Mawdudi based his claim to leadership on his promise to deliver Muslims from their political impotence."[63]

Sirhindi's tradition "has provided a powerful paradigm for activism," and Mawdūdī saw "himself as a part of this tradition, and was viewed as a part of it by his followers, as their documentation of all of his statements and his every decision attests."[64] He himself identified a number of other *mujaddids* responsible for calling Muslims back to the Shari'a, shunning innovations, and returning to pure Islam of the *salaf*.

Mawdūdī on Jihād

Introductory books on Mawdūdī rarely refer to his views on *jihād*. These views are uncompromising, unapologetic, and very disturbing in their implications. Mawdūdī begins his short treatise, *Jihād in Islam*, with a definition of religion and a definition of nation:

> But the truth is that Islam is not the name of a "Religion", nor is "Muslim" the title of a "Nation." In reality Islam is a revolutionary ideology and programme which seeks to alter the social order of the whole world and rebuild it in conformity with its own tenets and ideals. "Muslim" is the title of that International Revolutionary Party organized by Islam to carry into effect its revolutionary programme. And "*Jihād*" refers to that revolutionary struggle and utmost exertion which the Islamic Party brings into play to achieve this objective.[65]

Muslims shun the ordinary word for war, *harb*, for wars have traditionally been fought between nations, but Islam does not wage war for the sake of a nation. Mawdūdī declares:

---

62 Seyyed Vali Reza Nasr, *Mawdudi and the Making of Islamic Revivalism* (Oxford and New York: Oxford University Press, 1996), 115.

63 Ibid., 126.

64 Ibid., 136.

65 Syed Abul A'la Maududi, *Jihād in Islam* (Beirut: The Holy Koran Publishing House, 1980), 5.

Islam has no vested interest in promoting the cause of this or that Nation. The hegemony of this or that State on the face of this earth is irrelevant to Islam. The sole interest of Islam is the welfare of mankind. Islam has its own particular ideological standpoint and practical programme to carry out reforms for the welfare of mankind. Islam wishes to destroy all states and governments anywhere on the face of the earth which are opposed to the ideology and programme of Islam regardless of the country or the Nation which rules it. The purpose of Islam is to set up a state on the basis of its own ideology and programme, regardless of which nation assumes the role of the standard-bearer of Islam or the rule of which nation is undermined in the process of the establishment of an ideological Islamic State. Islam requires the earth—not just a portion, but the whole planet—not because the sovereignty over the earth should be wrested from one nation or several nations and vested in one particular nation, but because the entire mankind should benefit from the ideology and welfare programme or what would be truer to say from "Islam" which is the programme of well-being for all humanity. Towards this end, Islam wishes to press into service all forces which can bring about a revolution and a composite term for the use of all these forces is "*Jihād.*"[66]

The message could not be clearer: Islam must conquer the globe, and the purpose of *jihād* is totalitarian—it demands the engagement of all Muslims until Earth is ruled according to the precepts of Islam. All other ideologies, as systems where man-made laws rule, are enemies. Mawdūdī wishes to replace them with God-made laws: the Shari'a.

Mawdūdī and Shari'a

The Shari'a, for Mawdūdī, governs everything on earth, as it is but the will of God. One must submit to it, or be led astray into *jahiliyya*. The highest court of appeal is the Koran and the *Sunna* of the Prophet. To impugn them would be an unpardonable sin and result in the transgression of *shirk*, embodied in the principle of *tawhīd*:

> Tawhīd means that only God is the Creator, Sustainer and Master of the universe and of all that exists in it—organic

---
66 Ibid., 6–7.

and inorganic....He alone has the right to command or forbid. Worship and obedience are due to Him alone... It is not for us to decide the aim and purpose of our existence or to set the limits of our authority; nor is anyone else entitled to make these decisions for us. This right rests only with God.... This principle of the unity of God totally negates the concept of the legal and political independence of human beings.... No individual, family, class or race can set themselves above God. God alone is the Ruler and His commandments are the Law.[67]

The source of "all evil and mischief," wrote Mawdūdī, "is the domination of man over man, be it direct or indirect....If you do not believe in God, some artificial god will take His place in your thinking and behavior. It is even possible that instead of one real God, a number of false gods, 'ilahs' and 'rabbs' may impose themselves upon you."[68]

More than a guide to one's personal behavior, the Shari'a is also meant for the collective life, and prescribes all-encompassing directives, which for Mawdūdī include "family relationships, social and economic affairs, administration, rights and duties of citizens, judicial system, laws of war and peace and international relations....The Shari'a is a complete scheme of life and an all-embracing social order where nothing is superfluous and nothing lacking."[69]

Without the establishment of the entire Islamic system, the provisions of Islamic law cannot be properly implemented. The Shari'a does not recognize any division between religion and other aspects of life, and between religion and state. Secularism, which

> Mawdūdī equated with the separation of religion and state or with religionlessness, he considered to be the very contrary of Islam since it opened the way...to the exclusion of all morality, ethics, or human decency from the controlling mechanisms of society. This...was precisely what happened in the Western world whose governments and social bases he

---

[67] Syed Abul A'la Maududi, *The Islamic Way of Life*, ed. Khurshid Ahmad and Khurram Murad (Leicester, UK: The Islamic Foundation, 1992), 29–30. First Urdu edition, 1948; first English edition, 1967.

[68] Maududi, *Political Theory of Islam*, 13.

[69] Syed Abul A'la Maududi, *Islamic Law and Constitution* (Lahore, IL: Islamic Publications, 1967), 53.

never tired of condemning as unutterably and irredeemably corrupt. In his mind, morality of any kind was simply inconceivable without religion and the sanction of eternal punishment to support it.[70]

And to implement the Shari'a, political power embodied in an Islamic State is necessary: "the reforms which Islam wants to bring about cannot be carried out merely by sermons. Political power is essential for their achievement."[71]

The "materials for the constitution of an Islamic state are to be found in four principle sources, the Koran, the *Sunna* of the Prophet, the conventions and practices of the Four Rightly Guided Caliphs, and in the rulings of the great jurists of the Islamic tradition."[72]

As discussed earlier in these pages, the first basic principle of the Islamic State is the recognition of the sovereignty of God.

The second basic principle is the authority of the Prophet: "Whoso obeys the Messenger obeys God" (Q4. *an-Nisā'*, the Women, 80). The Prophet is the perfect model to be emulated.

The third basic principle of the Islamic State is its status as the viceregent of God, for the Islamic state does not make its own laws but enforces God-made laws for His sake. The Koran vests vicegerency in the entire Muslim citizenry of the Islamic state (Q24. *an-Nūr*, the Light, 55). As Mawdūdī wrote: "The power to rule over the earth has been promised to the whole community of believers; it has not been stated that any particular person or class among them will be raised to that position. From this it follows that all believers are repositories of the Caliphate."[73]

The fourth principle is that the Islamic State must conduct its affairs by mutual consultation (*shura*) among all the Muslims. Mawdūdī calls this system of government a "theo-democracy," although he is aware of the totalitarian aspect of the Islamic State—and is totally unapologetic. The Islamic State "cannot…restrict the scope of its activities….It seeks to mould every aspect of life and activity in consonance with its moral norms and programme of social reform. In such a state no one can regard any field of his affairs as personal and private. Considered from this aspect the Islamic state bears a kind of resemblance to the Fascist

---

70 Charles Adams, "Mawdudi and the Islamic State," in *Voices of Resurgent Islam*, ed. John L. Esposito (Oxford and New York: Oxford University Press, 1983), 113.
71 Maududi, *Islamic Law and Constitution*, 177.
72 Adams, "Mawdudi and the Islamic State," 114.
73 Maududi, *Political Theory of Islam*, 35.

and Communist states."⁷⁴ In this Mawdūdī makes it clear that Islam is "the very antithesis of secular Western democracy. The philosophical foundation of Western democracy is the sovereignty of the people."⁷⁵ He calls the Islamic State an ideological society: "All...who... surrender themselves to the will of God are welded into a community and that is how the 'Muslim society' comes into being. Thus, this is an ideological society—a society radically different from those spring from accidents of races, colour, or country."⁷⁶

Revivalist movements and the ideas of Muslim reformers in India bear a remarkable resemblance to each other, and to revivalist movements in other parts of the Islamic world, such as Wahhabism in eighteenth century Arabia. These reformers believed that Islam was in danger, and was being slowly corrupted by non-Muslim civilizations, whether Hindu, Buddhist or Western. Unacceptable innovations (*bida'*) had been introduced, and they had to be removed and a pristine Islam of the ancestors restored. *Tawhīd* (oneness of God) must be respected, and *shirk* (polytheism, idolatry, association of partners to God) extirpated. Despite the fact they had been initiated into various Sufi brotherhoods, and despite their qualified admiration for some of the Sufi thinkers, these reformers considered that the Koran, the *Sunna* and Sharī'a overrode all Sufi experiences, and principles. And above all, being a Sufi did not absolve one from waging *jihād* in the military sense. Sayyid Ahmad Brēlwī reminds us that *jihād* was not waged for the sake of booty, but to extend the frontiers of Islam, until it covered the entire world. There was no question of Islam accommodating itself to Hinduism or the Christianity of the British in India; on the contrary, Islam had to dominate. Finally, Mawdūdī admitted that Islam was a totalitarian ideology akin to Fascism and Communism, where the individual owes total allegiance to Islam, and Islam only, and where he loses his individuality and finds relief in submerging himself in the Islamic community (*umma*).

---

74 Ibid., 30.
75 Ibid., 21.
76 Maududi, *Islamic Law and Constitution*, 50.

CHAPTER 16
BRIGADIER S.K. MALIK AND
THE QUR'ANIC CONCEPT OF WAR

PRESIDENT ZIA AL-HAQ [1924 – 1988], who was President of Pakistan from 1978 to 1988 vowed to run the country on Islamic principles, and said, "Pakistan which was created in the name of Islam will continue to survive only if it sticks to Islam. That is why I consider the introduction of [an] Islamic system as an essential prerequisite for the country."[1] Thus while he began the Islamization of Pakistan in earnest, Zia al-Haq took time to write what, at first sight, might seem an extraordinary endorsement of *The Qur'anic Concept of War* (1979), by Brigadier S.K. Malik, which has become, according to Sebastian Gorka, who holds the Major General Matthew C. Horner Distinguished Chair of Military Theory at the Marine Corps University, "the most influential treatise on why *Jihād* is necessary and how it must be fought."[2] It is constantly quoted and referred to by modern jihādists. However, given the President's Islamization programme for Pakistan and the fact that *jihād* is the quintessential Islamic duty, Zai al-Haq's stamp of approval of Brigadier Malik's treatise makes perfect sense.

Little information is available on Brigadier Malik, and yet, as Patrick Poole and Mark Hanna point out in their publisher's preface:

> The continued relevance of *The Qur'anic Concept of War* is indicated by the discovery by US military officials of summa-

---

[1] Ian Talbot, *Pakistan, a Modern History* (New York: St.Martin's Press, 1998), 251.

[2] Sebastian Gorka, "Grandmasters of Jihad," *The Counter Jihad Report*, May 16, 2015, https://counterjihadreport.com/tag/s-k-malik/.

ries of this book published in various languages on captured and killed *jihādist* insurgents in Afghanistan. This is hardly a surprising development as Malik finds within the Quran a doctrine of aggressive, escalating and constant *jihād* against non-Muslims and the religious justification of terrorism as a means to achieving the dominance of Islam around the world—dogmas that square with the Islamist ideology driving terrorism worldwide.[3]

The endorsements of Zia al-Haq and Allah Bukhsh K. Brohi, the late advocate-general of Pakistan and former Pakistani ambassador to India, "established Malik's views on *jihād* as national policy and gave his interpretation official state sanction."[4] For Zia al-Haq, the book is essential for soldier and civilian:

> This book brings out with simplicity, clarity and precision the Quranic philosophy on the application of military force within the context of the totality that is *Jihād*. The professional soldier in a Muslim army, pursuing the goals of a Muslim state, cannot become "professional" if in all his activities he does not take the "colour of Allah." The nonmilitary citizen of a Muslim state must, likewise, be aware of the kind of soldier that his country must produce and the only pattern of war that his country's armed forces may wage.[5]

In his enthusiasm, Zia al-Haq would change the motto of the Pakistani army to "Islam, Piety, and *Jihād*."[6]

The Qur'anic Concept of War is replete with quotes from the Holy Book exhorting men to wage war in the name and for the cause of God. The most quoted suras include Q2. *al-Baqara*, the Cow; Q3. *'āl 'Imrān*, the Family of Imran; Q8. *al-'anfāl*, the Spoils of War / Voluntary Gifts; Q9. *at-Tawba*, the Repentance / *al-Barā'at*, the Immunity; Q48. *al-Fath*, the Victory; Q4. *an-Nisā'*, the Women. Eleven other suras are cited to a

---

[3] Patrick Poole and Mark Hanna, "Publishers Preface" to Brigadier S. K. Malik, *The Qur'anic Concept of War* (1992; Delhi: Adam Publishers & Distributors, 2008), http://www.discoverthenetworks.org/Articles/Quranic%20Concept%20of%20War.pdf.
[4] Ibid.
[5] General M. Zia-ul-Haq, "Foreword," in Malik, *Qur'anic Concept of War*.
[6] Ayesha Jalal, *Partisans of Allah: Jihad in South Asia* (Cambridge, MA: Harvard University Press, 2010), 275.

lesser degree. Malik offers a close analysis of all of Muhammad's battles, and his bibliography refers to the works of Mawdūdī, namely *Tafhīm al-Qurān* and *al-Jihād fī 'l-Islām*, which, as discussed, have had an enormous influence in Pakistan in general, and on Zia al-Haq in particular.

One of Malik's distinctive doctrines is the importance of using terror as its own end:

> [W]hen God wishes to impose His will upon the His enemies, He chooses to do so by casting terror into their hearts…."Let not the Unbelievers think," God commands us directly and pointedly, "that they can get better (of the Godly): they will never frustrate them. Against them make ready your strength to the utmost of your power, including steeds of war, to strike terror into (the hearts of) the enemies of Allah and your enemies, and others besides, whom ye may not know, but whom Allah doth know." (Q8. *al-'anfāl*, the Spoils of War / Voluntary Gifts, verses 59–60).[7]

Malik explains this approach:

> The Quranic military strategy thus enjoins us to prepare ourselves for war to the utmost in order to strike terror into the hearts of the enemies, known or hidden, while guarding ourselves from being terror stricken by the enemy….[G]uarding ourselves against terror is the "Base"; preparation for war to the utmost is the "Cause"; while the striking terror into the hearts of the enemies is the "Effect."…. In war, our main objective is the opponent's heart or soul, our main weapon of offence against this objective is the strength of our own souls, and to launch such an attack, we have to keep terror away from our own hearts.

And for Malik psychological preparation for war is all important:

> So spirited, zealous, complete and thorough should be our preparation for war that we should enter upon the "war of muscles" having already won the "war of will." Only a strategy that aims at striking terror into the hearts of the enemies

---

7 Malik, *Qur'anic Concept of War*, 57–58.

from the preparation stage can produce direct results.[8]

"Terror struck into the hearts of the enemies is not only a means, it is the end itself," Malik states, "It is the point where the means and the end meet and merge. Terror is not a means of imposing decision on the enemy; it is the decision we wish to impose on him."[9]

And what is the ultimate purpose of terror and terrorist action? To destroy the enemy's faith:

> Psychological dislocation is temporary; spiritual dislocation is permanent. Psychological dislocation can be produced by a physical act but this does not hold good of spiritual dislocation. To instill terror into the hearts of the enemy, it is essential, in the ultimate analysis, to dislocate his Faith. An invincible Faith is immune to terror. A weak Faith offers inroads to terror. The Faith conferred upon us by the Holy Quran has the inherent strength to ward off terror from us and to enable us to strike terror into the enemy.[10]

Malik constantly quotes Western experts on the causes of war such as Geoffrey Blainey, Bernard Brodie, and Liddel Hart only to dismiss their sociopolitical arguments as irrelevant to Islam: "[T]he central theme behind the causes of wars, as spelt out by the Holy Quran, was the cause of Allah. This cause manifested itself in different shapes and forms at different stages in the history of Islam. In pursuit of this cause, the Muslims were first granted *permission* to fight but were later *commanded* to fight in the Way of God as a matter of religious obligation and duty" (emphasis in original).[11]

Malik clearly sees the Koranic concept of war as humanitarian, noble, and righteous, freeing humanity from tyranny and injustice, but a careful reading reveals that by justice and peace he means the imposition of Islam on the whole of humanity, until everyone submits. For Muslims the Koran is the word of God, and it must be borne in mind constantly that Malik is addressing committed Muslims:

> [T]he fountain-head of the Quranic dimension of war lies in

---

8 Ibid., 58.
9 Ibid., 59.
10 Ibid., 60.
11 Ibid., 20.

the fact that war is waged for the cause of Allah, and with the object of imposing conditions of justice and peace. To those who fight for this noblest heavenly cause, the Book promises handsome heavenly assistance. The index of fighting for Allah's Cause is Man's total submission to His will. Those who fail to submit themselves fully and completely to the Will of God run the risk of incurring heavenly wrath. Nature has no particular or specific liking for any community of people as such; it helps only those who qualify themselves for it, and punishes the rest. Fighting involves risk to life and property that must be accepted willingly and cheerfully. Death in this world is inevitable; life in the Hereafter is certain; and the reward of those who fight for the cause of Allah is safe, splendid and sure. Our reward is in direct proportion to our performance. Those who die fighting for the cause of Allah never actually die."[12]

A little later, he adds, "A victory in Islam is a victory for the cause of Islam."[13]

Malik explains that the Koran

> gives us a distinctive concept of total war. It wants both, the nation and the individual, to be at war "in toto," that is, with all their spiritual moral and physicalresources....Practised in their totality, the Quranic dimensions of war provide complete protection to the *Muslim* armies against any psychological breakdown....It is on the strength of our Faith, and the weakness of that of our adversary, that we can initiate plans and actions calculated to strike terror into the hearts of our adversaries.[14] (Emphasis added.)

In his preface to Malik's book Allah Bukhsh K. Brohi, a former diplomat and advocate general of Pakistan, is even more explicit in his defense of Islam and its arguments for *jihād*. After thanking Malik for his "valuable contribution to Islamic jurisprudence" and "'analytic Re-statement' of the Quranic wisdom on the subject of war and peace," Brohi introduces and then unfurls an ingenious new definition of "de-

---

12 Ibid., 44.
13 Ibid., 50.
14 Ibid., 144.

fensive":

> When a believer sees that someone is trying to obstruct another believer from travelling on the road that leads to God, spirit of *Jihād* requires that such a man…be prevented from doing so and the obstacles…be removed, so that mankind may freely be able to negotiate its own path that leads to Heaven. To omit to do this is a culpable omission, if only because we…become passive spectators of the…forces imposing a blockade in the way of those who mean to keep their faith with God. Then ordinary wars which mankind has been fighting for…revenge or securing satisfaction of their desire of getting more land or more booty are not allowed in Islam. This is so because here the rule is, all striving must be for the sake of God….The wars in the theory of Islamic law are in the nature of an undertaking to advance God's purpose on earth, and invariably they are defensive in character.

Now comes Brohi's definition of "defensive":

> It is a duty of a believer to carry forward the Message of God and to bring it to the notice of his fellow-men in handsome ways. But if someone attempts to obstruct him from doing so he is entitled, as a measure of defense, to "retaliate." In other words, a Muslim has the right to fight anyone who stops him for spreading Islam and its message, and that is defined as a defensive measure.[15]

Thus it is a duty for all Muslims to spread the Message of the Quran, of Islam, and anyone who stands in the way must be fought in the military sense, if words do not suffice:

> In Islam war is waged to establish supremacy of the Lord only when every other argument has failed to convince those who reject His Will and work against the very purpose of the creation of mankind. Indeed, the person who goes to holy war virtually is offering testimony regarding the paramountcy and supreme authority of God's law by giving up the most precious thing he has, namely, his life….Indeed the very

---

15 Allah Bukhsh K. Brohi, "Preface," in Malik, *Qur'anic Concept of War*, iii.

word "*Shahīd*" which is roughly taken to mean as a martyr, literally signifies the idea that he has borne testimony as a witness that God's law is supreme and anyone who attempts to obstruct the progress of those who are taking their path to God will be dealt with sternly—for that is the only way in which to restore and rehabilitate the authority of God on Earth.[16]

In other words, do not get in the way of the so-called "suicide bomber," for he is a martyr in the cause of Islam clearing the path for those who want to get to God.

Brohi dismisses those Western critics who believe that Islam is in perpetual struggle with the non-Islamic world by arguing that because man is a slave to God, and defying God is treason under Islamic law, it is a Muslim's duty to remove those who defy God:

> Many Western Scholars have pointed their accusing fingers at some of the...verses in the Qur'an....As to them it is sufficient answer to make...that the defiance of God's authority by one who is His slave exposes that slave to the risk of being held guilty of treason and such a one, in the perspective of Islamic law, is indeed to be treated as a sort of...cancerous growth on that organism of humanity....It thus becomes necessary to remove the cancerous malformation even if it be by surgical means (if it would not respond to other treatment), in order to save the rest of Humanity.[17]

Brigadier Malik makes it clear that *jihād* is essential for the spread of Islam, and it is a duty incumbent on all Muslims until Islam covers the whole surface of the earth. Brohi also underlines another totalitarian aspect of Islam: Islam demands the total surrender of oneself to the cause of Islam, the individual sacrifices himself, and is sacrificed, for the sake of the Islamic community (*umma*).

---

16 Ibid., v.
17 Ibid., vii.

CHAPTER 17
HASAN AL-BANNA AND THE MUSLIM BROTHERHOOD

HASAN AL-BANNA was born in 1906 in Mahmudiyya, a village north of Cairo. His father, a watch repairer, devoted his spare time to religious studies and fulfilled the duties of an imam for the local mosque. Egypt was at the time effectively under British control—a constant source of humiliation for al-Banna and his fellow countrymen. Al-Banna took part in demonstrations against the British when he was thirteen years old.

According to his memoirs, al-Banna took seriously the Islamic principle of Commanding Right and Forbidding Wrong at an early age. For instance, he denounced some workmen who had sculpted a nude wooden figure for the prow of a boat to the local police. Later, he, his brother, and some friends founded the Society for the Prevention of the Forbidden, believing it their religious duty to write to those they felt were not following Islamic teachings in their behavior.

By age thirteen al-Banna was also deeply influenced by the Hasafiyya Brotherhood, a Sufi order and offshoot of the larger Shadhiliyya order whose founder, Shaykh Hasanayn al-Hasafi (1848/9–1910), was an Azhar scholar of the Shafi'i school who took Commanding Right and Forbidding Wrong seriously. Al-Banna made many friends in this *tarīqa* (Sufi order) for example, Ahmad al-Sukkari, who later became a leading figure in the Society of the Muslim Brotherhood.

At seventeen, al-Banna decided to enter Dar al-'Ulum, a teacher-training college in Cairo. For him, teaching was a religious calling; he believed education was the transmission of the truths of Islam, which was all-embracing. Al-Banna saw himself as a *murshid* (religious guide and teacher) and would later demand total loyalty and obedience from his followers. After graduating in 1927, he began teaching in Ismāʻīlīyya, in the Suez Canal Zone, where al-Banna encountered what he felt was Western dominance and Muslims who had shamelessly adopted Western civilization's worst aspects: its secularism and decadence.

He detested the cultural influences of the West over Muslims who were being tempted into abandoning Muslim ethics and the Islamic way of life. Al-Banna founded the Muslim Brotherhood (*Jamʻiyyat al-Ikhwān al-Muslimīn*) in 1928, when a group of laborers pleaded with him to do something about their constant humiliation from foreigners in their own land.

Al-Banna labored tirelessly to build a tight organization with a broad base of members who were enjoined to work for the good of the ordinary Egyptian at all levels, providing schools and medical aid, and ameliorating social conditions in the villages—in effect establishing a social welfare program. The political situation was unstable; though nominally independent since 1922, the real power in Egypt was divided among the Egyptian monarchy, the nationalist Wafd Party, and the British, with conflicts of interest that led to constantly shifting alliances. Corruption was rife. With the advent of World War II and the rise in nationalist agitation, the British tried desperately to maintain control and ensure that Egypt join the Allied cause.

It was at this moment that al-Banna began participating in Egyptian politics at the national level. He wanted to run for public office in 1941, but he was persuaded by the Wafd Party to step aside, in return for the lifting of restrictions on the Muslim Brotherhood. All along al-Banna's main goal had been more than independence from Britain: the installation of a truly Islamic government inspired by the Koran, the *Sunna*, and the *Shariʻa*. He obtained a promise from the Wafd Party to ban alcohol and prostitution as a step in the right direction.

Al-Banna was also unsuccessful in the election of 1945, and henceforth concentrated on agitating for the introduction of Islam into the private and public domain. In doing so he did not hesitate to use increasingly violent means to achieve his goals.

Brotherhood Ideology

At its fifth conference in 1939 the Muslim Brotherhood announced its basic ideology:

1. Islam as a total system, complete unto itself, and the final arbiter of life in all its categories;
2. An Islam formulated from and based on its two primary sources, the Koran as God's revelation, and His *ipsissima verba*, and the perfect example of the Prophet, as found in the *sunna*;
3. An Islam that was universal: applicable to all times and places, for the whole of humanity.[1]

Al-Banna explicitly defined the Muslim Brotherhood as "a Salafiyya message, a Sunni way, a Sufi truth, a political organization, an athletic group, a cultural-educational union, an economic company, and a social idea."[2] The Brotherhood was tightly run: patient planning, organization, program, and action—this alone could guarantee victory.

When in 1943 he thought he was about to be arrested by for nationalist agitation that would have led to the harassment of the British occupation, al-Banna wrote a message to his followers, which reads in part:

> My Brothers: you are not a benevolent society, nor a political party, nor a local organization having limited purposes. Rather, you are a new soul in the heart of this nation to give it life by means of the Qur'an; you are a new light which shines to destroy the darkness of materialism through knowing God; and you are the strong voice which rises to recall the message of the Prophet....You should feel yourselves the bearers of the burden which all others have refused. When asked what it is for which you call, reply that it is Islam, the message of Muhammad, the religion that contains within it government, and has one of its obligations freedom.[3]

In late 1942-early 1943, a new unit developed, called "the special section" (*al-nizam al-khass*) by Muslim Brotherhood insiders and "the secret apparatus" (*al-jihaz al-sirri*) by outsiders. The Brotherhood was not averse to using violence to achieve its aims, and was "were more effectively violent than other groups" since members had been taught that

---

[1] "Al-Mu'tamar al-Khāmis," quoted in Richard P. Mitchell, *The Society of Muslim Brothers* (1969; Oxford: Oxford University Press, 1993), 14.

[2] Ibid.

[3] Quoted in Mitchell, *Society of Muslim Brothers*, 30.

militancy and martyrdom were Islamic virtues as found in the notion of *jihād*. As al-Banna wrote,

> *Jihād* is an obligation from Allah on every Muslim and cannot be ignored nor evaded. Allah has ascribed great importance to *jihād* and has made the reward of the martyrs and the fighters in His way a splendid one. Only those who have acted similarly and who have modelled themselves upon the martyrs in their performance of *jihād* can join them in this reward. Furthermore, Allah has specifically honoured the *Mujahideen* with certain exceptional qualities, both spiritual and practical, to benefit them in this world and the next. Their pure blood is a symbol of victory in this world and the mark of success and felicity in the world to come.
>
> Those who can only find excuses, however, have been warned of extremely dreadful punishments and Allah...has reprimanded them for their cowardice and lack of spirit, and castigated them for their weakness and truancy....The weaknesses of abstention and evasion of *jihād* are regarded by Allah as...one of the seven sins that guarantee failure.
>
> Islam is concerned with the question of *jihād* and the drafting and the mobilisation of the entire *Umma* into one body to defend the right cause with all its strength....The verses of the Qur'an and the *Sunnah* of Muhammad (PBUH) are overflowing with all these noble ideals and they summon people in general (with the most eloquent expression and the clearest exposition) to *jihād*, to warfare, to the armed forces, and all means of land and sea fighting.[4]

Al-Banna goes onto quote verses from the Koran exhorting Muslims to *jihād*,[5] and *hadīth* from the six canonical collections of of Sunni Islam, followed by scholars from the various law schools.

Al-Banna rules out the pacific interpretation of *jihād* as an internal struggle against one's lower instincts. For him, that particular *hadīth* is inauthentic, not in the canonical collection, but "even if it were a sound

---

4 *Complete Works of Hasan al-Banna*, vol. 10, "al-Jihad.," 4.
5 Verses cited: *suras* 2:216; 3:156–58, 169–70; 4:74; 8:60, 65; 9:14–15, 29, 41, 81–83, 88–89, 111; 47:20–21; 48:18–19; 61: 4.

tradition, it would never warrant abandoning *jihād* or preparing for it in order to rescue the territories of the Muslims and repel the attacks of the disbelievers."[6]

While emphasizing the principle of Commading Right and Forbidding Wrong, he states, "It is said in the *hadīth*: 'One of the greatest forms of *jihād* is to utter a word of truth in the presence of a tyrannical ruler.' But nothing compares to the honour of *shahadah kubra* (the supreme martyrdom) or the reward that is waiting for the *Mujahideen*."[7] Muslims should therefore seek an honorable death:

> My brothers! The *ummah* that knows how to die a noble and honourable death is granted an exalted life in this world and eternal felicity in the next. Degradation and dishonour are the results of the love of this world and the fear of death. Therefore prepare for *jihād* and be the lovers of death....
>
> ...[O]ne day you will face death and this ominous event can only occur once. If you suffer on this occasion in the way of Allah, it will be to your benefit in this world and your reward in the next. And remember brother that nothing can happen without the Will of Allah....
>
> You should yearn for an honourable death and you will gain perfect happiness. May Allah grant myself and yours the honour of martyrdom in His way![8]

Violence Necessary

The Muslim Brotherhood came to believe that only in the period of the four orthodox caliphs (*al-khulafā' ar-Rāshidūn*) was the state "truly representative of Islam as a faith and a system"; thereafter the Islamic community began its decline and disintegration.[9] Al-Banna was totally disillusioned with al-Azhar, which the Brothers later took to task for failing to speak for a dynamic Islam and keep foreign influences at bay, and ultimately held responsible for the decline in Egypt's religious and cultural life.[10] Their ultimate goal was the creation of an Islamic order:

---

6 *Complete Works of Hasan al-Banna*, vol. 10, "*al-Jihad*," 20.
7 Ibid.
8 Ibid.
9 Mitchell, *Society of Muslim Brothers*, 210.
10 Ibid., 212.

a state run according to the *Shari'a*, derived from the Koran, the *Sunna*, and *hadīth*. There was no danger of theocratic tyranny, the Brothers argued, since there is no religious class in Islam.

The Muslim Brotherhood held that women are equal to men in the eyes of Islam, and any discrimination that exists (in inheritance, legal hearings, prayer) is a function of the greater responsibility of men, and due to the differences in mental and emotional capacities of men and women.

Violence was necessary to operations. It was seen as a way to defend the Brotherhood's ideas, derived, as discussed, from the Islamic concept of *jihād* in the military sense. The Brothers were "an Islamic army for the protection of the message," the late Richard P. Mitchell explains in his classic work, *The Society of the Muslim Brothers* (1969).[11] Though there were political elements in their acts of violence, the religious dimension, Mitchel believed, had a wider significance: "[O]ut of the fact of power in being, and in use in defence of 'eternal' goals, emerged a self-righteous and intolerant arrogance which opened an unbridgeable gap between the Society and its fellow citizens."[12]

Al-Banna and the Brothers created a sense of group and religious exclusiveness in which political opponents became the objects of violence. Though al-Banna was perhaps more moderate on the issue of commanding right and forbidding wrong, the Brothers generally took a more aggressive line. While this brutality was not unique to the Brothers, their apporach contained an Islamic dimension that led to all kinds of political and social violence and further intolerance.[13] For example, the Brotherhood was responsible for the assassination of Prime Minister Ahmad Mahar in February 1945 just after he had read Egypt's declaration of war on the Axis (the Brotherhood was pro-Nazi; al-Banna received regular subsidies from Hitler). Government minister Amin Uthman was murdered in January 1946, British soldiers were attacked regularly from 1946 onward, and in March 1948, "a respected judge was murdered by two members of the secret apparatus":

> Two more attempts were made on sometime Prime Minister Nahhas Pasha [1879–1965]. In June, houses were blown up in the Jewish quarter of Cairo, two large Jewish-owned department store were bombed. Cinemas were dynamited, and

---

11 Ibid., 319.
12 Ibid.
13 Ibid., 320.

hotels and restaurants catering to the "infidels and the heretics" were set on fire. Women wearing "inadequate dress" were the victims of knife attacks, and homes said to belong to apostates were raided and ransacked by angry believers gathering for "spontaneous demonstrations." In December, widespread riots brought the university to a stop. The Cairo police chief was killed by a bomb. Dozens of of other officials, businessmen, and intellectuals were likewise killed. Prime Minister Nuqrashi Pasha [1888–1948, the second prime minister of Egypt] finally ordered the society dissolved—he was gunned down twenty days later. As al-Banna had said, "The dagger, poison, the revolver....These are the weapons of Islam against its enemies."[14]

On January 25, 1952, British forces attempted to disarm some of the auxiliary police by attacking the Ismāʿīlīyya police headquarters; more than forty people were killed in the ensuing battle. Mitchell describes the following day:

> [T]he heart of modern and westernized Cairo was left a charred ruin in the wake of the most devastating riot in modern Egyptian history. In the early morning members of the auxiliary police in Cairo marched across the bridges to the university in Giza and with students and soldiers collected along the way, returned to the parliament where demands were voiced for an immediate declaration of war on Britain. At the same time other groups, well-organized and well-equipped, began the systematic burning of the centre of the city. The fire consumed department stores, cinemas, bars, nightclubs, social clubs, luxury food and clothing establishments, novelty shops, automobile showrooms and garages, airline offices, and the like.[15]

This was actually a well-planned operation organized by the Brotherhood.

The Brotherhood and the Totalitarian Core of Islam

The Egyptian government accused the Muslim Brotherhood of be-

---
14 Murawiec, *Mind of Jihad*, 34–35.
15 Mitchell, *Society of Muslim Brothers*, 92.

ing Khawarij—the Khārijite movement was often evoked as a model. In *al-Mabāhith* (May 1950–January 1951), a weekly news magazine edited by Muslim Brotherhood acting head Salih 'Ashmawi, he actually praised the "rectitude" of the Khārijites and their spirit of "struggle in the path of God."[16] And "in that sweep of developments in the Arab world beginning with movement of the Wahhābiyya in the late eighteenth century," Mitchell observes, "the Society of the Brothers emerges as the first mass-supported and organized, esentially urban-oriented effort to cope with the plight of Islam in the modern world. This fact complicates the attempt to trace its geneology, but does not osbscure the general harmony of its aims with those of earlier reform movements."[17]

And while they admired earlier reformers such as Jamal al-Din al-Afghani (d. 1897), Muhammad 'Abduh (d. 1905), and Rashid Rida (d. 1935), the Brothers felt that their reforms were inadequate because they failed to see Islam in the totality.[18] While al-Banna's father had been a student of Abduh, and he himself an avid reader of Rida's *al-Manar*, he remained critical of these reformers, who he felt lacked the Brothers' comprehensive view:

> We believe the provisions of Islam and its teachings are all inclusive, encompassing the affairs of the people in this world and the hearafter. And those who think that these teachings are concerned only with the spiritual or ritualistic aspects are mistaken in this belief because Islam is a faith and a ritual, a nation (*watan*) and a nationality, a religion and a state, spirit and deed, holy text and sword….The Glorious Qur'an…considers [these things] to be the core of Islam and its essence.[19]

To preserve a vital Islamic tradition the Brothers urged all Muslims to relate to their own heritage, but al-Banna bequeathed the Brotherhood a rigidity and puritanism that rendered its followers impatient of all dissent—or as Mitchell put it, "Profoundly genuine though it was, the call to return to Islam and its code of behaviour was nevertheless vitiated by a sterility born of obedience to inherited forms and a self-righteousness born of sanctimonious claims to omniscience."[20]

---

16 Ibid., 320n63.
17 Ibid., 321.
18 Ibid.
19 Ibid., 232-23.
20 Ibid., 325.

As discussed, there was a marked preference among the Brothers for action: "Our message means *jihād*, struggle and work…it is not a philosophical message."[21] They talked of "programme" versus "ideology," and Mitchell's harsh judgment on the Brothers' anti-intellectualism is important: "[T]his outlook reflected a modern and mass expression of classical Islamic thought patterns. Al-Banna was steeped in both the theological and Sufi traditions, and from both he absorbed, and in his teachings demonstrated, the non-rationalist, even non-intellectaulist quality which has been observed to be an aspect of Muslim thought." Significantly, "neither Banna nor the movement produced any work remotely identifiable as theology or philosophy."[22]

In his unjustly neglected *The Politics of Social Change in the Middle East and North Africa* (1963), the late Princeton professor of politics Manfred Halpern does not hesitate to name the Muslim Brotherhood, Mawdūdī's *Jamaʿat –i-Islam*, and the Khaksar Movement responsible for the assassination of Pakistani Liaqat Ali Khan in 1951, or to label several others groups in the Islamic world as neo-Islamic totalitarian and fascist.[23] The totalitarian nature of such groups and movements becomes clear when contrasted with extreme nationalism, because the latter limits itself geographically, while the neo-Islamic variety has universal ambitions where Islam is the defining element.

For Sa'id Ramadan, who was the son-in-law of al-Banna and a leader of the Muslim Brotherhood, nations have became idols—"[M]y religion is dearer to me than my family and clan. My religion is the first country that I take shelter in"[24]—therefore all nations that were once Muslim must return to Islamic sovereignty. According to *The Call of the Moslem Brotherhood*:

> the Moslem faith makes it the clear duty of every strong Moslem whose soul has drenched in the doctrines of the Koran to consider himself the protector of every other Moslem whose soul has also been drenched in …in Islam. The doctrine is everything. And is faith anything other than love and hate? Hereafter, we want the banner of Allah to fly high once more in those regions which were once happy in Islam….But ill

---

21 Ibid., 326.
22 Ibid., 326-27.
23 Manfred Halpern, *The Politics of Social Change in the Middle East and North Africa* (Princeton, NJ: Princeton University Press, 1963), 134, 135.
24 Ibid., 135.

luck deprived them of the light....Anadalusia, Sicily, the Balkans, the Greek Islands—all these are Moslem colonies which must come back into the Moslem fold. The Mediterranean and the Red Sea must be two Muslim lakes, as they were before.... Following that, we would want to issue our call to the world, and subdue every powerful man to it completely, that there may be no confusion, and that all religions may be Allah's.[25]

The neo-Islamic totalitarian movements are fascist, Halpern explains, because "they concentrate on mobilizing passion and violence to enlarge the power of their charismatic leader and the solidarity of the movement. They view material progress primarily as a means for accumulating strength for political expansion, and entirely deny individual and social freedom." And while they "champion...a heroic past," these movements "repress all free critical analysis of either past roots or present problems."[26]

Referring to the work of the late British historian Norman Cohn,[27] Halpern was the first to point out the similarities between these Middle Eastern fascist movements and certain religiopolitical movements in Western Europe at the beginning of the Modern Age, when groups adopted a militant social chiliasm (the doctrine that at some future time Christ will reign bodily upon the earth for 1000 years).[28] This was a theme taken up more recently by the French neoconservative Laurent Murawiec.[29]

Neo-totalitarian movements urge the individual to merge his destiny with the group struggling to resurrect the past. The movement then becomes the whole life of its members. Unable to cope with modernity, neo-Islamic totalitarianism pursues its vision "through nihilistic terror, cunning, and passion."[30] The leadership demands absolute obedience, and as members lose their individuality they identify with the leader, "whose power, emotion, and style of living pantomime the yearning of

---

25 *The Call of the Moslem Brotherhood*, Cairo, October 1938; quoted in Halpern, *Politics of Social Change*, 147–48.
26 Halpern, *Politics of Social Change*, 135–36.
27 Norman Cohn, *The Pursuit of the Millennium: Revolutionary Millenarians and Mystical Anarchists of the Middle Ages* (London: Secker & Warburg, 1957).
28 Halpern, *Politics of Social Change*, 136.
29 Murawiec, *Mind of Jihad*.
30 Halpern, *Politics of Social Change*, 140.

his followers," thereby stimulating "an intoxicating sense of nihilism in which the willingess to sacrifice one's self becomes more important than the object for which the sacrifice is made. Those who are sent to death as robots have the illusion of dying as martyrs."[31] At meetings, religious slogans are chanted over and over:

> God is our goal!
> The Prophet is our leader!
> The Koran is our constitution!
> Holy War is our path!
> Death in God's service is our loftiest hope!
> God is greatest, God is greatest!

Dangerous in their exclusivism, intolerance, and sacrifice of the individual, unable to answer difficult questions or brook opposition, these neo-Islamic totalitarian movements can only resort to violence.

---

31 Ibid., 142.

CHAPTER 18
Grand Mufti Haj Amin al-Husaini and the Nazis

I N *NAZIS, ISLAMISTS, and the Making of the Modern Middle East* (2014), Barry Rubin and Wolfgang Schwanitz cogently argue that the Grand Mufti Haj Amin al-Husaini (also "el-Husseini," 1895–1974) was an important figure in the founding of modern Arab and Islamist politics who "played a central role in the Islamist movement's survival during the 1950s and 1960s," making it possible for "the movement's revival in the 1970s to gain hegemony in Iran, Turkey, and much of the Arabic-speaking world and Iran by the early twenty-first century."[1] This alone warrants al-Husaini's inclusion in this study, but his collaboration with the Nazis, which has been misinterpreted by some recent scholars such as Matthias Küntzel,[2] must also be taken into consideration.

Historians like Küntzel claim that modern Islamic antisemitism was derived entirely from the Nazis. But as Rubin and Schwanitz repeatedly emphasize, al-Husaini and later Islamists such as al-Banna, Sayyd Qutb, and the Ayatollah Khomeini all drew on their own backgrounds, traditions, and doctrines to spread their antisemitism. Al-Husaini advocated

genocide even before the Nazi government did so. His 1937

---

1 Barry Rubin and Wolfgang G. Schwanitz, *Nazis, Islamists, and the Making of the Modern Middle East* (New Haven, CT: Yale University Press, 2014), 87.

2 Matthias Küntzel, *Jihad and Jew-Hatred: Islamism, Nazism and the Roots of 9/11* (New York: Telos Press Publishing, 2009).

Appeal to All Muslims of the World urged them to cleanse their lands of the Jews, and it was translated into German in 1938. Urging the use of force against all Jews in the Middle East, al-Husaini both gave his parallel version of Hitler's doctrine and laid the foundation for the antisemitic arguments used by radical Arab nationalists and Islamist down to this day. A half-century later, every speech and sermon from Hamas, Hizballah, Iran's regime, the Muslim Brotherhood, and al-Qaeda echoed all of the grand mufti's main points in his declaration.³

In his analysis, Rubin and Schwanitz explain, al-Husaini "combined traditional Islamic hatred of Jews with arguments framed by modern political concepts."⁴ He quoted constantly from the Koran, *Sira*, and *hadīth* to lay out his claims: Jews are cursed and evil; they were expelled from Egypt because they exploited the Egyptian people; (citing al-Tabarī) they tried to kill Moses; they were punished by God for their sins; they spread disease; they hated, tried to discredit, and, finally, tried to poison Muhammad; they are out to destroy Islam. The Grand Mufti's diatribe ends thus:

> I present to my Muslim brothers in the entire world the history and the true experience which the Jews cannot deny. The verses from the Koran and hadith prove that the Jews have been the bitterest enemies of Islam and continue to try to destroy it. Do not believe them. They know only hypocrisy and guile. Hold together, fight for Islamic thought, fight for your religion and your existence! Do not rest until your land is free of the Jews. Do not tolerate the plan of division, for Palestine has been an Arab land for centuries and shall remain Arab.⁵

Rubin and Schwanitz conclude: "It is wrong to see al-Husaini and his fellow radicals as merely importing European antisemitism or being influenced by the Nazis. The two groups' ideas developed in parallel from their own histories and political cultures....The two sides came together

---

3 Rubin and Schwanitz, *Nazis, Islamists*, 94–95.

4 Ibid., 95.

5 Andrew G. Bostom, *The Mufti's Islamic Jew-Hatred: What Nazis Learned from the 'Muslin Pope'* (Washington, DC: Barvura Books, 2013), 25–33.

on the basis of both common interests and similar worldviews."[6]

In an October 1944 speech to the imams of the Bosnian SS Division fighting for the Nazis, al-Husaini stated: "Nearly one-third of the Koran concerns the Jews. The Koran calls upon all Muslims to protect themselves against the Jews and to fight them wherever they may meet."[7]

Al-Husaini, Islam, and Violence

On the whole, al-Husaini's role as the father of modern, violent Arab radical movements has been overlooked because he allied himself with the Nazis and the losing side in World War II, and was implicated in the humiliating defeat of the Arabs by the Israelis in 1948. He was too closely identified with the Palestinian cause, when he was actually the leader of the international radical Arab forces, both Islamist and nationalist. When the nationalists gained power, al-Husaini's earlier part in keeping the two factions together was again forgotten. And, as noted above, al-Husaini was responsible for fundamentalism Islam's survival in the 1950s and 1960s and its 1970s revival.[8]

Muslims from many Muslim countries recognized al-Husaini's leadership and came to pay their respects in Jerusalem, his personal base. He was in close contact with the Muslim Brotherhood through Muhammad Mustafa al-Maraghi. In 1931, al-Husaini organized the General Islamic Congress in Jerusalem, which resulted in the formation of the Islamic World Congress and his election as president. Several international branches contributed funds to the head office in Jerusalem.

At first, al-Husaini concentrated in building a strong united state that would be nationalist and Islamist, and playing both cards, garnered mass support from a religiously oriented public that was not ready to accept secular nationalism. He also persuaded the Nazis that he was leader of the world's Muslims and Arabs. Al-Husaini's and the radical faction's most significant tactic at this stage "was to make militancy the test for legitimacy. The most extreme stance became the legitimate mainstream one; anything more moderate was portrayed as treason to Islam and the Arab people. Using this standard, al-Husaini and his allies could blackmail and intimidate Arab governments, threatening to discredit or even assassinate anyone who wanted to compromise with the West or to oppose their goals."[9]

---

6 Rubin and Schwanitz, *Nazis, Islamists*, 95.
7 Quoted in Bostom, *Mufti's Islamic Jew-Hatred*, 19.
8 Rubin and Schwanitz, *Nazis, Islamists*, 87.
9 Ibid., 89.

Al-Husaini was also able to impose his will on how the Palestinian cause would be handled. He and his allies were now in a position to influence and galvanize the masses through sermons at mosques, rousing speeches, "intimidating mobs, and demonstrations."[10] Al-Husaini also demonized the British and Americans, presenting them as enemies of Islam and simultaneously convincing his followers that Germany would soon rule the world. The result was an alliance of Palestinian Arabs, Syrian and Iraqi nationalists, and Egyptian Islamists with Hitler's regime.

Whereas the earlier German-Ottoman bond "had been built on defending the status quo in the Ottoman Empire while destroying their rivals' colonies, [t]he new Nazi-Arab nationalist and Islamist alliance... sought revolutionary political and social change everywhere in the Middle East."[11] The radicals, with their intransigence and violence, were obviously at odds with the moderate politicians and leaders who doubted that a hardline approach could succeed, but al-Husaini believed he could win because Allah was on the side of the Muslims. This indicates how al-Husaini's influential tactics would determine the future of the Middle East: "The basic approach of al-Husaini and his comrades continued through the careers of such leaders as Abd an-Nasir, Arafat, the al-Assad family, al-Qaddafi, Saddam Hussein, and bin Ladin, as well as with Iranian Islamists like Khomeini and Mahmud Ahmadinejad."[12]

Al-Husaini laid down the halt to the exodus of Jews from Germany as a condition for his support for Hitler, and bargained in the same way with the Allies—any migration from Germany would mean the migration to Palestine. The British had to close all migration of Jews to Palestine as well in order to keep the ambiguous support of the Grand Mufti and the Arabs. Al-Husaini, thus, can be justly held accountable for his role in the Holocaust.

Nazi Germany launched a well-organized campaign in the Middle East, urging the elite in the respective countries to embrace pro-Nazi, antisemitic sentiments. "In Beirut and Baghdad, Cairo and Jerusalem, Kabul and Tehran, Tripoli and Tunis, local Nazi Party branches coordinated military and SS intelligence, businessmen, and academics to spread the influence of Hitler's regime. There were also Nazi Party branches in Alexandria and Port Said; Haifa and Jaffa; and Adana, Ankara, Istanbul, and Izmir."[13] It was Nazi policy to subsidize and use ideo-

---

10 Ibid., 90.
11 Ibid., 91.
12 Ibid., 92.
13 Ibid., 110.

logically compatible Islamist and nationalist groups such the Muslim Brotherhood, the fascist Young Egypt Party, al-Husaini's forces in Palestine, and various other groups in Iraq and Syria.

In Iran one of the students to benefi from German training was Nawab Safavi, who later became the main radical Islamist leader and al-Husaini's closest ally. But it was in Iraq that Germany held the greatest influence, since the Iraqi nationalists were hoping for help to develop their economy. Acting for the Abwehr, German military intelligence, al-Banna received about one thousand Egyptian pounds a month from 1939, and perhaps earlier, from the German News Bureau in Cairo.[14]

In June 1940, when the war seemed to be going Germany's way, al-Husaini wrote to Franz von Papen, the German ambassador to Turkey, offering him his support. Unlike the nationalists, al-Husaini dreamed of an Islamic caliphate with himself as the caliph ruling over the Islamic *umma*. His short-term goal was the creation of a fully independent state comprising Syria, Lebanon, Palestine, Jordan, and Iraq, which he would lead. Having already created a popular network throughout the Arabic-speaking world and Muslim countries further East, al-Husaini had managed to unite, for the moment, the nationalists and Islamists.[15]

By March 1941 Hitler accepted al-Husaini as the *de facto* leader of the Muslims of the entire Middle East, and accordingly gave his total support to the Grand Mufti, praising the Arabs as an ancient civilization. The Germans gave al-Husaini a hundred thousand reichsmarks,[16] with twenty thousand more every month paid equally by Germany and Italy.[17]

Pro-German forces were now on the rise in the Middle East. Ba'th, a Pan-Arab nationalist party closely based on the fascist model, had been founded in November 1940, Alfred Rosenberg's antisemitic 1930 work on racial theory, *The Myth of the Twentieth Century* (*Der Mythus des 20. Jahrhunderts*), having influenced the party's founders.

As Rubin and Schwanitz point out, for both Hitler and al-Husaini the Jews were the arch-villains responsible for the sorry state of their respective countries and civilizations:

For Islamists, hostility to Jews and other infidels was root-

---

14 Ibid., 118.
15 Ibid., 119.
16 In 1930s, one reichsmark was worth $4.20, so 100,000 reichsmarks would have been worth $420,000.00.
17 Ibid., 127.

ed in their reading of Muslim texts but they identified the modern turning point [in their recent decline] as the 1924 decision to abolish the caliphate. Ignoring the fact that this system had not functioned for centuries, al-Husaini argued that to dissolve Islam's unique global bond was suicidal, especially given its clash with Anglo-American democracies and their "Jewish advocates."....

...So while Hitler and the Nazis blamed the Jews for the fate of Germans and "Aryans" generally, al-Husaini and the radical nationalists and Islamists did the same thing regarding the fate of Arabs and Muslims. They did not need the Nazis to teach them this idea. They had already invented stories using elements from their own religious, cultural, and historical traditions.[18]

Al-Husaini asked Hitler's help in destroying the Jews in Palestine, and beseeched him to stop Jews from leaving Germany. Hitler had allowed 537,000 Jews to leave Germany between 1933 and 1941, but with al-Husaini's antisemitic rhetoric and his insistence on eliminating Jews "fresh in his ears," Hitler made the decision to prepare the "final solution of the Jewish question."[19]

A True Radical Muslim Hero

After the war, al-Husaini escaped prosecution as a war criminal because Western powers calculated that such prosecution would harm their geopolitical standing in the Middle East. The Muslim Brotherhood, and the rest of the Muslim world, considered al-Husaini a true Muslim hero because of his past radicalism. Al-Banna wrote:

> Great welcome should be extended to him wherever he goes, as a sign of appreciation for his great services for the glory of Islam and the Arabs....What a hero, what a miracle of a man. We wish to know what the Arab youth, cabinet ministers, rich men, and princes of Palestine, Syria, Iraq, Tunis, Morocco, and Tripoli are going to do to be worthy of this hero. Yes, this hero who challenged an empire and fought Zionism, with the help of Hitler and Germany. Germany and Hitler are

---

18 Ibid., 158, 159.
19 Ibid., 162.

gone, but Amin al-Husaini will continue the struggle.[20]

After returning to Egypt, al-Husaini continued his struggles in the name of Islam with Arabs who had been Nazi collaborators and now served as his military commanders, men such as al-Qawuqji, 'Abd al-Qadir al-Husaini, and Salama. In 1939 the Nazis had sent the Arabs some arms that were hidden in the Egyptian desert. These were recovered by al-Husaini with the help of the Muslim Brotherhood, and used to drill the Holy Jihad Troops (*al-Jihad al-Muqaddas*), organized by Abd al-Qadir, who had fought in Iraq as a pro-Nazi, in a secret training camp near the Libyan border.

Al-Qadir was killed leading al-Husaini's main army in the Palestine War in 1948, but al-Husaini continued to intimidate Arab leaders to accept his uncompromising position: "Like al-Husaini and his own movement, most of the other forces pushing for intransigence and war over the Palestine issue also came from the same radical Arab and Islamist faction that had cooperated with the Nazis: the Muslim Brotherhood in Egypt and Syria as well as militant nationalists and Islamists in Syria and Iraq."[21]

After the Arab's disastrous defeat by newly-created Israel in 1948, al-Husaini devoted the next twenty-five years to promoting radical Islamism in order to take revenge not only on the West and Israel, but also the Arab nationalists. He kept the movement alive, though savagely repressed by its former radical nationalist partners, looking to create a worldwide radical Islamist movement—a goal that today no longer seems impossible. Al-Husaini began by founding the League of Jihad Call in Cairo in 1951, which reestablished his ties with the Muslim Brotherhood and the fascist Young Egypt Party.

Consolidating Efforts

Al-Husaini was undoubtedly behind the assassinations of moderate leaders from Jordan and Lebanon who wanted to establish some sort of peace with Israel. He also helped former German Nazis, some of whom he managed to convert to Islam, to obtain new identities and jobs in the Middle East. (It is forgotten that nearly four thousand Germans involved in war crimes escaped to the Middle East, finding welcome and work. The number of German war criminals who escaped to South America was considerably smaller: between 180 and 800.)

---

20 Quoted in ibid., 199.
21 Ibid., 201.

Al-Husaini maintained his contacts in Pakistan, where he organized annual meetings of his Islamic World Congress from 1949 to 1952. In Iran he consolidated his standing with Islamists such as Nawab Safavi, the ex-Nazi agent. At the 1953 Islamic World Congress in east Jerusalem, al-Husaini met and encouraged the Iranians 'Abd al-Qasim al-Khasani, the leading Islamic cleric, and Safavi, the leader of the radical Islamist group, *Fidaiyyun al-Islam*. He reestablished his friendship with the Egyptian Said Ramadan, who worked with al-Husaini and the Muslim Brotherhood. Also present was Sayyid Qutb, the Brotherhood's leading ideologue who would become the godfather of modern Islamist ideology.

Despite a short-term decline of the Islamist groups due to Safavi's execution, Kashani's withdrawal from politics, and Qutb's eventual imprisonment and execution, it was clear that al-Husaini had planted the seeds of revolution and violence, for "one of al-Kashani's disciples was Khoemini; Safavi's example inspired revolutionary terrorist Islamist groups in Iran.... The Muslim Brotherhood, its many even more radical spin-offs, and indeed all the revolutionary Islamist groups of the late twentieth and early twenty-first centuries owe a big debt to al-Husaini's and Qutb's innovative thinking."[22]

Just as the Muslim Brotherhood was about to takeover in Egypt in 2011, Tariq Ramadan, the highly regarded Islamist intellectual living and teaching in the West, wrote an op-ed in the *New York Times* claiming that the Muslim Brotherhood and its leader, his grandfather, had never been Nazi collaborators. He even insisted that the Brotherhood was an antifascist organization that had wished to emulate "the British parliamentary model" during the 1930s and 1940s. But Rubin and Schwanitz have carefully demonstrated otherwise:

> [T]he Brotherhood was clearly well financed and armed by the Nazis before and during the World War II. Collaborating with the Germans and al-Husaini, it planned an uprising to support the German army's conquest of Egypt as well as to kill Cairo's Jews and Christians. The only reason this plot failed was that the British stopped the German advance and forced King Faruq to replace pro-German politicians in the government. One aspect of the Brotherhood's campaign to portray itself as moderate in the early twenty-first century

---

22 Ibid., 206.

was to rewrite its history.[23]

The cooperation of Said Ramadan, who, it has been mentioned was Hasan al-Banna's son-in-law and Tariq Ramadan's father, with al-Husaini was noted by the CIA in 1953. Ramadan acted as al-Husaini's agent, running messages to Iran's al-Kashani. Later, Al-Husaini "selected Said Ramadan as his successor to lead the European-based Islamist movement."[24] He was al-Husaini's protégé, and would eventually inherit the ex-grand mufti's "Islamist network, financial base, and institutional assets in Switzerland and elsewhere."[25] Al-Husaini made him a member of the secretariat of the World Muslim Congress, and two years later its secretary general. Ramadan moved to Syria, where he continued working for al-Husaini and the Brotherhood. Al-Husaini helped finance his magazine, *al-Muslimin*, a vehicle for the ideas of the Syrian Muslim Brotherhood.

When the Arab nationalist regimes began repressing the Islamists, the latter retreated to Europe, where they began a relentless campaign of Islamic propaganda, building mosques, founding Islamic institutes, and taking control of Muslim associations and journals. Said Ramadan's decades of activity and energy saw to it that by the year 2000 many Islamic communities were led by Brotherhood members. Ramadan's primary concern was to keep control of the Munich mosque built by Syrian-born Ali Ghalib Himmat and an Uzbek, Nur ad-Din Namanjani. When Himmat took over in 1973, Ramadan was able to found the Islamic Center in Geneva with funds from Saudi Arabia. A similar center appeared in London, but the Munich center remained the most important to Islamism and the Brotherhood in West Germany.[26]

The ideological parallels between the Nazis and the Muslim Brotherhood, and in fact all Islamist movements, are striking, and compounded by the Brotherhood's collaboration with the Nazis. A comparison of statements and declarations by key Islamist ideologues reveals their resemblence to one another, and to those of al-Husaini. For example, Sayyid Qutb wrote:

> The Jews did indeed return to evil-doing, so Allah gave to the Muslims power over them. The Muslims then expelled them

---

23 Ibid., 234.
24 Ibid., 233.
25 Ibid., 248.
26 Ibid., 249.

from the whole of the Arabian Peninsula....Then the Jews again returned to evil-doing and consequently Allah sent against them others of his servants, until the modern period. Then Allah brought Hitler to rule over them. And once again today the Jews have returned to evil-doing, in the form of "Israel" which made the Arabs, the owners of the land, taste of sorrows and woe.[27]

For many Islamists, the Holocaust enjoyed divine sanction.

---

27 Ronald L. Nettler, *Past Trials and Present Tribulations: A Muslim Fundamentalist's View of the Jews* (Oxford: Pergamon Press, 1987), 86–87; quoted in Rubin and Schwanitz, *Nazis, Islamists*, 251.

CHAPTER 19

SAYYID QUTB

SAYYID QUTB (1906–1966) was a prominent thinker who is seen as the primary influence on many contemporary Islamic terrorists. He wrote extensively on what he believed was the cause of the present malaise in Islamic societies, and offered a reasoned solution to restore the glory of Islam. He had contempt for the West and it "decadent" values, and hated democracy, which he regarded as a tyranny of man-made laws.

Qutb was born in Middle Egypt in 1906, went to local schools, and got involved in his father's anti-British Egyptian nationalist political activities at a young age. His family moved to Cairo, where he went to a teacher's college and eventually obtained a B.A. in education. Qutb worked for the Ministry of Public Instruction, serving as a ministry inspector between 1940 and 1948. Qutb had developed a love for literature, particularly poetry, and considered himself a man of letters. He wrote novels and short stories, but after 1945 Qutb's writings dwelt more on political matters. In 1948 he was sent to the United States to study the American system of education, and earned an M.A. in education from the Teachers College at the University of Northern Colorado. He also spent time in New York, San Francisco, and other cities.

Qutb wrote about his stay in Greeley, Colorado, by all accounts, "a very conservative town, where alcohol was illegal," according to Robert Seigel, senior host of NPR's *All Things Considered*. "It was a planned community, founded by Utopian idealists looking to make a garden out of the dry plains north of Denver using irrigation. The founding fathers of Greeley were by all reports temperate, religious and peaceful people."[1]

At a gentle church dance, Qutb was appalled by what he saw as sexual promiscuity and the mingling of the sexes, which disgusted his reawakened Islamic sensibilities:

> The American girl is well acquainted with her body's seductive capacity. She knows it lies in the face, and in expressive eyes, and thirsty lips. She knows seductiveness lies in the round breasts, the full buttocks, and in the shapely thighs, sleek legs—and she shows all this and does not hide it.[2]

The whole scene's immorality was compounded by the pastor of the church dimming the lights!

Qutb also complains of the racism he encountered, and yet he is able to write racist diatribes against "jazz" such as the following: "This is that music that the Negroes invented to satisfy their primitive inclinations, as well as their desire to be noisy on the one hand and to excite bestial tendencies on the other."[3]

Qutb is often said to have a profound knowledge of history, and yet he mangles American history. "He informed his Arab readers that it began with bloody wars against the Indians, which he claimed were still underway in 1949," Siegel reports, and wrote that before independence, American colonists pushed Latinos south toward Central America—even though the American colonists themselves had not yet pushed west of the Mississippi... Then came the Revolution, which he called 'a destructive war led by George Washington.'"[4]

On his return to Egypt in 1951, Qutb began frequenting the meetings of the Muslim Brotherhood, which he joined.[5] He and many other

---

[1] Robert Siegel, "Sayyid Qutb's America: Al Qaeda Inspiration Denounced U.S. Greed, Sexuality" May 6, 2003, *All Things Considered*, NPR, http://www.npr.org/templates/story/story.php?storyId=1253796.

[2] Quoted in Robin Wright, *Dreams and Shadows: The Future of the Middle East* (New York: Penguin Press, 2008), 107. Wright is quoting Qutb's essay, "The America I Have Seen: In the Scale of Human Values," 1951, available at https://archive.org/stream/SayyidQutb/The%20America%20I%20have%20seen_djvu.txt.

[3] Quoted in James A. Nolan Jr., *What They Saw in America* (Cambridge and New York: Cambridge University Press, 2016), 196.

[4] Siegel, "Sayyid Qutb's America."

[5] Albert J. Bergesen, "Sayyid Qutb in Historical Context," in *The Sayyid Qutb Reader: Selected Writings on Politics, Religion, and Society*, ed. Albert J. Bergesen (London: Routledge, 2008), 3.

members opposed the ongoing presence of the British in Egypt, and thus at first were enthusiastic about the 1952 coup that brought Gamal 'Abd al-Nasser to power and put an end to colonialism. But Nasser was essentially secular; he certainly did not envisage an Islamic state for Egypt. In fact, he began arresting the leaders of the Brothers, and Qutb was imprisoned and tortured several times, suffering three heart attacks as a result.

In 1964, Qutb was arrested for the third and last time, just after the publication of his book, *Ma 'alim fi'l-tariq* (*Signposts Along the Road*). Accused of participating in a conspiracy against government, his book was used as evidence against him. Qutb was sentenced to death in 1966 and hanged soon after the verdict.

Core Ideas

Like all Salafists, Qutb believed that the Koran, the *Sunna*, and the society established by the Prophet and the Companions in seventh-century Arabia provided adequate guidance on how to bring about an Islamic polity. Religion and politics were inexorably connected. The ideal Islamic society and political system, as seen in the days of the Prophet, were based on the Koran, which was the *ipsissima verba* of God. "What an amazing phenomenon in the history of mankind," Qutb wrote, "a nation emerging from the text of a Book, living by it, and depending on its guidance as the prime mover!"[6]

The "later generations drifted away from the Koran," he continued, so that "today we see mankind in a miserable condition." Qutb's ambitious project to bring mankind back to Islam is based on three concepts, which are presented and explained by University of Arizona sociologiy professor Albert J. Bergesen, in "Sayyid Qutb in Historical Context":

> First, there are the divine revelations of the Koran, and the Islamic concept of life that they specify and imply. Second, there are socio-political obstacles in the form of existing socio-political systems, from race and economic relations to the power of the modern state. All of this he characterizes as *jahiliyya* (ignorance of God). This existing state of the world actively opposes God's will. Third, given that such *jahili* societies actively resist the implementation of the word of God, there must be an equivalent power, in the form of an Islamic

---

6 Sayyid Qutb, *The Islamic Concept and Its Characteristics* (Plainfield, IN: American Trust Publications, 1991), 2; quoted in Bergesen, *Sayyid Qutb Reader*, 14.

social movement, to remove these socio-political obstacles, thereby liberating mankind to realize the way of life God has designed. In short, there is (1) goal to be realized, (2) obstacles to be overcome, and (3) a means to overcome these obstacles and realize that goal.[7]

For Qutb, the effort to return mankind to Islam begins with the understanding that sovereignty over people is the major attribute of divinity. Thus, when man rules over man, as in a democracy or kingship, man is usurping God's role: "If only God is to exercise sovereignty over people, then when humans claim sovereignty over each other this implicitly takes people away from God. This, of course is the mirror opposite of the Western separation of the religious and the political: leave to Caesar what is Caesar's and to God what is God's. But in Qutbian Islam, what is Caesar's is God's, and to leave it to Caesar is to take it from God."[8]

And what God wants for humanity is found in the Koran, and should be followed. To exercise some level of political authority is to exercise sovereignty, and if sovereignty is a core attribute of God, then in accordance with *tawhīd* ("the unity or oneness of God") it cannot, and must not be divided with others. Therefore, only God is to exercise sovereignty through His laws as found in the Koran. We cannot follow the laws of the state—that would mean that the state is usurping the prerogative of God. Qutb wrote:

> This religion is really a universal declaration of the freedom of man from servitude to other men and from servitude to his own desires, which is also a form of human servitude; it is a declaration that sovereignty belongs to God alone and that He is the Lord of all the worlds. It means a challenge to all kinds and forms of systems which are based on the concept of the sovereignty of man; in other words, where man has usurped the Divine attribute. Any system in which the final decisions are referred to human beings, and in which the sources of all authority are human, deifies human beings by designating others than God as lords over men.[9]

This principle stemming from *tawhīd* leads to practical conse-

---

7 Ibid.
8 Bergesen, *Sayyid Qutb Reader*, 18.
9 Ibid., 37.

quences, political action. In Qutb's words, "[T]o proclaim the authority and sovereignty of God means to eliminate all human kingship and to announce the rule of sustainer of the universe over the entire earth.... Anyone who serves someone other than God in this sense is outside God's religion, although he may claim to profess this religion."[10]

For Qutb, democracy and its separation of religion and politics is a direct challenge to God. "This means that to bear behavioral witness that 'there is no deity but God' means to take political action, for if there is no deity but God, there is no sovereignty but God, and to bear witness to that is to avoid submission to other sovereignties, which means to defy existing secular political authorities."[11] As Qutb himself wrote:

> The nature of the Islamic concept is not to remain hidden in the human mind. It must be translated immediately into action and become a concrete reality in the world of events. The believer cannot be content to have his faith remain concealed in his heart, because he feels compelled to make his faith an effective force in changing his own life and the lives of the people around him.[12]

Thus God's plan for mankind has been revealed to Muhammad and is in the Koran. Earlier prophetic revelations to the Jews and Christians have been fatally compromised and distorted. God expects man to translate his faith into action. The duty of all Muslims is to guide all humanity back to God. It is a revolutionary project of universal significance.[13]

Normally, the Arabic term *jāhilīya* (also *jahiliyya, jahiliyyah*) means "a state of ignorance; pre-Islamic paganism, pre-Islamic times,"[14] but Qutb expands its meaning to signify the condition where one submits to an authority other than God, creating a "servitude of servants":

> If we look at the sources and foundations of modern ways of living, it becomes clear that the whole world is steeped in *jahiliyyah*, and all the marvelous material comforts and high-level inventions do not diminish this ignorance. This *jahiliyyah* is based on rebellion against God's sovereignty

---
10 Sayyid Qutb, *Milestones* (Damascus, Syria: Dar al-Ilm, n.d.), 57–60.
11 Bergesen, *Sayyid Qutb Reader*, 19.
12 Qutb, *Islamic Concept*, 155; quoted in Bergesen, *Sayyid Qutb Reader*, 19–20.
13 Bergesen, *Sayyid Qutb Reader*, 31.
14 Wehr, *Dictionary of Modern Written Arabic*, s.v. "*jāhilīya.*"

on earth. It transfers to man one of the greatest attributes of God…and makes some men lords over others. It…now…takes the form of claiming that the right to create values, to legislate rules of collective behavior, and to choose any way of life rests with men, without regard to what God has prescribed. The result of this rebellion against the authority of God is the oppression of His creatures.[15]

In other words, *jahiliyyah* is the wilful ignoring of God's guidance, which leads to a totally different political system, a state of error. Qutb argues:

There are only two possibilities for the life of a people, no matter in what time and place they live. These are the state of guidance or the state of error, whatever form the error may take; the state of truth or the state of falsehood, whatever may be the varieties of falsehood…the state of obedience to the Divine guidance or the state of following whims, no matter what varieties of whim there may be; the state of Islam or the state of *jahiliyyah*, without regard to the forms of *jahiliyyah*; and the state of belief or the state of unbelief, of whatever kind. People either live either according to Islam, following it as a way of life and a socio-political system, or else in the state of unbelief, *jahiliyyah*, whim, darkness, falsehood, and error.[16]

The Solution: *Jihād*

The first generation of Muslims, Muhammad's Companions, looked in the Koran for guidance on how to act, and as Qutb points out, "this Koran does not open its treasures except to him who accepts it with this spirit…of knowing with the intention of acting upon it. It did not come to be a book of intellectual content, or a book of literature, or to be considered as a book of stories or history, although it has all these facets. It came to become a way of life, a way dedicated to God."[17]

The Islamic movement must confront the *jahiliyyah* state using the "methods of preaching and persuasion for reforming ideas and beliefs," but Qutb clearly states that it must also use "physical power and *jihād* for

---

15 Qutb, *Milestones*, 10–11.
16 Qutb, *Islamic Concept*, 78; quoted in Bergesen, *Sayyid Qutb Reader*, 22.
17 Qutb, *Milestones*, 18.

abolishing the organizations and authorities of the *jahili* system which prevents people from reforming their ideas and beliefs but forces them to obey their erroneous ways and make them serve human lords instead of the Almighty Lord."[18] Qutb is critical of those putative Muslims

> who are a product of the sorry state of the present Muslim generation, have nothing but the label of Islam and having laid down their spiritual and rational arms in defeat. They say, "Islam has prescribed only defensive war"! and think they have done some good for their religion by depriving it of its method, which is to abolish all injustice from the earth, to bring people to the worship of God alone, and to bring them out of servitude to others into the servants of the Lord. Islam does not force people accept its belief, but it wants to provide the free environment in which they will have the choice of beliefs."[19]

For Qutb, *jihād* and faith are fundamentally linked, and those "persons who attempt to defend the concept of Islamic *jihād* by interpreting it in the narrow sense of the current concept of defensive wars…lack understanding of the nature of Islam and its primary aim…to spread the message of Islam throughout the world."[20]

If anything, defensive *jihād* diminishes the Islamic way of life: "Those who say that Islamic *jihād* was merely for the defense of the 'homeland of Islam' diminish the greatness of the Islamic way of life and consider it less important than their 'homeland.'"[21] *Jihād* must involve the use of force to remove all the obstacles to establishing an environment where all can choose freely. Islamic history is full of *jihād* in the military sense, and the early Muslim conquests are examples of successful *jihād* for the sake of Islam. Qutb explains:

> The reasons for *jihād* which have been described in (surahs, Q3. *'āl 'Imrān*, the Family of Imran; Q8. *al-'anfāl*, the Spoils of War / Voluntary Gifts; Q9. *at-Tawba*, the Repentance / *al-Barā'at*, the Immunity) are these: to establish God's authority in the earth; to arrange human affairs according to the true

---

18 Ibid., 55.
19 Ibid., 56.
20 Ibid., 62.
21 Ibid., 71.

guidance provided by God; to abolish all the Satanic forces and Satanic systems of life; to end the lordship of one man over others, since all men are creatures of God and no one has the authority to make them his servants or to make arbitrary laws for them. These reasons are sufficient for proclaiming *Jihād*.[22]

Qutb's view of Islam leads to direct challenge of the established political order, a challenge that can only end in some form of struggle:

When the purpose is to abolish the existing system and to replace it with a new system which in its character, principles and all its general and particular aspects, is different from the controlling *jahili* system, then it stands to reason that this new system should also come into the battlefield as an organized movement…with a determination that its strategy, its social organization, and the relationship between its individuals should be firmer and more powerful than the existing *jahili* system.[23]

In Qutb's world, religion and politics are one. *Jihād* "is a witnessing of the faith; it is inherent in the faith; to have the faith is to struggle for its sociological implementation in an existing *jahili* world."[24] *Jihād* exists, therefore, "not because of any threat of aggression against Islamic lands or against the Muslims residing in them. The reason for *jihād* exists in the nature of its message and in the actual conditions it finds in human societies and not merely in the necessity for defense, which may be temporary and of limited extent."[25]

In fact, according to Qutb, Islam has the right to initiate *jihād* since it is "in the very nature of Islam to take initiative for freeing the human beings throughout the earth from servitude to anyone other than God," and "Islam has a right to remove all those obstacles…so that it may address human reason and intuition with no interference and opposition from political systems," which means that "it is the duty of Islam to annihilate all such systems…as they are obstacles in the way of freedom."[26]

---

22 Ibid., 70.
23 Ibid., 47.
24 Bergesen, *Sayyid Qutb Reader*, 27.
25 Qutb, *Milestones*, 71.
26 Ibid., 74-75.

In his commentary on the Koran, Qutb states that "to fight for Islam is to fight for the implementation of this way of life and its systems. Faith, on the other hand, is a matter for free personal conviction, after the removal of all pressures and obstacles."[27] It is a universal struggle: "It is not possible that Islam will confine itself to geographical boundaries, or racial limits, abandoning the rest of mankind and leaving them to suffer from evil, corruption and servitude to lords other than God Almighty."[28] Therefore, "when we understand the nature of Islam...we realize the inevitability of *jihād*, or striving for God's cause, taking a military form in addition to its advocacy form."[29]

---

27 Sayyid Qutb, *In the Shade of the Qur'an*, trans. Adil Salahi, sura 8 (Leicester: The Islamic Foundation, 2003), 7:24.
28 Ibid., 22.
29 Ibid., 12.

CHAPTER 20
MUHAMMAD 'ABD AL-SALĀM FARAJ AND *THE NEGLECTED DUTY*

IT IS OFTEN argued that a cause of Islamic terrorism is the Arab-Israel conflict, and it was assumed that when President of Egypt Anwar Sadat was assassinated by an Islamic fundamentalist group in October 1981, it was because of Sadat's rapprochement with Israel. And yet, as Johannes J.G. Jansen pointed out in the preface to his translation of *The Neglected Duty*, a tract that spelled out that group's ideology, their statements "hardly mentioned Israel—and even stated that the war against the Zionist enemies of Islam ought to be postponed until after a more important question could be resolved: Egypt must first introduce the *Sharia*, the detailed Islamic legal system, as the law of the land.... 'Reintroduction of application of the *Sharia*,' the assassins believed took precedence over any other duty.'"[1]

The fifty-five page tract, written in Cairo, probably in 1980, explained the group's theology and ideology. It was authored by Muhammad 'Abd al-Salām Faraj (executed in 1982), who titled it *al-Farīda al-Ghā'iba*, variously translated as "The Absent Precept," "The Forgotten Obligation," or "The Neglected Duty." The title refers to *jihād*, which was, in Faraj's opinion, a religious duty, regrettably neglected: "The failure to apply the *Sharia* had rendered *Jihād* the sacred individual duty of every Muslim."[2] *The Neglected Duty*, Jansen states, "contains all ideological material needed to justify the attacks of 9/11 or any other recent

---

[1] Johannes J.G. Jansen, *The Neglected Duty: The Creed of Sadat's Assassins* (1986; New York: RVP Publishers, 2013), viii.

[2] Ibid., xi.

act of terror committed to frighten non-Muslims." And he thinks the document explains the criminal behavior of suburban and center-city immigrant youngsters in many European cities; its author clearly "sees Islam as a license to kill, rob, and commit arson."[3]

What makes *The Neglected Duty* particularly interesting is that it was not written for outsiders. Nor it is an apology or a justification of an assassination—Sadat is never mentioned. It is an internal memo circulated among strict Muslims. It does not sugarcoat or omit potentially offensive matter, but offers readers a glimpse of what the Islamic militants are really thinking, without euphemism or subterfuge.

As might be expected, the tract's 143 paragraphs are interlaced with quotes from the Koran (verses from more than fifteen suras are cited, with suras 2 and 9 predominating) and the *hadīth* as reported by Ibn Hanbal, Muslim, Bukhārī, and many others, as well as references to founders of schools of Islamic law such as al-Shāfiʿī, and to Muslim theologians and scholars such as Ibn Qayyim, Ibn Kathir, and above all Ibn Taymiyya, who is quoted several times.

After a quote from sura Q57 (*al-Hadīd*, Iron, 16) exhorting Muslims not to be like earlier generations, followed by praise of God and Muhammad, *The Neglected Duty* denounces innovations: "every novelty is an innovation (*bidʿa*) and every innovation is a deviation, and all deviation is in Hell" (para. 2). Then in paragraph 3 it launches into how *jihād* has been neglected:

> *Jihād* (struggle) for God's cause [*jihād fī sabīl Allāh*], in spite of its extreme importance and its great significance for the future of this religion, has been neglected by the *'ulamāʾ* (leading Muslim scholars) of this age. They have feigned ignorance of it, but they know that it is the only way to the return and the establishment of the glory of Islam anew. Every Muslim preferred his own favorite ideas and philosophies above the Best Road, which God—Praised and Exalted He is— drew Himself (a road that leads back), to (a state of) Honor for His Servants.[4]

Paragraphs 4 and 5 emphasize the power of the sword, which alone can rid the world of idols, and the importance of *tawhīd*, God's uni-

---

3 Ibid., xxi.

4 Ibid., 153. All further references to this work are cited parenthetically by paragraph number in the text.

ty, quoting a *hadīth* from Ibn Hanbal, where Muhammad says: "I have been sent with the Sword at this Hour, so that God alone is worshipped, without associate to Him, He put my daily bread under the shadow of my lance, He brings lowness and smallness to those who disagree with what I command." Paragraph 5: "God sent [Muhammad] to call with the sword for (acknowledgment of) God's unity."

The next topic is the establishment of an Islamic state, and the reintroduction of the caliphate, abolished in 1924. Paragraphs 8 to 13 describe how the glory of Islam is destined to return, while paragraph 14 deals with the despair that many Muslim activists have fallen into, counseling patience, because God has promised Muslims success. Paragraph 14 ends with quotes from al-Tirmidhī and others. Paragraph 16 argues for the Muslim duty of the establishment of an Islamic State, while paragraph 18 makes it clear that they are not yet living in an Islamic State, since (para. 19) "a House must be categorized according to the laws by which it is ruled. If (a House) is ruled by the laws of Islam, then it is the House of Islam. If (a House) is ruled by the laws of Unbelief, it is the House of Unbelief." *The Neglected Duty* supports this view with quotes from Ibn Taymiyya and Abu Hanifah: Rulers who do not rule by the laws of Islam must be considered apostates, and apostasy is punishable by death.

Faraj himself lists seventeen objections to his own views and then answers them one by one. He does not accept, for instance, the Sufi's personal piety as the answer to all the ills of Egypt, since a life of private devotion would mean neglecting a Muslim's highest duty— *jihād*—as long as long as all the other pillars of Islam are respected (para. 50). *The Neglected Duty* rejects the notion that *jihād* can be interpreted to mean "struggle to obtain knowledge." Faraj quotes the Koran, "Prescribed for you is fighting" (Q2. *al-Baqara*, the Cow, 216), and "Scholarship is not the decisive weapon which will radically put an end to paganism" (para. 64). Faraj also refutes the argument that it is only permissible to fight under a caliph or a commander, and ends by quoting Ibn Taymiyya, who wrote, "Any group of people that rebels against any single prescript of the clear and reliably transmitted prescripts of Islam has to be fought, according to the leading scholars of Islam, even if the members of this group pronounce the Islamic Confession of Faith" (para. 66).

Paragraph 68 introduces the idea of the near and the far enemy: "To fight an enemy who is near is more important than to fight an enemy who is far." Muslims must not waste their energies fighting imperialism, for example, but first concentrate on their own situation, that is, to establish the Rule of God's Religion in their own country, and make the Word of God supreme (para. 70).

The Neglected Duty rejects the idea that *jihād* is for defensive purposes only. The Prophet was asked "What is *jihād* for God's cause?" He replied, "Whosoever fights in order to make the Word of God supreme is someone who really fights for God's cause": "To fight is, in Islam, to make supreme the Word of God in this world, whether it be attacking or by defending....Islam was spread by the sword....It is obligatory for the Muslims to raise their swords against the Leaders who hide the Truth and spread falsehoods." (para. 71).

Faraj also denies the validity of the distinction between the greater and lesser jihād, a distinction, as Ibn al-Qayyim showed, was a fabrication put into circulation in order "to reduce the value of fighting with the Sword, so as to distract the Muslims from fighting the infidels and the hypocrites." (para. 90).

Paragraphs 98 and 99 make clear the rewards for those who fight in the Cause of God. Muhammad said, "God turns towards whomever goes out for His cause. He will not send someone out but to wage jihad for His cause and for belief in Him and for accepting the truthfulness of His Apostle. He guarantees that He will (either) make him enter Paradise or will make him come back to his home from which he went out with whatever reward or booty he obtained" (para. 98). Muhammad also said, "A martyr has six virtues in the eyes of God. He will be forgiven upon the first drop of blood. His seat will be in Paradise. He will be free from the punishment of the grave. He will be safe from the Great Fright. He will be dressed in the garb of faith. He will marry the heavenly dark-eyed virgins. He will intercede for 70 of his relatives" (transmitted by al-Tirmidhī, para. 99).

Equally, there are punishments for neglecting the duty of *jihād*, which is also the cause of humiliation and dissension in the Muslim world. *The Neglected Duty* quotes sura Q9. *at-Tawba*, the Repentance/ *al-Barā'at*, the Immunity, 38–39:

> O ye who have believed, what is the matter with you? When one says to you: "March out in the way of God," ye are weighed down to the ground: are you satisfied with this nearer life as to neglect the Hereafter [*l-ākhirati*]? The enjoyment of this nearer life is in comparison with the Hereafter only a little thing. If you do not march out He will inflict upon you a painful punishment, and will substitute for you another peo-

ple; ye will not injure Him at all. God over everything has power. (para. 100)

Contempt for this world is clearly quite common among the *jihadist* groups.

Another problem that *The Neglected Duty* addresses is that of Muslims engaged in *jihād* who may have to fight an enemy army with Muslims in its ranks, potentially killing fellow Muslims. Once again, Faraj turns to Ibn Taymiyya:

> Whoever doubts whether he has to fight them is most ignorant of the religion of Islam. Since fighting them is obligatory, they have to be fought, even if there is amongst them someone who has been forced to join their ranks. On this the Muslims are in agreement. Al-'Abbās (once) said, when he was taken prisoner on the Day of Battle of Badr: "O Apostle of God, I was forced to go out." Then the Apostle of God said: "Outwardly you were against us. Only God knows what is in your heart." (para. 103)

Lying to the enemy is perfectly acceptable; war is deceit (paras. 107–9). But is it permitted to a Muslim to serve in a non-Muslim army? The question's relevance is obvious, given that those involved in Sadat's assassination were officers in the Egyptian army. (Remember that Egypt is considered a non-Muslim country, as it is not ruled under *Shari'a*.) *The Neglected Duty* answers affirmatively, citing Ibn Taymiyya: "Muslim transmitted...the story of the people of the Trench, wherein (there is mention of) the youth who was ordered to kill himself for the benefit of the religion, and therefore the four Imams permit a Muslim to penetrate into the ranks of the infidels even if he considered it probable that they would kill him, when this (penetration) is to the advantage of the Muslims" (para. 118).

Jansen discusses the implications of such a policy: "It is easy to imagine how army activists were indeed in need of pastoral advice. Many of them must at times have wondered whether they should remain where they are, wait for things to come, and hope for the best. If this impression is right, there may be more potentially militant activists in the Egyptian army than anyone suspects."[5]

Many paragraphs are devoted to military tactics and ethics. Faraj

---

5 Ibid., 29.

quotes various Muslim theologians and scholars to justify the total destruction of enemy property. Innocent bystanders, women, and children may accidentally be killed in an attack. This cannot be helped, and the *jihadists* are not cuplable for such casualties.

Then Faraj returns to the true nature of *jihād*. In paragraph 130, Ibn al-Jawzī is cited: "Satan deceived many people so that they went out to wage *jihad*, their intention being vainglory and pride, hoping that it would be said that So-and-so is a Fighter for God. Probably, however, the real intention was that (they hoped that) people would say that So-and-So was a hero, or in pursuit of booty. Deeds, however, are (to be judged) according to their intentions."

Finally, the leaders of Islamic organizations must strive to be above reproach, but they cannot be on the right path as long as they do not prepare for true *jihād*. The real aim all along is to establish a true Islamic state in Egypt.

CHAPTER 21
ABDULLAH AZZAM AND
DEFENSE OF THE MUSLIM LANDS

SINCE 1979, Abdullah Yusuf Azzam (1941–1989) has had an enormous influence on the *jihādi* movement born in the wake of Soviet intervention in Afghanistan. Azzam was able to use his mastery of Islamic texts and jurisprudence for propaganda to recruit vacillating Muslims to the cause of fighting for Allah, to expel foreigners from Afghanistan, and to seek to reestablish Islam as the dominant creed worldwide. As there was no caliph, he argued that there was no need for permission from an imam. His Islamic scholarship added much to his prestige.

Abdullah Azzam was born in the village of Silat al-Harithiyain, in the Janin district of the West Bank. After earning a degree from Khaduri College, an agricultural college in Tulkarm, and a short teaching stint, Azzam began his Islamic studies in the *Shari'a* Faculty at Damascus University in Syria in 1963. He had already been deeply influenced by and joined the Muslim Brotherhood during the 1950s. The writings and political activities of Hasan al-Banna also made a particular impression on Azzam, but his personal mentor was Shafiq Asad 'Abd al-Hadi, who gave him direction and convinced him to fight for the cause of Islam.

Azzam received his B.A. in Shari'a, Islamic Law in 1966. After the 1967 Six-Day War, when Israel took over the West Bank, Azzam and his family settled in Jordan. Thereafter, Azzam took part in military actions against Israel, but he soon became disillusioned with the secular and entirely parochial nature of the PLO. Azzam began formulating ideas of a Pan-Islamic movement that would restore pride and glory to the

Islamic *umma*, and cut across the artificial political boundaries drawn up by colonialists.

Azzam continued his Islamic studies at Cairo's Al-Azhar University, acquiring an M.A. in Shari'a. After teaching briefly at the University of Jordan in Amman, Azzam returned to Al-Azhar on a scholarship, where he obtained his Ph.D. in the principles of Islamic jurisprudence in 1973. These are important details, and serve as a counterargument to those who pretend that *jihādists* know nothing of Islam and are not competent to pass judgment on any aspect of Islamic law or theology.

Azzam returned to teaching at the University of Jordan, but was forced to leave because of his radical views. He found a warm welcome in Saudi Arabia, where he became a lecturer at King Abdul Aziz University in Jeddah. He remained at the university until 1979, when he was expelled, and it is possible during his tenure Azzam met Osama bin Laden. Then things happened in 1979 in the larger world that decided his destiny.

What happened in 1979 that was so decisive?

It turned out to be the most important year in the modern history of Islamic radical movements because of three key events: the success of the Islamic Revolution in Iran when the Ayatollah Khomeini introduced a theocracy (although a Sh'ite revolution, this had an enormous impact on all Islamic movements); the Soviet Union's decision to send troops into Afghanistan to support a Marxist regime (marking the beginning of modern global *jihādist* movements); and the seizure of the Grand Mosque at Mecca by armed extremists demanding the overthrow of the Saudi regime (Saudi Arabia ended the siege after two weeks but with great loss of lives).

Azzam moved to Pakistan where he began teaching, but then devoted all his energies to fighting the Soviets and formulating his philosophy of *jihād*. Azzam published his best-known tract, *Defense of the Muslim Lands*, sometime between 1979 and 1984. Like *The Neglected Duty*, Azzam's *Defense* brims with citations from the Koran, *hadīth*, and Islamic scholars and theologians such as Ibn Kathir and, inevitably, Ibn Taymiyya. Indeed, chapter 1 opens with an Ibn Taymiyya quote: "The first obligation after *Iman* [faith, belief, right belief] is the repulsion of the enemy aggressor who assaults the religion and the worldly affairs."

Allah, according to Azzam, has chosen Islam for the entire world, through the last Prophet on earth, Muhammad,

[t]o bring it victory by the sword and the spear, after he had

clearly expounded it with evidences and arguments. The Prophet (saw) said in a *Saḥīḥ* [authentic] *hadith* narrated by Ahmad and Tabarani: "I have been raised between the hands of the Hour with the sword, until Allah the Exalted is worshipped alone with no associates. He has provided sustenance from beneath the shadow of spears and has decreed humiliation and belittlement for those who oppose my order. And whoever resembles a people, he is of them."[1]

Allah does not like those who turn away from their duty of *jihād*. He will replace them with those who are braver, and punish cowardice. But despite clear rules and guidance, Muslims have fallen away from their religion, which explains why they are now lost, humiliated by infidels and imperialists. Only a return to religion and reestablishment of the caliphate will restore Islam's glory.

What of this neglected duty? "One of the most important lost obligations is the forgotten obligation of fighting. Because it is absent from the present condition of the Muslims, they have become as rubbish of the flood waters."[2] Azzam quotes the Prophet, who said, "'Allah will put *Wahn* [weakness, feebleness] into your hearts and remove the fear from the hearts of your enemies because of your love for the world and your hate of death.' In another narration it was said: 'and what is the *Wahn*, O messenger of Allah?' He (pbuh) said: 'love of the world and the hate for fighting.' (Abu Dawud)."[3]

The theme of true Muslims loving death as others love life, as has been shown throughout this text, appears in the Koran and reaches back to the earliest Islamic traditions, which the quote above from Abu Dāwūd reminds us. Martyrdom is the highest honor of a Muslim fighting in the cause of Allah. As Azzam writes:

> History does not write its lines except with blood. Glory does not build its lofty edifice except with skulls. Honour and respect cannot be established except on a foundation of cripples and corpses. Empires, distinguished peoples, states and societies cannot be established except with examples. Indeed,

---

[1] Abdullah Azzam, *Defense of the Muslim Lands: The First Obligation after Imam*, trans. Brothers in Ribatt, 1979–1984, 11–12, https://islamfuture.files.wordpress.com/2009/11/defence-of-the-muslim-lands.pdf.

[2] Ibid., 13.

[3] Abū Dāwūd, *Sunan*, hadīth 4284, 3:1196.

those who think that they can change reality, or change societies, without blood, sacrifices and invalids, without pure, innocent souls, then they do not understand the essence of this *dīn* [religion, that is, Islam] and they do not know the method of the best of the Messengers (may Allah bless him and grant him peace).[4]

Scholar's Ink, Martyr's Blood

For Azzam, both offensive and defensive *jihād* are obligatory. Offensive *jihād* becomes *fard kifaya* (a collective obligation fulfillable by some members of the community on behalf of the community at large) and its object can be to collect the poll tax (*jizya*), terrorize the enemy, and "*da'wah* [call, invitation, or missionary activity for the cause of Islam] with a force," which believers are obliged "to perform with all available capabilities, until there remain only Muslims or people who submit to Islam."[5] Defensive *jihād* is *fard ayn* (an obligatory duty of every Muslim) to expel unbelievers from Muslim lands, and furthermore, "It has been made clear to us that no permission is required for anyone when *jihād* is *fard ayn*, as no permission is required from the father, the sheikh or the master for the obligatory morning prayer before the rising of the sun."[6] At the moment, the most urgent problem for a Muslim to deal with is Afghanistan, and then Palestine.

But as Gorka points out, Azzam is fully aware of the necessity of scholar's ink as well as martyr's blood:[7]

> Indeed nations are only brought to life by their beliefs and their concepts and they die only with their desires and their lusts....As for the Muslim *Umma*, it does continue to exist in the course of history of humankind, except by a divine ideology and the blood which flows as a result of spreading this divine ideology and implanting it into the real World. The life of the Muslim *Umma* [community] is solely dependent on the ink of its scholars and the blood of its martyrs.

---

4 Abdullah Azzam, "Document—Martyrs: The Building Blocks of Nations," *Religioscope*, February 1, 2002, http://english.religion.info/2002/02/01/document-martyrs-the-building-blocks-of-nations/. Also quoted by Sebastian Gorka, *Defeating Jihad: The Winnable War* (Washington, DC: Regnery Publishing, 2016), 88.
5 Azzam, *Defense of Muslim Lands*, 14.
6 Ibid., 34.

What is more beautiful than the writing of the *Umma*'s history with both the ink of a scholar and his blood, such that the map of Islamic history becomes coloured with two lines: one of them black, and that is what the scholar wrote with the ink of his pen; and the other one red, and that is what the martyr wrote with his blood. And something more beautiful than this is when the blood is one and the pen is one, so that the hand of the scholar which expends the ink and moves the pen, is the same as the hand which expends its blood and moves the *Umma*. The extent to which the number of martyred scholars increases is the extent to which nations are delivered from their slumber, rescued from their decline and awoken from their sleep.[8]

In his 1987 work, *Join the Caravan*, Azzam goes through the same arguments justifying *jihād*, citing by now familiar quotes from the Koran, *hadīth*, and Islamic scholars. He gives sixteen reasons for carrying out *jihād*:

1. In order that the Disbelievers do not dominate.
2. Due to the scarcity of men.
3. Fear of Hell-fire.
4. Fulfilling the duty of *Jihād*, and responding to the call of the Lord.
5. Following in the footsteps of the Pious Predecessors.
6. Establishing a solid foundation as a base for Islam.
7. Protecting those who are oppressed in the land.
8. Hoping for martyrdom.
9. A shield for the *Umma*, and a means for lifting disgrace off them.
10. Protecting the dignity of the *Umma*, and repelling the conspiracy of its enemies.
11. Preservation of the earth, and protection from corruption.
12. Security of Islamic places of worship.
13. Protection of the *Umma* from punishment, disfiguration and displacement.
14. Prosperity of the *Umma*, and surplus of its resources.
15. *Jihād* is the highest peak of Islam.

---

[8] Azzam, "Document—Martyrs."

16. *Jihād* is the most excellent form of worship, and by means of it the Muslim can reach the highest of ranks.[9]

Azzam's immediate concern was to defend Islamic lands from infidels in Afghanistan. This should, in his scheme of things, be followed by the establishment of a caliphate, and eventually an *umma* ruled solely by God's law as manifested in the Koran, *sunna*, and developed by the religious scholars. Only then, would Muslims regain freedom from colonialists and man-made laws, and Islam her past glory and dignity.

Azzam was assassinated by a car bomb in 1989. It remains unsolved who was responsible; everyone from Osama bin Laden to the Iranians to the CIA to Mossad has been accused at one time or another.

---

9 Shaykh Abdullah Azzam, *Join the Caravan*, 1987, archived at https://archive.org/stream/JoinTheCaravan/JoinTheCaravan_djvu.txt.

CHAPTER 22

AYMAN AL-ZAWAHIRI AND
KNIGHTS UNDER THE PROPHET'S BANNER

AYMAN AL ZAWAHIRI (b. 1951) has been the leader of al-Qaeda since Osama bin Laden's death on May 2, 2011. Al-Zawahiri was born into an upper-middle-class family in the Maadi district of Cairo, Egypt. Both of his parents came from wealthy families—an important point to bear in mind when encountering the cliché that poverty creates Islamic terrorism. Ayman studied medicine in Cairo, earned a degree in 1974, and went on to earn an advanced degree in surgery a few years later. Along the way al-Zawahiri acquired considerable knowledge of Islamic theology and jurisprudence.

Religiously and politically active in his teens, al-Zawahiri joined the Muslim Brotherhood at fourteen. He was deeply affected by Qutb's execution in 1966, and would later write, "The Nasserite regime thought that the Islamic movement received a deadly blow with the execution of Sayyid Qutb and his comrades, but the apparent surface calm concealed an immediate interaction with Sayyid Qutb's ideas and the formation of the nucleus of the modern Islamic *jihād* movement in Egypt."[1]

That same year, according to Lawrence Wright in *The Looming Tower: Al-Qaeda and the Road to 9/11* (2007), al-Zawahiri, age fifteen, "helped form an underground cell devoted to overthrowing the government and establishing an Islamic state."[2]

Like all Islamic fundamentalists, al-Zawahiri dreamed of restoring the caliphate, which had been dissolved in 1924. Once it was reestab-

---

1 Quoted in Wright, *Looming Tower*, 37.
2 Ibid.

lished, and the secular regime replaced with one ruled under *Shari'a*, Egypt would become the rallying point for the Islamic world. As he wrote in *Knights under the Prophet's Banner* in 2001, "Armies achieve victory only when the infantry takes hold of land. Likewise, the *mujahid* Islamic movement will not triumph against the world coalition unless it possesses a fundamentalist base in the heart of the Islamic world. All the means and plans that we have reviewed for mobilizing the nation will remain up in the air without a tangible gain or benefit unless they lead to the establishment of the state of caliphate in the heart of the Islamic world."[3] But al-Zawahiri was also aware that the conditions were not quite right yet for the establishment of the caliphate. He counseled patience.

At the same time, there can be no solution without *jihād*: "With the emergence of this new batch of Islamists, who have been missing from the nation for a long time, a new awareness is increasingly developing among the sons of Islam, who are eager to uphold it: namely, that there is no solution without *jihād*."[4] For Zawahiri,

> [J]ihād in the path of Allah is greater than any individual or organisation. It is a struggle between Truth and Falsehood, until Almighty inherits the earth and those who live on it.... There is no reform without *jihād* in the path of Allah. And every call seeking reform without *jihād* condemns itself to death and failure.[5]

In *Knights under the Prophet's Banner*, al-Zawahiri summarized the strategies necessary to win this fight:

> The Islamic movement in general and the *jihād* in particular must launch a battle for orienting the nation by: exposing the rulers who are fighting Islam; highlighting the importance of loyalty to the faithful and relinquishment of the infidels in the Muslim creed; holding every Muslim responsible for

---

3 Ayman al-Zawahiri, *Knights under the Prophet's Banner*; quoted in Walter Laqueur, ed., *Voices of Terror: Manifestos, Writings and Manuals of Al Qaeda, Hamas, and Other Terrorists from Around the World and Throughout the Ages* (New York: Reed Press, 2004), 432.

4 Ibid., 428.

5 Ayman al-Zawahiri, "Interview," in *The Al-Qaeda Reader: The Essential Texts of Osama Bin Laden's Terrorist Organization*, ed. and trans. Raymond Ibrahim (New York: Broadway Books, 2007), 182–86.

defending Islam, its sanctities, nation, and homeland; cautioning against the *'ulama'* of the sultan and reminding the nation of the virtues of the *'ulama'* of *jihād* and the imams of sacrifice and the need for the nation to defend, protect, honor, and follow them; and exposing the extent of the aggression against our creed and sanctities and plundering of our wealth.[6]

In his book that first began circulating around 1991, *The Bitter Harvest: The [Muslim] Brotherhood in Sixty Years*, al-Zawahiri laments that the Brotherhood had lost its way by agreeing to participate in so-called democratic elections instead of performing their Islamic duty of waging a *jihād* against the current regime in Egypt, which must be considered un-Islamic, and hence apostate.[7] He bases this accusation of betrayal of on two principles: (1) if a ruler of a putative Islamic country does not govern according to the *Shari'a*, which is God-given law, then Muslims have an obligation to overthrow such a ruler, and (2) "democracy and Islam are antithetical and thus can never coexist,"[8] since democracy makes humans sovereign, putting man-made laws above those of God, as enshrined in the *Shari'a*. He writes at the end of *The Bitter Harvest*: "Thus whoever claims to be a 'democratic-Muslim', or a Muslim who calls for democracy, is like one who says about himself 'I am a Jewish Muslim,' or 'I am a Christian Muslim'—the one worse than the other. He is an apostate infidel."[9]

Here are some further thoughts from al-Zawahiri on democracy and Islam, and their incompatibility:

> The current rulers of Muslim countries who govern without the *sharia* of Allah are apostate infidels. It is obligatory to overthrow them, to wage *jihād* against them, and to depose them, installing a Muslim ruler in their stead.[10]

> These rulers must be considered apostates for the following reasons:
> [because they] abandon the *sharia* of Allah...

---

6 Al-Zawahiri, *Knights*, 432.
7 See al-Zawahiri, "Interview," 116.
8 Ibid., 117.
9 Quoted in ibid., 119.
10 Ibid., 122.

[because they] ridicule the *sharia*...

[because they] institute democratic rule, which is, as Abu al-Ali al-Mawdudi described in his book *Islam and Modern Civilization*, "rule of the masses" and "the deification of man."[11]

Under Islamic rule Allah alone is the legislator. Otherwise, *Under the Prophet's Banner* is filled with the by-now familiar quotes from and references to the Koran, *hadīth*, and various Islamic theologians and scholars such as Ibn Kathir and Ibn Taymiyya.

---

11 Ibid., 123.

CHAPTER 23
AYATOLLAH RUHOLLAH KHOMEINI AND THE IRANIAN REVOLUTION

Historical and Political Background to Khomeini's Rise to Power: Nawab Safavi and the *Fidā'īyīn-i Islam*

ACCORDING TO Farhad Kazemi,[1] Mojtaba Nawab Safavi [also Navvab Safavi] was born in 1923[2] in Tehran in a religious family, that claimed descent from the Prophet, and on the mother's side from the Safavids, who had made Shi'ism the state religion of Iran in the sixteenth century.

Nawab Safavi left for Najaf at an early age to become a theology student. Here, Nawab encountered the works of Ahmad Kasravi, who had advocated Islamic reformation, and later proved to be very hostile to Shi'ism in general. Kasravi was also very critical of the clergy in Iran, holding them responsible for Iran's backwardness. He believed the clergy were parasites who exploited the illiterate masses by playing on their fears of hell, and by promising them the delights of paradise. Kasravi had been a brilliant student at the Tehran Law Faculty and the Sorbonne in

---

1 Farhad Kazemi, "The *Fada'iyan-e Islam*: Fanaticism, Politics and Terror," in ed. Said Amir Arjomand, *From Nationalism to Revolutionary Islam* (State University of New York Press, 1985), 160.
2 According to Sohrab Behdad, Safavi was born in 1924, see Sohrab Behdad, "Islamic Utopia in Pre-Revolutionary Iran: Navvab Safavi and the Fad'ian-e Eslam", in *Middle Eastern Studies*, Vol.33, No.1, January 1997, 40. Amir Taheri seems to think Safavi was born at the beginning of the twentieth century, see Amir Taheri, *Holy Terror. The Inside Story of Islamic Terrorism*, (London: Sphere Books Ltd., 1987), 51.

Paris, credentials which gave his writings much authority and credibility. Essentially, Kasravi hoped for the eventual de-Islamization of Iran.

Very disturbed by what he had read, Nawab Safavi returned to Tehran to "take care of" Kasravi, and begin a campaign of terror. The clerical establishment was angered by Kasravi's writings, and the Ayatollah Khomeini replied to Kasravi's "They Read and Judge" with "Read and Act", which criticized Muslims for not taking any action against Kasravi. In 1944, Khomeini published *Kashf al-Asrar* (*The Unveiling of Secrets*), which condemned in forthright terms Kasravi and, more indirectly, other Islamic reformists, without naming them. How is that you Muslims have not risen up against this shameful book? asked Khomeini. He wrote,

> Our faithful believers, our honourable brothers, our Persian-speaking friends, our courageous youth! Read these manifestations of crime, these shameful publications, these kernels of division and animosity, these invitations to Zoroastrianism, ... these condemnations of our sacred religion, and try to do something; with a national uprising, with a religious uprising, ... with a strong will, with an iron fist, rid the earth of the seeds of these dishonourable, shameless beings, ... we are condemned in the court of our religion, we are disgraced in the eye of the prophet of Islam. Yes! Rise up courageously and honourably, so that the arrogant do not make you surrender.[3]

Khomeini found these attacks on Islam as "corrupt on earth" (*mofsed fi al-arz*) and wished that "the scholars ... who see themselves as guardians of the faith, the Qur'an and the religious sacred beliefs, to shatter the teeth of these jerks with their iron fists and to crush their heads under their courageous feet". He knew that an Islamic government would have executed "these offenders in front of the supporters of the faith."[4]

Khomeini continued, "The rules of Islam do not provide a cure for your diseases, which are the love of debauchery and fornication as well as compulsive lying and cheating. The rule of Islam declares your blood

---

3 Khomeini, *Kashf al-Asrar*, 74, quoted in Sohrab Behdad, "Islamic Utopia in Pre-Revolutionary Iran: Navvab Safavi and the Fad'ian-e Eslam", 43

4 Quoted in Sohrab Behdad, "Islamic Utopia in Pre-Revolutionary Iran: Navvab Safavi and the Fad'ian-e Eslam", 43.

to be worthless and shall cut off your thieving arms. This is why you are fighting [Islam]. The mullahs want to block your path to treachery. They want to remove from behind the desks those beautiful women who are, as we all know, used for certain purposes, so that they return to their veils...."[5]

It is unlikely that Nawab Safavi had any direct contact with Khomeini, though it is very probable that he had read the latter's *Kashf al-Asrar*. Safavi debated Kasravi in public but found the experience frustrating, coming to the conclusion that the only solution was to assassinate him. Safavi bought a gun and shot Kasravi on 28 April 1945 but did not manage to kill him. That task was accomplished by two of Safavi's followers, Seyyed Hosein Emami and Seyyed Ali Muhammad Emami on 11 March, 1946, when they shot and killed Kasravi. Nawab Safavi was imprisoned for two months, while Seyyed Hosein was sentenced to death.

The assassins became instant heroes, and the clergy rejoiced. "It was the most beautiful day in my life," recounted Ayatollah Shaikh Sadeq Khalkhali, one of Khomeini's closest friends. "We all know that the miscreant had been struck by the hand of Allah, so that Islam could begin to live again." Shaikh Sadeq decided to join Safavi's group, *Fedayeen-i Islam*[6] that seems to have been formed sometime in 1945. On its formation, Nawab Safavi declared,

> We are alive and God, the revengeful, is alert. The blood of the destitute has long been dripping from the fingers of the selfish pleasure seekers, who are hiding, each with a different name and in a different colour, behind the black curtains of oppression, thievery and crime. Once in a while the divine retribution puts them in their place, but the rest of them do not learn a lesson .... Damn you! You traitors, impostors, oppressors! You deceitful hypocrites! We are free, noble and alert. We are knowledgeable, believers in God and fearless. [This declaration was an attack on those who damaged] the foundation of the faith and Qur'anic knowledge in the name of religion, ... have no mercy on the privation of the poor, throw dirt on the blessed blood of Hosein (peace on him) ... make deals with robber barons and know of the degenerate

---

5 Amir Taheri, *Holy Terror*, 57.

6 Also spelt: *Fadi'ian-e Eslam; Fada'iyan-e Islam*; however the strict Arabic transliteration should be *Fidā'īyīn-i Islām*.

morality of the youth of today and of their disgust with religion when they sow the seeds [of ruin and division].⁷

The declaration was full of quotes from the Koran, including one from Q3. *āl 'Imrān*, the Family of Imran:169: "Never think that those who were slain in the cause of God [*fī sabīli llāhi*] are dead. They are alive, and well-provided for by their Lord." The declaration calls on all the Muslims of the world to shatter their chains of subjugation: "These chains are made and set by those who have been living in ignorance and savagery years after the coming of the Islamic civilization and the call of the Qur'an.... Muslim people of the world, rise up! Come to life! So that we can win back our rights."⁸

The declaration began with the words "*huwa l-'azīz*", a reference to God, meaning the "All Powerful" or "Almighty", which appears frequently in the Koran. It served as the group's slogan and appeared at the head of their pamphlets, leaflets, and above the title of their newspapers.

In 1946, Ayatollah Khasani took an active interest in the activities of the *Fedayeen-i Islam*, helping to promote their goals, but also using them for his own ends—that is, to rouse the masses. In 1949, the *Fedayeen-i Islam* assassinated Abdolhosein Hazhir, the court minister, and later General Haj-Ali Razmara, and Education Minister Ahmad Zangeneh. After the assassination of Razmara, Nawab Safavi declared his commitment to the creation of an Islamic state: "Now, you the son of Pahlavi, and you the deputies in the Majlis and members of the Senate... you and your associates must know that if you do not follow all the precepts of Islam, one by one, according to the book of the *Fada'ian-e Islam* you would be approaching the fall into hell." In the addenda to his book, *Barnameh-ye Enqelabi*, Nawab Safavi warns opposition groups that "Iran is the country of the followers of Muhammad and his descendants, and whoever takes the smallest step in violation of Islamic law will be dealt with the rules of Islam."⁹

In another speech, Safavi related how he dreamt that the light of Muhammad would one day shine on the land of Iran.¹⁰ Safavi was able to attract to his Fedayeen just what he needed, dedicated fighters ready to die for the cause of Islam. "Throw away your worry beads and buy a gun," he said. "For worry beads keep you silent while guns silence the

---

7 Sohrab Behdad, "Islamic Utopia in Pre-Revolutionary Iran," 45.
8 Quoted in Sohrab Behdad, "Islamic Utopia in Pre-Revolutionary Iran," 46.
9 Ibid., 49.
10 Amir Taheri, *Holy Terror*, 59.

enemies of Islam."¹¹ As Khomeini had said, be ready to act.

Safavi appealed to that principle in Islam of Commanding Right and Forbidding Wrong, that enjoins all Muslims to fight evil, that exhorts them to action; he wrote, "Islam asks us to Command Good and prevent Evil. Now Good and Evil involve men and women and not objects. All we have to do is to ask followers of Evil to stop and cross over to the side of Good. It is only when our advice is not heeded that we have no choice but to take action, including of men of Evil."[12]

After the coup that overthrew Mossadeq, there was a massive purge of communist and fundamentalist militants, over a thousand were arrested, of which a quarter were members of the *Fedayeen-i Islam*. Nine members of the *Fedayeen* were hanged, including Nawab Safavi. Those who escaped hanging, lived on to join Khomeini twenty years later.

In 1944, there had been seventy members, but the membership grew to three hundred within a few years. They terrified politicians during the 1940s and 1950s, when dozens were assassinated. The group's support seems to have come from small shopkeepers, bazaar apprentices, and those considered at the edge of society. Nawab Safavi was certainly charismatic, and he gave rousing speeches on the corruption of Iranian society under the grip of the iniquitous influence of the West, which was particularly degrading Muslim women.

Sohrab Behdad ends his article with the following observation, "There was a historical link connecting the Islamic Republic to the *Fada'ian-e Eslam*, as demonstrated by Ayatollah Khomeini's preference to sit under a *huwa l-'azīz* sign in his public appearances. It all began with Khomeini's *Kashf al-Asrar*."[13] However, Khomeini's admiration was revealed in a far more direct way when he tried to save Nawab Safavi from the gallows. As Con Coughlin pointed out, "While the rest of the country's leading clergy, including Grand Ayatollah Borujerdi, sought to distance themselves from the extremists, Khomeini stood apart as he mounted a spirited campaign to save Safavi's life. He personally lobbied Borujerdi, who turned down his entreaties to petition the Shah for Safavi's release. And when that failed he wrote to several leading members of the Shah's court appealing for clemency."[14] It was to no avail, as Safavi

---

11 Quoted in Amir Taheri, *Holy Terror*, 50.
12 Quoted in ibid., 53.
13 Sohrab Behdad, "Islamic Utopia in Pre-Revolutionary Iran, 62.
14 Con Coughlin, *Khomeini's Ghost. The Definitive Account of Ayatollah Khomeini's Islamic Revolution and its Enduring Legacy* (London: Macmillan, 2009), 87.

was hanged in January 1956.[15] Certainly, Safavi's militancy was a stirring example for Khomeini, who insisted that Muslims put their beliefs into action, and actively sought ways to bring about an Islamic revolution. Safavi's uncompromising Islamic agenda was very much in line with Khomeini's wishes for an Islamic republic.

The Influence of the 1979 Iranian Revolution in the Islamic World

The Iranian Revolution of 1979, when the Ayatollah Ruhollah Khomeini returned to Iran from exile and set about creating an Islamic republic, has been very influential throughout the Islamic world, even though it was a theocracy of a Shi'ite kind. (It was often argued that because Iran was Shi'ite, it could not possibly have any impact on the Sunni world. It was also assumed that Sunnis and Shi'ites would never collaborate.) Henceforth, whenever riots with pretentions to revolutionary movements broke out in Muslim countries from Bangladesh to Morocco, portraits of the glowering and formidable figure of Khomeini were defiantly brandished and translations of his works into the local languages were distributed among protesters.

The assassins of Egyptian president Anwar Sadat invoked Khomeini's name at their 1981 trial, and King Hasan of Morocco held the Ayatollah responsible for the kingdom's 1983 riots. As Amir Taheri explained in *The Spirit of Allah: Khomeini & the Islamic Revolution* (1986):

> It became evident that Khomeini's appeal was not limited to Sh'ites. Sunni radicals also adopted his slogans in their efforts to mobilize popular support. Fear of Khomeini was in part responsible for the sudden and almost concerted reintroduction of strict Islamic laws in Malaysia, Bangladesh, Pakistan, Abu Dhabi, Jordan, Yemen, Iraq, Egypt, Sudan, Somalia, Tunisia, Morocco and Mauritania. Even secular Turkey had to move some steps away from Kemalism in order to accommodate the new mood of Islamic militancy exported by Iran.[16]

Ruhollah Khomeini

Ruhollah Khomeini was born on September 24, 1902, in Khomein (also Khumayn), a town approximately a hundred kilometers southwest

---

15 According to Con Coughlin, Safavi was hanged in January 1956, (Con Coughlin, op.cit., 87). But according to Sohrab Behdad, he was hanged in December 1955, (Sohrab Behdad, op.cit., 51.)

16 Taheri, *Spirit of Allah*, 296-97.

of Tehran, into a fairly affluent family with religious traditions. His father, Sayyid Mostafa (d. 1902) studied in Najaf, a prestigious center of Shi'ite learning where he obtained a higher theology degree. Khomeini's paternal grandfather, Sayyid Ahmad (d. 1868) had also studied in Najaf.

Khomeini began his own religious studies in 1920 as the pupil of a famous high-ranking cleric, Shaykh Abdul-Karim Ha'eri (Ha'iri), who eventually settled in Qom, which became Iran's major scholastic center. Khomeini followed, and taught at the recently revived seminary, the Faizziyah, in the 1930s, publishing commentaries on *hadīths*, ethics, and mysticism, all in Arabic, which he had learned in his local school during his youth.[17] Khomeini's works included the *Misbah al-Hidaya* (*Book of Guidance*), *Shahar Do'ay al-Sahar* (*Interpretation of the Dawn Prayer*), *Shahar Arbe'en* (*Hadīth Explanations*), and *Adab as-Salat* (*Prayer Literature*). Khomeini also wrote poetry in Persian, which was only published posthumously. At this period, the clerics of Qom largely remained apolitical and refrained from criticizing the monarchy.

In 1937, Khomeini went on a pilgrimage to Mecca, and on the way back spent several months in Najaf to visit some holy shrines. His first timid foray into politics took the form of a tract, *Kashf al-Asrar* (*Secrets Unveiled*) published in 1943, in which he was very critical of contemporary secularists, particularly Reza Shah and the Pahlavi regime, but also Shariat Sangalaji, a reform-minded cleric who had supported the previous monarch, and Ahmad Kasravi, a historian of Shi'ism and Iran and truly anti-clerical supporter of democracy and admirer of the West.

In *Kashf al-Asrar* Khomeini attributed the lamentable state of Iran to the Shah's policy of ignoring Islamic precepts and weakening the *ulama'*, thereby undermining Islam itself. He also broached a subject that he would return to over and over throughout his life—the evil intentions of the Jews: "Jews and their foreign backers are those who are opposed to the very foundations of Islam and want to establish an international Jewish Government; and since they are a crafty and active lot, my fear is that, may Allah forbid it, they may one day succeed."[18] But on the whole, Khomeini avoided politics, and spent his time teaching at the Faizziyah during the 1950s, and working on *Towzih al-Masa'el* (*Questions Clarified*), which was published in 1961. His true entry into politics began in 1963.

In October 1962, the government had approved a law that pro-

---

17 Ervand Abrahamian, *Khomeinism: Essays on the Islamic Republic* (Berkeley: University of California Press, 1993), 7.

18 Quoted in Taheri, *Spirit of Allah*, 155.

vided for the election of representative local councils throughout the nation. Khomeini and other religious leaders found the law un-Islamic for three reasons: (1) it gave women the right to vote, (2) "it did not require adherence to Islam as a necessary qualification for either voters or candidates," and (3) it ruled "that elected councillors would take oath of office, not on the Koran, but on 'the holy book,' a wording that permitted the swearing in of councilors belonging to non-Muslim denominations."[19]

Khomeini considered the law an effort to corrupt chaste Muslim women, a sinister attempt to remove religion from its central place in national life, and a door being opened to "apostates," the Bahā'īs, giving them the possibility of elected seats on the councils. He wrote that the local council's law "was perhaps drawn up by the spies of the Jews and the Zionists.... The Koran and Islam are in danger. The independence of the state and the economy are threatened by a takeover by the Zionists, who in Iran have appeared in the guise of the Bahā'īs."[20] Khomeini was prepared to oppose even the constitution if it proved to be "contrary to the Koran."[21]

Nor did Khomeini remain politically passive when the Shah launched a series of reforms in 1963, later called the White Revolution. When seminary students protested, the Shah authorized army commandos to attack and harsass them over several days in March. Khomeini accused the Shah of violating the commandments of Islam and the rights of Muslims. He delivered a sermon on June 3 defending the religious classes, the *ulama'*, and again accused the Shah of trying to destroy Islam. Khomeini argued that the Shah was colluding with Israel, which did "not want the Koran to survive in this country," which "through its black agents, crushed the Faizziyah seminary. It crushes us. It crushes you, the nation. It desires to take over the economy. It desires to destroy our commerce and agriculture. It desires to seize the country's wealth."[22]

Khomeini was arrested a few days after giving the sermon, along with many other religious figures. He was visited by many emissaries from the Shah, who tried to persuade him to renounce politics. When the chief of Savak, the much feared Iranian secret police, told Khomeini,

---

19 Shaul Bakhash, *The Reign of the Ayatollahs Iran and the Islamic Revolution* (London: Unwin Paperbacks, 1985), 24.
20 Quoted in ibid., 26.
21 Quoted in ibid., 27.
22 Quoted in ibid., 29.

"Politics is lies, deception, shame and meanness. Leave politics to us," Khomeini replied, rather ambiguously, "All of Islam is politics."[23]

Khomeini was detained for two months, and then released. In 1964, he was rearrested for continued criticism of the Shah's policies and his continued claim that the Shah was trying to destroy Islam and the Koran. This time Khomeini was deported to Turkey, from whence he made his way to Najaf, Iraq, where he would spend the next thirteen years.

In Najaf Khomeini taught Islamic jurisprudence (fiqh), and wrote manuals on the rituals of pilgrimage (*jaj*) and on trade. In 1970, Khomeini gave a series of lectures denouncing the clergy, who compromised with the monarchy in Iran and remained aloof from politics. The lectures were collected, published, and circulated in Iran under the title *Vilāyat-i faqīh: Hukumat-i Islami* (*Islamic Government by the Jurist*). After spending a few months in France, Khomeini returned in triumph to Iran. Throughout the last ten years of his life he gave lectures, talks, and sermons, all consistently continuing the theme of the dangers to Islam and the threats to the independence of Iran.

An Islamic Revolution

Some modern scholars such as Ervand Abrahamian have argued that Khomeini was not an Islamic fundamentalist but more akin to a Latin American populist. Inevitably, such scholars downplay the importance of religion, in general, and Islam in particular in their analysis of Khomeini's ideas. I completely disagree with Abrahamian—it seems to me he misreads the spiritual core of Khomeini's political activism. Khomeini explicitly rejected the notion that the Islamic Revolution of 1979 was brought about for socioeconomic reasons; it was for Islam.

Consider this excerpt from Khomeini's September 8, 1979, address to the Iranian people broadcast on Tehran Radio:

> I would like to see everyone believe that our movement... for which considerable efforts were made, sacrifices given, young people killed and families ruined...was only for Islam....I do not accept that any prudent individual can believe that...we sacrificed our young men to have less expensive housing. No one in his right mind would lose young men simply to acquire less expensive housing. There is a false log-

---

23 Quoted in Bernard Lewis, *Islam in History: Ideas, People, and Events in the Middle East* (Chicago and La Salle, IL: Open Court 1993), 390.

ic promoted perhaps by some self-seeking individuals...that the aim of our sacrifices is to improve agriculture. No one would give his life for better agriculture....Islam has put an end to means that lead our young men to corruption. Islam wants fighters to stand up to the unbelievers, to those attacking our country. Islam wants to create *mujahid* [one engaged in *jihād*]; it has no intention of making revelers, so that while they are engaged in having a good time, others denigrate and dishonor them. Islam is a serious religion...The only games allowed by Islam are shooting and horse racing, and only for fighting....However, the West wants to keep us as before.... We must try to implement the true nature of the Islamic Republic....Certain drastic and profound changes have taken place that give rise to hopefulness.[24]

Other scholars of Iranian origin also emphasized the Islamic nature of the revolution. For example, Shaul Bakhash in a much lauded work gives unequivocal importance to the role of Islam in the newly created Islamic Republic of Iran:

[A] secular state has given way to a quasi-theocracy. Islamic law codes have replaced secular statutes....Due to its specifically Islamic character, the Iranian revolution has also galvanized Islamic communities in the Persian Gulf and the Middle East. The revolution appeared to provide evidence of the ability of Islam to mobilize millions, to overthrow an autocratic government, to humiliate the United States, to defend the national frontiers, to wage foreign war, and to begin the task of realizing the ideal of an Islamic state.[25]

Bakhash underlines that it is in Iran "that the most comprehensive efforts to forge Islamic legal and economic institutions and to establish an Islamic state is underway."[26] One simply cannot ignore "the powerful

---

24 Ayatollah Ruhollah Khomeini, speech, Tehran Radio, September 8, 1979, trans. Foreign Broadcast Information Service (FBIS), September 10, 1979; quoted in Rubin and Rubin, *Anti-American Terrorism*, 35–36. FBIS, an open source intelligence component of the CIA's Directorate of Science and Technology, monitored, translated, and disseminated within the U.S. government openly available news and information from media sources outside the United States.

25 Bakhash, *Reign of the Ayatollahs*, 4.

26 Ibid., 5.

pull of Islamic ideology"[27] in what is happening in Iran, though admittedly there are other complex factors in play in the upheavals.

As the revolution progressed after February 1979, Khomeini skillfully used each crisis "to consolidate his hold on the country and to pursue, single-mindedly, his aim to establishing an Islamic state."[28] Even a cursory glance at Khomeini's central work, *Vilāyat-i faqīh: Hukumat-i Islami* (*Islamic Government by the Jurist*), reveals the importance of "Islam" in an "Islamic government." As Hamid Algar, British-American professor emeritus of Persian studies at the University of California, Berkeley, observes, three major points that emerge from this treatise: "The first is the necessity for the establishment and maintenance of Islamic political institutions...[i.e.,] the need for subordinating political power to Islamic goals, precepts, and criteria. The second is the duty of the religious scholars (*fuqaha*) to bring about an Islamic state, and to assume legislative, executive, and judicial positions within it—in short the doctrine of the 'governance of the *faqih*' (*vilayat-i faqih* [vice-regency government of the Islamic jurists)."[29] The third is the need for a program of action for the establishment of an Islamic state.

Islamic Government begins with an attack: "From the very beginning, the historical movement of Islam has had to contend with the Jews, for it was they who first established anti-Islamic propaganda and engaged in various strategems, and as you can see, this activity continues down to the present."[30] There is a tendency to downplay that antisemitism is central to Islamic fundamentalism, and is not merely a matter of Israel's existence, but part of the Islamic myth derived from the Koran, *hadīth*, and *Sira*. Khomeini returns to the theme of the Jews and their evil ways throughout *Islamic Government*, four times at great length.[31]

Khomeini explains in *Islamic Government* that the Prophet Muhammad appointed a successor to do more than expound Islamic law: Muhammad "implemented the penal provisions of Islam: he cut off the hand of the thief and administered lashings and stonings. The successor to the Prophet must do the same; his task is not legislation, but the implementation of the divine laws that the Prophet has promulgated."[32]

---

27 Ibid.
28 Ibid., 6.
29 *Islam and Revolution: Writings and Declarations of Imam Khomeini (1941–1980)*, trans. with annotations Hamid Algar (North Haledon, NJ: Mizan Press, 1981), 25.
30 Ibid., 27.
31 Ibid., 89, 109, 113, 127.
32 Ibid., 37.

Addressing the religious class, Khomeini tells them that it is their duty to establish an Islamic government and that there is no separation of religion and politics.[33] He emphasizes the universality, comprehensiveness, and eternal validity of Islamic law:

> According to one of the noble verses of the Qur'an, the ordinances of Islam are not limited with respect to time or place; they are permanent and must be enacted until the end of time....The claim that the laws of Islam may remain in abeyance or are restricted to a particular time or place is contrary to the essential creedal basis of Islam. Since the enactment of laws, then is necessary after the departure of the Prophet from this world, and indeed, will remain so until the end of time, the formation of a government and the establishment of executive and administrative organs are also necessary.[34]

For Khomeini, as for so many Islamists such as Mawdūdī, Islamic law amounts to a complete social system in which "all the needs of man have been met: his dealings with neighbors, fellow citizens, and clan, as well as children and relatives; the concerns of private and marital life; regulations concerning war and peace and intercourse with other nations; penal and commercial law; and regulations pertaining to trade and agriculture."[35] This explains its totalitarian nature.

And it is all contained in the Koran and the *Sunna*. Sovereignty belongs to God alone and law is His decree and command. "It is an established principle that the *faqih* [expert in Islamic jurisprudence] has authority over the ruler. If the ruler adheres to Islam, he must necessarily submit to the *faqih*, asking him about the laws and ordinances of Islam in order to implement them. This being the case, the true rulers are the *fuqaha* [pl. of *faqih*] themselves, and rulership ought officially... to apply to them, not to those who are obliged to follow the guidance of the *fuqaha* on account of their own ignorance of the law."[36]

Growing with Blood

Because of its universality, and because God intended the world to follow Islam, it is the duty of all Muslims and especially the scholars

---

33 Ibid., 37-38.
34 Ibid., 41-42.
35 Ibid., 43.
36 Ibid., 60.

to disseminate knowledge of Islam to the world.[37] It is a Muslim's duty to preserve Islam, and to this end, blood must sometimes be shed. "The *fuqaha* by means of *jihad* and enjoining good and forbidding the evil, must overthrow tyrannical rulers and rouse the people so that the universal movement of all alert Muslims can establish Islamic government in place of tyrannical regimes."[38] And Khomeini never hid the fact that

> Islam grew with blood....The great prophet of Islam on one hand carried the Koran and in the other a sword; the sword for crushing the traitors and the Koran for guidance. For those who could be guided, the Koran was their means of guidance, while as for those who could not be guided and were plotters, the sword descended on their heads.... Islam is a religion of blood for the infidels but a religion of guidance for other people.[39]

In the crucial year 1978, Khomeini kept up the pressure, continuing to criticize the Shah, the monarchy, the constitution, and the United States, while emphasizing Islam's centrality to the opposition movement and even warning against groups with non-Islamic tendencies.[40] In a July 27 proclamation Khomeini established the Islamic nature of the anti-regime movement, giving the clerics their due: "Iran's recent, sacred movement...is one hundred percent Islamic. It was founded by the able hand of the clerics alone, and with the support of the great, Islamic nation. It was and is directed, individually or jointly, by the leadership of the clerical community. Since this...movement is Islamic, it continues and shall continue without the interference of others in the leadership."[41]

For Khomeini, "The whole nation, throughout Iran, cries out: 'We want an Islamic Republic,'"[42] and he vigorously urged the clerics not to cede in their demand for the same. In June 1979 Khomeini uged the religious scholars of Islam to review and correct the draft constitution, without giving in to outside voices:

---

37 Ibid., 70.
38 Ibid., 108-9.
39 Ayatollah Ruhollah Khomeini, from a speech at Feyziyeh (Fayziyyah) Theological School, August 24, 1979; quoted in Rubin and Rubin, *Anti-American Terrorism*, 32–33.
40 Bakhash, *Reign of the Ayatollahs*, 47.
41 Ibid., 48.
42 Ibid.

This right belongs to you. It is those knowledgeable in Islam who may express an opinion on the law of Islam. The constitution of the Islamic Republic means the constitution of Islam. Don't sit back while foreignized intellectuals, who have no faith in Islam, give their views....Pick up your pens and in the mosques, from the altars, in the streets and bazaars, speak of the things that in your view should be included in the constitution.[43]

A Constitution of Islam

Heeding Khomeini's advice, the Congress of Muslim Critics of the Constitution entered the fray, and "sought to enshrine Islam as the basis of the constitution, the institutions of the state, its economic and judicial system, and even the institution of the family."[44] They rejected the idea of equality of men and women; they rejected the idea of the sovereignty of the people. Many clerics reminded the people of Iran that Islam is universal and does not recognize borders. Others stated that by its very nature Islam is domineering, and one had a duty to spread it. When the Assembly of Experts met on August 18, Khomeini reminded the delegates that the constitution must be "one hundred per cent Islamic," and that "discussion of proposals contrary to Islam lies outside the scope of [its] mandate." Furthermore, only the leading Islamic jurists could decide whether the articles constitution met Islamic criteria.[45]

By November 15, the assembly had drawn up the new draft constitution, which essentially laid the foundation for a theocratic state. The *faqih* was henceforth the central figure in the political order, which

> enshrined the dominance of the clerical community over the institutions of the state, entrenched Islamic jurisprudence as the foundation over the country's laws and legal system, and limited the individual freedoms to what was considered permissible under Islam. The constitution provided for a twelve-man Council of Guardians empowered to veto all legislation in violation of Islamic or constitutional principles and reserved to the six Islamic jurists on the council the power to declare laws in conflict with Islam.[46]

---

43 Quoted in ibid., 7.
44 Ibid., 78.
45 Ibid., 81.
46 Ibid., 83.

As article 4 of the constitution stated, "All civil, penal, financial, economic, administrative, cultural, military, political and other laws and regulations must be based on Islamic criteria."[47]

The constitution that emerged despite a certain ambiguity as to whom sovereignty really belonged—God or the people—was largely a product of Khomeini's concept of Islamic government, with the clerical class clearly in charge.

By 1982, Khomeini was in control; his religious lieutenants ran the country. He trusted only clerics, having always believed that they were the class most qualified to govern and bring about the Islamic state. Khomeini

> attached overriding importance to the spread of Islamic teaching, to ideological orthodoxy, and to political conformity. He was relentless in his pursuit of those he regarded as the enemies of the Islamic Republic. Because Islamic government to him was synonymous with the rule of Islamic law, he devoted careful attention to appointment of judges, the elaboration of an Islamic court system, and the legislation of Islamic law codes. He took care that internal security remained in the hands of trusted lieutenants. Increasingly, he was committed to exporting revolution.[48]

That Khomeini's main concern was establishing an Islamic State is underlined by the fact that he showed little to no interest in economic policy.[49]

The Islamic Republic of Iran

Once the clerics were in command, the Islamic Republic of Iran began eliminating all opponents and all Khomeini deemed apostates. Blood had to be spilled to protect Islam, and Islam was not a religion of pacifists. Back in 1942 Khomeini had written: "Islam's *jihād* is a struggle against idolatry, sexual deviation plunder, repression, and cruelty. The war waged by conquerors…aims at promoting lust and animal pleasures. They care not if whole countries are wiped out and many families left homeless. But those who study *jihād* will understand why Islam wants to conquer the whole world. All the countries conquered by Is-

---

47 Ibid.
48 Ibid., 241-42.
49 Ibid., 242.

lam...will be marked for everlasting salvation."⁵⁰

Khomeini then poured scorn on those who have a pacifist interpretation of Islam and *jihād*:

> Those who know nothing of Islam pretend that Islam counsels against war....Islam says: Kill all unbelievers just as they would kill you all!...Does this mean sitting back until [non-Muslims] overcome us? Islam says: Kill in the service of Allah those may want to kill you! Does this mean we should surrender [to the enemy]? Islam says: Whatever good there is exists thanks to the sword and in the shadow of the sword! People cannot be made obedient except with the sword! The sword is the key to paradise, which can be opened only for holy warriors! There are hundreds of other psalms and *hadiths* urging Muslims to value war and to fight. Does all that mean that Islam is a religion that prevents men from waging war? I spit upon those foolish souls who make such a claim.⁵¹

A Disregard for Human Rights

Whenever and wherever Islamic principles are invoked, there is inevitably a disregard for the human rights of women, religious minorities, gays and lesbians, apostates, and freethinkers. The Iran Human Rights Documentation Center (IHRDC), which has carefully monitored human rights abuses in Iran since the 1979 Revolution, states

> The Islamic Republic of Iran executes the second-highest number of people annually in the world: in 2011, for instance, the Islamic Republic of Iran executed 660 people. In Iran, capital punishment can be imposed on appeal, thereby acting as a deterrent to appeals in criminal cases. Juveniles can also be subjected to capital punishment, in violation of peremptory norms.⁵² Moreover, capital punishment is not limited to violent crimes. Adultery, drug offenses, sodomy (consensual or otherwise), apostasy (conversion from Is-

---

50 Ayatollah Ruhollah Khomeini; quoted in Rubin and Rubin, *Anti-American Terrorism*, 29.

51 Ibid.

52 A peremptory norm (also called *jus cogens or ius cogens*, "compelling law") is a fundamental principle of international law accepted by the international community of states as a norm from which no derogation is permitted.

lam), "insulting the prophet," and vague national security crimes like "sowing corruption on Earth" are all punishable by death. Meanwhile, capital punishment cases are often marked by weak evidentiary standards.[53]

Capital punishment may be imposed for rape, murder, drug trafficking, apostasy, and illicit sex (adultery, sodomy). Amnesty International has reported seventy-six cases of lethal stoning between 1980 and 1989 in Iran, while the International Committee against Execution (ICAE) has reported that seventy-four others were stoned to death in Iran between 1990 and 2009.[54]

Estimates by human rights activists and opponents of the Islamic Republic of Iran of the number of gay men and lesbians executed for crimes related to their sexual orientation since 1979 vary between several hundred to as many as six thousand.[55] According to the Boroumand Foundation, records exist for at least 107 executions with charges related to homosexuality between 1979 and 1990.[56] Iran is one of eight countries in the world where homosexual acts are punishable by death; all are Islamic.[57] According to a 2013 report from the IHRDC:

---

[53] "Executions," Iran Human Rights Documentation Center, n.d., http://www.iranhrdc.org/english/executions.html.

[54] Hamid R. Kusha1 and Nawal H. Ammar, "Stoning Women in the Islamic Republic of Iran: Is It Holy Law or Gender Violence?" *Arts and Social Sciences Journal* 5, no. 1 (2014), https://www.omicsonline.com/open-access/stoning-women-in-the-islamic-republic-of-iran-is-it-holy-law-or-gender-violence-2151-6200.1000063.pdf. See also, Farshad Hoseini, "List of Known Cases of Death by Stoning Sentences in Iran, 1980–2010," International Committee against Execution, July 2010, http://stopstonningnow.com/wpress/SList%20_1980-2010__FHdoc.pdf.

[55] "Iran: UK Grants Asylum to Victim of Tehran Persecution of Gays, Citing Publicity," (London) *Telegraph*, February 4, 2011, http://www.telegraph.co.uk/news/wikileaks-files/london-wikileaks/8305064/IRAN-UK-GRANTS-ASYLUM-TO-VICTIM-OF-TEHRAN-PERSECUTION-OF-GAYS-CITING-PUBLICITY.html. See also: Arhsam Parsi, "Iranian Queers and Laws: Fighting for Freedom of Expression," *Harvard International Review* 36, no. 2 (Fall 2014/Winter 2015), http://hir.harvard.edu/iranian-queers-and-laws-fighting-for-freedom-of-expression/; "Denied Identity: Human Rights Abuses against Iran's LGBT Community," Iran Human Rights Documentation Center, November 7, 2013, http://www.iranrights.org/library/document/2636.

[56] Omid: A Memorial in Defense of Human Rights, Human Rights and Democracy in Iran, Abdorrahman Boroumand Foundation, https://www.iranrights.org/memorial

[57] Yemen, Mauritania, and Saudi Arabia: death by stoning; Qatar, Afghanistan, Somalia, Sudan. Certain states in Nigeria where Islamic laws have been passed also prescribe the death penalty for homosexual acts.

In 1982 the Iranian parliament passed the Law of Hodud and Qisas. This law was the first legislation that codified punishments based on Shariʻa law. A supplementary law was enacted in 1983. The Islamic Republic of Iran [IRI] merged these laws into a single code in 1991. The Iran Penal Code, which came into effect in that year, explicitly codified punishments for adultery, sodomy and other homosexual acts. According to this code, anyone convicted of sodomy would be sentenced to death. The method of the execution was left to the judge's discretion. Islamic law grants extensive discretion to a judge in determining the method of execution for a person convicted of sodomy. Although in practice most offenders are executed by hanging, Ayatollah Khomeini previously stated that in cases of sodomy the judge can order the offender to be beheaded by a sword, burned alive, stoned or thrown off of a mountain or another high place with his hands and feet tied, or even have a wall demolished over his head.[58]

In the months following February 1979, the Islamic Republic executed 757 Iranians for "sowing corruption on earth."[59] Between 1981 and 1985, the regime executed thousands of its political opponents. One prisoner remembers spotting Ayatollah Qaffari, a noted cleric and revolutionary, walking through Evin's atrium [the central courtyard of the main prison located in northwestern Tehran] and stopping at a water spigot. The prisoner, a royalist, reported that "[Qaffari's] whole body was covered in blood, which he had to wash off in order to go and pray. They were doing some mind-boggling killing of the Mojahedin."[60]

However, as the IHRDC reports,

[T]he 1988 massacre stands out for the systematic way in which it was planned and carried out, the short time period in which it took place throughout the country, the arbitrary method used to determine victims, the sheer number of victims, and the fact that the regime took extensive measures to keep the executions secret and continues to deny that

---

58 Iran Human Rights Documentation Center, "Denied Identity."
59 Ervand Abrahamian, *Tortured Confessions: Prisons and Public Recantations in Modern Iran* (Berkeley: University of California Press, 1999), 124–25.
60 Iran Human Rights Documentation Center, telephone interview with Bahman Rahbari, April 19, 2009.

they took place. The executions began pursuant to a fatwa issued by Ayatollah Khomeini immediately following Iran's announcement that it had agreed to a cease-fire in the devastating eight-year Iran-Iraq war. The fatwa created three-man commissions to determine who should be executed. The commissions, known by prisoners as Death Commissions, questioned prisoners about their political and religious beliefs, and depending on the answers, determined who should be executed and/or tortured. The questioning was brief, not public, there were no appeals, and prisoners were executed the same day or soon thereafter. Many who were not executed immediately were tortured.[61]

Here is Khomeini's decree:

In the Name of God, the Compassionate, the Merciful.

As the treacherous *Monafeqin* [*Munāfiqūn*, "The Hypocrites," but here refers to the Mojahedin] do not believe in Islam and what they say is out of deception and hypocrisy, and as their leaders have confessed that they have become renegades, and as they are waging war on God, and as they are engaging in classical warfare in the western, the northern and southern fronts, and as they are collaborating with the Baathist Party of Iraq and spying for Saddam against our Muslim nation, and as they are tied to the World Arrogance, and in light of their cowardly blows to the Islamic Republic since its inception, it is decreed that those who are in prisons throughout the country and remain steadfast in their support for the *Monafeqin*, are waging war and are condemned to execution.

The task of implanting the decree in Tehran is entrusted to Hojjatol-Islam Nayyeri, the religious judge, Mr Eshraqi, the Tehran prosecutor, and a representative of the Intelligence Ministry.

Even though a unanimous decision is better, the view of the

---

[61] "Deadly Fatwa: Iran's 1988 Prison Massacre," Iran Human Rights Documentation Center, n.d., http://www.iranhrdc.org/english/publications/reports/3158-deadly-fatwa-iran-s-1988-prison-massacre.html.

majority of the three must prevail. In prisons in the provinces, the views of a majority of a trio consisting of the religious judge, the revolutionary prosecutor, and the Intelligence Ministry representative must be obeyed. It is naïve to show mercy to those who wage war on God. The decisive way in Islam which treats the enemies of God is among the unquestionable tenets of the Islamic regime. I hope that with your revolutionary rage and vengeance toward the enemies of Islam, you would achieve the satisfaction of the Almighty God. Those who are making the decisions must not hesitate, nor show any doubt or be concerned with details. They must try to be "most ferocious against infidels."

To have doubts about the judicial matters of revolutionary Islam is to ignore the pure blood of martyrs.[62]

Khomeini's Victims

The number of Khomeini's victims is hard to estimate. According to Christina Lamb in a 2001 *Daily Telegraph* article, basing her figures on the memoirs of Grand Ayatollah Hossein Ali Montazeri: "More than 30,000 political prisoners were executed in the 1988 massacre—a far larger number than previously suspected. Secret documents smuggled out of Iran reveal that, because of the large numbers of necks to be broken, prisoners [including children] were loaded onto forklift trucks in groups of six and hanged from cranes in half-hourly intervals."[63]

The National Council of Resistance of Iran Foreign Affairs Committee gives a thorough analysis of events in all of Iran's prisons in 1988 and confirms the 30,000 figure.[64] It also quotes Montazeri's memoirs, which detail the systematic rape of women, some as young as thirteen. In his letter to Khomeini, Montazeri aked, "Did you know that in Mashad prison, some 25 girls had to have their ovaries or uterus removed

---

62 Quoted in Foreign Affairs Committee, *Crime against Humanity: Indict Iran's Ruling Mullahs for Massacre of 30,000 Political Prisoners* (Auvers-sur-Oise, France: National Council of Resistance of Iran, 2001), 2.

63 Christina Lamb, "Khomeini Fatwa 'Led to Killing of 30,000 in Iran'" (London) *Telegraph*, February 4, 2001, http://www.telegraph.co.uk/news/worldnews/middleeast/iran/1321090/Khomeini-fatwa-led-to-killing-of-30000-in-Iran.html. See also Geoffrey Robertson QC, *The Massacre of Political Prisoners in Iran, 1988, Report of an Inquiry* (Washington, DC: Abdorraham Boroumand Foundation, 2016), http://www.iranrights.org/library/document/1380.

64 Foreign Affairs Committee, *Crime against Humanity*, 21–26.

as result of what had been done to them, and because there were no physicians and medical care?"[65]

In its 2015 annual report, the United States Commission on International Religious Freedom (USCIRF) paints a grim picture of conditions in Iran:

> Poor religious freedom conditions continued to deteriorate in 2014, particularly for religious minorities, especially Baha'is, Christian converts, and Sunni Muslims. Sufi Muslims and dissenting Shi'a Muslims also faced harassment, arrests, and imprisonment. Since President Hassan Rouhani assumed office in August 2013, the number of individuals from religious minority communities who are in prison because of their beliefs has increased. The government of Iran continues to engage in systematic, ongoing, and egregious violations of religious freedom, including prolonged detention, torture, and executions based primarily or entirely upon the religion of the accused.[66]

On May 13, 2016, the Religion News Service reported:

> The eighth anniversary this Saturday (May 14) of Iran's imprisonment of seven Baha'i leaders is an opportune time to refocus attention on the plight of their people. Dominated by an extremist interpretation of Shiite Islam, Iran's government has a long-term goal to eradicate the more than 300,000-member Baha'i community, the country's largest non-Muslim religious minority. While pursuit of that goal remains, its intensity ebbs and flows in response to the level of world attention and outrage. Unfortunately, there are signs from this past year that persecution is on the upswing, calling for greater world outrage at Iran's abuses of this peaceful religious community. Since Iran's Khomeini revolution of 1979, authorities have killed more than 200 Baha'i leaders, and more than 10,000 have been dismissed from government

---

65 Ibid., 27.
66 United States Commission on International Religious Freedom, Annual Report 2015 (Washington, DC: U.S. Commission on International Religious Freedom, 2015), http://www.uscirf.gov/sites/default/files/USCIRF%20Annual%20Report%202015%20%282%29.pdf

and university jobs. Baha'is effectively are prohibited from attending colleges, chartering their own worship centers or schools, serving in the military, and obtaining various kinds of jobs. Even Baha'i marriages are not recognized.

Over the past 10 years, about 850 Baha'is arbitrarily have been arrested. As of February 2016, more than 80 remain imprisoned, including the Baha'i Seven.[67]

The rest of the report makes it clear that the situation is similar for Christians, Jews and Zoroastrians, all of whom are subject to arbitrary arrest, imprisonment and torture.

The IHRDC has closely monitored the worsening situation of women in the Islamic Republic of Iran (IRI). Following a detailed report, it concludes:

> The IRI legal system recognizes women as dependent upon men and incomplete human beings who need to be supervised and controlled by men and the State. While the IRI Constitution claims to guarantee equality…women are still treated as second class citizens under the IRI legal system. For instance…under the Islamic Penal Code, the value of a woman's worth is only half that of a man's.…The same view… is rooted in the IRI Civil Code and family law which provide that women may inherit half of what men do. Similarly, it gives far greater rights in marriage and divorce to men than to women. Most notably, only a man can contract more than one marriage at a time (up to four permanent marriages and an unlimited number of temporary marriages are allowed for men), and only men have unilateral and unconditional divorce rights, while a woman cannot terminate the marriage contract without her husband's agreement, or in specific circumstances by permission of the judge. These gender inequalities have often been rationalized and justified by arguments based on assumptions about innate, natural differences between the sexes.…It is also claimed that women are

---

67 Robert P. George and Katrina Lantos Swett, "Iran Wants to Eradicate Baha'is: We Should Demand Their Religious Freedom," Religion News Service, May 13, 2016, http://religionnews.com/2016/05/13/iran-wants-to-eradicate-bahais-we-should-demand-their-religious-freedom.

created solely for the purpose of giving pleasure to men and child-bearing—functions that confine them to the home—which means that men must protect and provide for them. This construction of gender roles and the patriarchal control of women have produced a framework that demands women's obedience to their husbands and has its roots in the idea of male superiority...and results in the economic, social and political predominance of men and dependency of women. The IRI legal system still retains this traditional patriarchal bias that can be described as nothing but the systemic subordination of women, which is undoubtedly a human rights violation. In addition, the IRI is not meeting its obligations of equal treatment of both genders required by international human rights instruments including the Universal Declaration of Human Rights (1948) and the International Covenant on Civil and Political Rights.[68]

State Terror

Iran is representative of what Islamic fundamentalists desire, an Islamic State, and the consequence of achieving it: State Terror. Instead of utopia, Iran is an Islamic totalitarian nightmare, a predictable outcome, given its premises. There is no ambiguity in this statement. Ayatollah Khomeini was born into an affluent family and became a scholar with a profound knowledge of the Koran and *sunna* who studied and taught Islam all his life. Thus we may eliminate poverty and ignorance of Islam—two popular explanations for Islamic terrorism—as the motivating impulses behind Khomeini's desire for an Islamic State.

Khomeini and his clerics wished to implement Islamic laws in an Islamic State, which they managed to install. The ensuing state terrorism followed naturally from Islamic laws. In other words, Islam was and is responsible for Islamic terrorism, precisely the thesis I set out to demonstrate.

Of course, some scholars have convinced themselves, if not everyone else, that the Islamic Revolution was actually "a movement for democratization in a society atrophied by tyranny."[69] But to pull off this

---

68 "Gender Inequality and Discrimination: The Case of Iranian Women," Iran Human Rights Documentation Center, March 8, 2013, http://iranhrdc.org/english/publications/legal-commentary/1000000261-gender-inequality-and-discrimination-the-case-of-iranian-women.html#19.
69 Taheri, *Spirit of Allah*, 20–21.

act of historical prestidigitation such scholars are obliged to minimize the role of Khomeini. Other historians who are unable to understand the role of religion in the Islamic world also relegate Khomeini to a supporting role and try their best to locate the Islamic Revolution in the scholar's habitual procrustean bed of historical materialism or socioeconomics. But the Islamic Republic of Iran exists and operates as what every Islamic fundamentalist dreams of, an Islamic state ruled by *Shariʿa*.

Certain pragmatic compromises have certainly been made, but the Islamic Republic of Iran is, essentially, an Islamic State. What followed its establishment was the inevitable consequence and inexorable logic of its Islamic premises: state terrorism, a merciless tyranny. Despite his compassion for the poor, Khomeini despised the comforts of this world, loathed "Western materialism," and had no interest in economic policy or concern for the "price of melons." For Khomeini—as for so many Islamic ideologues from Mawdūdī to Sayyid Qutb—we are on Earth to worship Allah, who needs, nay commands, constant, eternal flattery. We are here to follow His law as set down in the Koran and the *Sunna*, and it is the duty of all humanity to prepare for the Hereafter. Death should not be feared but welcomed as a means to fight for the sake of Allah.

Khomeini was fond of reciting the Persian poet Nasser Khosrow Qobadiani: "People's fear of death is a disease whose only cure is faith."[70] And in his talks to the people of Iran Khomeini tried to convince them that death is to be coveted and life shunned, for "[d]eath offered purification and the exalted status of the martyr, while life was pregnant with all manner of corruption and sin, the smallest of which would surely lead to hell....'You should pray to Allah to grant you the honor of becoming martyrs.'"[71]

In an address commemorating the seventh day of his son Mostafa's death in Najaf, Iraq, Khomeini said:

> This world is but a passage; it is not a world in which we ought to live. This [world] is but a way, it is the Narrow Path....True Life is that offered only in the Hereafter....We are here, in this low, earthly Life, only to perform the duties Allah has set for us to perform. We may, because of our ignorance, consider these duties to be onerous; but these are, verily, the best example of the Almighty's generosity....No one becomes a

---

70 Ibid., 121.
71 Ibid., 122.

true human being without first crossing the Narrow Path.[72]

At a meeting in Qom, Khomeini stated, "The aim of creation was for mankind to be put to the test through hardship and prayer. An Islamic regime must be serious in every field. There are no jokes in Islam. There is no humor in Islam. There can be no…joy in whatever is serious."[73]

Khomeini's vision did not end with the establishment of the Islamic Republic of Iran. He dreamed of creating a single universal Islamic State, and to that end encouraged revolution throughout the Islamic world. Only an Islamic superstate could take on the Jews, Crusaders, and the Satanic superpowers: the United States and the Soviet Union.

---

72 Ibid., 39.
73 Ibid., 259.

CHAPTER 24
CONCLUSION: "THE LIFE OF THE MUSLIM *UMMA* IS SOLELY DEPENDENT ON THE INK OF THE SCHOLARS AND THE BLOOD OF THE MARTYRS."

TO UNDERTAND the Islam in Islamic terrorism we need examine the continuities between contemporary *jihadists* and similar movements throughout Islamic history. It seems clear that these movements would not have existed without Islamic history, and would not have had the aims they do have without Islam. Not only do similarities exist between contemporary movements and the religious riots in seventeenth-century Istanbul, for example, but there is a causal, historical link between them. The Qādīzādeli movement in Istanbul influenced the movement initiated by Ibn ʿAbd al-Wahhāb in eighteenth-century Najd (Arabia), and Wahhābism has influenced modern movements in Egypt as well in India and Southeast Asia. All, in turn, were influenced by Ibn Taymiyya, the Islamic philosopher who died in 1328.

But to concentrate only on the influence of this medieval Islamic thinker, as many modern critics do, is to miss the point. For Ibn Taymiyya himself was drawing upon a long tradition derived from Ahmad Ibn Hanbal (d. 855)—and that tradition did not originate with Ibn Hanbal either, but reaches all the way back to early Islam, and its founding texts, the Koran, the *Sira*, and *hadīth*, and the model to be followed as found in the *Sunna*.

To understand the Islamic aims of ISIS or ISIL (the Islamic State of Iraq and the Levant), one only need ask what will ISIL do once Syria,

Iraq, and the Levant are conquered? The answer is obvious: ISIL will establish an Islamic State. That is exactly what happened in Iran: Khomeini took power and established an Islamic State, applying Islamic Law. As Khomeini said, Islam is politics. And as Mawdūdī, Hasan al-Banna, and Khomeini have pointed out, Islam is a total system that regulates every aspect of an individual's life—from cradle to grave.

Two important concepts in Islam are brought forth in the following quotes, the first from Ismail Faruqi, the late Palestinian-American professor of religion, the second from Michael Cook, British historian and scholar of Islamic history. "Islam teaches not only that the realization of the good is possible in this world," wrote Faruqi, "but that to bring it about here and now is precisely the duty of every man and woman....Hence, the good must be possible to actualize—indeed obligatory."[1] But this duty, this imperative of putting into action the principles of Islam is emphasized over and over again by all the thinkers and groups discussed in these pages: from the Khārijites, to Khomeini, from the Hanbalites, to the rioters in tenth century Baghdad, from Ibn 'Abd al-Wahhāb to Hasan al-Banna and Sayyid Qutb.

Meanwhile, Cook observes, "The difference between Muslim thinking and that of the modern West is thus not simply that there is no single Muslim concept corresponding to the Western notion of privacy; it is also that the Muslim concepts seem to be of a significantly different kind."[2] Combine these statements and it is but a short step to what Westerners, at least, would call interfering in the private lives of others. Thence ensues all kinds of mischief; these worldviews that cannot help but clash. As Thomas Hobbes once said, "Certainly, peace among citizens cannot endure while there is no consent about the factors thought necessary for eternal salvation."[3]

In the epilogue of his lucid *Radical Islam and the Revival of Medieval Theology*, Daniel Lav points out that radical Salafists are fighting a war on behalf of faith against unbelief:[4]

> It is a mistake then to ascribe to these radicals too great an interest in any specific grievance or too great a vendetta

---

[1] Al-Faruqi, *Islam*, 13, cited by Levtzion and Voll, *Eighteenth-Century Renewal*, 6.
[2] Cook, *Forbidding Wrong*, 62–63.
[3] Thomas Hobbes, *Opera Latina*, London: 1839–1845, 1:29; quoted by Daniel Lav, *Radical Islam and the Revival of Medieval Theology* (Cambridge and New York: Cambridge University Press, 2012), 203n4.
[4] Ibid., 201-3.

against any particular flesh-and-blood enemy in its normal, real world existence. These enemies are, first and foremost, ciphers of unbelief, and their specificity dissipates under a glaring ultrafidian light to reveal their primary identity as *tāghūt* [idol].[5]

For the Salafi jihadists, there are false idols everywhere, and these radicals are equally ready to displace themselves "to Somalia, Yemen, Iraq, or Waziristan, as these are, in their view, fundamentally one single *jihad*....They do not trust 'those who do not share this stark doctrine of total war between faith and unbelief.'"[6]

As Lav says, there are no specific grievances, it is not something we, in the West have done, it is simply the fact that we do not accept the Koran as a blueprint for a model society. Our simple existence is provocation enough. It is the duty of the Islamic terrorists to bring about a society ruled by God's laws as promulgated in the Koran. The Islamic terrorists throughout Islamic history are galvanized by the same concerns: a desire for a return to the purity of their ancestors (*salaf*), a rejection of innovations (*bidaʻ*), a rigorous adherence to the concept of *tawhīd* (Unicity of God), the duty to follow the principle of Commanding Right and Forbidding Wrong and the necessity of carrying out, for the sake of God, *jihād*, in its military sense. They all have recourse to the same sources, above all the Koran; they all quote the same verses from the same *suras*, page after page.

Finally, it is not as the journalistic cliché has it, a simple matter of "a few bad apples." There is something immanent in Islam that engenders radicals willing to kill and be killed in the name of Allah. Appeasing or attempting to negotiate with the "bad apples" will not work. Nor will piecemeal tinkering: while the *Shariʻa*, to paraphrase Martin Kramer, maybe open to some reinterpretation, it is not infinitely elastic. Islam will produce Islamic terrorists until Muslims take a critical look at the Koran, and no longer treat it as the word of God. Lav concludes "When considered in the *longue durée*, these Muslim radicals are only

---

5 Lav, *Radical Islam*, 202. Thomas Patrick Hughes gives this definition of *tāghūt*: "An idol mentioned in the Qurʾan: Q4. *an-Nisāʾ*, the Women 54; Q2. *al-Baqara*, the Cow 257; Q2. *al-Baqara*, the Cow 259....[As-Suyūtī] says *tāghūt* was an idol of the Quraish, whom certain renegade Jews honoured in order to please the tribe. Mr [E.W.] Lane observes that in the *Arabian Nights* the name is used to express the devil as well as an idol." Hughes, *Dictionary of Islam*, s.v. "*tāghūt*."

6 Lav, *Radical Islam*, 202.

one recent irruption of the belligerent potential inherent in every *strong monotheism*" (emphasis added).[7]

In the twenty-first century there is a world of difference between a (not so strong) monotheism (Christianity) that expresses sorrow when confronted with apostasy, and one that is indeed strong (Islam), and when confronted by the same phenomenon expresses anger by killing the apostate. In his epilogue to *Radical Islam*, Lav notes:

> Thomas Hobbes remarked that a state's monopoly on violence could not deter those motivated to fight over "the factors thought necessary for eternal salvation." For this reason, the civil commonwealth must circumscribe the ambit of revelation and establish its moral priority over religious claims to authority if it is to bring peace. Centuries later, this same basic conflict is unfolding in the Muslim world, however different the parameters may be.[8]

Islamic revivalists divide the world into the Near Enemy and the Far Enemy. The near enemy is represented by the urgent situation in present-day Islamic countries where Islamic law is no longer applied. Here the unbroken tradition that leads all the way back to early Islam comes to the fore. But the far enemy will have to be confronted one day, and is represented by paganism, *mushrikun*, all who stray from God's Unicity (*tawhīd*) such as Christians, Hindus, and even those who worship saints. It also means democracy and liberty, where sovereignty belongs to the people, a principle antithetical to Islam, where sovereignty belongs to God. They, too, will have to be fought.

Thus *jihadism* is destined to remain with us for many decades, since there is something inherent in Islam that demands action, an incumbent religious duty to combat unbelief until only Islam remains across the face of the earth.

Reading fundamentalist writers such as Mawdūdī, al-Banna, Qutb, or Khomeini, one is struck by their certainty that they possess the Truth—that they know the will of God and that it is their duty to implement His laws as laid down in the Koran and other revered texts. They reveal no shred of doubt. And because they are convinced they possess the Truth, they feel it is their duty to impose it on the world. They cannot rest until Islam dominates the globe. There is no subtlety

---

7 Ibid.
8 Ibid., 202-3.

or nuance in their thought, and they are mediocre thinkers rather than profound philosophers, despite the fact that they have seduced many Western intellectuals into believing that what the Islamists are proposing is perfectly civilized and acceptable.

Western civilization on the other hand is racked by doubt, and until we retrieve our civilizational self-confidence, the irresistible logic of things will mean we will surrender our freedoms without a murmur.

Why has *jihād* reemerged with particular ferocity in the last forty years? Prolific contributor to the *New English Review* and *Jihad Watch* Hugh Fitzgerald offers gives three reasons for its resurrection, to which I add one additional explanation.[9]

In my view, paradoxically, it was increasing literacy and education that led to a growing dissatisfaction with current conditions in Islamic countries, as well as a rise in fundamentalism. Before the rise in urbanization and literacy, Islam was divided between a folk variant and an Islam accessible only to a clerical elite who could read Classical Arabic. Now more people have access to their own High Culture. They can read Ibn Taymiyya, and recognize for themselves that their own societies have fallen away from the true Islam, the pristine Islam of Muhammad and his companions.

Fitzgerald argues that "[t]he doctrine of *Jihād* wasn't suddenly invented in the past fifty years. It's been the same, more or less, for 1350 years. It had fallen into desuetude, but did not, and could not, disappear. What happened to make things so very different? Well, some might point to the end of 'colonialism.' But that is not the main thing."[10] Three developments explain the reemergence of *jihād*.

Muslim countries in the Middle East became immensely rich thanks to geology. Fitzgerald writes, "Since 1973, the Arab and other Muslim-dominated oil states have received ten trillion dollars from the sale of oil and gas to oil-consuming nations, the greatest transfer of wealth in human history. The Muslims did nothing to deserve this, though many took the oil bonanza as a deliberate sign of Allah's favor."[11]

Apart from buying billions of dollars in arms, Saudi Arabia has spent millions on Islamic propaganda on the building of madrassas. During the campaign against the Soviet presence in Afghanistan, much

---

9 Hugh Fitzgerald, "Understanding the Resurgence of Islam," *New English Review* (July 2007), http://www.newenglishreview.org/Hugh_Fitzgerald/Understanding_The_Resurgence_Of_Islam/.
10 Ibid.
11 Ibid.

money was provided to *jihādi* groups for missiles and training. Saudi Arabia and other Islamic countries such as Iran and Brunei have corrupted Western universities by large donations with strings attached, so that Islam is only taught in a manner acceptable to them.

Second, there has been large-scale immigration into the West, from Islamic nations, often former colonies, of Muslims who are implacably hostile to the West, have no desire to learn why the West became so rich and tolerant, and certainly have no desire to assimilate. They feel no gratitude or allegiance to their Western host nations; their only obligations are to fellow Muslims.

The mere presence of so many Muslims in the West has affected the domestic and international behavior of governments, whose foreign policy is dominated by a fear of offending their own Muslim population, ready to riot on the slightest pretext. These unassimilated Muslims are committed to introducing Islamic laws in the West, and they are able to do so by cleverly exploiting the freedoms created over centuries by the infidels.

Third, advances in technology, from cell phones to the Internet, from satellite television to YouTube videos, has meant the spread of Islamic propaganda, reaching all believers. By now no Muslim can claim ignorance of his duties, from the daily five prayers to the duty of Commanding Right and Forbidding Wrong to *jihād*. Theoretically, the West could use the same technological advances, which it invented, to broadcast its own propaganda. But the West, lacking confidence in its own values and afraid of offending Islamic governments considered "allies," has not done so. No Western government dares point out the "connection between the political, economic, social, and intellectual failures of Muslim societies, and Islam itself."[12] In any case, Muslims only watch channels such as *al-Jazeera*, that are broadcast in their own languages.

The Internet presents young Muslims access to Islamic material that was totally unknown to their parents—everything from the Koran, *hadīth*, the life of Muhammad, and the history of Islam. Islam is a totalitarian system that demands the suppression of one's individuality, and as surprising as it may seem, there are thousands of Muslims willing to submerge their identities into the group, where all answers are handed down from on high. They breathe a sigh of relief as they join the collective, "the charismatic community" in Watt's description, a community whose actions are undergirded by God. All these traits of Islam make it a kind of fascism, and certainly a totalitarian construct. We defeated, in

---

12 Ibid.

the twentieth century, two such totalitarian systems, but not before it had destroyed the lives of many millions. Let us prepare to confront, and defeat, another such ideology in the twenty-first century.

Selected Bibliography

I HAVE LIMITED myself to the most important works consulted. I have left out the bibliographical material referred to by my secondary sources; for example, in the present work I consult and cite the article on "*djihād*", in the *Encyclopaedia of Islam* 2nd Edition, by Émile Tyan. Tyan gives bibliographical details of nearly twenty-five works, which I have given in a footnote. However, I do not repeat them here in this bibliography. I have also omitted many of the web-based sources; though, once again, they are to be found in the footnotes.

A. Reference

Encyclopaedia of Islam Ist Edn. Ed. M.T. Housma et al. (Leiden: E.J. Brill, 1913-1936).

Encyclopaedia of Islam 2nd Edn. Ed, H.A.R. Gibb et al. (Leiden: E.J. Brill, 1960-2004).

Hughes, Thomas Patrick. *Dictionary of Islam* (London: W.H. Allen, 1885; Delhi: Rupa & Co, 1988).

Netton, Ian Richard. *A Popular Dictionary of Islam* (Richmond, UK: Curzon Press, 1992).

Shorter Encyclopaedia of Islam, edd, H.A.R. Gibb and J.H. Kramers (Leiden: E.J.Brill, 1953).

B. Koran Translations and Concordance

Al-Hilali, Muhammad Taqi-ud-Din, & Khan, Muhammad Muhsin. *Interpretation of the Meaning of the Noble Qur'ān, in the English Language* (Delhi, India: Maktaba Darul Qur'ān. 1993).

Ali, Abdullah Yusuf. *The Holy Quran. Text, Translation & Commentary*, (Lahore: Shaikh Muhammad Ashraf, 1939-40).

Ali, Maulana Muhammad. *The Holy Qur'ān* (Columbus, Ohio: Ahmadiyyah Anjuman Isha'at Islam, 1995).

Arberry, A.J. *The Koran Interpreted* (Oxford: Oxford University Press, 1964, Ist edn.1955).

Bell, Richard. *The Qur'ān. Translated with a Critical Re-arrangement of the Suras* (Edinburgh: Clark, 1937).

Blachère, Régis. *Le Coran* (Paris: G.P.Maisonneuve & Cie, 1949)

Paret, Rudi. *Der Koran, Übersetzung* (Stuttgart: Kohlhammer, 1962).

Pickthall, Muhammad Marmaduke. T*he Meaning of the Glorious Koran: An Explanatory Translation* (Mecca al-Mukarramah, Saudi Arabia: Muslim World League, 1977; 1930, Ist edn.).

Kassis, Hanna E. *A Concordance of the Qur'an* (Berkeley: University of California Press, 1983).

C. Primary sources: Islamic
C.1. *Life of Muhammad*

Ibn Ishāq. *The Life of Muhammad*, trans. A. Guillaume (1955; Oxford: Oxford University Press, 1987).

Ibn Hisham. *al-Sira al-Nabawiyya* (Cairo: Mustafa Al Babi Al Halabi & Sons, 1955).

Ibn Sa'd. *Kitāb al-Tabaqāt al Kabīr*, trans. S. M. Haq (New Delhi: Kitab Bhavan, 1972).

Al-Tabarī. *The History of al-Tabarī*, trans. W. Montgomery Watt and M.V. McDonald, vol. VI, *Muhammad at Mecca* (Albany: State University of New York Press, 1985)

Al-Tabarī. *The History of al-Tabarī*, trans. W. Montgomery Watt and M.V. McDonald, vol. VII, *The Foundation of the Community* (Albany: State University of New York Press, 1987)

Al-Tabarī. *The History of al-Tabarī*, trans. Michael Fishbein, vol. VIII, *The Victory of Islam* (Albany: State University of New York Press, 1997).

Al-Tabarī. *The History of al-Tabarī*, trans. Ismail K. Poonawala, vol. IX, *The Last Years of the Prophet* (Albany: State University of New York Press, 1990).

Al-Wāqidī. *The Life of Muhammad: Kitāb al-Maghāzī*, ed. Rizwi Faizer, trans. Rizwi Faizer, Amal Ismail, and Abdul Kader Tayob, Routledge Studies in Classical Islam (Milton Park, Abingdon, Oxon, U.K. & New York: Routledge, 2011),

C2. Early Islamic Conquests

Al-Baladhuri. *The Origins of the Islamic State* (Kitāb Futūh al-Buldān), trans. P.K. Hitti, (Piscataway, NJ: Gorgias Press, 2002).

Blankinship, Khalid Yahya. *The End of the Jihâd State: The Reign of Hishām Ibn 'Abd al-Malik and the Collapse of the Umayyads* (Albany: State University of New York Press, 1994).

Al-Tabarī. *The History of al-Tabarī*, vol. 11, *The Challenge to the Empires*, trans. Khalid Yahya Blankinship (Albany: State University of New York Press, 1993).

Al- Tabarī. *The History of al- Tabarī*, vol. 12, *The Battle of a-Qadisiyya and the Conquest of Syria and Palestine*, trans. Yohanan Friedmann (Albany: State University of New York Press, 1991).

Al-Tabarī. *The History of al-Tabarī*, vol. 13, *The Conquest of Iraq, Southwestern Persia, and Egypt*, trans. Gautier H.A. Juynboll (Albany: State University of New York Press, 1989).

C3. Koranic Commentators and other Classical Islamic scholars

al-'Asqalānī, Ibn Hajar (1382–1449). *Fath-ul-Bari* (Cairo: Dar al-Kitab al-adid, 1390/ 1970)

al-Bayhaqī. *Kitāb al-zuhd al-kabir*, ed. 'Amir Ahmad Haydar (Beirut: Dar al-Jinan, 1987).

Ibn Battūta. *The Travels of Ibn Battuta, A.D. 1325–1354*, trans. by H.A.R. Gibb (Delhi: Munshiram Manoharlal Publishers, 1999).

Ibn 'Abd al-Hādī, Muhammad b. Ahmad (d. 744/1343). *Al-'Uqūd al-durriyya min manāqib Shaykh al-Islām Ahmad b. Taymiyya* (Beirut: Dār al-kutub al-'ilmiyya, n.d).

Abū l-Qāsim Abū l-Husayn ibn Muhammad, known as al-Rāghib al-Isfahānī. *Al-Mufradāt fī Gharīb al-Qur'ān*, ed. Muhammad Sayyid Kīlānī (Egypt: Mustafā al-Bābī al-Halabī, 1381 /1961 impression).

Al-Māwardi. *The Ordinances of Government*, trans. Wafaa H. Wahba, (Reading, UK: Garnet Publishing Ltd. 1996)

al-Qurtubi. *Tafsir: Classical Commentary of the Holy Qur'an*, trans. Aisha Bewley (London: Dar al-Taqwa, 2003), 127.

Al- Shāfi'ī, Risāla. *Treatise on the Foundations of Islamic Jurisprudence*, trans. Majid Khadduri (Baltimore: The Johns Hopkins University Press, 1961; Cambridge: The Islamic Texts Society, 1987).

C4. Ibn Taymiyya

Ibn Taymiyya. *The Criterion between the Allies of the Merciful and the Allies of the Devil : al-furqān bayna awliyâ'ar-rahman wa awliyā' as-shaytān*, trans. Salim AbdAllāh ibn Morgan (Birmingham, UK: Idara Ihya-us-Sunnah, 1993).

Ibn Taimiyah, Sheikh Al-Islam Ahmad. *Principles of Islamic Faith (Al-'Aqidah Al-Wasitiyah)*, trans. Assad Nimer Busool (Skokie, IL: IQRA' International Educational Foundation, 1992).

Ibn Taymiyya. *Majmū'at Fatāwā*, ed. 'A.R. b. M. Ibn Qāsim, 37 vols. (Rabat: Maktabat al-Ma'ārif, 1401/ 1981).

Ibn Taymiyya. *Iqtidā' al-sirāt al-mustaqīm li-mukhālafat ashāb al-jahīm* (Cairo, 1950); also ed. 'Isām Fāris al-Harastāni & Muhammad Ibrāhīm al-Zaghlī (Beirut: Dār al-Jīl, 1993).

Ibn Taymiyya. *al-Jawāb al-Sahīh li-man baddala dīn al-Masīh* (Cairo: Matba'at al-Nīl, 1905).

Ibn Taymiyya. *Mas'alat al-Kanā'is*, Paris Bibliothèque Nationale, no. 2962, ii.

Ibn Taymiyya. *al-Fatāwā al-kubrā*, (Cairo: Dār al-Kutub al-Hadītha, 1966).

Ibn Taymiyya. *al-Siyāsa al-shar'iyya fī iAlāh al-rā'ī wa-al-ra'iyya*, (*Le Traité de droit public d'Ibn Taimīya*), trans. Henri Laoust (Beruit: Institut français de Damas, 1948

D. Hadith

Abu Dāwūd, *Sunan*, trans. Ahmad Hasan, (New Delhi: Kitab Bhavan, 1997).

Bukhārī, *Sahīh*, trans. Muhammad Muhsin Khan (Riyadh, Saudi Arabia: Darussalam, 1997).

Ibn Māja, *Sunan*, trans. M. Tufail Ansari (New Delhi: Kitab Bhavan, 2008)

Mālik b. Anas. *Muwatta'*, Muhammad Rahimuddin (New Delhi: Kitab Bhavan, 2003)

Muslim ibn al-Hajjāj. *Sahīh, Kitāb al-Imara*, trans. 'Abdul Hamid Siddiqi, (New Delhi: Kitab Bhavan, 2000)

an-Nawawi. *Forty Hadith*, trans. Abdassamad Clarke (London: Ta Ha Publishers, 1998

Al-Tirmidhī. *Jamī': The Virtues of Jihād*, trans. Abu Khaliyl (Riyadh, Saudi Arabia: Darrusalam, 2007

E. Modern Radical Islam: Primary Sources

Azzam, Iman Abdullah. "Join the Caravan: Conclusion," *Religioscope*, February 1, 2002, http://english.religion.info/2002/02/01/document-join-the-caravan/

Azzam, Abdullah. *Defense of the Muslim Lands: The First Obligation after Iman*, trans. Brothers in Ribatt, 1979–1984, 11–12, https://islamfuture.files.wordpress.com/2009/11/defence-of-the-muslim-lands.pdf.

Azzam, Abdullah. "Document—Martyrs: The Building Blocks of Nations," *Religioscope*, February 1, 2002, http://english.religion.info/2002/02/01/document-martyrs-the-building-blocks-of-nations/.

al-Banna, Hasan. *Five Tracts of Hasan al-Bannā' (1906–1949): A Selection from the Majmū'at Rasā'il al-Shahīd Hasan al-Bannā'*, trans. with annotations Charles Wendell (Berkeley: University of California Press, 1978),

al-Banna, Hasan. *The Complete Works of Imam Hasan al-Banna: 1906–1949*, available at *The Quran Blog—Enlighten Yourself*, June 7, 2008, https://thequranblog.wordpress.com/2008/06/07/the-complete-works-of-imam-hasan-al-banna-10/.

Bin Laden, Osama. Interviewed by Tayser Allouni, *Al Jazeera*, October 21, 2001, ed., Lawrence, Bruce ed. *Messages to the World: The Statements of Osama Bin Laden*, trans. James Howarth (London: Verso, 2005).

Ghuniem, Wagdi. Speech delivered at "Palestine: 50 Years of Occupation," a program sponsored by the Islamic Association for Palestine and held in the Walt Whitman Auditorium, Brooklyn College, Brooklyn, NY, May 24, 1998.

Hamas Covenant 1988: "The Covenant of the Islamic Resistance Movement," August 18, 1988, text available at Yale Law School, Lillian Goldman Law Library, The Avalon Project: Documents in Law, History, and Diplomacy, http://avalon.law.yale.edu/20th_century/hamas.asp

Ibn 'Abd al-Wahhāb, Muhammad. *Mu'allafāt al-shaykh al-imām Muhammad ibn Abd al-Wahhāb*, including al-Rasā'il al-Shakhsiyya (RS), and *al-'Aqīda* (2 parts), *'Aqīda*, *al-Fiqh* (*Fiqh*), and *MukhtaAar Sīrat al-Rasūl* (*Sira*), ed. 'Abd al-'Azīz Zayd al-Rūmī et al. (Riyadh: Jāmi 'at al-Imām Muhammad b. Su 'ūd al-Islāmiyya, 1978.

Khomeini. *Islam and Revolution*, trans. Hamid Algar, (N. Haledon, NJ: Mizan Press, 1981).

Khomeini. *Mavaz'-e Imam Khomeini*, ed. Mohammad Reza Akbari (Isfahan, Iran: Payam-i 'Itrat, 1999).

Khomeini, S.R. (Ayatollah). *Principes, Politiques, Philosophiques, Sociaux et Religieux*, trans. and ed. J.-M. Xaviere (Paris: Libres-Hallier, 1979).

Khomeini, Ayatollah Ruhollah. Speech, Tehran Radio, September

8, 1979, trans. Foreign Broadcast Information Service (FBIS), September 10, 1979.

Khomeini, Ayatollah Ruhollah. From a speech at Feyziyeh (Fayziyyah) Theological School, August 24, 1979; quoted in Rubin and Rubin, *Anti-American Terrorism*, 32–33.

Malik, Brigadier S. K. *The Qur'anic Concept of War* (1992; Delhi: Adam Publishers & Distributors, 2008),

Maudoodi, Syed Abul 'Ala. *Islamic Law and Constitution*, trans. and ed. Khurshid Ahmad (Chicago: Kazi Publications, Inc., 1993).

Maudoodi, Abul Ala. "Twenty-Nine Years of the Jamaat-e-Islami," *Criterion* 5, no. 6 (November–December 1970).

Maududi, Syed Abul A'la. *Political Theory of Islam* (1960; Lahore: Islamic Publications Ltd., 1980), 27.

Maududi, Syed Abul A'la. *Jihad in Islam* (Beirut: The Holy Koran Publishing House, 1980), 5.

Maududi, Syed Abul A'la. *The Islamic Way of Life*, ed. Khurshid Ahmad and Khurram Murad (Leicester, UK: The Islamic Foundation, 1992. First Urdu edition, 1948; first English edition, 1967).

Maududi, Syed Abul A'la. *Islamic Law and Constitution* (Lahore, IL: Islamic Publications, 1967), 53.

Qutb, Sayyid. "The America I Have Seen: In the Scale of Human Values," 1951, available at https://archive.org/stream/SayyidQutb/The%20America%20I%20have%20seen_djvu.txt.

The Sayyid Qutb Reader: Selected Writings on Politics, Religion, and Society, ed. Albert J. Bergesen (London: Routledge, 2008), 3.

Qutb, Sayyid. *The Islamic Concept and Its Characteristics* (Plainfield, IN: American Trust Publications, 1991),

Qutb, Sayyid. *Milestones* (Damascus, Syria: Dar al-Ilm, n.d.)

Qutb, Sayyid. *In the Shade of the Qur'an*, trans. Adil Salahi, sura 8 (Leicester: The Islamic Foundation, 2003), 7:24

al-Zawahiri, Ayman. *Knights under the Prophet's Banner*; quoted in Walter Laqueur, ed., *Voices of Terror: Manifestos, Writings and Manuals of Al Qaeda, Hamas, and Other Terrorists from Around the World and Throughout the Ages* (New York: Reed Press, 2004), 432.

al-Zawahiri, Ayman. "Interview," in *The Al-Qaeda Reader: The Essential Texts of Osama Bin Laden's Terrorist Organization*, ed. and trans. Raymond Ibrahim (New York: Broadway Books, 2007), 182–86.

F. Secondary Sources

Abrahamian, Ervand. *Khomeinism: Essays on the Islamic Republic*

(Berkeley: University of California Press, 1993).

Abrahamian, Ervand. *Tortured Confessions: Prisons and Public Recantations in Modern Iran* (Berkeley: University of California Press, 1999).

Adams, Charles. "Mawdudi and the Islamic State," in *Voices of Resurgent Islam*, ed. John L. Esposito (Oxford and New York: Oxford University Press, 1983).

Afary, Janet and Anderson, Kevin B. *Foucault and the Iranian Revolution: Gender and the Seductions of Islamism* (Chicago: University of Chicago Press, 2005).

Ahmad, Irfan. "Mawdudi, Abu al-A 'la (1903–1979)," in *Princeton Encyclopaedia of Islamic Political Thought*.

Ahmed, Beenish. "How a Teenage Girl Goes from Listening to Coldplay and Reading Harry Potter to Joining ISIS," *Think Progress*, February 24, 2015, http://thinkprogress.org/world/2015/02/24/3626720/women-isis/

Aigle, Denise. "The Mongol Invasions of Bilād al-Shām [Syria] by Ghāzān Khān and Ibn Taymīyah's Three 'Anti-Mongol' Fatwas" *Mamluk Studies Review* 11, no. 2 (2007).

Ali, Syed Ameer. *The Life and Teachings of Mohammed: Or, The Spirit of Islam* (London: W.H. Allen & Co., Ltd., 1891).

Allen, Charles. God's Terrorists. *The Wahhabi Cult and the Hidden Roots of Modern Jihad* (Cambridge, MA: Da Capo Press, 2006),

Amayreh, Khaled. "Reality Behind the Image," *Jerusalem Post*, February 24, 1995.

Amin, Galal A. *Egypt's Economic Predicament: A Study in the Interaction of External Pressure, Political Folly and Social Tension in Egypt, 1960–1990* (Leiden: E.J. Brill, 1995).

Arjomand, Saïd Amir. *After Khomeini: Iran under His Successors* (Oxford and New York: Oxford University Press, 2009).

Arjomand, Saïd Amir. "Iran's Islamic Revolution in Comparative Perspective," *World Politics* 38, no. 3 (April 1986).

Arnold, Thomas Walker. *The Preaching of Islam: a History of the Propagation of the Muslim Faith*, 2nd ed. (London: A. Constable, 1913).

al-'Arrābī, Sultān Ibn 'Abd Allāh. "Dāmighat al-mubtadi 'īn wa-kāshifat butlān al-mulhīdīn. Al-Imām Muhammad b. Bīr 'Alī Iskandar al-Birgiwī: Dirāsa wa-tahqīq," (Master's thesis, Jāmi 'at Umm al-Qurā, Mecca 1425/2004).

Bakhash, Shaul. *The Reign of the Ayatollahs Iran and the Islamic Revolution* (London: Unwin Paperbacks, 1985).

Baljon, J.M.S. *Religion and Thought of Shāh Walī Allāh Dihlawī 1703-1762* (Leiden: E.J. Brill, 1986).

Banerjee, A.C. *Two Nations. The Philosophy of Muslim Nationalism* (New Delhi: Concept Publishing Company, 1981).

Barth, Karl. *The Church and the Political Problem of Our Day* (New York: Scribner's, 1939).

Bat Ye'or. *The Dhimmi: Jews and Christians under Islam* (London: Associated University Presses, 1996).

Bauer, Yahuda. *Rethinking the Holocaust* (New Haven, CT: Yale Nota Bene, 2002).

Bausani, A. "Farā'idiyya" in *Encyclopaedia of Islam* 2nd Edn., Vol. 2, s.v. 783 b.

Behdad, Sohrab. "Islamic Utopia in Pre-Revolutionary Iran: Navvab Safavi and the Fad'ian-e Eslam," in *Middle Eastern Studies*, Vol.33, No.1, January 1997

Berlin, Isaiah. *Liberty: Incorporating Four Essays on Liberty*, ed. Henry Hardy, 2nd ed. (Oxford: Oxford University Press, 2002).

Berlin, Isaiah. "A Message to the 21st Century," acceptance address upon receiving honorary Doctor of Laws, University of Toronto, November 25, 1994, reprinted in *New York Review of Books*, October 23, 2014, http://www.nybooks.com/articles/2014/10/23/message-21st-century/

Bird, Adam and Brown, Malcolm. "The History and Social Consequences of a Nationalized Oil Industry," June 2, 2005, available at https://web.stanford.edu/class/e297a/VENEZUELA%20OIL%20&%20LAND%20REFORM.htm

Birgili. *Tarikat-i Muhammediyye Tercümesi* (trans. from Arabic into Turkish by Celal Yildirim), (Istanbul, 1981).

Birnbaum, Jean. *Un silence religieux: La gauche face au djihadisme* (Paris: Éditions du Seuil, 2016).

Bostom, Andrew G. *The Mufti's Islamic Jew-Hatred: What Nazis Learned from the 'Muslin Pope'* (Washington, DC: Barvura Books, 2013).

Bostom, Andrew. *The Legacy of Islamic Antisemitism: From Sacred Texts to Solemn History* (Amherst, MA: Prometheus Books, 2008).

Bousquet, Georges-Henri. *L'Ethique sexuelle de l'Islam* (1966, Paris: Desclée de Brouwer, 1990).

Bousquet, Georges-Henri. "*Queleques remarques critiques et sociologiques sur le conquête arabe et les theories émises à ce sujet*," in *Studi Orientalistici in Onore di Giorgio Levi Della Vida* (Roma: Instituto per l'Oriente, 1956).

Bousquet, Georges-Henri. "*Observations sur la nature et causes de la conquête arabe,*" *Studia Islamica* 6 (1956).

Brohi, Allah Bukhsh K. "Preface," in Malik, *Qur'anic Concept of War.*

Brooks, Geraldine. *Nine Parts of Desire: The Hidden World of Islamic Women* (1994; New York: Anchor Books, 1996).

Caetani, Leone. *Annali dell'Islam,* 10 vols. (Milano: U. Hoepli, 1905–1926).

Caetani, Leone. *Studi di Storia Orientale I* (Milano: U. Hoepli, 1911).

Calder, Norman. "Law, Islamic philosophy of" *Islamic Philosophy Online,* 1998, http://www.muslimphilosophy.com/ip/rep/H015.html

Cantemir, Dimitrie. *The History of the Growth and Decay of the Othman Empire,* trans. N. Tindal (London, 1734).

Çelebi, Katib. *Fezleke-i Tarih,* 2 vols. (Istanbul, 1286/1870).

Christian-Muslim Relations: A Bibliographical History, ed. David Thomas, vol.4, *1200–1350,* ed. David Thomas and Alex Mallet (Leiden: E.J. Brill, 2009).

Cohn, Norman. *The Pursuit of the Millennium: Revolutionary Millenarians and Mystical Anarchists of the Middle Ages* (London: Secker & Warburg, 1957).

Commins, David. *The Wahhabi Mission and Saudi Arabia* (New York: I.B. Tauris, 2006).

Cook, David. *Understanding Jihād* (Berkeley: University of California Press, 2005).

Cook, David. "Muslim Apocalyptic and *Jihād,*" *Jerusalem Studies in Arabic and Islam* 20 (1996).

Cook, Michael. *Commanding Right and Forbidding Wrong in Islamic Thought* (Cambridge and New York: Cambridge University Press, 2001).

Cook, Michael, *Forbidding Wrong in Islam: An Introduction* (Cambridge and New York: Cambridge University Press, 2003).

Coughlin, Con. *Khomeini's Ghost. The Definitive Account of Ayatollah Khomeini's Islamic Revolution and its Enduring Legacy* (London: Macmillan, 2009).

Crawford, Michael. *Ibn 'Abd al-Wahhāb* (London: Oneworld Publications, 2014).

Crawford, Michael. "The Da'wa of Ibn 'Abd al-Wahhāb before the Al Sa'ūd," *Journal of Arabian Studies* 1, no. 2 (2011): 159–60.

Crone, Patricia. *God's Rule—Government and Islam: Six Centuries of Medieval Islamic Political Thought* (New York: Columbia University Press, 2004).

Crone, Patricia. "A Statement by the Najdiyya Khārijites on the Dispensability of the Imamate" *Studia Islamica*, no. 88 (1998).

Crossette, Barbara "Taliban Explains Buddha Demolition," *New York Times*, March 19, 2001, http://www.nytimes.com/2001/03/19/world/taliban-explains-buddha-demolition.html.

Digby, Simon. *Sufis and Soldiers in Awrangzeb's Deccan* (New York: 2001).

Diggins, John Patrick. "Fate and Freedom in History: The Two Worlds of Eric Foner," *National Interest*, no. 69 (Fall 2002).

Donner, Fred. ed., *The Formation of the Classical Islamic World*, vol. 5, *The Expansion of the Early Islamic State* (Burlington, VT: Ashgate, 2008).

Duran, Khalid. "How CAIR Put My Life in Peril," *Middle East Quarterly* 9, no. 1 (Winter 2002).

Eco, Umberto "Ur-Fascism," *New York Review of Books*, June 22, 1995, http://www.nybooks.com/articles/1995/06/22/ur-fascism/.

El Fadl, Khaled M. Abou. *The Great Theft: Wrestling Islam from the Extremists* (New York: Harper One, 2007).

El-Rouayheb, Khaled. "From Ibn Hajar al-Haytamī (d. 1566) to Khayr al-Dīn al-Ālūsī (d. 1899): Changing Views of Ibn Taymiyya among non-Hanbalī Sunni Scholars," in *Ibn Taymiyya and His Times*, ed. Yossef Rapoport and Shahab Ahmed (Oxford: Oxford University Press, 2010).

Encyclopaedia Iranica (www.iranicaonline.org/), s.v. "Amr be Ma'rūf," by Wilferd Madelung.

Euben, Roxanne L. and Zaman, Muhammad Qasim. *Princeton Readings in Islamist Thought: Texts and Contexts from al-Banna to Bin Laden* (Princeton, NJ: Princeton University Press, 2009).

Evstatiev, Simeon "The Qādīzādeli Movement and the Revival of *Takfīr* in the Ottoman Age," in *Accusations of Unbelief in Islam: A Diachronic Perspective on Takfīr*, ed. Camilla Adang et al. (Leiden: Brill, 2015).

al-Faruqi, Ismail R. *Islam* (Niles, IL: Argus Communications, 1979).

Firestone, Reuven. *Jihād: The Origins of Holy War in Islām* (Oxford: Oxford University Press, 1999).

Flemming, Barbara. "Die vorwahhabitische Fitna im osmanischen Kairo, 1711," in *Ord. Prof. İsmail Hakki Uzunçarşili'ya Ar-mağan* (Ankara: Türk Tarih Kurumu, 1976), 55-65.

Friedman, Yaron. *The Nusayrī-'Alawīs: An Introduction to the Religion, History and Identity of the Leading Minority in Syria* (Leiden and Boston: E.J. Brill, 2010).

Friedmann, Yohanan. *Shaykh Ahmad Sirhindi, An Outline of His Thought and a Study of His Image in the Eyes of Posterity* (Montreal: McGill-Queen's University Press, 1971),

Galland, Antoine. *De l'Origine et du progrez du café* (Caen. 1699).

Gardet, Louis. *La cité musulmane: vie sociale et politique*, 2nd edn. (Paris: Librairie Philosophique J. Vrin, 1961).

Ghanem-Yazbeck, Dalia. "The Decline of Islamist Parties in Algeria," Sada: Middle East Analysis, Carnegie Endowment for International Peace, February 13, 2014, http://carnegieendowment.org/sada/?fa=54510.

Gibb, H.A.R. *Modern Trends in Islam* (New York: Octagon Books, 1975).

Goldhagen, Daniel Jonah. *Hitler's Willing Executioners: Ordinary Germans and the Holocaust* (New York: Vintage Books, 1996).

Goldziher, Ignaz. *Introduction to Islamic Theology and Law*, trans. Andras and Ruth Hamori (Princeton, NJ: Princeton University Press, 1981).

Goldziher, Ignaz. "Review of Walter M. Patton, Ahmed Ibn Hanbal and the Mihna," in *Zeitschrift der Deutschen Morgenländischen Gesellschaft*, Bd. 52, (1898).

Goldziher, Ignaz. *Muslim Studies*, ed. S. M. Stern (London: George Allen & Unwin, 1967-1971), Vol.2.

Gorka, Sebastian. *Defeating Jihad: The Winnable War* (Washington, DC: Regnery Publishing, 2016).

Habib, Mohammad. *The Political Theory of the Delhi Sultanate*, (Allahbad: Kitab Mahal, 1961),

Halm, Heinz. *Shi'ism*, 2nd ed. (1991; New York: Columbia University Press, 2004).

Halpern, Manfred. *The Politics of Social Change in the Middle East and North Africa* (Princeton, NJ: Princeton University Press, 1963).

Hamid, Tawfik. *Inside Jihad: How Radical Islam Works; Why It Should Terrify Us; How to Defeat It* (Mountain Lake, MD: Mountain Lake Press, 2015).

Hardy, Peter. *The Muslims of British India* (Cambridge: Cambridge University Press, 1972)

Hardy, Peter. "Baranī, Diyā al-Dīn" in *Encyclopaedia of Islam* 2nd.

Edn., Vol. I   1036a.

Hawting, Gerald R. "The Significance of the Slogan '*lā hukma illā lillāh*' and the References to the '*Hudūd*' in the Traditions about the *Fitna* and the Murder of 'Uthmān," *Bulletin of the (University of London) School of Oriental and African Studies* 41, no. 3 (1978).

Haykel, Bernard. "Ibn 'Abd al-Wahhāb, Muhammad (1703–92)," in *Princeton Encyclopaedia of Islamic Political Thought*, ed. Gerhard Bowering (Princeton, NJ: Princeton University Press, 2013).

Haynes, John Earl and Klehr, Harvey. *In Denial: Historians, Communism, and Espionage* (New York: Encounter Books, 2003).

Hourani, Albert. *A History of the Arab Peoples* (London: Faber and Faber, 1991).

Hurgronje, C. Snouck. *Selected Works*, ed. Georges-Henri Bousqet and Joseph Schacht (Leiden: E.J. Brill, 1957).

Hurgronje, C. Snouck. *Politique Musulmane de la Hollande* (Paris: E. Leroux, 1911).

Ibn Bishr, 'Uthman. *'Unwān al-Majd fī Ta'rīkh Najd* (*Token of Glory: On the History of Najd*) (Beirut, 1967).

Ibn Ghannām, Husayn. *Ta'rīkh Najd al-Musmmā Rawdat al-Afhām li-Murtād Hāl al-Imām wa-Ta'dād Ghazawāt Dhawī 'l-Islām*, 2 vols. (Cairo, 1949).

Ibn Warraq, "Reason, Not Revelation," in Ibn Warraq, ed. *Virgins? What Virgins? And Other Essays* (Amherst, MA: Prometheus Books, 2010).

Ibn Warraq, *Why the West Is Best* (New York: Encounter Books, 2011).

Ibn Warraq, *Sir Walter Scott's Crusades and Other Fantasies* (Nashville, TN: New English Review Press, 2013).

Ibn Warraq, "Islam, Middle East, and Fascism," in ed. Ibn Warraq. *Virgins? What Virgins?*

Ibn Warraq, "Apologists of Totalitarianism: From Communism to Islam" in *Politcal Violence: Belief, Behavior and Legitimation*, ed. Paul Hollander (New York: Palgrave Macmillan, 2008).

Ibrahim, Saad Eddin. "Anatomy of Egypt's Militant Islamic Groups: Methodological Notes and Preliminary Findings," in *Egypt, Islam and Democracy: Critical Essays* (1996; Cairo: The American University in Cairo Press, 2002). First published under the same title in *International Journal of Middle East Studies* 12, no. 4 (December 1980).

Inayatullah, Sh. "Sayyid Ahmad Brēlwī" in *Encyclopaedia of Islam* 2nd Edn. Vol.1, 282a-282b.

Iskandar Beg Munshī. *Tārīkh-i 'Alam-ārā-yi 'Abbāsī*, trans. R.M. Savory, Persian Heritage Series, ed. Ehsan Yarshater, no. 28, 2 vols. (Boulder, CO: 1978).

Ismā'īl, Mahmūd. *al-Harakāt al-sirrīyah fī al-Islām: ru'yah 'asrīyah* (*Secret Movements in Islam: Modern View*) (Bayrūt: Dār al-Qalam, 1973).

Jalal, Ayesha. *Partisans of Allah: Jihad in South Asia* (Cambridge, MA: Harvard University Press, 2010).

Jansen, Johannes J.G. "The Early Islamic Movement of the Kharidjites and the Modern Moslem Extremists: Similarities and Differences," *Orient* 27, no. 1 (1986): 127–35.

Jansen, Johannes J.G. *The Neglected Duty: The Creed of Sadat's Assassins* (1986; New York: RVP Publishers, 2013).

Jones, Kenneth W. *Socio-religious Reform Movements in British India* (Cambridge: Cambridge University Press. (The New Cambridge History of India III.1),1989)

Jung, Carl. *The Collected Works*, vol. 18, *The Symbolic Life* (Princeton, NJ: Princeton University Press, 1939).

Juynboll, Th.W. *Handbuch des Islamischen Gesetzes Nach der Lehre der Schafi'itischen Schule Nebst Einer Allgemeinen Einleitung* (Leiden, E.J.Brill; Leipzig: Harrassowitz, 1910).

Karsh, Efraim. *The Tail Wags the Dog: International Politics and the Middle East* (New York: Bloomsbury, 2015).

Kazemi, Farhad. "The Fada'iyan-e Islam: Fanaticism, Politics and Terror," in ed. Said Amir Arjomand, *From Nationalism to Revolutionary Islam* (State University of New York Press, 1985).

Kepel, Gilles. *The War for Muslim Minds: Islam and the West* (Cambridge, MA: Belknap Press, 2006).

Khadduri, Majid. *War and Peace in the Law of Islam* (Baltimore: Johns Hopkins University Press, 1955; Clark, NJ: Lawbook Exchange, Ltd., 2006, 2010).

Küntzel, Matthias. *Jihad and Jew-Hatred: Islamism, Nazism and the Roots of 9/11* (New York: Telos Press Publishing, 2009).

Lane, Edward William. *An Arabic-English Lexicon*, part 4 (London: Williams & Norgate, 1872; Beirut: Librairie du Liban, 1968).

Laoust, Henri. "La Biographie d'Ibn Taimīya d'après Ibn Katīr," *Bulletin d'études orientales* 9 (1942–1943).

Laoust, Henri. *Essai sur les doctrines sociales et politiques de Takī-d- Dīn Ahmad b. Taimīya* (Cairo: Imprimerie de l'Institut Français d'Archéologie Orientale, 1939).

Lapidus, Ira M. "The Separation of State and Religion in the Development of Early Islamic Society," *International Journal of Middle East Studies* 6, no. 4 (October 1975): 363–85.

Lav, Daniel. *Radical Islam and the Revival of Medieval Theology* (Cambridge and New York: Cambridge University Press, 2012).

Lerner, Max. *Ideas Are Weapons: The History and Uses of Ideas* (New York: Viking Press, 1939).

Levtzion, Nehemia and Voll, John O., eds., *Eighteenth-Century Renewal and Reform in Islam* (Syracuse, NY: Syracuse University Press, 1987).

Lewis, Bernard. "Islam and Liberal Democracy," *Atlantic* (February 1993), http://www.theatlantic.com/magazine/archive/1993/02/islam-and-liberal- democracy/308509/.

Lewis, Bernard. *The Assassins: A Radical Sect in Islam* (London: Weidenfeld & Nicolson Ltd, 1967; New York: Basic Books, 2003).

Lewis, Bernard. *Islam and the West* (Oxford and New York: Oxford University Press, 1994).

Lewis, Bernard. *Islam in History: Ideas, People, and Events in the Middle East* (Chicago and La Salle, IL: Open Court 1993).

Little, D.P. "Religion under the Mamluks," *Muslim World* 73, no. 3–4 (October 1983).

Little, D.P. "Did Ibn Taymiyya Have a Screw Loose" in *Studia Islamica*, No. 41 (Paris, 1975), pp. 93-111

Madelung, Wilferd. *Religious Trends in Early Islamic Iran* (Albany, NY: Persian Heritage Foundation, 1988.

Madelung, Wilferd. "Amr be Ma'rūf," in *Encyclopaedia Iranica* (www.iranicaonline.org/).

Malia, Martin. *The Soviet Tragedy: A History of Socialism in Russia, 1917–1991* (New York: The Free Press, 1994).

Maloney, Suzanne. *Iran's Political Economy since the Revolution* (Cambridge: Cambridge University Press, 2015).

Meier, Fritz. *Die Vita des Scheich Abū Ishāq al-Kāzarūnī in der persischen Bearbeitung von Mahmūd b. 'Utmān* (Leipzig, 1948).

Metcalf, Barbara. *Islamic Revival in British India: Deoband 1860–1900* (Princeton, NJ: Princeton University Press, 1982).

Michot, Yahya. "Ibn Taymiyya," in *The Princeton Encyclopaedia of Islamic Political Thought*, ed. Gerhard Bowering (Princeton, NJ: Princeton University Press, 2013).

Mir, Mustansir. "Jihād in Islam," in *The Jihād and Its Times*, ed. Hadia Dajani-Shakeel and Ronald A. Messier (Ann Arbor, MI: Center for Near Eastern and North African Studies, University of Michigan, 1991).

Mitchell, Richard P. *The Society of Muslim Brothers* (1969; Oxford: Oxford University Press, 1993),

Monnerot, Jules. *Sociologie du Communisme* (Paris: Gallimard, 1949). Translated by Jane Degras and Richard Rees as *Sociology and Psychology of Communism* (Boston: Beacon Press, 1953).

Morabia, Alfred. "*Ibn Taymiyya: Dernier grand théoricien du Ǧihād médiéval*," *Bulletin d'études orientales*, *Mélanges offerts a Henri Laoust, tome 2*, 30 (1978).

Murād, Hasan Q. "*Mihan* of Ibn Taymiya: A Narrative Account Based on a Comparative Analysis of Sources" (Master's thesis, McGill University, 1968).

Murawiec, Laurent. *The Mind of Jihad* (Cambridge and New York: Cambridge University Press, 2008).

Murray, Douglas. *Neoconservatism: Why We Need It* (New York: Encounter Books, 2006).

Mussolini, Benito. "The Doctrine of Fascism" (1932), in Adrian Lyttleton, *Italian Fascisms: From Pareto to Gentile* (London, 1973).

Naima, Mustafa. *Tarih-i Naima*, 6 vols. (Istanbul, 1280/1863-64).

Nasr, Seyyed Vali Reza. "Mawdudi and the *Jam'at-i Islami*: The Origins, Theory and Practice of Islamic Revivalism" in *Pioneers of Islamic Revival*, ed. Ali Rahnema, Studies in Islamic Society (London: Zed Books Ltd).

Nasr, Seyyed Vali Reza. *Mawdudi and the Making of Islamic Revivalism* (Oxford and New York: Oxford University Press, 1996).

Neocleous, Mark. *Fascism* (Buckingham, UK: Open University Press, 1997).

Netanyahu, Benjamin. "Defining Terrorism," in *Terrorism: How the West Can Win*, ed. Benjamin Netanyahu (New York: Farrar, Starus, Giroux, 1986).

Netanyahu, Benjamin. *Fighting Terrorism: How Democracies Can Defeat Domestic and International Terrorism* (New York: Farrar, Straus and Giroux, 1995).

Nettler, Ronald L. *Past Trials and Present Tribulations: A Muslim Fundamentalist's View of the Jews* (Oxford: Pergamon Press, 1987), 86–87; quoted in Rubin and Schwanitz, *Nazis, Islamists*, 251.

Neumann, Peter R. ed., *Addressing the Causes of Terrorism*, Club de Madrid Series on Democracy and Terrorism, vol. 1 (Madrid: Club de Madrid, 2005). http://www.clubmadrid.org/img/secciones/Club_de_

Madrid_Volume_I_The_Causes_of_Terrorism.pdf.

Nolan Jr., James A. *What They Saw in America* (Cambridge and New York: Cambridge University Press, 2016).

Peters, Rudolph. "The Battered Dervishes of Bab Zuwyala: A Religious Riot in Eighteenth-Century Cairo," in Levtzion and Voll, *Eighteenth Century Renewal*, 93–115.

Peters, Rudolph. *Islam and Colonialism* (The Hague: Mouton Publishers, 1979).

Peters, Rudolph. *Jihad in Classical and Modern Islam* (Princeton, NJ: Markus Wiener Publishers, 1996).

Peters, Rudolph. *Jihād: A History in Documents* (Princeton, NJ: Markus Wiener Publishers, 2016).

Peters, Rudolph. "*Islamischer Fundamentalismus: Glauben, Handeln, Führung*," in *Max Webers Sicht des Islams: Interpretation und Kritik*, ed. Wolfgang Schlucter (Frankfurt: Suhrkamp, 1987), 217–42.

Pipes, Daniel. "We Free Them or They Destroy Us," *Lion's Den: Daniel Pipes Blog*, September 13, 2006, http://www.danielpipes.org/blog/2006/09/we-free-them-or-they-destroy-us.

Pipes, Daniel. "Bush Returns to the 'Religion of Peace' Formulation," *Lion's Den: Daniel Pipes Blog*, October 4, 2007, http://www.danielpipes.org/blog/2007/10/bush-returns-to-the-religion-of-peace.

Pipes, Daniel. "God and Mammon: Does Poverty Cause Militant Islam?" *National Interest*, no. 66 (Winter 2001/2002).

Pipes, Daniel. *Militant Islam Reaches America* (New York: W.W. Norton and Company, 2002).

Pohlmann, Marcus D., ed. and intro. *African American Political Thought*, vol.6, *Integration vs. Separatism: 1945 to the Present* (London: Routledge, 2003.)

Poliak, A.N. "*Les révoltes populaires en Égypte à l'époque des Mamelouks et leur causes economiques*," *Revue des Études Islamiques* 8 (1934).

Rahman, Fazlur. *Islam* (Chicago: Chicago University Press, 1966; 2nd Edn. 1979).

Reilly, Robert R. *The Closing of the Muslim Mind: How Intellectual Suicide Created the Modern Islamist Crisis* (Wilmington, DE: Intercollegiate Studies Institute, 2011).

Reilly, Robert R. "Thinking like a Terrorist," review of *Leaderless Jihad: Terror Networks in the Twenty-First Century* by Marc Sageman, and *The Mind of Jihad*, by Laurent Murawiec, 9, no. 2 (Spring 2009): 31–33, http://www.claremont.org/crb/article/think-like-a-terrorist/.

Rida, Muhammad Rashid. ed., *Majmū'at al-Tawhīd al-Najdiyya* (Riyadh: Al-Amana al-'Amma, 1999).

Riley-Smith, Jonathan. *The Crusades, Christianity, and Islam* (New York: Columbia University Press, 2008).

Rippin, Andrew. *Muslims: Their Religious Beliefs and Practices*, 2nd ed. (London: Routledge, 2001).

Rizvi, Saiyid Athar Abbas. *Muslim Revivalist Movements in Northern India in the Sixteenth and Seventeenth Centuries*, (New Delhi: Munshiram Manoharlal Publishers Pvt. Ltd. 1965).

Rizvi, Saiyid Athar Abbas. *Shah Wali-Allah and His Times*, (Lahore: Suhail Academy, 2004).

Rizvi, Saiyid Athar Abbas. *Shah 'Abd al-'Aziz*, (Lahore: Suhail Academy, 2004).

Robinson, F.C.R., "Mawdūdī, Sayyid Abu 'l-a'la" in *Encyclopaedia of Islam*, vol. 4, "*Iran–Kha*," ed. by E. van Donzel, B. Lewis, and Ch. Pellat, 2nd ed. (Leiden: Brill, 1978).

Rodinson, Maxime. *Islam and Capitalism*, trans. Brian Pearce (London: Allen Lane, 1974), 296ff. Originally published as *Islam et le capitalisme* (Paris: Editions du Seuil, 1966).

Rodinson, Maxime "Islam Resurgent?" *Le Monde*, December 6–8, 1978.

Roemer, H.R. 'Die turkmenischen Qizilbaš-Gründer und Opfer der safawidischen Theokratie,' in *Zeitschrift der Deutschen Morgenländischen Gesellschaft*, 135 (1985).

Rousseau, J.B.L.J. *Description du Pachalik de Bagdad Suivie d'une Notice Historique sur les Wahabis* (Paris: Treutel & Würtz, 1809).

Rubin, Barry and Schwanitz, Wolfgang G. *Nazis, Islamists, and the Making of the Modern Middle East* (New Haven, CT: Yale University Press, 2014).

Rubin, Barry. "The Truth about U.S. Middle East Policy," in *Anti-American Terrorism and the Middle East: A Documentary Reader—Understanding the Violence*, ed. Barry Rubin and Judith Colp Rubin (Oxford and New York: Oxford University Press, 2002). Originally published under the same title in *Middle East Review of International Affairs* 5, no. 4 (December 2001), http://www.rubincenter.org/meria/2001/12/brubin.pdf.

Russell, Bertrand. *The Practice and Theory of Bolshevism* (London: George Allen and Unwin, 1920).

Ruthven, Malise. *A Fury for God: The Islamist Attack on America* (London: Granta Books, 2002).

Rycaut, Paul. *The History the Turkish Empire from the year 1623 to the Year 1677*, 2 vols. in 1 (London, 1680).

Sageman, Marc. *Leaderless Jihad: Terror Networks in the Twenty-First Century* (Philadelphia: University of Pennsylvania Press, 2008).

Savory, Roger. *Iran under the Safavids* (1980; Cambridge: Cambridge University Press, 2007).

Schacht, Joseph "Islamic Religious Law," in *The Legacy of Islam*, ed. Joseph Schacht and C.E. Bosworth, 2nd ed. (Oxford: Oxford University Press, 1979).

Schacht, Joseph. *An Introduction to Islamic Law* (1964; Oxford: Clarendon Press,1991).

Scruton, Roger "The Glory of the West Is That Life Is an Open Book," *Sunday Times* (UK), May 27, 2007.

Siegel, Robert. "Sayyid Qutb's America: Al Qaeda Inspiration Denounced U.S. Greed, Sexuality" May 6, 2003, *All Things Considered*, NPR, http://www.npr.org/templates/story/story.php?storyId=1253796.

Sivan, Emmanuel. "Ibn Taymiyya: Father of the Islamic Revolution: Medieval Theology & Modern Politics," *Encounter* 69, no. 5 (May 1983).

Smith, Vincent A. *The Oxford History of India* (Delhi: Oxford University Press, 1981 [Ist edn. 1919]),

Solzhenitsyn, Alexsandr. *The Gulag Archipelago, 1918–1956*, 3 vols. (New York: Harper & Row, 1973–1978).

Speer, Albert. *Inside the Third Reich* (New York: Macmillan, 1970).

Stevenson, Leslie. "Conclusion: A Synthesis of the Theories," in Stevenson, Leslie; Haberman, David L., and Wright, Peter Mathew. *Twelve Theories of Human Nature*, 6th ed. (Oxford and New York: Oxford University Press, 2013).

Stevenson, Leslie and Haberman, David L. *Ten Theories of Human Nature*, 3rd ed. (Oxford: Oxford University Press, 1998).

Taheri, Amir. *Holy Terror: The Inside Story of Islamic Terrorism* (London: Sphere Books, 1987).

Taheri, Amir. *The Spirit of Allah: Khomeini & the Islamic Revolution* (Bethesda, MD: Adler & Adler, 1986).

Talbot, Ian. *Pakistan, a Modern History* (New York: St.Martin's Press, 1998).

Timani, Hussam S. *Modern Intellectual Readings of the Kharijites* (New York: Peter Lang, 2008).

al-'Uthaymīn, 'Abd Allāh Sālih. *Muhammad ibn 'Abd al-Wahhāb: The Man and His Works* (London and New York: I. B. Tauris, 2009).

Van der Hoeven, Jan Willem. "The Main Reason for the Present Middle East Conflict: Islam and Not 'The Territories," EretzYisroel.Org, 2000–2001, http://www.eretzyisroel.org/~jkatz/mainreason.html.

Van Ess, Josef. "*Une lecture a rebours de l'histoire du muʿtazilisme*," *Revue des études islamiques* 47, no. 1 (1979).

Vassiliev, Alexei. *The History of Saudi Arabia* (London: Saqi Books, 2000).

Voll, John. "Muḥammad Ḥayyā al-Sindī and Muhammad ibn 'Abd al-Wahhab: An Analysis of an Intellectual Group in Eighteenth-Century Madīna" in *Bulletin of the School of Oriental and African Studies* (University of London), Vol. 38, No. 1 (1975), 32-39.

Watson, Charles. *Muslim World* 28, no. 1 (January 1938).

Watt, W. Montgomery. *Islamic Political Thought* (Edinburgh: Edinburgh University Press, 1968).

Watt, W. Montgomery. *The Majesty That Was Islam* (London: Sidgwick & Jackson, 1974).

Watt, W. Montgomery. *The Formative Period of Islamic Thought* (Edinburgh: University of Edinburgh Press, 1973).

Wehr, Hans. *A Dictionary of Modern Written Arabic*, ed. Milton Cowan (Beirut: Librairie du Liban, 1974).

Wellhausen, Julius. *The Religio-Political Factions in Early Islam* (Amsterdam: North-Holland Publishing Company, 1975), 17. Originally published as *Die religiös—politischen Oppositionsparteien im alten Islam* (Göttingen, 1901).

Wright, Lawrence. *The Looming Tower: Al-Qaeda and the Road to 9/11* (New York: Vintage 2007).

Wright, Robin. *Dreams and Shadows: The Future of the Middle East* (New York: Penguin Press, 2008).

Wurmser, David. "The Rise and Fall of the Arab World," *Strategic Review* 21, no. 3 (Summer 1993).

Zia-ul-Haq, General M. "Foreword," in Malik, *Qur'anic Concept of War*.

Zilbergeld, George. *A Reader for the Politically Incorrect* (Santa Barbara, CA: Praeger, 2003).

Zilfi, Madeline C. "The Qāḍīzādelis: Discordant Revivalism in Seventeenth-Century Istanbul," *Journal of Near Eastern Studies* 45, no. 4 (October 1986).

Zilfi, Madeline C. *The Politics of Piety: The Ottoman Ulema in the Postclassical Age (1600–1800)* (Minneapolis, MN: Bibliotheca Islamica, 1988).

Index

Symbols
9/11 25, 34, 36, 45, 46, 55, 63, 289, 308, 320

A
Abbāsid 94, 173
'Abd Allah (d. 903) 176, 228
'Abd Allah ibn Dhahlān 224
Abd al-Latīf ibn 'Abd al-Rahman 241
'Abd al-Qadir al-Husaini 295
'Abd al-Qasim al-Khasani 296
'Abd al-Rahmān ibn Hasan (d. 1869) 241
Abd al-Razzāq (d. 826) 119
al-'Askarī, Shihāb al-Dīn Ahmad ibn 'Abd Allāh 224
Abdel Nasser, Gamal 40, 245
Abrahamian, Ervand 330, 332, 341
Abū Bakr 156, 176
Abu Bakr al-Khallāl (d. 924) 228
Abu Dāwūd 80, 120, 231, 316
Abu Dhabi 329
'Abduh, Muhammad (d. 1905) 285
Abu Hanifah 310
Abū Ja'far 181, 182, 183
Abū Mahammad al-Akfānī 179
Abu Muhammad al-Tamīmī 182
Abu Sa'd al-Baqqāl 181
Abū Ya 'lā b. al-Farrā' 176
Abwehr 293
Adana 292
Aden 34
Afghanistan 42, 90, 96, 272, 314, 315, 317, 319, 340, 353
ahl al-dīwān 192
Ahmad al-Rūmī al-Aqhizārī 216
Ahmad al-Sukkari 278
Ahmad ibn 'Atwa 224
Ahmad ibn Muhammad ibn Musharraf 224
Ahmadinejad, Mahmud 292
Ahmadiyya 262, 264

Ahmad Mahar 283
Ahmed, Beenish 32, 33
Ahram 33
Aigle, Denise 193
al-Adil Kitbugha 188
al-Afghani, Jamal al-Din 285
Al-Ahram 33
al-ākhira 32, 79
al-Amīn 171
al-'āshūrā' 178, 180
al-'Askarī, Shihāb al-Dīn Ahmad ibn 'Abd Allāh 224
al-Assad family 292
Al-Awzā'ī 119
al-Azhar 54, 143, 224, 246, 282
Aleppo 127, 227
Alexandria 26, 127, 292
Algeria 34, 47, 48
'Ali ibn Hajj 96
Allah's Government 261
All India Muslim League 243, 260
Almoravids 87
Alp Arslan 181
Al Sa'ud 228, 238
Amayreh, Khaled 28
Amin, Galal A. 27
Amman 28, 315
Amnesty International 340
Andalusia 40
Angel Gabriel 77
Ankara 211, 292
Ansār 148
antinomianism 198, 201
antisemitism 38, 63, 289, 290, 334
apostasy 55, 85, 162, 165, 310, 339, 340, 352
Arabia 18, 20, 30, 38, 41, 42, 48, 55, 75, 79, 80, 83, 95, 96, 98, 100, 102, 105, 110, 121, 133, 137, 151, 154, 215, 223, 226, 228, 230, 241, 244, 245, 253, 263,

270, 297, 301, 315, 340, 349, 353, 354
Arabic-English Lexicon 130, 131, 133, 165
Arab-Israeli conflict 24
Arafat, Yasir 41
Arjomand, Saïd Amir 31, 65, 69
Armed Islamic Group 47
Arnold, Sir Thomas 151
Aš'arites 197
Ash'arism 180, 181, 182
Ash'arites 181
'āshūrā' 178, 180
asl 81, 85, 207
'Asma' b. Marwan 83
'Assāf al-Nasrānī 186
the assassins 21, 308
Āšūrā' 199
Atlantic 21, 149
Aurangabad 259
Auschwitz 68
Awrangzeb 146
Aya Sofya 213
āyat al-sayf 87
Ayatollah Khasani 327
Ayatollah Qaffari 341
Ayatollah Shaikh Sadeq Khalkhali 326
'ayyārūn 179, 181
Azraqites 18, 159, 165, 166, 167, 243, 256
Azzam, Abdullah Yusuf 54, 57, 69, 143, 314- 319

B
Baathist 342
Baba Palangposh 146
Bab Zuwyala 219
Badjkam 176
Badr, Battle of 149, 312
Baeumler, Alfred 59
Baghdad 18, 20, 43, 95, 170- 172, 174, 175, 178, 179, 180- 183, 210, 227, 292, 350

Bahā'īs 331
Bakhash, Shaul 331, 333
al-Bakri 183
Balance of Truth, The 212
Bali 33
Balkans 40, 51, 287
Banū Hāshim 172
Banu 'l-Nadir 82
Banu Qurayza 82
Barak, Ehud 36
Barāthā, the mosque of 176, 180
Barbahārī 18, 170, 174-176, 178
al-Barm, Yūsuf 94
Barth, Karl 65, 67
Basra 166, 227, 229, 240
Ba'th 293
Bātiniyya 190
Bauer, Yahuda 63
Baybars 201
Bayhaq/Sabzavār 144
Bedouins 159, 199, 236, 238, 244
Beduin 88
Behesht Zahra 99
Beirut 36, 41, 117, 124, 130, 131, 139, 188, 199, 225, 266, 292
Bengal 246, 247, 248
Bergesen. Albert J. 300, 301
Berlin, Isaiah 59, 60, 61
Bhutto, Zulfiqar Ali 263
bid'a 134, 259
Bin Laden 37, 52, 265, 321
al-Birgawī 210
Birgili 177, 210- 213, 216, 219, 221, 222
Birgivi 210
al-Birgiwī 210, 216
Birkawī 210
Bitter Harvest, The 322
Blainey, Geoffrey 274
Blankinship, Khalid Yahya 152, 156
blood 31, 32, 80, 85, 97, 99, 100, 103, 118, 132, 133, 135, 229, 248, 259, 281, 311, 316- 318, 325, 326, 336, 341, 343, 349, 351

Boroumand Foundation 340, 343
Bosnia 42
Bostom, Andrew 38, 55, 67
Bousquet, Georges-Henri 65, 150, 151
British forces 284
Brodie, Bernard 274
Brohi, Allah Bukhsh K. 272, 275, 276
Brooks, Geraldine 28
Brotherhood, Muslim 26, 29, 40, 69, 96, 142, 154, 158, 246, 278-280, 282- 286, 290, 291, 293-297, 300, 314, 320
Brunei 354
Buddhas of Bamyan 90
Buffalo 264
Al-Bukhārī, 'Ala' al-Dīn 38, 80, 82, 98, 102- 104, 109, 120- 125, 130, 133, 135, 137, 186, 216, 231, 236, 309
Al-Burjumi 179, 181
Bush, George W. 45, 46
Buyid period 178

C
Caesar 125, 302
Caetani, Leone 150
Cairo 25, 26, 54, 82, 105, 107-109, 111, 125, 127, 135, 165, 185, 188, 190, 194, 199, 201, 203, 204, 218, 219, 222, 224, 227, 230, 246, 278, 283, 284, 287, 292, 293, 295, 296, 299, 308, 315, 320
Calder, Norman 135, 239
Caliph 'Ali 229
Call to Jihād 188
Cambodia 56
Camp David 36, 43
capital punishment 339, 340
Carter, Jimmy 42, 44
Caspian Sea 144
Cathars 49

Charlie Hebdo 54, 83
Chelebi, Katib 212
Chinggis Khan 196, 197
Chosroes 125
Christianity 50, 64, 66, 68, 76, 106, 202, 203, 206, 270, 352
Cilicia 188, 197, 207
Clinton, Bill 36, 41, 42, 62
Club de Madrid 73
Cohen, William 100
Cohn, Norman 287
Cold War 45, 61
collective obligation (*fard 'alā 'l-kifāya*) 89
Commanding Right and Forbidding Wrong 23, 87, 88, 95, 164, 171, 174, 178, 180, 182, 191, 206, 210, 211, 221, 240, 241, 278, 328, 351, 354
Communism 61, 62, 63, 64, 65, 66, 109, 270
Congress 259, 260, 291, 296, 297, 337
Congress of Muslim Critics of the Constitution 337
Conquest of Mecca 147
Cook, David 113, 115, 117, 139, 140, 194
Cook, Michael 88, 94, 161, 174, 178, 181, 191, 240, 350
Copts 187
Coulibaly, Amedy 96
Crawford, Michael 223, 233, 237
Crone, Patricia 161
Crusades 24, 49- 52, 118, 151

D
Daily Telegraph 343
Dallā' 176
Damascus 43, 54, 109, 185, 188, 190, 197, 198, 224, 227, 303, 314
Dar al-Hadith al-Sukkariyah 185
Dar al-Harb 115, 125, 126, 194, 256
Dār al-'ilm 178
Dar al-Islam 115, 125, 126, 194, 235,

249, 256, 258
Dar al-Sulh 125, 126
Dar al-'Ulum 278
Day of the Cave 179
Deccan 146
Defense of the Muslim Lands 314-317
Deobandi 18
al-Dhahabī 187, 188
dhikr 220, 221
The Dictionary of Islam 39, 84
Dictionary of Modern Written Arabic 130, 135, 165, 303
Digby, Simon 146
al-Dir'iyya 228
al-Djashnikir 201
Donner, Fred 150, 155

E
Eco, Umberto 64
Edirne 215
Egypt 25- 30, 33, 35, 40, 41, 43, 44, 45, 48, 65, 72, 73, 95, 111, 128, 141, 143, 150, 157, 184, 185, 187, 204, 219, 223, 224, 243, 245, 264, 278, 279, 282, 283, 284, 290, 293, 295, 296, 299- 301, 308, 310, 312, 313, 320- 322, 329, 349
Eisenhower, Dwight 48
El Fadl, Abou 237
Emami, Seyyed Ali Muhammad 326
Emirate of Diriyah 228
Encounter 35, 62, 95, 184
Encyclopaedia of Islam 21, 81, 86, 87, 104, 105, 107, 117, 118, 120, 125, 126, 136, 159, 160, 162, 165, 169, 174, 177, 180, 182, 183, 185, 189, 191, 198- 201, 204, 210, 228, 230, 246, 250, 257, 260, 264, 265
Erzurum 215
Eshraqi 342
esotericism 198, 201
Ettinger, Yoram 36

Evstatiev, Simeon 210, 215

F
Faizziyah 330, 331
Fakhr al-Mulk 180
Fallacy 24
Al-Fanniya al-'Askariya 25
faqih 334, 335, 337
Faraj, Muhammad 'Abd al-Salām 308
fard ayn 317
fard kifaya 317
Far Enemy 352
al-Farīda al-Ghā'iba 308
al-Faruqi, Ismail R. 217
Fascism 64, 70, 270
fatwa 186, 195, 197, 202, 204, 214, 221, 222, 238, 342, 343
Fidaiyyun al-Islam 296
Firestone, Reuven 139, 140
Fitzgerald, Hugh 353
Flemming, Barbara 211
Foner, Eric 62
Foucault, Michel 68
Four orthodox caliphs 282
Franks 196, 197, 207
free will 71, 195
Freud, S 71
Friedman, Thomas L. 54
Friedman, Yaron 202
fundamentalists 19, 20, 22, 30, 94- 96, 101, 114, 158, 209, 212, 251, 320, 346
furū' 135, 238

G
Al-Gama'a al-Islamiyya 33
Gardet, Louis 96
Gaza 31, 36, 41, 98
General Islamic Congress 291
geology 353
Georgians 145, 194, 197
German News Bureau 293
Germans 64, 68, 293, 294, 295, 296
Germany 66, 67, 292, 293, 294, 297

al-Ghāba 147
Ghadīr Khumm 178, 179
al-Ghazālī 91, 94, 200
Ghāzān Khān 193, 196
Ghuniem, Wagdi 35
Goldhagen, Daniel 64
Goldziher, Ignaz 107, 170, 171, 174, 214
Gorka, Sebastian 271, 317
greater *jihād* 108, 139, 142, 144, 146, 206
Gulf of al-'Aqaba 150

H
hadd 86, 261
al-Hādī 187, 188
hadīth 17, 38, 53, 80-84, 87, 89, 98, 101-104, 112, 114, 117, 119-125, 128- 130, 132-135, 137, 139-143, 146, 154, 155, 169, 170, 175, 185, 186, 195, 206, 226, 230, 231, 236, 259, 264, 281- 283, 290, 309, 310, 315, 316, 318, 323, 334, 349, 354
Haifa 292
Hā'il 223
al-Hajjāj 102- 104, 120, 124, 132, 137
al-Hallāj 182, 183, 227
al-Hamawiyya al-kubrā 188
al-Haythami 136
Halm, Heinz 144
Halpern, Manfred 65, 286
Hamadan 227
Hamas 39, 98, 99, 290, 321
Hamid, Tawfik 48, 49
Hamza 146
Hanafi 93, 134, 135, 136, 189, 216
Hanafites 134, 221
Hanbal 174, 181, 182, 185, 186, 192, 231, 309, 310, 349
Hanbali 170, 174, 175, 176, 183, 188, 200
Hanbalite 134, 174, 178, 180, 181, 182, 183, 185, 198

hand 19, 21, 49, 69, 81, 86, 88, 89, 90, 116, 125, 128, 169, 186, 191, 222, 226, 258, 300, 307, 318, 326, 334, 336, 353
Haney, Philip 55
Haniyeh, Ismail 98
Hanna, Mark 271, 272
al-Harbiyya 172
Harran 185
Hart, Liddel 274
Harun al-Rashid 83
Hasafiyya Brotherhood 278
Hasan, Ahmad 80, 83, 102, 103
Hasan al-Banna 18, 39, 40, 58, 59, 142, 154, 155, 278, 281, 282, 297, 314, 350
  agreement with Wafd Party 279
  basic ideology of Muslim Brotherhood 280
  dismisses distinction between greater and lesser *jihād* 142
  emphasis on action 286
  fascism of Muslim Brotherhood 287
  financed by Nazis 296
  founds Muslim Brotherhood 279
  hatred of Western influences on Islamic society 279
  importance of Koran for the nation 280, 281
  influenced by Sufis 278
  paid by Hitler 283, 293
  on *jihād* 281, 282, 286
  on martyrdom 154-155, 282
  on Principle of Commanding Right and Forbidding Wrong 278, 282
  necessity of violence 282, 283
  terrorism of Muslim Brotherhood 283, 284
  totalitarianism of Muslim Brotherhood 284, 285

on women 283
al-Hasan al-Harashi 171
Hasan-i Sabbah 21, 22
Hawting, Gerald 161
Haykel, Bernard 234
Haynes, John Earl 62, 63
al-Haythami 136
Hazhir, Abdolhosein 327
heart 31, 50, 89, 91, 108, 121, 142, 191, 198, 215, 218, 233, 273, 280, 284, 301, 303, 312, 321
Hegelian 261
Hegira 151
Hereafter 33, 79, 96, 97, 98, 99, 122, 155, 157, 208, 220, 275, 286, 311, 347
heretics 49, 50, 184, 190, 198, 205, 207, 284
Hijra 25, 163
Himmat, Ali Ghalib 297
al-Hīrah 156
hisba 192, 202
Hitchens, Christopher 36
Hitler, A 60, 62, 63, 64, 65, 66, 67, 68, 70, 283, 290, 292, 293, 294, 298
Hizb al-Tahrir al-Islami 26
Hobbes, Thomas 350, 352
Hojjatol-Islam Nayyeri 342
Hollander, Paul 53, 65
Holocaust 63, 64, 292, 298
Holy *Jihād* Troops 295
homosexual acts 340, 341
Hourani, Albert 27, 28
Hudaybiyah, Treaty of 150
hudud 86, 261
Hughes, Thomas Patrick 39, 101, 351
Human Rights 37, 339, 340, 341, 342, 346
Hunayn 147
al-Husaini, Grand Mufti Haj Amin 289-298
    accepted as leader of all Muslims 293
    advocates genocide of Jews before Hitler 289-290
    antisemitism derived from Islam not from Nazis 290, 291, 294
    holds Jews responsible for all ills of Islamic world 294
    in the pay of Nazis 293
    misinterpreted by Küntzel 289
    praised by Hasan al-Banna 294
    responsible for political assassinations 295
    responsible for Islamic fundamentalist revival of 1950s, 60s, 70s 291
    Said Ramadan's cooperation with al-Husaini 297
Hussein, Saddam 43, 292
Hyderabad 108, 259, 260

I
Ibādīs 89, 91, 94
Ibn 'Abd Al-Wahhāb 217, 226- 246, 349
    bedouin, considered infidel 237-238
    Commanding Right and Forbidding Wrong 240-241
    critical of Sufis 227
    debt to Ibn Qudama 227
    hostility to Shi'a 228-230
    ijtihād 239
    Ikhwan 243-245
    influence of 246-249
    influenced by Qādīzādeli movement 349
    influences on 228
    jihād 235-237
    massacre of Shi'a 229-230
    meeting with Mu¬hammad ibn Sa'ūd 228
    motivated by Muslim concerns 95

necessity for denunciation of unbelief 233-234
not motivated by anticolonial animus 48
pilgrimage to Mecca 226
social justice not a concern 242-243
takfir 234-235
taqlīd 239
taught by Muhammad Hayāt 226
tawhīd 230-234
tawhīd an outward activity 233
travels of 227
writings of 241-242
Ibn al-'Arabi 201
Ibn al-Azraq 166
Ibn al-Humām 108
Ibn al-Jawzī 182, 200, 313
Ibn al-Mubārak, Abd Allāh 117
Ibn al-Muqaffa' 173
Ibn al-Qitt 94
Ibn al-Qushayri 183
Ibn al-Walīd, Khālid 156
Ibn 'Aqīl 182, 183
Ibn-az-Zubayr 166
Ibn Batta al-'Ukbarī 176
Ibn Battūta 189
Ibn Baz 121
ibn Bishr 225, 237
Ibn Ghannām 225
Ibn Hanbal 174, 181, 182, 192, 231, 309, 310, 349
Ibn Ishāq 82, 83
Ibn Karrām 143
Ibn Kathir 186, 188, 309, 315, 323
Ibn Majā 119, 120, 133
Ibn Mas'ūd 179
Ibn Qayyim al-Djawziyya (al-Jawziyya) 222, 228
Ibn Qudāma 107, 205, 185, 227, 228, 242
Ibn Sab'īn 200

Ibn Sa'd 83
Ibn Salāma, Sahl 18, 170, 172
Ibn Sa'ūd 228
Ibn Sinā 200
Ibn Sukkara 181
Ibn Sunayna 82
Ibn Tabataba 171
Ibn Taymiyya 18, 107, 134, 141-142, 170-171, 174, 176- 177, 184-210, 215- 216, 222, 226- 228, 231, 235, 241- 242, 254, 309-310, 312, 315, 323, 349, 353
activist moralist 193
against Nusayris 190
anti-Mongol fatwas 193
as regenerator of *jihād* 205, 206
battles heretics 197
call to *jihād* 188
calls for death penalty for blasphemy 186
cited in *Defense of the Muslim Lands* (Azzam) 315
cited in *The Neglected Duty* (Faraj) 309, 310, 312
Commanding Right and Forbidding Wrong 191, 192
critical of *hadith* 186
dismisses distinction between greater and lesser *jihād* 141, 206
denounces excesses of Sufis, veneration of graves 199
early life 185
hatred of innovations 199
hatred of Shī'ites 201, 202, 203
his character 187-188
hostility to *kalam* 189
Ibn Battuta on 189
Ignaz Goldziher on 170
influenced by Ahmad ibn Hanbal
influenced by Koran 185, 186
in prison 186

jihād superior to pilgrimage 207
on Jews, Christians and *dhimmis* 203, 204, 205
Sivan on 184
Ibrāhīm 145
Ibrahim I 214
Ibrahim, Raymond 321
Ibrahim, Saad Eddin 25, 72
ibtidā' 81
Ideology 59, 63, 64, 154, 279
Ideology of Nazism 63
idolatry 77, 90, 91, 108, 125, 215, 244, 270, 338
ijmā' 85, 239
ijtihād 134, 221, 226, 239
Ijtihād and *Taqlīd* 238
ikhls 77
Ikhwān 243, 244, 245, 279
Ilkhan Ghazan 190
ilm al-bātin 190
Imāma 239
Imām al-Dīn 'Umar al-Qazwīnī 189
Imām al-Husayn 180
Imāmīs 89
Imam Malik 80
India 15, 18, 20, 23, 42, 75, 95, 101, 105, 116, 128, 146, 223, 242, 243, 246- 252, 254 -261, 265, 270, 272, 349
Indonesia 33, 95
infidels 42, 52, 61, 93, 102, 103, 104, 125, 130, 143, 165, 166, 194-196, 208, 218, 230, 238, 244, 257, 264, 284, 293, 311, 312, 316, 319, 321, 322, 336, 343, 354
innovations 18, 81, 95, 171, 174, 176, 185, 197, 199, 200, 202, 207, 212, 215, 225, 226, 228, 247, 251, 252, 254, 255, 256, 266, 270, 309, 351
International Committee against Execution 340

International Covenant on Civil and Political Rights 346
in the Path of Allah 105
Iqtidā' 199, 202, 204, 205
Iran 21, 23, 31, 32, 41- 44, 46, 49, 69, 95, 96, 99, 112, 120, 143-145, 159, 180, 196, 197, 260, 264, 289, 290, 293, 296, 297, 315, 324, 325, 327- 334, 336- 348, 350, 354
Iran Human Rights Documentation Center 339, 340, 341, 342, 346
Iranian Revolution 31, 68, 69, 324, 329
Iran Penal Code 341
Iraq 23, 26, 41- 45, 144, 156, 157, 159, 166, 171, 178, 204, 229, 243, 245, 293, 294, 295, 329, 332, 342, 347, 349, 350, 351
Isfahan 32, 227
ISIL (the Islamic State of Iraq and the Levant) 349
ISIS 17, 32, 33, 349
Iskandar Beg Munshī 145
Islamic Armed Movement 47
Islamic Republic of Iran 21, 333, 338-341, 345, 347-348
Islamic World Congress 291, 296
Ismā'īl, Mahmūd 158
'Ismat Allāh of Sharānpur 93
Israel 24, 28, 34- 38, 40, 42, 43, 295, 298, 308, 314, 331, 334
Israeli-Arab Conflict 34
Istanbul 18, 20, 95, 107, 108, 210-214, 219, 292, 349
isti'rād 165, 167
ittibā' 81
Ittihādiyya 201
Izmir 211, 292

J

Jaffa 292
jāhada 108, 111, 149
jāhilīya 303

al-jāhilīyah 196, 197
jahiliyya 225, 267, 301, 303
jahiliyyah 303, 304
Jahm ibn Safwān 94
Jalal, Ayesha 251, 252, 258, 259, 272
Jalāl al-Dīn Ahmad al-Rāzī 189
Jamāʿat-i Islāmī 261, 263
Jāmiʿat-Tirmidhī 120
Jamʿiyyat al-Ikhwān al-Muslimīn 279
Janin district 314
Johannes, J.G. Jansen 308
Jassās 93
al-Jazeera 354
Jemaah Islamiyah 33
Jerusalem 28, 37, 38, 41, 49, 63, 124, 131, 180, 199, 200, 227, 291, 292, 296
Jerusalem Post 28
Jews 35, 38, 39, 59, 63, 78- 80, 82, 83, 96, 116, 123- 125, 129, 134, 181, 190, 200- 204, 229, 290- 294, 296- 298, 303, 330, 331, 334, 345, 348, 351
Jihād 17, 23, 29, 30, 32, 38, 49, 58, 97, 99, 101, 103, 104, 107, 109- 111, 113- 126, 128- 131, 133- 141, 143, 144, 146, 148, 149, 154, 155, 188, 194, 205, 207, 232, 235, 236, 248, 251, 252, 253, 255, 257, 258, 266, 267, 271- 273, 276, 281, 304, 305, 306, 308, 309, 318, 319, 353
   Bukhārī on 120-123
   Cook, David on 113
   creating terror part of 124
   of crucial importance in Islamic culture 114
   definition in *Dictionary of Islam* 101- 104
   definition in *Encyclopaedia of Islam* Ist Edn. 104-105
   Encyclopaedia of Islam 2nd Edn. 105-107
   end of the world and 129
   Fighting Jews a part of 123- 124
   greater and lesser *jihād* 138- 143
   Hadīth on 120ff
   Ibn al-Mubarak on 117-118
   Khadduri, Majid on 107-109
   in the Koran 115-116
   law schools on 134-136
   Mālik b. Anas on 119
   martyr and 130-131
   Mir, Mustansir on 109-111
   Peters, Rudolph on 111-113.
   Rahman, Fazlur on 109
   reason for 123
   redemptive character of 117- 118
   rewards of martyrdom 131- 134
   spiritual goals of 130, 136-138
   sufism and 143-146
jihādists 20, 21, 23, 24, 77, 98, 271, 315
al-jihādu 'l-Akbar 102
al-jihādu 'l-asghar 102
Jihad Watch 353
jizya 85, 87, 112, 134, 154, 156, 317
Join the Caravan 143, 318, 319
Judaism 36, 202, 203
Jund al-Khalifa 48
Jung, Carl 65, 66, 67

K

Kaʿba 147, 256
Kaba 100
Kaʿb ibn al-Ashraf 82
Kadizade 19
kalām 182, 189, 199, 228
Karbala 178, 179, 180, 229, 238, 255
Karsh, Efraim 47
Kashf al-Asrar 325, 326, 328, 330
Kasravi 324, 325, 326, 330
Kasrawān 202
Kayhan 99

Kāzarūn 143
al-Kāzarūnī, Abū Isḥāq 143
Kemalism 329
Kenya 36
Kerry, Secretary John 54
Khadduri, Majid 107
Khaduri College 314
Khaled El-Rouayheb 216
Khālid al-Daryūs 171
Khamīs ibn Sulaymān 224
Khan, General Ayub 263
Khan, Liaqat Ali 286
Khan, Muhammad Muhsin 38, 98, 102, 121, 122
Khan, Sayyid Ahmad 259
Khan, Zafar'ullah 262
Khandaq 147
kharāj 85
Khārijites 20, 94, 116, 158-169, 173, 193, 208, 285, 350
Khawāridj 161
Khaybar 147
Khilafat movement 259
Khobar Towers 36
Khomein 329
Khomeini, Ayatollah Ruhollah 15, 18, 31, 32, 80, 96, 99, 289, 292, 315, 324-326, 328 329- 339, 341- 344- 348, 350, 352
   accuses the Shah of colluding with Israel 331
   admiration for Nawab Safavi 328
   assassins pf Sadat invoke the name of 329
   Bahā'īs as apoatates 331
   beliefs must lead to action 329
   Constitution of Islam 337-338
   disregard for human rights 339-343
   Fa¬da'ian-e Eslam's link to 328
   his victims 343-346
   impact of Islamic Revolution 315
   in Najaf 332
   in praise of the Hereafter 99
   influence throughout Islamic world 329
   Islamic character of Islamic Revolution 333
   Islamic Revolution not made for price of melons 31-32
   Islamic state means state terror 346
   Kashf al-Asrar (*The Unveiling of Secrets*) 325, 330
   Koran in danger 331, 332
   non-muslims unclean 80
   on Jews 331
   on *Jihād* 338-339
   pilgrimage to Mecca 330
   replies to Kasravi 325
   true aim of Islamic Revolution 333
   Vilāyat-i faqīh: Hukumat-i Islami (*Islamic Government by the Jurist*) 332, 334-346
   works of 330, 334-336
Khruschev, N 62
Khumayn 329
Khurasan 172, 173
khutba 178
Khwādja Ali 145
King Faysal 245
King Hasan 329
kitāb al-Īmān 120
Kitāb al-Mabsūt 135
Kitāb al-Maghāzī 83, 147
Kitāb al-Muwatta' 118, 119
Kitāb al-Risāla fī Usūl al-Fiqh 135
Klehr, Harvey 62, 63
Knights under the Prophet's Banner 320, 321
Koch, Tom 54, 55
Koran 15, 17, 23, 24, 29, 38, 46, 53, 54, 57, 76- 79, 84- 89, 97, 101, 105, 111, 114- 117, 120, 122-

125, 128, 131, 134- 136, 138, 146- 147, 154-155, 159-167, 169, 170, 172, 175, 179, 180, 185, 186, 189, 195, 203, 207, 211, 215, 219, 226, 230, 231, 236, 238-239, 240, 252, 253, 261, 264, 266- 267, 269, 270, 274, 275, 279- 281, 283, 286, 288, 290- 291, 301-304, 307, 309- 310, 315, 316, 318- 319, 323, 327, 331-332, 334- 336, 346-347, 349, 351-352, 354
Hereafter extolled in 79, 96
ipsissima verba of God 23, 77, 280, 301
jihād in 115
source of guidance 301, 304, 336
Q1. *al-fātiha*, The Opening 78[1]
Q2. *al-Baqara*, the Cow 78, 79, 97, 102, 108 fn.17, 112, 116, 156, 272, 310, 351 fn.5
Q3. *'āl 'Imrān*, the Family of Imran 78, 79, 88, 89, 111, 122, 124, 132, 132, 136, 272, 305, 327
Q4. *an-Nisā'*, the Women 77, 78, 87, 102, 135 fn.24, 141, 163, 198, 269, 272, 351 fn.5
Q5. *al-Mā'ida*, the Table 78, 148
Q7. *al-'A'raf*, the Heights 162
Q8. *al-'anfāl*, the Spoils of War / Voluntary Gifts 78, 102,112, 123, 125, 236, 272, 273, 305
Q9. *at-Tawba*, the Repentance / *al-Barā'at*, the Immunity 78, 79, 88, 97, 102, 108 fn.17, 111, 112, 115, 116, 122, 132, 135 fn.24, 141, 155, 163, 203, 272, 305, 311

Q12. *Yūsuf*, Joseph 128, 169
Q16. *An-Nahl*, the Bee 79, 97
Q17. *al-'Isrā'*, The Night Journey 175
Q22. *al-Hajj*, the Pilgrimage 128
Q24. *an-Nūr*, the Light 269
Q25. *al-Furqān*, The Discrimination 78 fn.2
Q29. *al-'Ankabūt*, The Spider 79,
Q33. *al-'Ahzāb*, Confederates 122, 195
Q40. *Ghāfir*, the Forgiver 79, 128
Q42. *ash-Shūrā*, Counsel 128, 189
Q43. *az-Zukhruf*, Gold 128
Q45. *al-Jātiya*, the Kneeling 128
Q47. *Muhammad*, Muhammad 128
Q48. *al-Fath*, the Victory 78, 79, 111, 203, 231, 272
Q49. *al-Hujurāt*, The Dwellings 162
Q54. *al-Qamar*, the Moon 128
Q57 *al-Hadīd*, Iron 309
Q 61. *As-Saff*, The Row/ The Ranks 79, 108
Q66. *at-Tahrīm*, the Prohibition 108 fn. 17
Q 85, *al-Buruj*, The Mansions of the Stars 219 fn.10
Q87. *'al-A'lā*, The Most High 97
Q109. *al-Kāfirūn*, The Disbelievers 78
Kosovo 42
Kramer, Martin 29, 30, 351
Krieck, Ernst 59
Kufa 160, 171, 229
kufr 81, 100, 235
Kurdistan 227

---

[1] Just a reminder that these figures refer to the page numbers in the book, NOT verses of the Koran

Kurds 88, 199
Kuwait 41, 42, 43, 44

L
Lahore 253, 263, 264, 268
Lala Mustafa Pasha mosque 215
Lamb, Christina 343
Lane, Edward William 130, 131, 133
Laoust, Henri 174, 175, 177, 178, 183, 185, 197, 201, 205, 230
Lapidus, Ira M. 171
Last Judgment 79
Lav, Daniel 350
League of *Jihād* Call 295
Lebanon 36, 41, 44, 293, 295
Lenin 60
Lesser *Jihād* 138
Levi Della Vida, Giorgio 150, 159, 165
Levtzion, Nehemia 217
Lewis, Bernard 20, 21, 40, 73, 74, 332
Liaqat Ali Khan 286
Libya 26, 34, 246
Lorenz, Konrad 71
Lucknow 259
lute 181
Luxor Massacre 33

M
MA 25
Maadi district 320
Ma'alim fi'l-tariq [Qutb] 301
Macdonald, D.B. 104, 105
Madelung, Wilferd 143
madhab 134, 187
madhahib 134
madrasa 178, 188, 248
madrassas 353
mafsada 191
Mahdi 129
Mahmood, Aqsa 32
Mahmudiyya 278
al-Majma'a 226
Makdisi, George 182, 185, 228

Malfuzat-i Naqshbandiyya 146
Malia, Martin 61
Malik, Brigadier S.K. 271
Al Malik al-Mansur Lajin 188
Mālik b. Anas 118, 119
Mālikī 134
Mālikīs 94, 118
Malik Shah 181
Mamluk 185, 187, 188, 190, 191, 193, 196, 207
al-Ma'mūn 171-173
Al-Ma'mūn 171
al-Manar 285
manāsib dīniyya 192
Manāsik al-hajj 185
Mānkdīm 91
Shams al-Din 'Abd al Rahman al-Maqdisi 185
Mardin 194
Mar'ī ibn Yūsuf 224
ma'rūf 88, 175, 191
Marx, Karl 53, 54, 57, 60, 66, 69, 71
Marxism 57, 61, 64, 69, 76
mashāyikh 192
al-masīh 196
maslaha 191
Maulana Inyadullah 99
Mauritania 329, 340
Mawdūdī 58, 59, 70, 250, 259-270, 273, 286, 335, 347, 350, 352
  beliefs 264-265
  campaigns against Ahmadiyya 262, 263
  critical of Congress 260
  distrust of All India Muslim League 260
  dogmatic certainty of 352
  early education 259
  founds *Jamā'at-i Islāmī* (JI) 261
  founds *Tarjumanul Qur'an* 259
  hostility to Sufis 265
  Islam antithesis of democracy

270
Islam as total, holistic system 260, 350
Islam corrupted by West 259, 260
Islamic state an ideological state 262, 265
jihād and 266-267
not concerned with socio-economic problems 262
on women 263
says Islamic state similar to fascist state 70
sharī'ia and 267-269
uses Hegelian and Marxist analyses 261
Zia al-Haq and 264
Mawlid 199
Māzandarān 144
Mecca 43, 48, 109, 116, 147, 148, 166, 180, 185, 195, 197, 216, 223, 226- 228, 244, 246, 247, 248, 255, 315, 330
Medina 19, 43, 48, 109, 125, 148, 150, 159-160, 180, 213, 223, 226, 244-245, 252, 256, 263
melons 32, 347
Merah, Mohamed 99
Metcalf, Barbara 18
Michot, Yahya 184, 185
Middle East Policy 37, 40, 41, 44, 45, 46
Middle East Quarterly 29, 31
Milosz, Czeslaw 65
Mir, Mustansir 107, 109, 140
Mir Shihab al-Din 146
Mirza Ghulam Ahmad 262
Mitchell, Richard P. 280, 283
al-Mizzī 187
Moharram 199
Monafeqin 342
Mongol 187, 190, 193- 197
Mongols 50, 185, 187, 190, 193- 199, 207

monism 198, 201
Monnerot, Jules 65, 66
Montazeri 343
Montenegro 42
Morabia, Alfred 197, 198
Mostafa 347
Mu'āwiya 160
Mubarqa' 94
Al-Mughirah b.Shu'bah 156
muhājirūn 148
Muhammad (Prophet) 17, 19, 23, 38, 53, 54, 66, 67, 74, 77, 79-84, 89, 101, 102, 104, 108, 115-117, 123, 124, 128, 129, 135-137, 146-153, 160, 167, 179, 189, 190, 197, 199, 200, 203, 204, 213, 214, 223, 232, 243, 273, 280, 281, 290, 303, 304, 310, 311, 315, 327, 334, 353, 354.
assassinations of opponents 83
centrality of for Muslims 23
compared to Hitler 66, 67
declared Islam cannot tolerate other religions 79
example of his cruelty 82
hatred of Jews 82
his battles 147, 273
Muhammad Hayāt al-Sindī 226, 252
Muhammad ibn 'Īd 230
Muhammad ibn Ismā'īl 224
Muhammad Mustafa al-Maraghi 291
Muhriz b. Nadla 147
Munāfiqūn 342
munkar 88, 171, 191, 195, 241
al-Muqtadir 176
al-Murabitun 48
Murawiec, Laurent 58, 97, 287
al-Muraysī' 147
murshid 279
Murshidiyya 143
murtaddūn 203
Mus'ab b.Zubayr 179
mushrikīn 190

Muslim Brotherhood 26, 29, 40, 69, 96, 142, 154, 158, 246, 278-280, 282- 286, 290-291, 293-297, 300, 314, 320
Muslim Brothers 27, 28, 245, 280, 282- 284
Muslimin 297
Musnad 78, 185
Mussolini 69, 70
Mustafa, Shukri 26
mut'a 229
mutawwi'in 240
Mu'tazilīs 86
Muwahhidūn 86
Muyyad Mosque 219

N
Nahhas Pasha 283
al-Nahrawan 161
Najaf 324, 330, 332, 347
Najd 20, 95, 124, 223, 224, 225, 226, 227, 230, 232, 236, 237, 238, 243, 349
Najdiyya 162, 233, 235, 236
Nur ad-Din Namanjani 297
Naqshbandis 227
Naqshbandiyya-Mujaddidiyya 146
Al-Nasā'ī 120, 129
Nasr ibn Shabath 171
Nasr, Seyyed Vali Reza 260, 266
Nasser Khosrow Qobadiani 347
National Council of Resistance of Iran 343
Nazis 59, 63, 289, 290, 291, 294, 295, 296, 297, 298
Nazism 38, 63, 64, 65, 66, 70, 289
Near Enemy 352
Neglected Duty, The 308-313
Nejd 223
Netanyahu, Benjamin 34, 35, 36
Nettler, Ronald L. 298
Netton, Ian Richard 49, 220, 239
New English Review 49, 64, 353
New York Times 33, 54, 55, 90, 296

Nietzsche, Friedrich 59
Nizām al-Mulk 181
Nizāmīya 181
Nolan Jr., James A. 300
Nuqrashi Pasha 284
Nusayris 190
Nusayrīs 202
Nusayrīyya 190

O
Obama, Barack 45
Oslo talks 36
Ottoman Empire 18, 47, 48, 55, 223, 292
Oxus 149

P
Pact of 'Umar 204
Pahlavi regime 330
Pakistan 42, 75, 158, 260, 261, 262, 263, 264, 271- 273, 275, 296, 315, 329
Palestine 32, 35, 38-41, 51, 69, 94, 185, 290, 292, 293- 295, 317
Palestinian 26, 28, 37, 39, 41, 69, 98, 99, 143, 217, 291, 292, 350
Partition of India 261
Peres, Shimon 36
Peters, Rudolph 60, 111, 113, 140, 211, 218, 219
Pipes, Daniel 29, 30, 31, 40, 45
PLO 36, 41, 44, 314
Politics of Piety, The 19
Pol Pot 60
polytheism 77, 87, 205, 215, 220, 225, 227, 229- 233, 235, 240, 241, 243, 247, 265, 270
Poole, Patrick 271, 272
Port Said 292
privacy 92
    Western notion of 92, 350
Punjab 149, 257
Pyrenees 149

Q

Qabīsah 156
al-qadā 195
al-qadar 195
al-Qaddafi 292
qadhf 85
qādī askar 222
al-Qādir 178, 180, 181
Qadiris 227
Qādīzāde 177, 212, 213, 214, 216
Qādīzādeli 18, 95, 210, 211, 212, 213, 214, 215, 216, 349
Qādīzāde Mehmed b. Mustafa 212
al-Qaeda 20, 33, 48, 54, 290, 320
Qarāmita 190
al-Qassim 223
qat' al-tarīq 86
al-Qawuqji 295
Qibjaq 190
qital 234
qiyās 85, 174
Qom 31, 227, 330, 348
qudra 191
quietist moralists 193
Qurayza 82, 147
al-Qurtubī 78
Qutb, Sayyid 58- 59, 69, 96, 144, 225, 246, 289, 296, 297, 299- 307, 320, 347, 350, 352
   contempt for West 299
   debt owed to Marxism and fascism 69
   duty to interfere when Islamic precepts not obeyed 96
   Greeley, Colorado 299-300
   al-Husaini and 296
   ignorance of American history 300
   jahiliyya 301, 303-304
   jihād as a solution 305-307
   Koran 301, 302, 303
   on an Islamic polity 301
   on Jews 297-298
   racism of 300
   tawhid 302-303

R

al-Rādī 176
Rahman, Fazlur 107, 109, 110, 140
Ramadān 116, 154, 220, 247, 286, 296, 297
Ramadan, Sa'id 286
Ramadan, Tariq 296, 297
Rand Corporation 75
Rashid al-Din 21
rawāfid 200
al-Rāzī, Jalāl al-Dīn Ahmad 189
Razmara, General Haj-Ali 327
razzia 111, 148, 149
Reagan, R 42
Red Sea 149, 287
Reductionist 71
Reilly, Robert 58
Religion 39, 45, 72, 75, 79, 121, 171, 172, 191, 198, 202, 203, 207, 254, 266, 300, 301, 311, 344, 345
Religion News Service 344, 345
Repentance and Holy Flight (RHF) 25, 26
revivalism 146, 218, 222, 260
Reza Shah 330
Rida, Muhammad Rashid 233
Riley-Smith, Jonathan 49, 50
riots 20, 179, 180, 181, 183, 284, 329, 349
Risale-i Birgili Mehmed 211
Riyadh 36, 38, 80, 98, 121, 129, 133, 137, 223, 224, 233, 235, 244
Rodinson, Maxime 60, 65, 68, 69, 71
root cause 34, 46, 58
Rosenberg, Alfred 59, 70, 293
Rouhani, Hasan 344
Rousseau, J.B.L.J. 229, 230
Rubin, Barry 37, 40, 289
Russell, Bertrand 65, 66
Rustam 156, 157
Ruthven, Malise 69

S

sabr 191
Sadat, Anwar 184, 308, 309, 312, 329
Sadr al-Din Musa 144
Safavid dynasty 144
Safaviyya 144, 145
Safaviyya Sufi order 144
Safi ad-din Ardabili 144
Šāfi'tes 197
Sageman, Marc 17, 30, 57, 58
Sahar 28, 29, 330
Sahīh 38, 80, 82, 98, 102, 103, 104, 109, 120, 121, 122, 123, 124, 132, 137, 201, 202, 204, 206, 208, 316
Sahīh al-Bukhārī 38, 98, 120
Sahīh Muslim 120, 132, 202
Sahl ibn Salāma al-Ansārī 18, 170, 172
Salafī 211, 216
Salafiyya 280
Salama 295
Salih 'Ashmawi 285
Sallam ibn Abu'l-Huqayq 82
Sāmarrā, Great Mosque of 180
al-Sarakhsī 135, 136
sariqa 86
Saudi Arabia 30, 38, 41, 42, 48, 55, 75, 80, 96, 98, 100, 121, 133, 137, 154, 223, 226, 228, 230, 241, 244, 245, 263, 297, 315, 340, 353, 354
Savory, R.M. 145
al-sawād al-a'zam 230
Sayyid Ahmad 248, 254- 259, 265, 270, 330
Sayyid Ahmad Khan 259
Sayyid Mostafa 330
Schacht, Joseph 65, 84
Schmalenbach, Herman 59
Schmitt, Carl 59
Schwanitz, Wolfgang 289
Scott, Sir Walter 49, 51
Scruton, Sir Roger 95, 96

secret apparatus" (*al-jihaz al-sirri*) 280
separation of religion and politics 303, 335
September 11, 2001 24, 37, 48, 62
Serbia 42
Serbs 42
Shadhiliyya order 278
al-Shāfi'ī 81, 136, 309
Shafiq Asad 'Abd al-Hadi 314
Shahīd 142, 277
Shah Walli Allah 265
Shakhab 190
Shari'a 17, 54, 55, 56, 79, 80, 84, 94, 95, 97, 115, 125, 188, 202, 215, 238, 239, 240, 260- 262, 264- 269, 279, 283, 312, 314, 315, 321, 322, 341, 347, 351
Shari'a Faculty at Damascus University 314
Shariat Sangalaji 330
Sharif Abū Dja'far al-Hāshimī 176
Sharīf Abū Ja'far 181
Shaykh 'Abd Allah 226, 228
Shaykh 'Abd Allah ibn Ibrāhīm ibn Sayf 226
Shaykh Abdul-Karim Ha'eri 330
Shaykh Abū Hāmid al-Isfarā'inī 179
Shaykh Ahmad al-Nafrawi 221
Shaykh Hasan-i Jūrī 144
Shaykh-i-Khalīfa 144
Shaykhiyya-Jūriyya 144
Shaykh Junayd 145
Shaykh al Mufīd 179
Shaykh Muhammad al-Khabbāz 201
Shaykh Nasr al-Din al-Manbidji 201
Shekau, Abubakar 99
Shi 'ism 324
shirk 77, 87, 90, 205, 215, 220, 230, 231, 240, 247, 252, 267, 270
Shorter Encyclopaedia of Islam 81, 104
shurb al-khamr 85
Sicily 40, 128, 287

Siddiqi, Abdul Hamid 102, 103, 124
Silat al-Harithiyain 314
Sind 23
Singer, Alan 63
sira 53, 241
Sirhindi, Ahmad 251, 259, 265
Salih Siriya 25
Sivan, Emmanuel 184
Six-Day War 314
sixth pillar of Islam 171
Skinner, B.F. 71
sodomy 241, 339, 340, 341
softa 219, 220, 221, 222
Solzhenitsyn, A 62
Somalia 42, 329, 340, 351
Sorbonne 324
Sorel, Georges 70
south Italy 40
Soviet Union 57, 61, 62, 315, 348
Spears, Britney 24
special section (*al-nizam al-khass*) 280
Speer, Albert 68
Spirit of Allah: Khomeini & the Islamic Revolution, The 99, 329
Stalin 60, 62
Stevenson, Leslie 64, 71
Sudan 246, 329, 340
Sudayr 226, 240
Suez Canal 48, 279
Suez Canal Zone 279
Suez crisis 40
Sūfīs 93
Sulayman ibn ʿAbd al-Qawi al-Tuft 185
Sulaymān ibn ʿAlī 224
Sultān Ibn ʿAbd Allāh al-ʿArrābī 216
Sultan Murad IV 214, 216
Sunan Abu Dāwūd 80, 120
Sunan al-Sughra 120
Sunan Ibn Māja 120
sunna 38, 81, 82, 85, 86, 107, 120, 170, 171, 172, 175, 187, 211, 222, 236, 240, 251, 252, 280, 319, 346
Syed Ameer Ali 243
Syria 22, 32, 43, 44, 51, 127, 145, 160, 185, 186, 190, 193, 202, 204, 224, 264, 293, 294, 295, 297, 303, 314, 349

T
al-Tabari 175
Tabuk 141, 150, 206
Taheri, Amir 22, 99, 324, 326- 329
al-Tāʾif 147
tāʾifa 192
takfīr 162, 218, 230, 234, 235, 236, 237, 238
Takfīr and *Qitāl* 234
Al-Takfīr wa-l-Hijra 25
Taliban 17, 20, 90, 96
Talisman, The 51
al-Tamīmī, Zuhrah b. Hawiyyah 157
Tanzania 36
taqiyya 229
Taqlīd 238, 239
al-Tarīqa al-Muhammadiyya, or Tarikat, 211
tarīqas 144
Tarjumanul Qurʾan 259
tashbīh 176, 189
tawhīd 77, 86, 87, 90, 215, 222, 226, 230-231, 232, 233, 235- 237, 240, 241, 247, 267, 302, 309, 351, 352
Tawhīd al-asmāʾ wa-a-sifāt 231
tawhīd al-ʿibāda 231
Tawhīd al-ilāhiyya 231
Tawhīd al-kuffar 232
Tawhīd al-rubūbiyya 231
Technical Military Academy 25
Tehran 44, 99, 144, 292, 324, 325, 330, 332, 333, 340, 341, 342
Tel Aviv 29
terrorism 17, 23, 24, 28, 29, 33, 34, 36, 37, 41, 42, 44, 45, 46, 48, 49, 53, 54, 57, 58, 64, 73, 97,

166, 174, 183, 272, 308, 320, 346, 347, 349
theocracy 163, 164
theodicy 176, 202
al-Tirmidhī 133, 136, 139, 231, 310, 311
tongue 89, 108, 191, 233
totalitarianism 287
Tours, Battle of 68
Tripoli 292, 294
Tughril Beg 181
Tulkarm 314
Tunis 292, 294
Tunisia 34, 329
Turkey 30, 42, 46, 105, 185, 289, 293, 329, 332
Twelver Shī'ias 179

U

'Ubayd-Allah ibn-Zayid 166
UCLA 237
Uhud 146, 147
Ukl 82
'ulamā' 112, 187, 188, 198, 221, 222, 244, 251, 253, 257, 309
'Umar 177, 204, 229
umarā' 192
Umayyad 94, 152, 163, 173, 185
Umma 190, 281, 317, 318
'Umras 147
United Nations (U.N.) 38, 43, 75
United States 24, 31, 33, 35, 37, 40, 41, 42, 43, 44, 45, 46, 48, 55, 63, 299, 333, 336, 344, 348
United States Commission on International Religious Freedom 344
Universal Declaration of Human Rights 346
U.S. Aid 45
USS Cole 36
usūl 81, 85, 134, 207
usūl al-fiqh 134
al-'Uthaymīn, Abd Allāh Sālih 224, 230, 231
'Uthman 160, 161, 168
'Uthmān ibn Qā'id 224
al-'Uyayna 224, 226, 227, 228, 240

V

van der Hoeven, Jan Willem 38, 39
van Ess, Josef 171
Vienna 50, 67, 215
Vietnam 56
Voll, John O. 217

W

Wādī al-Qurā 147
Wafd Party 279
wahdat al-shuhūd 182
Wahhābī 18, 218, 225, 229, 235, 238, 241, 242, 243, 244
Wahhābism 48, 95, 223, 224, 228, 237, 242, 243, 244, 245, 349
Wall Street Journal 28
al-Wāqidī 83, 147
Watson, Charles 65
Watt, W. Montgomery 111, 147, 148, 159
Waziristan 351
Wehr, Hans 130, 135
Wellhausen, Julius 160, 163, 164
West Bank 28, 30, 41, 314
White Revolution 331
women 328, 331, 337, 339, 343, 345, 346
World Muslim Congress 297
World War II 45, 68, 279, 291, 296
Wright, Lawrence 34, 320
Wright, Robin 300
Wurmser, David 31

Y

Yarmuk 151
yāsā 196, 197
Yazid 166
Yemen 34, 54, 119, 329, 340, 351
Young Egypt Party 293, 295

al-Yusayr 83

Z
Zafar'ullah Khan 262
Zahirite 134
Zamakhshari 151
Zangeneh, Ahmad 327
al-Zawahiri, Ayman 30, 99, 320, 321
Zayd ibn 'Alī 229
Zaydīs 89, 91, 94
Zia al-Haq 264, 271, 272, 273
Zilfi, Madeline C. 18, 19, 211
zinā 85, 195
zindīqs 198
Zionism 36, 294
Zoroastrians 49, 93, 143, 205, 345
zuhūr 144

www.ingramcontent.com/pod-product-compliance
Lightning Source LLC
Chambersburg PA
CBHW020633230426
43665CB00008B/162